XML
HACKS™

Michael Fitzgerald

O'REILLY®

Beijing · Cambridge · Farnham · Köln · Paris · Sebastopol · Taipei · Tokyo

XML Hacks™

by Michael Fitzgerald

Copyright © 2004 O'Reilly Media, Inc. All rights reserved.
Printed in the United States of America.

Published by O'Reilly Media, Inc., 1005 Gravenstein Highway North,
Sebastopol, CA 95472.

O'Reilly books may be purchased for educational, business, or sales promotional use. Online editions are also available for most titles (*safari.oreilly.com*). For more information, contact our corporate/institutional sales department: (800) 998-9938 or *corporate@oreilly.com*.

Editor:	Simon St.Laurent	**Production Editor:**	Reg Aubry
Series Editor:	Rael Dornfest	**Cover Designer:**	Hanna Dyer
Executive Editor:	Dale Dougherty	**Interior Designer:**	David Futato

Printing History:

July 2004:	First Edition.

 This book uses RepKover,™ a durable and flexible lay-flat binding.

ISBN: 0-596-00711-6
[C]

Contents

Credits

Author

Michael Fitzgerald is principal of Wy'east Communications (*http://www. wyeast.net*), a writing, training, and programming consultancy specializing in XML. In addition to this book, he is the author of *Learning XSLT* (O'Reilly), *XSL Essentials* (Wiley & Sons), and *Building B2B Applications with XML: A Resource Guide* (Wiley & Sons). Mike is the creator of Ox, an open source Java tool for generating brief, syntax-related documentation at the command line (*http://www.wyeast.net/ox.html*). He was also a member of the original RELAX NG technical committee at OASIS (2001–2003). A native of Oregon, Mike now lives with his family in Mapleton, Utah. You can find his technical blog at *http://www.oreillynet.com/weblogs/author/ 1365*.

Contributors

- Timothy Appnel has 13 years of corporate IT and Internet systems development experience and is the principal of Appnel Internet Solutions, a technology consultancy specializing in Movable Type and Type-Pad systems. In addition to being a technologist, Tim has a background in publications which includes cofounding and managing *Oculus Magazine*, a free indie music and arts 'zine, for over seven years. He is an occasional contributor to the O'Reilly Network and maintains a personal weblog of his thoughts at *http://www.timaoutloud.org/*.

- Tara Calishan is the editor of the online newsletter *ResearchBuzz* (*http:// www.researchbuzz.com*) and the author or coauthor of several books, including the bestselling *Google Hacks* (O'Reilly) and *Spidering Hacks* (O'Reilly). A search engine enthusiast for many years, she began her foray into the world of Perl when Google released its API in April 2002.

- John Cowan is the senior Internet systems developer for Reuters Health, a very small subsidiary of Reuters, a wire service and financial news company. He was responsible for Reuters Health's current news publication system, which distributes about 100 articles per day to about 200 wholesale news customers, mostly in XML. (Yes, so most of them want HTML and get XHTML. Deal.) John is a member of the W3C XML Core WG (and the editor of the XML Infoset and XML 1.1 specifications) and the closed Unicore mailing list of the Unicode Technical Committee. He also hangs out on far too many other technical mailing lists, masquerading as the expert on A for the B mailing list and the expert on B for the A mailing list. His friends say that he knows at least something about almost everything, while his enemies say that he knows far too much about far too much. In his copious spare time, John constructed and maintains TagSoup, a SAX-compatible Java parser for ugly, nasty HTML, and the Itsy Bitsy Teeny Weeny Simple Hypertext DTD, a small subset of XHTML Basic suitable for adding rich text to otherwise bald and unconvincing document types (now available in RELAX NG, too). He is interested in languages—natural, constructed, and computer—and is the author of *The Complete Lojban Language*. He is also the current maintainer of FIGlet, the world's only Unicode rendering engine that uses ASCII characters instead of pixels.

- Leigh Dodds is an application developer and designer specializing in Java and XML. He currently manages a small engineering team at Ingenta (*http://www.ingenta.com/*), and is responsible for developing bibliographic content management and document delivery systems and services. Leigh is also a freelance author and has contributed numerous articles and tutorials to xmlhack.com, XML.com, and IBM developerWorks. Leigh is based in Bath, United Kingdom.

- Micah Dubinko is a software engineer who lives in Phoenix, Arizona, with his wife and child, and works for Verity, Inc. (*http://www.verity.com/*). He is the author of *XForms Essentials* (O'Reilly), available online at *http://xformsinstitute.com*. He also served as an editor and author of the W3C XForms specification (*http://www.w3.org/TR/xforms/*), and participated in the XForms effort beginning in September 1999, nine months before the official Working Group was chartered. He was awarded CompTIA CDIA (Certified Document Imaging Architect) certification in January 2001.

- Bob DuCharme (*http://www.snee.com/bob*) is the author of *XSLT Quickly* (Manning Publications), *XML: The Annotated Specification* (Prentice Hall), *SGML CD* (Prentice Hall), and *Operating Systems Handbook* (McGraw Hill). He writes the monthly "Transforming XML" column for XML.com and has contributed to *XML Magazine*, *XML Journal*, IBM developerWorks, XML Developer, and *XML Handbook* (Prentice Hall). A consulting software engineer at LexisNexis, Bob received his BA in religion from Columbia University and his master's in computer science from New York University.

- Hans Fugal is the author of *desert.vim*, the number-one rated color scheme at vim.org (*http://www.vim.org/scripts/script.php?script_id=105*). He also wrote *rnc.vim*, a Vim syntax highlighting specification for the RELAX NG compact syntax (*http://www.vim.org/scripts/script.php?script_id=387*). He is the author of the gdmxml schema, an XML implementation of the GENTECH Genealogical Data Model (*http://gdmxml.fugal.net*). He has a bachelor's degree in computer science from Brigham Young University and is preparing to pursue a PhD in computer science. He is very interested in computer music and maintains a few computer music–related packages in Debian. He plays the piano and the organ. He is presently employed as a system administrator at Wencor West, Inc. (*http://www.wencor.com/*).

- Jason Hunter is the author of *Java Servlet Programming* (O'Reilly) and coauthor of *Java Enterprise Best Practices* (O'Reilly). He's an Apache Member, and as Apache's representative to the Java Community Process Executive Committee, he established a landmark agreement for open source Java. He is publisher of Servlets.com and XQuery.com, an original contributor to Apache Tomcat, creator of the *com.oreilly.servlet* library, and a member of the Expert Groups responsible for servlet, JSP, JAXP, and XQJ API development, and he sits on the W3C XQuery Working Group. He co-created the open source JDOM library to enable optimized Java and XML integration. He works at Mark Logic (*http://www.marklogic.com/*), where he has been working on their XQuery implementation since June 2002.

- Rick Jelliffe is CTO of Topologi Pty. Ltd. (*http://www.topologi.com*), a company making XML-related desktop tools, and spends most of his time working on editors, validators, and publishing-related markup. His current main standards project is editing an upcoming ISO standard for the Schematron schema language (*http://www.ascc.net/xml/schematron*), which he originally developed. As well as his work with ISO SC34 and the original XML group at W3C, Rick was a sporadic member of the W3C Schema Working Group and the W3C Internationalization Interest Group. He is the author of *XML & SGML Cookbook: Recipes on Structured Information* (Prentice Hall PTR). He lead the Chinese XML Now project at Academia Sinica Computing Centre (*http://www.ascc.net/xml*). He lives in Sydney, Australia, and has an economics degree from Sydney University.

- Sean McGrath is CTO of Propylon, an XML solutions company. He is an internationally acknowledged authority on XML and related standards. He served as an invited expert to the W3C's Expert Group that defined XML in 1998. He is the author of three books on markup languages published by Prentice Hall and writes the weekly "e-business in the enterprise" newsletter for ITWorld (*http://www.itworld.com/*). His blog is at *http://seanmcgrath.blogspot.com*.

- Sean Nolan founded Software Poetry (*http://www.softwarepoetry.com/*), and was the CTO for drugstore.com, where he was the fifth employee and led the design and implementation of their award-winning e-commerce systems. While at drugstore.com, Sean was honored as one of the nation's Premier 100 IT Leaders for 2001 by *Computerworld* magazine.

- Thomas Passin is a systems engineer with Mitretek Systems (*http://www.mitretek.org/*), a nonprofit systems and information engineering company. He graduated with a BS in physics from the Massachusetts Institute of Technology, and studied graduate-level physics at the University of Chicago. He has been active in XML-related work since 1998. He helped to develop XML versions of message standards for Advanced Traveler Information Systems (*http://www.sae.org/its/standards/atishome.htm*), including translations of the message schemas from ASN.1 to XML. He developed an XML/XSLT-based questionnaire generation system. He is also active in the area of Topic Maps, and developed the open source TM4JScript Javascript topic map engine. Mr. Passin is the author of *Explorer's Guide to the Semantic Web*, forthcoming from Manning in 2004 (*http://www.manning.com/passin*).

- Dave Pawson is from Peterborough in the United Kingdom. He has an aerospace background, and is currently working for *http://www.rnib.org.uk* on web standards accessibility. In his spare time, he maintains the XSLT FAQ (*http://www.dpawson.co.uk/xsl/xslfaq.html*) and a DocBook FAQ (*http://www.dpawson.co.uk/docbook/*). His interest in DSSSL and XSL-FO led to the publication of the O'Reilly book *XSL-FO*.

- Dean Peters is a graying code-monkey who by day is a mild-mannered IIS/.NET programmer, but by night becomes a not-so-evil Linux genius as he develops software and articles for his blogs, *http://HealYourChurchWebSite.com* and *http://blogs4God.com*.

- Eddie Robertsson finished his master's degree in computer science at the Lund Institute of Technology in Sweden in 1999. Shortly thereafter he moved to Sydney, Australia for employment at Allette Systems, where he worked as an XML developer and trainer specializing in XML schema languages. During his last few years in Sydney, Eddie worked very closely with Rick Jelliffe and Topologi with the design and implementation of Topologi's suite of XML tools. In mid-2003, Eddie moved back to Sweden, where he continues to work with software engineering and XML-related technologies.

- Richard Rose began life at an early age and rapidly started absorbing information, finding that he liked the taste of information relating to computers the best. He has since feasted upon information from the University of Bristol in the United Kingdom, where he earned a BSc with Honors. He lives in Bristol but currently does not work, and he will be returned for store credit as soon as somebody can find the receipt. Richard writes programs for the intellectual challenge. He also turns his hand to system administration and has done the obligatory time in tech support. For fun, he juggles, does close-up magic, and plays the guitar badly. He can also be found on IRC, where he currently is a network operator known as rik on the Open and Free Technology Community (*irc.oftc.net*).

- Michael Smith is a software non-executive living and working in Tokyo, with a particular fondness for RELAX NG and DocBook. He's a member of the DocBook Technical Committee (*http://www.oasis-open.org/committees/tc_home.php?wg_abbrev=docbook*), is involved with the DocBook Open Repository development team, and is the owner/moderator of the xml-doc mailing list (*http://groups.yahoo.com/group/xml-doc/*). In the good old days, he wrote for the xmlhack.com web site in some pretty select company, among whom were Uche Ogbuji, Edd Dumbill, Micah Dubinko, Simon St.Laurent, and Eric van der Vlist.

- Simon St.Laurent is an editor with O'Reilly Media, Inc. Prior to that, he'd been a web developer, network administrator, computer book author, and XML troublemaker. He lives in Dryden, New York. His books include *XML: A Primer*, *XML Elements of Style*, *Building XML Applications*, *Cookies*, and *Sharing Bandwidth*. He is an occasional contributor to XML.com.

Preface

Extensible Markup Language or XML (*http://www.w3.org/TR/REC-xml/*) appeared as a recommendation of the World Wide Web Consortium (*http://www.w3.org*) in early 1998. XML is a restricted subset of Standard Generalized Markup Language or SGML (ISO/IEC 8879). By some grace, XML has enjoyed considerable popularity and has been almost universally received as an interoperability solution for heterogeneous computer systems. Although not without shortcomings, XML is probably the best thing we have going for us to deal with software interoperability issues, mainly because of its wide acceptance and presence.

Today, you can find XML just about anywhere you find software. To name a few examples:

- OpenOffice's file format **[Hack #65]** consists of a set of ZIP-archived XML files.

- Ant's build file format **[Hack #91]** is written in XML, as are Microsoft Visual Studio .NET project files (*http://msdn.microsoft.com/vstudio/*).

- Mac plist configuration files **[Hack #44]** are also written in XML.

- Web pages now increasingly use Extensible Hypertext Markup Language (XHTML) **[Hack #61]**, an XML version of HTML.

- XML User Interface Language (XUL) is a Mozilla project that allows you to define applications with XML (*http://www.mozilla.org/projects/xul/*). Likewise, Extensible Application Markup Language (XAML) is an XML-based language for defining user interfaces for the Avalon framework, part of Microsoft's upcoming release of Windows code-named "Longhorn" (*http://msdn.microsoft.com/longhorn/*).

XML is by no means a panacea for all the ills of interchange, but it's becoming an increasingly practical option for packaging and moving data in and out of systems or for representing data in a consistent, readable way.

And it can be fun to use, too, as many of the hacks in this book demonstrate.

The XML specification defines a syntax for creating markup. *Markup* consists of elements, attributes, and other structures that allow you to label documents and data in a way that can give them meaning that other human beings or software can understand and interpret. Because reliable XML parsers are readily and often freely available in a variety of programming languages, it is relatively easy to integrate XML processing into just about any application.

This book's mission is to give you a running start at doing many of the things that are commonly—and sometimes uncommonly—done with XML. While you'll find beginning, intermediate, and advanced hacks between the covers, this book is not an exhaustive treatment of *everything* you can do with XML. Instead, it focuses on the mainstream, core tasks found in XML territory. These tasks can be accomplished quickly and usually use downloadable, open source software or software that is available for free trial.

Why XML Hacks?

The term *hacking* has a bad reputation in the press. They use it to refer to someone who breaks into systems or wreaks havoc with computers as their weapon. Among people who write code, though, the term *hack* refers to a "quick-and-dirty" solution to a problem, or a clever way to get something done. And the term *hacker* is taken very much as a compliment, referring to someone as being creative and having the technical chops to get things done. The Hacks series is an attempt to reclaim the word, document the good ways people are hacking, and pass the hacker ethic of creative participation on to the uninitiated. Seeing how others approach systems and problems is often the quickest way to learn about a new technology.

XML Hacks is for folks who like to cobble together a variety of free or low-cost tools and techniques, with XML as the touchstone, to get something practical done. This book is designed to meet the needs of a broad audience: from those who are just cutting their teeth on XML to those who are already familiar with it. Even experts will find new approaches to solving interesting challenges among these hacks—for example, Rick Jelliffe's hack on converting Wiki to XML via SGML [Hack #94]. Because it covers a lot of ground, this book will probably meet some need, no matter at what level you are hacking with XML.

How This Book Is Organized

This book is divided into seven chapters, each of which is briefly described here:

Chapter 1, *Looking at XML Documents*
Contains a series of introductory hacks, including an overview of what an XML document should look like, how to display an XML document in a browser, how to style an XML document with CSS, and how to use command-line Java applications to process XML.

Chapter 2, *Creating XML Documents*
Teaches you how to edit XML with a variety of editors, including Vim, Emacs, <oXygen/>, and Microsoft Office 2003 applications. Among other things, shows you how to convert a plain text file to XML with xmlspy, translate CSV to XML, and convert HTML to XHTML with HTML Tidy.

Chapter 3, *Transforming XML Documents*
Explores many ways that you can use XSLT and other tools to transform XML into CSV, transform an iTunes library (plist) file into HTML, transform XML documents with grep and sed, and generate SVG with XSLT.

Chapter 4, *XML Vocabularies*
Helps you get acquainted with namespaces and RDDL, and describes how to use common XML vocabularies and frameworks such as XHTML, DocBook, RDDL, and RDF in the form of FOAF.

Chapter 5, *Defining XML Vocabularies with Schema Languages*
Covers the creation of valid XML using DTDs, XML Schema, RELAX NG, and Schematron. It also explains how to generate schemas from instances, how to generate instances from schemas, and how to convert a schema from one schema language to another.

Chapter 6, *RSS and Atom*
Teaches you how to subscribe to RSS feeds with news readers; create RSS 0.91, RSS 1.0, RSS 2.0, and Atom documents; and generate RSS from Google queries and with Movable Type templates.

Chapter 7, *Advanced XML Hacks*
Shows you how to perform XML tasks in an Ant pipeline, how to use Cocoon, and how to process XML documents using DOM, SAX, Genx, and the facilities of C#'s System.Xml namespace, among others.

Conventions Used in This Book

The following is a list of typographical conventions used in this book:

Italic

> Used to indicate new terms, URLs, filenames, file extensions, directories, commands and options, and program names, and to highlight comments in examples. For example, a path in the filesystem may appear as *C:\Hacks\examples* or */usr/mike/hacks/examples*.

`Constant width`

> Used to show code examples, XML markup, Java package or C# namespace names, or output from commands.

`Constant width bold`

> Used in examples to show emphasis.

`Constant width italic`

> Used in examples to show text that should be replaced with user-supplied values.

Color

> The second color is used to indicate a cross-reference within the book.

↵ A carriage return (↵) at the end of a line of code is used to denote an unnatural line break; that is, you should not enter these as two lines of code, but as one continuous line. Multiple lines are used in these cases due to page-width constraints.

You should pay special attention to notes set apart from the text with the following icons:

> This is a tip, suggestion, or general note. It contains useful supplementary information about the topic at hand.

> This is a warning or a note of caution.

The thermometer icons, found next to each hack, indicate the relative complexity of the hack:

 beginner   moderate   expert

Using Code Examples

This book is here to help you get your job done with XML. In general, you may use the markup, stylesheets, and code in this book in your programs and documentation (all available for download in a ZIP archive from *http:// www.oreilly.com/catalog/xmlhks*—most of the hacks assume that these example files are in place in a working directory). You do not need to contact us for permission unless you're reproducing a significant portion of the code. For example, writing a program that uses several chunks of code from this book does not require permission. However, selling or distributing a CD-ROM of examples from an O'Reilly book does require permission. Answering a question by citing this book and quoting an example does not require permission, but incorporating a significant amount of examples from this book into your product's documentation does require permission.

We appreciate, but do not require, attribution when using code. An attribution usually includes the title, author, publisher, and ISBN. For example: "*XML Hacks* by Michael Fitzgerald. Copyright 2004 O'Reilly Media, Inc., 0-596-00711-6."

If you feel your use of code examples falls outside fair use or the permission given above, feel free to contact us at *permissions@oreilly.com*.

How to Contact Us

We have tested and verified the information in this book to the best of our ability, but you may find that some software features have changed over time or even that we have made some mistakes. As a reader, you can help us to improve future editions of this book by sending us your feedback. Let us know about any errors, inaccuracies, bugs, misleading or confusing statements, and typos that you find anywhere in this book.

Also, please let us know what we can do to make this book more useful to you. We take your comments seriously and will try to incorporate reasonable suggestions into future editions. You can write us at:

O'Reilly Media, Inc.
1005 Gravenstein Highway North
Sebastopol, CA 95472
(800) 998-9938 (in the U.S. or Canada)
(707) 829-0515 (international/local)
(707) 829-0104 (fax)

To ask technical questions or to comment on the book, send email to:

bookquestions@oreilly.com

The web site for *XML Hacks* offers a ZIP archive of example files, as well as errata, a place to write reader reviews, and much more. You can find this page at:

> *http://www.oreilly.com/catalog/xmlhks/*

For more information about this and other books, see the O'Reilly web site:

> *http://www.oreilly.com*

Got a hack?

To explore other hacks books or to contribute a hack online, visit the O'Reilly hacks site at:

> *http://hacks.oreilly.com*

Acknowledgments

Thanks to Simon St.Laurent for giving me the opportunity to write this book and for being a sane voice in a crazy world. It was a privilege to write for O'Reilly again. Thanks are also due to Jeni Tennison and Jeff Maggard for their many helpful comments on the technical content of this book. I also want to thank all the contributors—Timothy Appnel, Tara Calishan, John Cowan, Leigh Dodds, Micah Dubinko, Bob DuCharme, Hans Fugal, Jason Hunter, Rick Jelliffe, Sean McGrath, Sean Nolan, Tom Passin, Dave Pawson, Dean Peters, Eddie Robertsson, Richard Rose, Michael Smith, and once again Simon St.Laurent—for making this book better than it would otherwise be. Finally, I want to thank Cristi—my wife of 25 years—for believing in and supporting me, no matter how difficult it may have been.

## CHAPTER ONE

Looking at XML Documents
Hacks 1–10

Just because you can find XML in any nook and cranny you find software these days doesn't mean that everyone is an expert on the subject. That's why the hacks in this chapter were written: they are for readers who are just getting up to speed with XML. If that's you, read on; if that's not you, you can skip ahead to Chapter 2.

These hacks introduce you to the basics of XML: what an ordinary XML document looks like [Hack #1], how to display an XML document in a variety of browsers [Hack #2], how to style an XML document with CSS [Hack #3], how to use character and entity references [Hack #4], how to check an XML document for errors, both online [Hack #8] and on a command line [Hack #9], and how to run Java programs that process XML [Hack #10].

All the files mentioned in this chapter are in the book's file archive, downloadable from *http://www.oreilly.com/catalog/xmlhks/*. These hacks assume that you have extracted this archive into a working directory where you can exercise the examples.

Read an XML Document

Before you can do much with an XML document, you need to understand its basic parts. This hack explores the most common structures found in XML.

This hack lays the basic groundwork for XML: what it looks like and how it's put together. Example 1-1 shows a simple document (*start.xml*) that contains some of the most common XML structures: an XML declaration, a comment, elements, attributes, an empty element, and a character reference. *start.xml* is *well-formed*, meaning that it conforms to the syntax rules in the XML specification. XML documents must be well-formed.

Example 1-1. start.xml

```
1   <?xml version="1.0" encoding="UTF-8"?>
2
3   <!-- a time instant -->
4   <time timezone="PST">
5    <hour>11</hour>
6    <minute>59</minute>
7    <second>59</second>
8    <meridiem>p.m.</meridiem>
9    <atomic signal="true" symbol="&#x25D1;"/>
10  </time>
```

The XML Declaration

The first line of the example contains an XML declaration, which is recommended by the XML spec but is not mandatory. If present, it must appear on the first line of the document. It is a human- and machine-readable flag that states a few facts about the content of the document.

> An XML declaration is not a processing instruction, although it looks like one. Processing instructions are discussed in "Apply Style to an XML Document with CSS" [**Hack #3**].

In general, an XML declaration provides three pieces of information about the document that contains it: the XML version information; the character encoding in use; and whether the document stands alone or relies on information from an external source.

Version information. If you use an XML declaration, it must include version information (as in version="1.0"). Currently, XML Version 1.0 is in the broadest use, but Version 1.1 is also now available (*http://www.w3.org/TR/xml11/*), so 1.1 is also a possible value for version. The main differences between Versions 1.0 and 1.1 are that 1.1 supports a later version of Unicode (4.0 instead of 2.0), has a more liberal policy for characters used in names, adds a couple space characters, and allows character references for control characters that were forbidden in 1.0 (for details see *http://www.w3.org/TR/xml11/#sec-xml11*).

The encoding declaration. An optional encoding declaration allows you to explicitly state the character encoding used in the document. Character encoding refers to the way characters are represented internally, usually by one or more 8-bit bytes or *octets*. If no encoding declaration exists in a document's XML declaration, that XML document is required to use either UTF-8

or UTF-16 encoding. A UTF-16 document must begin with a special character called a Byte Order Mark or BOM (the zero-width, no break space
U+FEFF; see *http://www.unicode.org/charts/PDF/UFE70.pdf*). As values for
encoding, you should use names registered at Internet Assigned Numbers
Authority or IANA (*http://www.iana.org/assignments/character-sets*). In addition to UTF-8 and UTF-16, possible choices include US-ASCII, ISO-8859-1,
ISO-2022-JP, and Shift_JIS (*http://www.w3.org/TR/2004/REC-xml-20040204/
#charencoding*). If you use an encoding that is uncommon, make sure that
your XML processor supports the encoding or you'll get an error. You'll find
more in the discussion on character encoding [Hack #27]; also see *http://www.
w3.org/TR/REC-xml#charencoding*.

The standalone declaration. An optional standalone declaration (not shown in
Example 1-1) can tell an XML processor whether an XML document
depends on external markup declarations; i.e., whether it relies on declarations in an external Document Type Definition (DTD). A DTD defines the
content of valid XML documents. This declaration can have a value of yes or
no.

Don't worry too much about standalone declarations. If you don't use external markup declarations, the standalone declaration has no meaning,
whether its value is yes or no (standalone="yes" or standalone="no"). On the
other hand, if you use external markup declarations but no standalone document declaration, the value no is assumed. Given this logic, there isn't
much real need for standalone declarations—other than acting as a visual
cue—unless your processor can convert an XML document from one that
does not stand alone to one that does, which may be more efficient in a net-
worked environment. (See *http://www.w3.org/TR/REC-xml#sec-rmd*.)

Comments

Comments can contain human-readable information that can help you
understand the purpose of a document or the markup in it. A comment
appears on line 3 of Example 1-1. XML comments are generally ignored by
XML processors, but a processor may keep track of them if this is desired
(*http://www.w3.org/TR/REC-xml.html#sec-comments*). They begin with a
<!-- and end with -->, but can't contain the character sequence --. You can
place comments anywhere in an XML document except inside other
markup, such as inside tag brackets.

Elements

A legal or compliant XML document must have at least one element. An element can have either one tag—called an empty element—or two tags—a start tag and an end tag with content in between.

The first or top element in an XML document—such as the time element on line 4—is called the *document element* or *root element*. A document element is required in any XML document. The content of the time element consists of five child elements: hour, minute, second, meridiem, and atomic.

Element content includes text (officially called *parsed character data*), other child elements, or a mix of text and elements. For example, 11 is the text content of the hour element. Elements can contain a few other things, but these are the most common as far as content goes.

The atomic element on line 9 in Example 1-1 is an example of an empty element. Empty elements don't have any content; i.e., they consist of a single tag (`<atomic signal="true" symbol="&#x25D1;"/>`). The other elements all have start tags and end tags; for example, `<hour>` is a start tag and `</hour>` is an end tag.

XML documents are structured documents, and that structure comes essentially from the parent-child relationship between elements. In Example 1-1, hour, minute, second, meridiem, and atomic are the children of time, and time is the parent of hour, minute, second, meridiem, and atomic. The depth of elements can go much deeper than the simple parent-child relationship. Such elements are called *ancestor elements* and *descendant elements*.

Mixed content. The document *start.xml* in Example 1-1 doesn't show mixed content. The document *mixed.xml* in Example 1-2 shows what mixed content looks like.

Example 1-2. mixed.xml

```
<?xml version="1.0" encoding="UTF-8"?>

<!-- a time instant -->
<time timezone="PST">The time is: <hour>11</hour>:<minute>59</minute>: <second>
59</second> <meridiem>p.m.</meridiem></time>
```

The time element has both text (e.g., "The time is:") and child element content (e.g., hour, minute, and second).

Attributes

XML elements may also contain attributes that modify elements in some way. In *start.xml*, the elements time and atomic both contain attributes. For example, on line 4 of Example 1-1, the start tag of the time element contains a timezone attribute. Attributes may occur only in start tags and empty element tags, but never in end tags (see *http://www.w3.org/TR/REC-xml#sec-starttags*). An *attribute specification* consists of an attribute name paired with an attribute value. For example, in timezone="PDT", timezone is the attribute name and PDT is the value, separated by an equals sign (=). Attribute values must be enclosed in matching pairs of single (') or double (") quotes.

Whether to use elements or attributes, and when and where they should be used to represent data, is the subject of long debate **[Hack #40]**. To illustrate, some prefer that the data in the document *time.xml* be represented as:

```
<time hour="11" minute="59" second="59"/>
```

After considering the problem for several years, my conclusion is that it seems to be more of a matter of taste than anything else. The short answer is: do what works for you.

Character references. The attribute symbol on line 9 of Example 1-1 contains something called a character reference **[Hack #4]**. Character references allow access to characters that are not normally available through the keyboard. A character reference begins with an ampersand (&) and ends with a semicolon (;). In the character reference ◑, the hexadecimal number 25D1 preceded by #x refers to the Unicode character "circle with right half black" (*http://www.unicode.org/charts/PDF/U25A0.pdf*), which looks like this when it is rendered: ◑.

CDATA Sections

One structure not shown in the example (see **[Hack #43]**) is something called a *CDATA section*. CDATA sections in XML (*http://www.w3.org/TR/REC-xml/#sec-cdata-sect*) allow you to hide characters like < and & from an XML processor. This is because these characters have special meaning: a < begins an element tag and & begins a character reference or entity reference. A CDATA section begins with the characters <![CDATA[and ends with]]>. For example, the company element in the following fragment contains a CDATA section:

```
<company><![CDATA[Fitzgerald & Daughters]]></company>
```

When munched, the & character in the CDATA section is hidden from the processor so that it isn't interpreted as markup the way the start of an entity reference or character reference would be.

You now should understand the basic components of an XML document.

See Also

- *Learning XML* by Erik Ray (O'Reilly)
- *XML: A Primer* by Simon St.Laurent (Hungry Minds, Inc.)
- *XML 1.1 Bible* by Elliotte Rusty Harold (Hungry Minds, Inc.)

Display an XML Document in a Web Browser

The most popular web browsers can display and process XML natively. Nowadays, it's just a matter of opening a file.

XML is now mature enough that recent versions of the more popular web browsers support it natively. At the time of writing, the most recent versions of these browsers include:

- Microsoft Internet Explorer 6 (*http://www.microsoft.com/windows/ie/*)
- Mozilla 1.7 and Mozilla Firefox 0.9 (*http://www.mozilla.org*)
- Netscape 7.1 (*http://channels.netscape.com/ns/browsers/download.jsp*)
- Opera 7.51 (*http://www.opera.com*)
- Apple's Safari 1.2 (*http://www.apple.com/safari/*)

This means that you can display raw, unstyled XML documents (files) directly in web browsers, with varying results.

The browsers use their own internal mechanisms to display XML. Internet Explorer (IE), for example, uses the default stylesheet *defaultss.xsl*, which is stored in a MSXML dynamic link library (DLL)—*msxml.dll*, *msxml2.dll*, or *msxml3.dll*. You can examine this stylesheet in IE by entering *res://msxml3. dll/DEFAULTSS.xsl* in the address bar. (This works for *msxml.dll*, *msxml2. dll*, or *msxml3.dll*, but not *msxsml4.dll*, the latest version.) If you have Visual Studio (*http://msdn.microsoft.com/vstudio/*), you can use the Resource Editor to edit and save this stylesheet back in the DLL (*http://netcrucible.com/xslt/ msxml-faq.htm#Q19*).

To open an XML document such as *time.xml* (similar to *start.xml*), go to File → Open File or File → Open, depending on the browser, and select the document.

Figures 1-1, 1-2, 1-3, and 1-4 show *time.xml* displayed in IE, Mozilla, Opera, and Safari, respectively. (Mozilla, Firefox, and Netscape have very similar output, so only Mozilla is shown in Figure 1-2. All three of these browsers do not show the XML declaration of *time.xml*.)

IE and Mozilla show a tree representation of *time.xml*, but Opera and Safari only show the text content of the elements in the document.

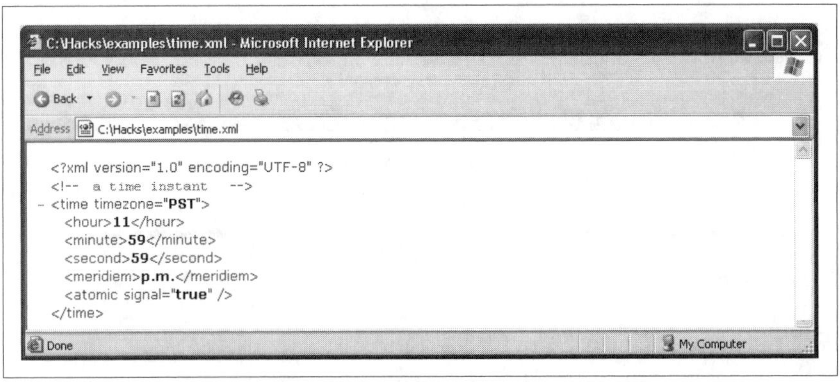

Figure 1-1. time.xml in Internet Explorer

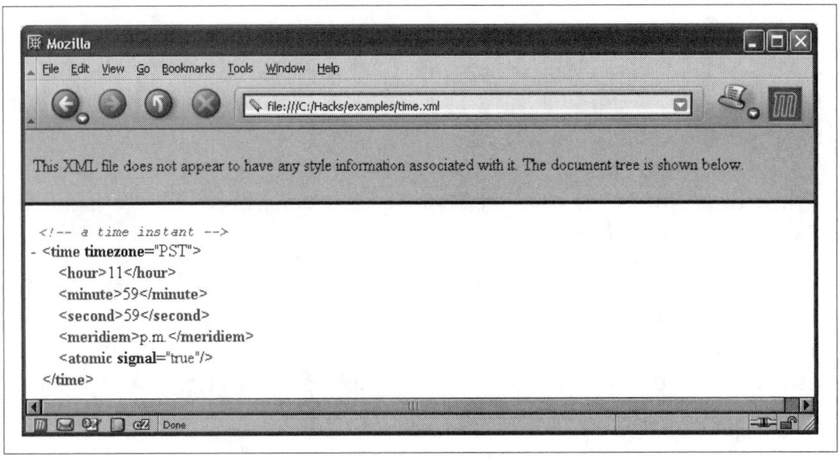

Figure 1-2. time.xml in Mozilla

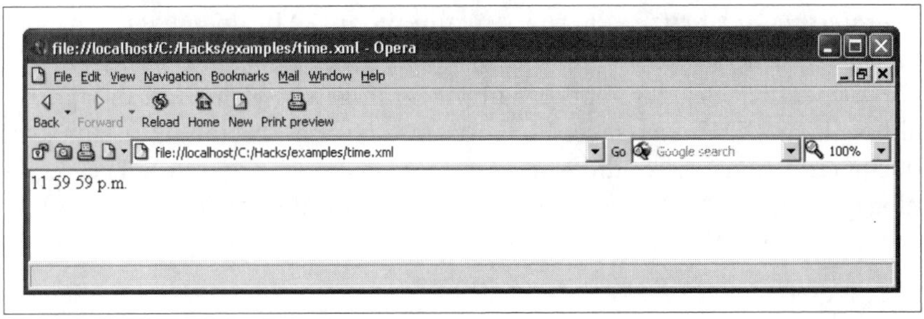

Figure 1-3. time.xml in Opera

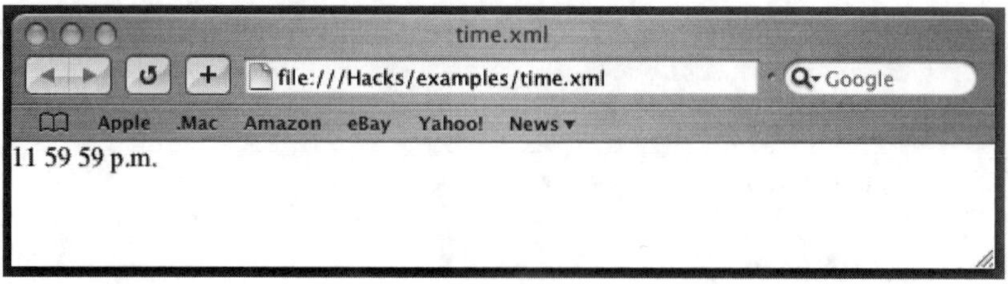

Figure 1-4. time.xml in Safari

Apply Style to an XML Document with CSS
HACK #3

Make an in-browser XML document more appealing by applying a CSS stylesheet to it.

Cascading Style Sheets (CSS) is a W3C language for applying style to HTML, XHTML, or XML documents (*http://www.w3.org/Style/CSS/*). CSS Level 1 or CSS/1 (*http://www.w3.org/TR/CSS1*) came out of the W3C in 1996 and was later revised in 1999. CSS Level 2 or CSS/2 (*http://www.w3. org/TR/CSS2/*) became a W3C recommendation in 1998. CSS/3 is under construction (*http://www.w3.org/Style/CSS/current-work*). Understandably, CSS/1 enjoys the widest support.

To apply CSS to an XML document, you must use the XML stylesheet processing instruction, which is based on another recommendation of the W3C (*http://www.w3.org/TR/xml-stylesheet*). The XML stylesheet processing instruction is optional unless you are using a stylesheet that you want to associate with an XML document in a standard way.

Processing Instructions

A *processing instruction* (PI) is a structure in an XML document that contains an instruction to an application (*http://www.w3.org/TR/REC-xml#sec-pi*). Generally, PIs can appear anywhere that an element can appear, although the XML stylesheet PI must appear at the beginning of an XML document (though after the XML declaration, if one is present). The beginning part of an XML document, before the document element begins, is called a *prolog*.

Here is an example of a PI:

```
<?xml-stylesheet href="time.css" type="text/css"?>
```

A PI is bounded by `<?` and `?>`. The term immediately following `<?` is called the *target*. The target identifies the purpose or name of the PI. Other than the XML stylesheet PI, you can find PIs used in DocBook files **[Hack #62]** and in

XML-format files used by Microsoft Office 2003 applications, such as Word [Hack #14] and Excel [Hack #15].

The purpose of the XML stylesheet PI is to associate a stylesheet with an XML document. The semantics of the XML stylesheet PI are like those of the HTML or XHTML link element. The structures href and type are called *pseudo-attributes*. The PI actually has six pseudo-attributes, but, to be brief, we'll discuss only href and type here (for information on the others—title, media, charset, and alternate—see *http://www.w3.org/TR/xml-stylesheet*).

In the example just shown, href identifies a relative URI for the stylesheet *time.css*, and type defines a media type for the stylesheet, namely text/css (see *http://www.ietf.org/rfc/rfc2318.txt*).

Cascading Style Sheets

In HTML or XHTML, you can declare CSS properties within a style attribute, the style element, or an external document associated with the HTML document by a link element. However, in XML you usually need to use CSS properties that are defined in an external document.

Here are a few CSS basics as a refresher. The external stylesheet *time.css* in Example 1-3 contains nine CSS statements.

Example 1-3. time.css

```
1  time {font-size:40pt; text-align: center }
2  time:before {content: "The time is now: "}
3  hour {font-family: sans-serif; color: gray}
4  hour:after {content: ":"; color: black}
5  minute {font-family: sans-serif; color: gray}
6  minute:after {content: ":"; color: black}
7  second {font-family: sans-serif; color: gray}
8  second:after {content: " "; color: black}
9  meridiem {font-variant: small-caps}
```

Each line of *time.css* contains a CSS statement or statements. Line 1 begins with the selector time (the name of the time element) followed by a declaration enclosed in braces. A declaration consists of one or more property/value pairs; the property and value pair are separated by a colon. If there is more than one pair, they are separated by a semicolon.

The declaration on line 1 consists of two properties: font-size followed by the value 40pt, and text-align with a value of center. The first statement says that all text found inside the time element should be rendered with a point size of 40; the second statement indicates that the content of the element should be centered.

Properties on lines 2, 4, 6, and 8 place generated text before and after the given element, using the content property, together with the :before and :after pseudo-elements, all three of which are part of CSS/2. A pseudo-element in CSS allows you to apply styles to abstractions of elements, such as the first line in an element, the first letter in an element, and before and after an element (see *http://www.w3.org/TR/CSS21/selector.html#pseudo-elements*).

 IE does not support the :before and :after pseudo-elements along with the content property, so *style.xml* will not look the same in IE as it does in Firefox (Figure 1-5).

Lines 3, 5, and 7 assign a generic sans serif font using the font-family property, and a gray color using the color property, to the hour, minute, and second elements. Text contained in meridiem (line 9) is to be rendered in small caps, as specified with the font-variant property.

Applying a Stylesheet to an XML Document

Now let's hook up the stylesheet *time.css* to the document *style.xml* (Example 1-4). We'll do it with the XML stylesheet PI, shown here in bold on the second line of *style.xml*.

Example 1-4. style.xml

```
<?xml version="1.0" encoding="UTF-8"?>
<?xml-stylesheet href="time.css" type="text/css"?>

<!-- a time instant -->
<time timezone="PST">
 <hour>11</hour>
 <minute>59</minute>
 <second>59</second>
 <meridiem>p.m.</meridiem>
</time>
```

When you display *style.xml* in the Firefox browser, for example, the XML processor in the browser interprets the stylesheet PI and applies the named stylesheet to the XML document. The result in Firefox is shown in Figure 1-5.

With just a few lines of CSS and a PI to pick it up, you can make your XML documents much more readable.

Figure 1-5. style.xml in Firefox

See Also

- Eric Meyer's CSS1 reference: *http://www.meyerweb.com/eric/css/references/css1ref.html*
- Eric Meyer's CSS2 reference: *http://www.meyerweb.com/eric/css/references/css2ref.html*
- The css-discuss mailing list: *http://www.css-discuss.org/*
- A great CSS design site: *http://www.csszengarden.com/*
- *Cascading Style Sheets: The Definitive Guide* by Eric Meyer (O'Reilly)
- *Core CSS* by Keith Schengili-Roberts (Prentice Hall PTR)

HACK #4 Use Character and Entity References

Not all characters are available on the keyboard! This hack shows you how to represent such characters in an XML document by using decimal and hexadecimal character references, and how to represent entities by using entity references.

In XML, character and entity references are formed by surrounding a numerical value or a name with & and ;—for example, © is a decimal character reference and © is an entity reference. This hack shows you how to use both.

Character References

According to the third and latest edition of the XML 1.0 specification (*http://www.w3.org/TR/REC-xml/*), XML processors must accept over 1,000,000 hexadecimal characters (*http://www.w3.org/TR/REC-xml/#charsets*). It's possible that you won't be able to find all those characters on your keyboard! Don't worry. You can use character references instead.

You can look up the semantics of individual Unicode characters at *http://www.unicode/org/charts/*.

You can reference characters using either decimal or hexadecimal numbers. Which one you use is a matter of style. The document *Namen.xml* uses both (Example 1-5); it contains some German names enclosed in German language tags.

Example 1-5. Namen.xml

```
1   <?xml version="1.0" encoding="UTF-8"?>
2   <?xml-stylesheet href="Namen.css" type="text/css"?>
3
4   <Namen xml:lang="de">
5   <Name>
6    <Vorname>Marie</Vorname>
7    <Nachname>M&#252;ller</Nachname>
8    <Geschlecht>&#9792;</Geschlecht>
9   </Name>
10  <Name>
11   <Vorname>Klaus</Vorname>
12   <Nachname>M&#xfc;ller</Nachname>
13   <Geschlecht>&#x2642;</Geschlecht>
14  </Name>
15  </Namen>
```

On lines 7 and 8 are the decimal character references ü and ♀, respectively. The first one refers to the letter u with an umlaut (ü) and the second one is a female sign. Lines 12 and 13 use the hexadecimal character references ü (ü) and ♂ (male sign), respectively. You can see how these character references are rendered in Opera in Figure 1-6.

Figure 1-6. Namen.xml in Opera, styled by Namen.css

The xml:lang attribute. Incidentally, the xml:lang attribute on line 4 is a special language identification attribute in XML 1.0 (*http://www.w3.org/TR/*

REC-xml/#sec-lang-tag). Its value de is a language identifier as defined by RFC 3066 (*http://www.ietf.org/rfc/rfc3066.txt*) and ISO 639 (search *http://www.iso.ch*). Other examples of language identifiers are en (English), fr (French), and es (Spanish).

Entity References

XML has five predefined entities, listed in Table 1-1. These predefined entities can be used where the equivalent literal character is forbidden. For example, an attribute value cannot contain a less-than sign (<), because it looks too much like the beginning of a tag to an XML parser. No problem: you can use < instead. Likewise, you cannot use an ampersand in parsed character data, the text content of an element. Why? Again, it looks like the beginning of a character or entity reference to an XML parser. Again, no problem: you can use & instead.

Table 1-1. XML predefined entities

Entity reference	Description
&lt;	Less-than sign or open angle bracket (<)
&gt;	Greater-than sign or close angle bracket (>)
&amp;	Ampersand (&)
&apos;	Apostrophe or single quote (')
&quot;	Quote or double quote (")

The following document, *copy.xml* in Example 1-6, uses a predefined entity and also declares and references a new entity.

Example 1-6. copy.xml

```
1  <?xml version="1.0" encoding="UTF-8"?>
2  <?xml-stylesheet href="copy.css" type="text/css"?>
3  <!DOCTYPE time [<!ENTITY copy "&#169;">]>
4
5  <!-- a time instant -->
6  <time timezone="PST">
7   <hour>11</hour>
8   <minute>59</minute>
9   <second>59</second>
10  <meridiem>p.m.</meridiem>
11  <atomic signal="true"/>
12  <copyright>&copy; O'Reilly &amp; Associates</copyright>
13 </time>
```

The entity copy is declared in the document type declaration on line 3. The keyword is ENTITY; it is followed by the entity name copy; and this is followed by the value or content of the entity in quotes, "©". (This entity comes standard in HTML and XHTML.) Line 12 of this document references the entity declared on line 3 (©) and also references the XML 1.0 predefined entity for an ampersand (&). Open this document in Firefox (it is styled by the CSS stylesheet *copy.css*) and it will appear like Figure 1-7.

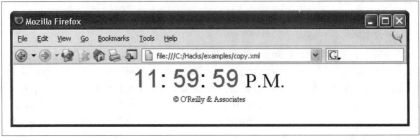

Figure 1-7. copy.xml in Firefox

Character references provide a convenient means to access a very large number of characters. Entities [Hack #25] are also a convenient means to store information and access it elsewhere, even multiple times if necessary.

Examine XML Documents in Text Editors

#5   Even plain-text editors offer features that make editing XML documents a pleasure. This hack introduces two options, Vim and Emacs with nXML.

XML has been called "Unicode with pointy brackets." As such, XML documents can be displayed in your average, run-of-the-mill, non-graphical text editor. Of course you could view, create, and edit XML documents in Notepad on Windows, but it's not a very exciting editing environment (see *http://tucows.com/htmltext95_default.html* for examples of other text editors).

There are a number of text editors that are quite suitable for working with XML. We'll talk about two of them here: Vim (Vi improved, a clone of Vi) and Emacs. Both are free for the downloading.

> If you are accustomed to a point-and-click, graphical user interface for editing text [Hack #6], you probably won't like using Vim or Emacs with XML. If, however, you prefer typing at the keyboard over clicking the mouse (like me), this hack is for you.

Vim

Vim (*http://www.vim.org*) is a derivative of the Unix screen editor, Vi. It is currently at Version 6.3 and is developed under the leadership of Bram

Moolenaar. You can get flavors of Vim that run on Unix (such as Red Hat, Sun Solaris, or Debian), Windows, MS-DOS, the Mac, OS/2, and even Amiga (downloads available at *http://www.vim.org/download.php*). If you are running recent versions of Red Hat (*http://www.redhat.com*) or Cygwin for Windows (*http://www.cygwin.com*), you likely already have Vim installed on your system.

Vi was developed by Bill Joy et al. in the late 1970s for Unix (*http://www.cs. pdx.edu/~kirkenda/joy84.html*). Vi was the first screen editor I ever used— back in 1983—and I still use Vim almost every day. Vim is powerful, and without elaborating on all the reasons why I like to use Vim, I will mention just one: syntax highlighting.

Sure, syntax highlighting is available in other editors, but Vim supports over 300 languages with syntax highlighting. Syntax highlighting helps you see clearly that what you are typing is correct because it assigns colors to the correct syntax of a given language, such as XML. This can help you detect typing errors readily. (See a FAQ on Vim syntax highlighting at *http:// vimdoc.sf.net/cgi-bin/vimfaq2html3.pl#24.1*.) Hans Fugal's advanced hack on Vim is available in the next chapter ("Edit XML with Vim" **[Hack #13]**).

If Vim is already installed and in the path, type the following line:

```
vim -h
```

This will return Vim's command-line options. If you need help installing Vim, see *http://vimdoc.sourceforge.net/htmldoc/usr_90.html*.

To bring up the XML file *time.xml* in Vim, type the following on a command line while in the working directory:

```
vim time.xml
```

Figure 1-8 shows Vim in a terminal window under Gnome on Red Hat.

Emacs with nXML

Another text editor that you might consider for editing XML is Emacs. For simple installation on Windows or Unix/Linux, try the Text Coding Initiative's (TEI) version of Emacs (*http://www.tei-c.org/Software/tei-emacs/*); otherwise, try GNU Emacs for Windows, Unix/Linux, and an even broader range of platforms (*http://www.gnu.org/software/emacs/emacs.html*). Emacs is a rich and powerful editing environment. It was the second editor I used, also in 1983, under the TOPS 20 operating system on a DEC 20 system. (Yes, I know I'm dating myself.)

Editing XML with Emacs is a pleasure with James Clark's nXML **[Hack #12]**. It's included in the TEI version, but you can also obtain a copy of nXML

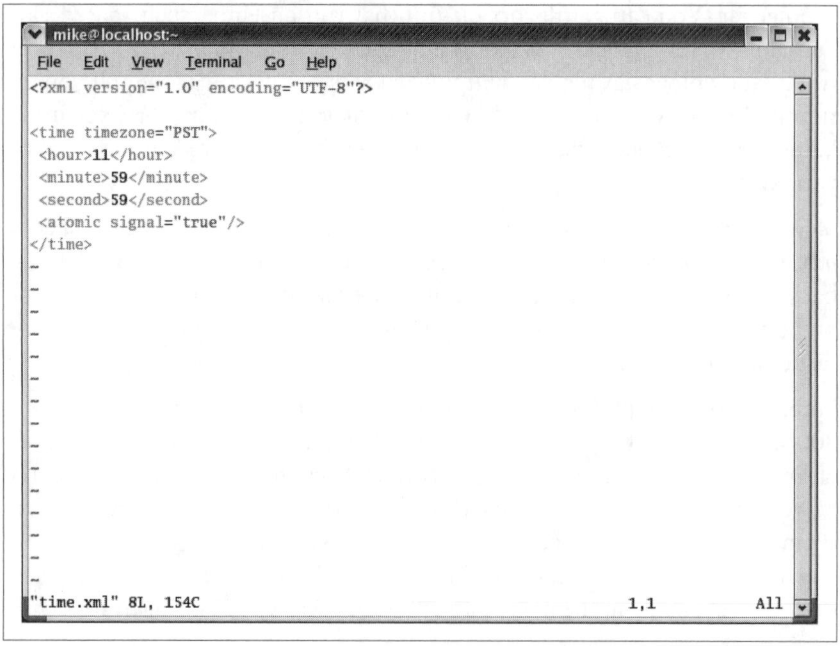

Figure 1-8. Vim in a terminal window under Gnome on Red Hat

from *http://www.thaiopensource.com/download/*). Figure 1-9 shows TEI's Emacs in nXML mode. The nXML mode offers features like context-sensitive completion of tag names based on schemas, and schema-sensitive validation using RELAX NG compact schemas [Hack #72].

Another important major mode for editing XML in Emacs is Lennart Staflin's PSGML (*http://www.lysator.liu.se/~lenst/about_psgml/* and *http://psgml.sourceforge.net/*). This major mode for Emacs provides structural editing, built-in validation with a DTD (for both XML and SGML), menus and commands for inserting tags, error reporting, and more.

Figure 1-9 shows TEI Emacs with nXML editing *time.xml* on Windows XP.

See Also

- Vim documentation: *http://vimdoc.sourceforge.net/*
- The Vim FAQ: *http://vimdoc.sourceforge.net/cgi-bin/vimfaq2html3.pl*
- Lennart Staflin's "Editing SGML with Emacs and PSGML": *http://www.lns.cornell.edu/public/COMP/info/psgml/psgml_toc.html*
- Bob DuCharme's PSGML tricks: *http://www.snee.com/bob/sgmlfree/emcspsgm.html*

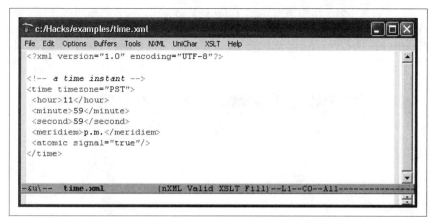

Figure 1-9. TEI Emacs with nXML editing time.xml

HACK #6 Explore XML Documents in Graphical Editors

Text editor not enough for you? This hack looks at XML documents with graphical editors.

Along with XML has come a thundering horde of graphical XML editors that do everything short of buttering your toast. Many editors are readily available (see *http://www.xmlsoftware.com/editors.html* for a comprehensive though not exhaustive list), but I'll mention only a few safe bets here.

xmlspy

xmlspy 2004 by Altova (*http://www.xmlspy.com*) is a feature-rich, graphical editor for XML for the Windows environment. xmlspy has also been tested on Red Hat Linux running Wine, and Mac OS/X running Microsoft Virtual PC for Mac. The Home Edition of this popular editor is available for free, but you must pay for licensess for Professional and Enterprise editions. I'll give you a quick feature fly-over of xmlspy—though there are a number of features I won't get around to mentioning.

xmlspy can help you create documents and schemas by hand or from templates (examples), organize work into projects, and import text and database files. You can view documents as text with syntax highlighting or in a grid view, check spelling, validate against DTDs and XML Schema documents, perform XSLT transformations **[Hack #33]** and evaluate XPath location paths. xmlspy provides support for WSDL (*http://www.w3.org/TR/wsdl*) and SOAP **[Hack #63]**. You can also use xmlspy to generate Java, C++, or C# code **[Hack #99]** from DTDs or XML Schema documents.

Figure 1-10 shows the document *valid.xml* in xmlspy with helper panes on the right. These panes let you insert elements, attributes, and entities with a single click. The Project pane on the left gives you quick access to all kinds of templates.

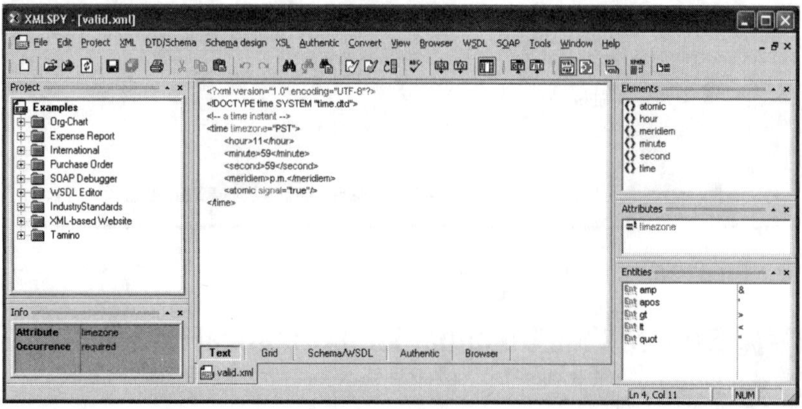

Figure 1-10. valid.xml in xmlspy 2004

xRay2

xRay2 is a free, Windows-only graphical XML editor from Architag (*http://architag.com/xray/*). Figure 1-11 displays *time.xml* in xRay2. It's a small download (a little over 5 megabytes) and comes with only a handful of files. This editor is a great learning tool because it checks your XML as you type. It uses syntax highlighting, and the shaded pane at the bottom of the editing window shows a red, yellow, or green background color depending on what you're typing (think traffic light). The status bar also reports whether your document is well-formed. You can check your XML in real time or at measured intervals, or turn it off altogether. xRay2 also recognizes and checks against DTD and XML Schema documents and can perform XSLT transformations [Hack #33].

is supported on Windows, the Mac, and Linux and other flavors of Unix. This editor is written in Java and has lots of useful features. And the price is right: you can get a 30-day trial, and a single license costs only $74 USD. (It's cheaper in quantity.) Norm Walsh wrote a glowing little review of worth reading (*http://norman.walsh.name/2004/01/22/oxygen*). Figure 1-12 shows *time.xml* in .

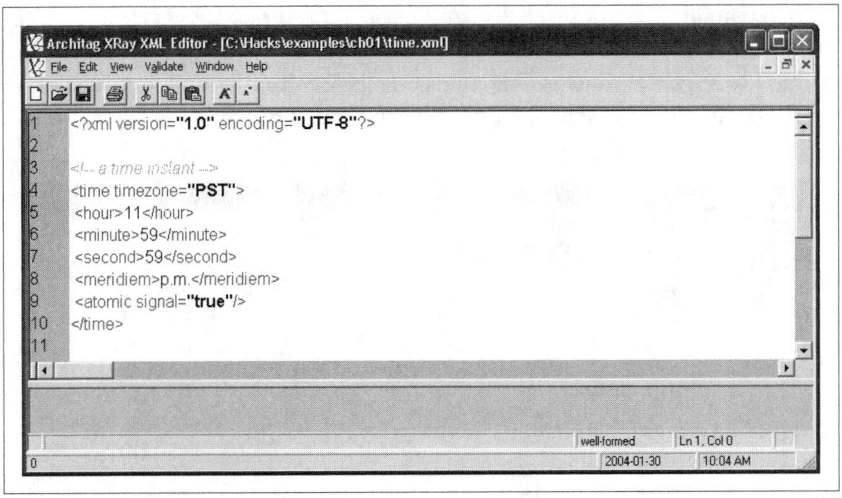

Figure 1-11. time.xml in xRay2

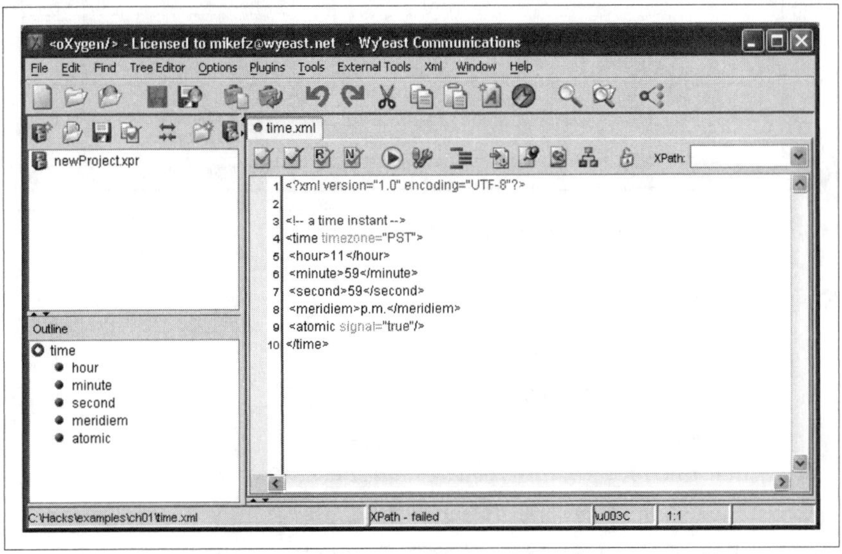

Figure 1-12. time.xml in <oXygen/> 3.0

lets you create XML documents or schemas from templates or from scratch, and then use projects to organize your work. You can view documents with syntax highlighting or with a tree editor (see Figure 1-13); check spelling; validate against DTDs, XML Schema, RELAX NG in both XML and compact syntax, even Namespace Routing Language (see *http://www.thaiopensource.com/relaxng/nrl.html*); perform XSLT transformations [Hack #33]; and evaluate XPath location paths. Two features that I particularly like are the ability to use FTP (*http://www.ietf.org/rfc/rfc959.txt*) and Web-DAV (*http://www.webdav.org/*) and to save a document to a URL from within <oXygen/>, and seeing the code point for the Unicode character where the cursor is flashing displayed in the status bar.

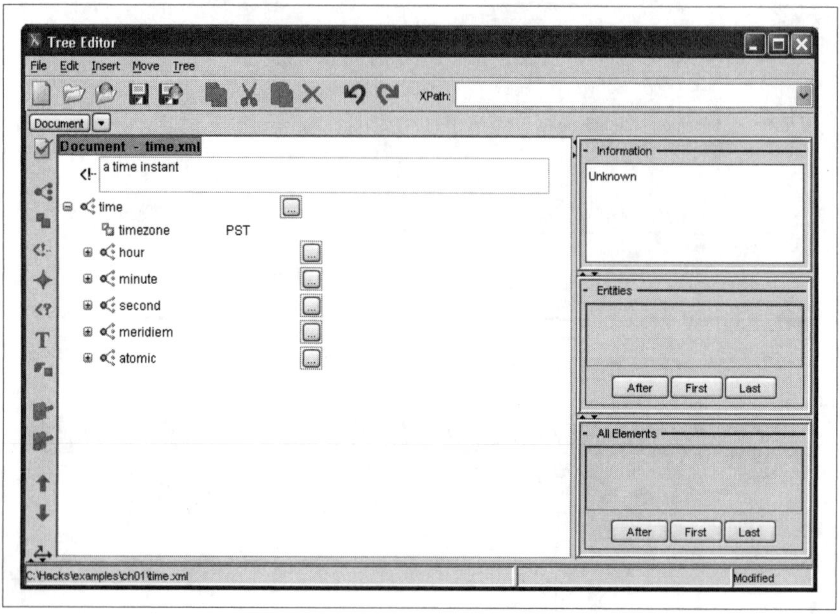

Figure 1-13. Tree Editor view of time.xml in <oXygen/> 3.0

See Also

- jEdit: *http://www.jedit.org*
- Armed Bear: *http://armedbear-j.sourceforge.net/*
- XML Cooktop: *http://www.xmlcooktop.com*
- XMLDistilled Editor: *http://www.xmldistilled.com/tools/*
- SysOnyx's xmlHack: *http://www.sysonyx.com*
- Bob Foster's XML Buddy and XML Buddy Pro, an Eclipse (*http://www. eclipse.org/*) IDE plug-in: *http://www.xmlbuddy.com*
- Xopus browser-based editor for Internet Explorer: *http://xopus.com/*
- XMLmind: *http://www.xmlmind.com/xmleditor/*
- XMLwriter XML Editor: *http://www.xmlwriter.net/*
- Blast Radius' XMetal 4: *http://www.sq.com*
- Sonic Stylus Studio: *http://www.stylusstudio.com/index.html*

- Tibco TurboXML: *http://www.tibco.com/solutions/products/extensibility/turbo_xml.jsp*
- Topologi's Collaborative Markup Editor: *http://www.topologi.com*
- Editing XML documents in Microsoft Word 2003 **[Hack #14]**

HACK #7 Choose Tools for Creating an XML Vocabulary

XML provides the syntax necessary to create your own vocabulary or dialect of XML. Here are a few things you need to know about namespaces and schemas.

One of the best things about XML is that you can create your own tags—a vocabulary or dialect—if you want. To create a vocabulary, you should understand a couple of things about schemas and namespaces. You can use XML without schemas or namespaces, but sometimes you want to use one, the other, or both. This hack explains when you'll want to use schemas and namespaces and when you'll want to avoid them.

Well-Formedness, Validation, and Schemas

XML documents must be *well-formed*. This means that they must adhere to the syntax defined in the XML specification (*http://www.w3.org/TR/REC-xml/*). This syntax mandates such things as matching case in tag names, matching quotes around attribute values, restrictions on what Unicode characters may be used, and so on.

An XML document may also be *valid*. This means that such a document must conform to the restrictions laid out in an associated schema. Basically, a *schema* declares or defines what elements and attributes are allowed in a valid instance, including in what order the elements may appear. Governing document layout with schemas can greatly increase the reliability, consistency, and accuracy of exchanged documents.

DTD. The native schema language of XML is the document type definition or DTD **[Hack #68]**, which is part of the XML specification and which XML inherited, in simplified form, from SGML. The document *valid.xml* in Example 1-7 uses a document type declaration (shown in boldface) to associate a DTD with itself.

Example 1-7. valid.xml

```
<?xml version="1.0" encoding="UTF-8"?>
<!DOCTYPE time SYSTEM "time.dtd">

<!-- a time instant -->
```

Example 1-7. valid.xml (continued)

```
<time timezone="PST">
 <hour>11</hour>
 <minute>59</minute>
 <second>59</second>
 <meridiem>p.m.</meridiem>
 <atomic signal="true"/>
</time>
```

The document type declaration states that the document element for *valid. xml* is the time element and that it is an instance of the DTD *time.dtd*. SYSTEM indicates that the DTD will be found as indicated in the filename that follows, in this case, relative to the location of *valid.xml* (in this case, in the same directory). The simple DTD *time.dtd* is shown in Example 1-8.

Example 1-8. time.dtd

```
1  <!ELEMENT time (hour,minute,second,meridiem,atomic)>
2  <!ATTLIST time timezone CDATA #REQUIRED>
3  <!ELEMENT hour (#PCDATA)>
4  <!ELEMENT minute (#PCDATA)>
5  <!ELEMENT second (#PCDATA)>
6  <!ELEMENT meridiem (#PCDATA)>
7  <!ELEMENT atomic EMPTY>
8  <!ATTLIST atomic signal CDATA #REQUIRED>
```

The DTD is not written in XML syntax: it has its own structural rules. This DTD uses what are called *markup declarations* for elements and attributes to spell out how the elements and attributes should appear in an instance. For example, the element declaration on line 1 indicates that the time element will contain only child elements, and that exactly one occurrence of each of these child elements will appear in the exact order hour, minute, second, meridiem, and atomic.

The element declaration on line 3 tells the XML processor that the hour element will contain parsed character data or text (the same goes for the minute, second, and meridiem elements declared on lines 4, 5, and 6). The atomic element is declared empty on line 7 (no content).

Two attributes are declared on lines 2 and 8. These *attribute-list declarations*, probably so called because you can list more than one attribute at a time, first name the element that is linked to the attribute (time with timezone, atomic with signal), followed by the kind of value allowed for the attribute (CDATA is text, basically). Finally, a token is given that indicates that the attribute is required and must appear on the element (#REQUIRED).

Other schema languages. XML Schema [Hack #69] was developed by the W3C, reaching recommendation status in May 2001 (*http://www.w3.org/XML/ Schema*). Written in XML, it is a grammar-based schema language that aims to provide more expressive power than DTDs, which it succeeds in doing to a degree. One of the most popular features of XML Schema is extensive datatypes (*http://www.w3.org/TR/xmlschema-2/*). DTDs offer less than 10 types for attributes only, but XML Schema provides a broad range of standard types—string, date, boolean, integer, and byte, to name a few—for both elements and attributes. XML Schema's structures recommendation (*http://www.w3.org/TR/xmlschema-1*), where its elements and attributes are specified, is long and very complex, even somewhat obfuscated, and mournfully so. It is widely used because of the W3C imprimatur, though other schema languages seem more popular in certain circles. Take RELAX NG [Hack #72], for example.

RELAX NG (*http://www.relaxng.org* and *http://www.oasis-open.org/ committees/tc_home.php?wg_abbrev=relax-ng*) is also a grammar-based schema language, and was developed by James Clark and Murata Makoto at OASIS (*http://www.oasis-open.org*). It is a remarkably intuitive language that is easy to grasp yet has sound mathematical underpinnings, which makes it very popular with users and developers alike. It has great expressive power; for example, you can do things like validate interleaved elements that can appear in any order. It's modular, too: it implements XML Schema's datatypes, for instance, though you can implement your own datatypes if you like. RELAX NG has recently become an ISO standard as part 2 of the Document Schema Definition Language or DSDL (ISO/IEC 19757-2:2003 Information technology—Document Schema Definition Language (DSDL)—Part 2: Regular-grammar-based validation—RELAX NG). Search for DSDL at *http://www.iso.ch*.

Unlike its grammar-based cousins, Schematron [Hack #77] (*http://www. schematron.com*) is an assertion-based language that works well with other schema languages. As its creator Rick Jelliffe has said, it's the feather duster that reaches into the corners of documents that other languages can't reach. Assertions are expressed as paths, and reference implementations for Schematron are written in XSLT, a natural language for analyzing paths. Along with RELAX NG, Schematron is being standardized as part of ISO's DSDL.

There are other schema languages for XML, but DTDs, XML Schema, RELAX NG, and Schematron are the most popular.

Namespaces

Namespaces in XML provide a way to disambiguate names in XML documents, thus helping avoid the collision of names when one or more vocabularies are combined in a document. The following document, *namespace.xml* (Example 1-9), shows a default namespace declaration, which declares a namespace for the document element `time` and all of its children using the special attribute `xmlns` and the URI value `http://www.wyeast.net/time`.

Example 1-9. namespace.xml

```
<?xml version="1.0" encoding="UTF-8"?>

<!-- a time instant -->
<time timezone="PST" xmlns="http://www.wyeast.net/time">
 <hour>11</hour>
 <minute>59</minute>
 <second>59</second>
 <meridiem>p.m.</meridiem>
 <atomic signal="true"/>
</time>
```

You can also use a prefix with a namespace instead of a default namespace declaration. This is shown in *prefix.xml* (Example 1-10), which associates the prefix `tz` with namespace URI `http://www.wyeast.net/time` using the `xmlns:tz` attribute. Any child element of `tz:time` that doesn't use the prefix will not be in the `http://www.wyeast.net/time` namespace.

Example 1-10. prefix.xml

```
<?xml version="1.0" encoding="UTF-8"?>

<!-- a time instant -->
<tz:time timezone="PST" xmlns:tz="http://www.wyeast.net/time">
 <tz:hour>11</tz:hour>
 <tz:minute>59</tz:minute>
 <tz:second>59</tz:second>
 <tz:meridiem>p.m.</tz:meridiem>
 <tz:atomic tz:signal="true"/>
</tz:time>
```

"Use XML Namespaces in an XML Vocabulary" **[Hack #59]** goes into more depth about namespaces in XML.

See Also

- XML Schema primer: *http://www.w3.org/TR/xmlschema-0/*
- RELAX NG tutorial: *http://www.oasis-open.org/committees/relax-ng/tutorial.html*

- Eddie Robertsson's introduction to Schematron: *http://www.xml.com/pub/a/2003/11/12/schematron.html*
- A presentation on namespaces by Simon St.Laurent: *http://simonstl.com/articles/namespaces/*

HACK #8 Test XML Documents Online

Are your XML documents syntactically correct? Find out how and where to check XML documents using online resources.

Several web sites allow you to test your XML documents online to make sure that they are well-formed and/or valid. This hack introduces three such sites: RUWF, RXP, and Brown University's XML validation form.

RUWF

One site that does well-formedness checks is XML.com's RUWF—Are You Well-Formed? (*http://www.xml.com/pub/a/tools/ruwf/check.html*)—which is implemented in Perl using XML::Parser (*http://www.perl.com/pub/a/1998/11/xml.html*). RUWF accepts a URL for an XML document or allows you to paste an XML document into a text box.

Figure 1-14 shows a copy of *time.xml* pasted into the text box, and Figure 1-15 shows the result of clicking the RUWF? button. (You could also test an online copy of *time.xml*, *http://www.wyeast.net/time.xml*, by entering the URL into the "Your URL" text box.)

RXP

Richard Tobin of the University of Edinburgh has created RXP, a validating XML processor that is available online (*http://www.cogsci.ed.ac.uk/~richard/xml-check.html*) or from the command line **[Hack #8]**.

As mentioned earlier, the document *time.xml* is available on my web site at *http://www.wyeast.net/time.xml*. Figure 1-16 shows you how to check this document for well-formedness using the online version of RXP. Enter the URL in the text box, and then click the button labeled "check it."

The result is displayed as canonical XML (*http://www.w3.org/TR/xml-c14n*) in Figure 1-17. Canonical XML defines a method for outputting XML in a consistent, reliable way, leaving some things behind in output, such as the XML declaration and, optionally, comments.

You can also use this form to check a document for validity. The document shown in Example 1-11, *online.xml*, is located at *http://www.wyeast.net/online.xml*.

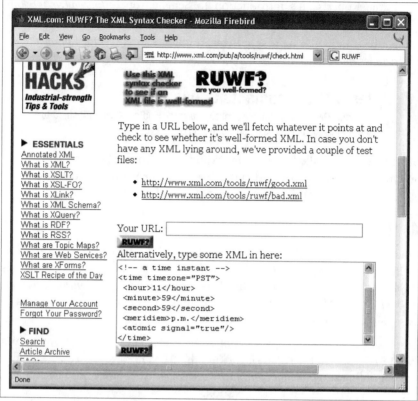

Figure 1-14. XML.com's RUWF

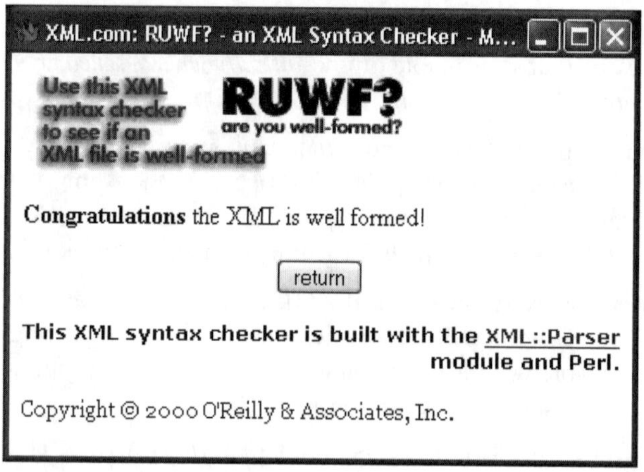

Figure 1-15. Results of checking time.xml with RUWF

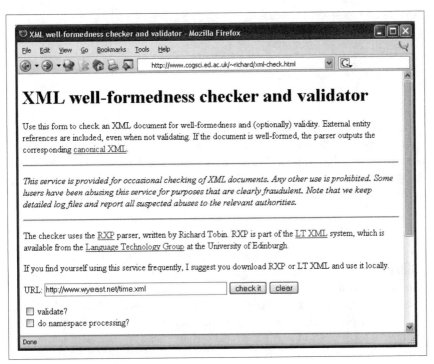

Figure 1-16. RXP online

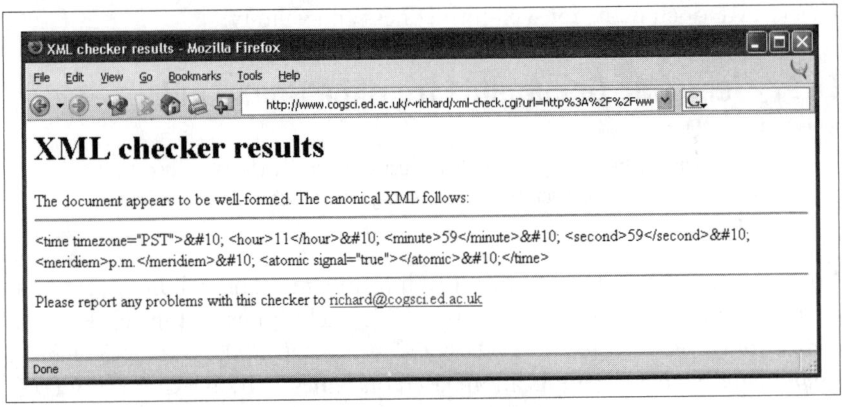

Figure 1-17. Results of checking time.xml with RXP online

Example 1-11. online.xml

```
<?xml version="1.0" encoding="UTF-8"?>
<!DOCTYPE time SYSTEM "http://www.wyeast.net/time.dtd">

<!-- a time instant -->
<time timezone="PST">
```

Example 1-11. online.xml (continued)

```
    <hour>11</hour>
    <minute>59</minute>
    <second>59</second>
    <meridiem>p.m.</meridiem>
    <atomic signal="true"/>
</time>
```

Its document type declaration references the DTD *time.dtd*, which is also available online. Place the URL *http://www.wyeast.net/online.xml* in the URL text box. Click the "validate?" checkbox below the URL text box, then click the "check it" button. The well-formedness and validity checks should report no errors.

Brown University's Validation Form

Brown University's Scholarly Technology Group (STG) provides an online validation form at *http://www.stg.brown.edu/service/xmlvalid/*. Naturally, it does a well-formedness check as well because a valid XML document must also be well-formed. This form allows you to check and validate a local file, a URL, or a pasted document. Place the URL *http://www.wyeast.net/online.xml* in the form as shown in Figure 1-18, then click the *Validate* button. The result is shown in Figure 1-19.

If you have Internet access, these online tools are an easy, no-fuss way to check XML documents for well-formedness and validity.

HACK #9 Test XML Documents from the Command Line

A number of free, easy-to-use XML processors are available for use on the command line. This hack shows where to get four such tools and how to use them.

You can check XML documents for well-formedness and validity using tools on the command line or shell prompt. This hack discusses four tools: Richard Tobin's RXP, Elcel's XML Validator (*xmlvalid*), Daniel Veillard's *xmllint*, and *xmlwf* (an application based on James Clark's Expat C library).

RXP

You've already seen the online version of RXP [Hack #8]. This hack shows you how to use the command-line version, available free at *http://www.cogsci.ed.ac.uk/~richard/rxp.html*. For Windows and other platforms, you can download the C source and compile it yourself (*ftp://ftp.cogsci.ed.ac.uk/pub/richard/rxp.tar.gz*) or, if you are on Windows, you can simply download the executable *rxp.exe* (*ftp://ftp.cogsci.ed.ac.uk/pub/richard/rxp.exe*).

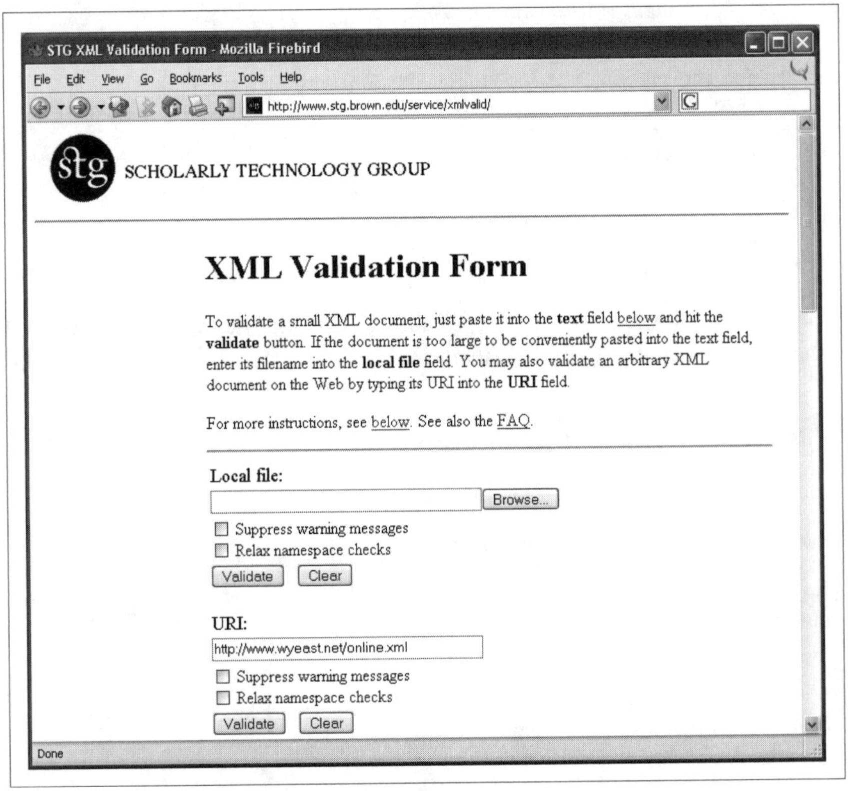

Figure 1-18. Brown University's XML validation form

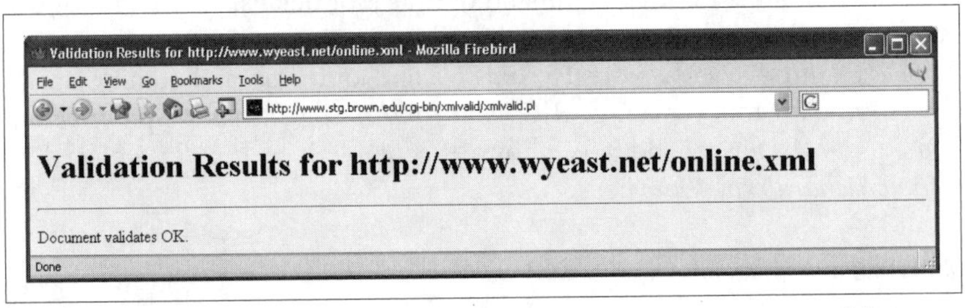

Figure 1-19. Results of validating online.xml with Brown University's XML validation form

Once you've downloaded RXP and placed it in your path, you can check XML documents for well-formedness at a command prompt with this:

```
rxp time.xml
```

Upon success, this command will produce the output shown in Example 1-12.

Example 1-12. Output of RXP with time.xml

```
<?xml version="1.0" encoding="UTF-8"?>
<!-- a time instant -->
<time timezone="PST">
    <hour>11</hour>
    <minute>59</minute>
    <second>59</second>
    <meridiem>p.m.</meridiem>
    <atomic signal="true"/>
</time>
```

You can also check a document for validity by using the -V option, provided it has an accompanying DTD (as *valid.xml* does):

```
rxp -V valid.xml
```

When successful, you will see the output in Example 1-13.

Example 1-13. Output of RXP with valid.xml

```
<?xml version="1.0" encoding="UTF-8"?>
<!DOCTYPE time SYSTEM "time.dtd">
<!-- a time instant -->
<time timezone="PST">
        <hour>11</hour>
        <minute>59</minute>
        <second>59</second>
        <meridiem>p.m.</meridiem>
        <atomic signal="true"/>
</time>
```

RXP has a number of other command options; for details, see *ftp://ftp.cogsci. ed.ac.uk/pub/richard/rxp.txt*. Also, there is a version of RXP that supports XML 1.1 (*http://www.w3.org/TR/xml11/*) and other up-and-coming specs. The source for this version of RXP is at *ftp://ftp.cogsci.ed.ac.uk/pub/richard/ rxp-1.4.0pre10.tar.gz*, and a Windows executable is at *ftp://ftp.cogsci.ed.ac. uk/pub/richard/rxp140pre4.exe*.

xmlvalid

Elcel Technologies offers XML Validator (*xmlvalid*), a free command-line XML checker and validator (*http://www.elcel.com/products/xmlvalid.html*). You have to register to download the software. *xmlvalid* runs on Windows, Linux, Solaris, and other operating systems.

Once *xmlvalid* is downloaded, installed, and in the path, you can use it on the command line in this way to check a document for well-formedness (the -v switch means "don't validate"):

```
xmlvalid -v time.xml
```

whereupon *xmlvalid* reports:

```
time.xml is well-formed
```

To check a document for validity, simply type:

```
xmlvalid valid.xml
```

and, assuming that the DTD is within reach of the processor, you get this response:

```
valid.xml is valid
```

For more command-line options, just type:

```
xmlvalid -h
```

Elcel also offers the C++ XML Toolkit (*http://www.elcel.com/products/xmltoolkit.html*) and OpenTop (*http://www.elcel.com/products/opentop/index.html*), a cross-platform C++ class library that is available under both commercial and free (GNU General Public License or GPL) licenses. The free version is available on Sourceforge (*http://sourceforge.net/projects/open-top/*).

xmllint

Another option for XML processing is *xmllint*, an application based on Daniel Veillard's C library *libxml2* (*http://www.xmlsoft.org*). *xmllint* comes with Cygwin and Red Hat, but can be downloaded separately along with the *libxml2* library (*http://xmlsoft.org/downloads.html*). *libxml2* is supported on Red Hat, Windows, Solaris, Max OS X, and HP-UX.

Assuming that *xmllint* is installed, you can type this command at a command prompt to check a document for well-formedness:

```
xmllint time.xml
```

time.xml is well-formed, so the result will be a copy of the document (Example 1-14).

Example 1-14. Output of xmllint with time.xml

```
<?xml version="1.0" encoding="UTF-8"?>
<!-- a time instant -->
<time timezone="PST">
 <hour>11</hour>
 <minute>59</minute>
 <second>59</second>
 <meridiem>p.m.</meridiem>
 <atomic signal="true"/>
</time>
```

You can also check a document for validity by using the `--valid` switch:

```
xmllint --valid valid.xml
```

If the command is successful, it yields Example 1-15.

Example 1-15. Output of xmllint with valid.xml

```
<?xml version="1.0" encoding="UTF-8"?>
<!DOCTYPE time SYSTEM "time.dtd">
<!-- a time instant -->
<time timezone="PST">
 <hour>11</hour>
 <minute>59</minute>
 <second>59</second>
 <meridiem>p.m.</meridiem>
 <atomic signal="true"/>
</time>
```

xmllint has many other options, which you can find by typing only `xmllint` at a prompt. *xmllib2* documentation is at *http://xmlsoft.org/html/index.html*. In addition to validating against a DTD, *xmllint* can also do validation against XML Schema **[Hack #69]** and RELAX NG **[Hack #72]** .

xmlwf

Another well-formedness checker is *xmlwf*, an application of the Expat C library for parsing XML (*http://expat.sourceforge.net*) that was originally written by James Clark. It comes with packages such as Cygwin on Windows and Red Hat Linux, you can also download it separately from Sourceforge as a Windows 32 executable (*xmlwf.exe*) and for other platforms.

With *xmlwf* installed and in the path, type:

```
xmlwf -v
```

xmlwf will report version and other information:

```
xmlwf using expat_1.95.7
sizeof(XML_Char)=1, sizeof(XML_LChar)=1, XML_DTD, XML_CONTEXT_BYTES=1024
```

Version 1.95.7 is the latest version as of this writing. To run *xmlwf* against a file, type this command:

```
xmlwf time.xml
```

If the file is well-formed, *xmlwf* is silent. However, if *xmlwf* finds a well-formedness error, it reports it and exits. For example, if you enter this line:

```
xmlwf bad.xml
```

xmlwf will report this error:

```
bad.xml:5:11: mismatched tag
```

This error message reports that on line 5, column 11 of *bad.xml*, *xmlwf* found a mismatched end tag (</howr>), which should have matched a previous start tag (<hour>).

Run Java Programs that Process XML

Open source, command-line Java programs that process XML are abundant. This hack shows you how to use them.

The Java programming language (*http://java.sun.com*) has been a popular object-oriented language since it was unveiled by Sun in the mid-1990s. One key idea behind Java was that it made it possible to write and compile a program once, and then run it on any machine that supports a Java interpreter ("write once, run anywhere"). Note that it's not a perfect programming language—I've heard Ted Ts'o (*http://thunk.org/tytso/*) say of Java, "Write once, run screaming."

Nonetheless, Java is widespread and generally well liked, and you'll find many command-line Java programs that can process XML in one way or another. A number of these programs appear in this book, so this hack walks you through how to use them.

 This hack assumes that you know little to nothing about Java. If you are entirely new to Java, the information at *http://java.sun.com/learning/new2java/* will also help you get up to speed quickly.

To get a Java program to run on your system, you need a Java virtual machine (VM), part of the Java runtime environment (JRE). One may already be on your system, but to get the latest JRE anyway, go to *http://java.sun.com* and find the link for the Java VM download. (There are alternatives to Sun's VM, such as one offered on *http://www.kaffe.org/*, but I'm only going to talk about the Sun VM here.) In a few clicks, the new VM will be downloaded to your machine. You should then be able to go to a command prompt and type:

```
java -version
```

and get a response that looks something like the following:

```
java version "1.4.2_03"
Java(TM) 2 Runtime Environment, Standard Edition (build 1.4.2_03-b02)
Java HotSpot(TM) Client VM (build 1.4.2_03-b02, mixed mode)
```

A more recent version may be available, but if you get a reply similar to this, you're in business. If not, consult the installation instructions for

Windows (*http://java.sun.com/j2se/1.4.2/install-windows.html*), the Mac (*http://developer.apple.com/java/download.html*), general Unix (*http://java. sun.com/j2se/1.4.2/install-linux.html*), or Solaris (*http://java.sun.com/j2se/ 1.4.2/install-solaris.html*).

JAR Files

In the file archive for this book (mentioned at the beginning of this chapter) is the Java archive or JAR file *wf.jar*. This JAR contains all the compiled Java classes from the XML Object Model or XOM (*http://www.cafeconleche.org/ XOM/*). XOM is a simple, open source, tree-based application programming interface (API) for XML, written in Java. *wf.jar* also contains a little program called *Wf.class* that does a well-formedness check on an XML document. Type in this line:

```
java -jar wf.jar
```

The program echoes back usage information, letting you know that it expects a URL as an argument:

```
Usage: java -jar wf.jar URL
```

Try it with a file:

```
java -jar wf.jar time.xml
```

Because it is well-formed, *time.xml* is written to standard output. If it were not well-formed, *Wf.class* would display an error. Try this program with *bad.xml*, which contains a fatal well-formedness error:

```
java -jar wf.jar bad.xml
```

You should get an error like:

```
nu.xom.ParsingException: Expected "</hour>" to terminate element starting on
line 5. at line 5, column -1.
```

Once again, try it with a web resource:

```
java -jar wf.jar http://www.wyeast.net/time.xml
```

If it finds no errors, the program will echo the file to standard output (the console).

> *Wf.class* uses what is know as the *JAR method*. This technique relies on an entry (Main-Class: Wf) in the manifest file that is stored in the JAR. This points the Java interpreter to *Wf.class*, which contains the main( ) method, the entry point of a Java program.

The Java Classpath

Class files contain compiled bytecode that can be executed by the Java interpreter. The interpreter has to be able to "see" where the class files are in order to execute them. That's why there's such a thing as a *classpath*. You have to place the needed Java classes in the classpath so that the interpreter can see them.

The file *Wf.class* comes with the book's file archive and should have been extracted into your working directory. Even when a class file is in the same directory where you are running the Java interpreter, you can't execute it unless it's in the classpath. In addition, the class file *Wf.class* also needs the XOM JAR to run.

Assuming that you have downloaded and stored *xom.jar* (renamed to *xom.jar* from a version available at writing time, *xom-1.0d24.jar*) in the working directory, place it directly in the classpath on the command line by using the -cp switch. On Windows, you do it like this:

```
java -cp .;xom.jar Wf worksheet.xml
```

Or on Unix, you do it like this:

```
java -cp .:xom.jar Wf worksheet.xml
```

The difference between the Windows and Unix commands is the colon versus the semicolon (: or ;). The current directory is represented by a period (.).

If a directory contains the actual classes, all you have to do is place the directory in the classpath; if the classes are contained in a JAR file, you have to place the path to the JAR file, including the JAR filename, in the classpath.

There are several other solutions for placing class files in the classpath. On Windows, you could place the JAR file in the classpath using this line at a command prompt or in *autoexec.bat*:

```
set CLASSPATH=%CLASSPATH%;".;C:\Hacks\examples\xom.jar"
```

This puts the current directory (.) and C:\Hacks\examples\xom.jar in the CLASSPATH environment variable. %CLASSPATH% prepends the current classpath to the new value of CLASSPATH.

The following command works on Unix (this line could be added to a shell setup file, such as *.profile* or *.cshrc*):

```
classpath="$CLASSPATH:/usr/mike/hacks/examples/xom.jar"
```

$CLASSPATH adds the current classpath to the new value of classpath. Another way to put classes in the classpath is to place a copy of the JAR file in the *jre/lib* directory where your JRE is installed. For example, wherever the JRE is installed, it will have the subdirectory *jre/lib*, such as *C:\Program Files\Java\j2sdk1.4.2_03\jre\lib* on Windows.

If you are using Windows XP, you can also set the CLASSPATH environment variable by choosing Start → Control Panel → System, clicking the Advanced tab, and then clicking the Environment Variables button (Figure 1-20). Select the existing CLASSPATH variable and add the classpath information to it. If the classpath variable does not already exist, you can create it by clicking the New button (Figure 1-21). You can select or add a CLASSPATH variable either for an individual user or, if you have administrator privileges, for the whole system (system variables).

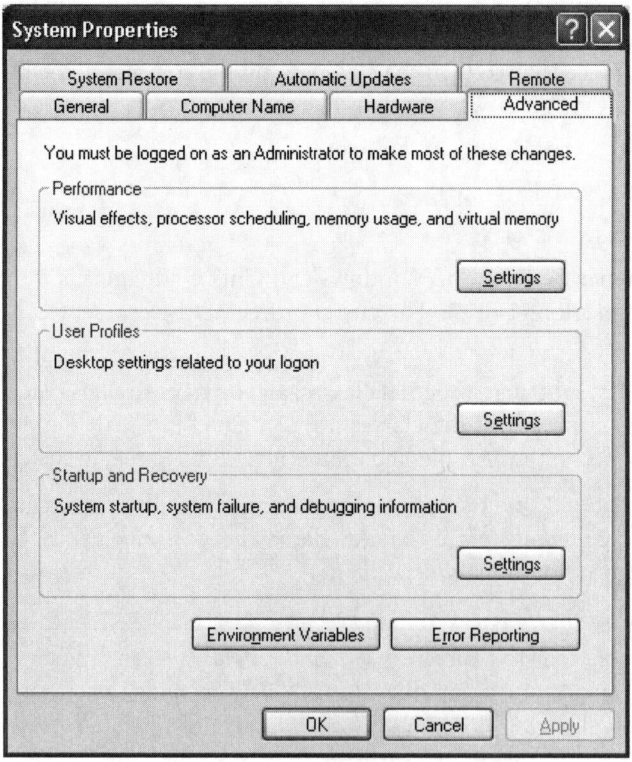

Figure 1-20. System Properties dialog box on Windows XP

Using a JAR File as an Executable on Windows 2000 or XP

With a little setup, you can use a JAR file that uses the JAR method—one that has the Main-class: field in its manifest file—like a normal executable file (*.exe*) on a Windows 2000 or XP command line. James Clark explained

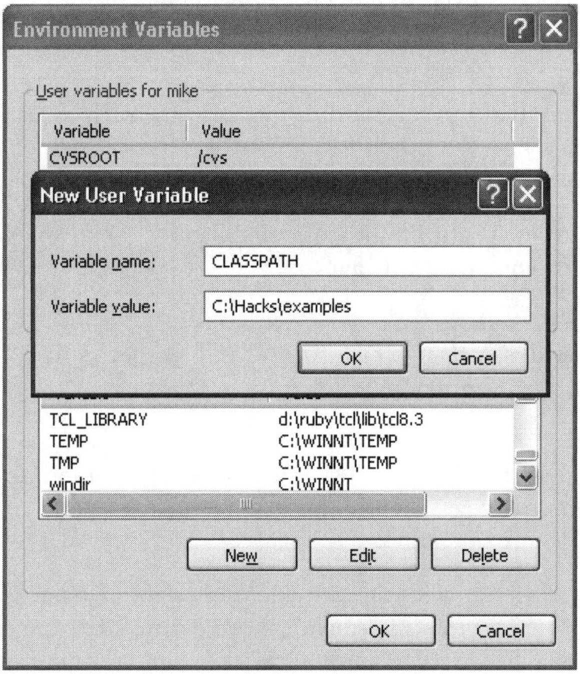

Figure 1-21. Entering a new CLASSPATH variable in Windows XP

this technique on the RELAX NG mailing list a few years ago (*http://lists. oasis-open.org/archives/relax-ng/200203/msg00037.html*). This is how you do it.

In a command prompt window, go to the working directory where you extracted the file archive for the book, then type:

```
assoc .jar
```

This helps you find out what name is associated with the *.jar* extension, if any (to backtrack, write it down if it is already associated with some name). Now type this in:

```
assoc .jar=jarfile
```

This command associates the extension *.jar* with the name *jarfile*. Then enter:

```
ftype jarfile=C:\Program Files\Java\j2sdk1.4.2_03\bin\java -jar %1 %*
```

ftype displays or modifies the file types that are used with file extension associations. This command associates the name *jarfile* with *java.exe* using the replaceable parameters %1 and %* for the JAR filename and for the input files, respectively.

Next, set the path extension like this, which prepends the *.jar* extension to the current path extensions (%pathext%):

```
set pathext=.jar;%pathext%
```

Also make sure that the current directory is in the path by using this command:

```
set path=.;%path%
```

This prepends the path of the current directory (.) to the current path (%path%). Now, enter the following:

```
wf
```

This will execute *Wf.class*, which Main-Class: Wf points to in the manifest file. You will see this response:

```
Usage: java -jar wf.jar URL
```

Try this command with other JARs, such as *jing.jar* or *trang.jar*, to see what kind of response you get. To turn this feature off, just type:

```
assoc .jar=
```

This disassociates files with the *.jar* extension with the name *jarfile*, or any other name. If *.jar* was associated with another name (determined in the first step when you typed assoc .jar), you can reenter that name now.

## CHAPTER TWO

Creating XML Documents

Hacks 11–30

The collection of hacks in this chapter introduces you to different ways to edit and create XML documents. You'll get more detailed introductions to editing XML with <oXygen/> **[Hack #11]**, with Emacs plus nXML **[Hack #12]**, and with Vim **[Hack #13]**. You'll also get exposure to three Microsoft Office 2003 applications: Word **[Hack #14]**, Excel **[Hack #15]**, and Access **[Hack #16]**.

Several hacks show you how to create XML from plain text **[Hack #18]** and **[Hack #19]** and from comma-separated values (CSV) **[Hack #21]** files. You'll execute an XQuery **[Hack #24]**, and learn about encoding documents **[Hack #27]** and including text and documents with entities **[Hack #25]** and XInclude **[Hack #26]**.

Reminder: all the example files mentioned in this chapter are available from the file archive that can be downloaded from *http://www.oreilly.com/catalog/ xmlhks/*.

Edit XML Documents with

#11 Quickly learn how to edit XML documents with .

In Chapter 1, you got an introduction to a few graphical editors **[Hack #6]**. This hack provides more highlights on how to edit documents using the graphical editor (*http://www.oxygenxml.com/*). I have chosen because it runs on multiple platforms, is inexpensive (it has a free trial and its license is less than $100 USD), and offers many useful features.

Figure 2-1 shows editing *time.xml* and *valid.xml*, both part of the project *time.xpr*. Note the project pane (upper left) and the tabs above the document pane. The lower-left pane shows an outline view of *valid.xml* (note that the hour element is highlighted in both the outline and document panes). Beneath the document pane is a tabbed pane that shows the result of a transformation of *valid.xml* with XSLT.

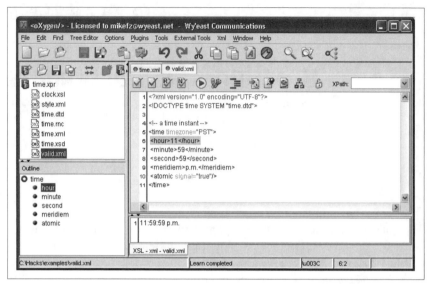

*Figure 2-1. *

Like any editor, allows you to do normal editing tasks, such as undo and redo, spell check, and so forth. Here is a list of some of 's more important features.

Projects

can organize files into groups called *projects* (see the File menu). These projects can be named and saved in simple XML project files that have an *.xpr* file extension. All the files in a project can be validated in one fell swoop. When you reopen a project, it remembers some state information, such as what file was last opened and whether it had focus.

Document creation

provides templates for creating XML documents in a variety of vocabularies: DocBook, SMIL, SVG, TEI, VoiceXML, WML, WSDL, and XHTML, to name but a few. It also has syntax highlighting, which can be edited under Options → Preferences → Colors. Syntax highlighting works not only for XML, but also batch files, C, C++, DTD, Java, PHP, RNC, SQL, and shell. The Xml → Format and Indent command quickly formats your XML to make it more readable. An outline pane allows you to highlight the structure of a document by selecting an item in the outline, and with the click of a button, you can lock elements so that they cannot be edited, although element content still can. The Tree Editor is a fully graphical landscape for inserting or adding XML structure by merely clicking buttons. File → Save to URL allows you to save a document on the Web using FTP/WebDAV.

Well-formedness and validation

has a well-formedness checker (Xml → Check document form), and can validate against a DTD or XML Schema (Xml → Validate document), RELAX NG—both XML and compact versions (Xml → RELAX NG validation)—and even Namespace Routing Language (Xml → NRL validation; see also *http://www.thaiopensource.com/relaxng/nrl. html*). A special command provides a quick way to associate a schema with an instance (Xml → Associate schema). Because RELAX NG does not have its own method for associating schemas, <oXygen/> uses its own processing instruction **[Hack #3]** that appears as follows: `<?oxygen RNGSchema="file:/C:/Hacks/examples/time.rnc" type="compact"?>`. Schemas can be local or across the Web. You can generate documentation about your schemas, too.

XSLT and XPath support

offers several built-in XSLT processors. You can create and name a variety of transformation scenarios (Xml → Create transformation scenario), and include parameters with the command as well as insert headers and footers for output. These scenarios can be imported and exported (Options → Import transformation scenarios and Options → Export transformation scenarios). has a built-in XSL-FO processor (FOP) with PDF, PostScript (ps), or text output. You can also specify output be sent to a browser or saved in a file (you can choose to be prompted for a name). Transformation results are displayed in tabbed panes and can be saved in files. can also evaluate XPath paths to see if they exist in a given document (with the results shown in a tabbed pane).

Trang converter

provides an interface to James Clark's Trang conversion tool (*http://www.thaiopensource.com/relaxng/trang.html*). Trang is a handy tool that can accept a DTD, a RELAX NG schema in XML or compact syntax, or an XML document as input, and then output a DTD, a RELAX NG schema (XML or compact), or an XML Schema.

HACK #12 Edit XML Documents with Emacs and nXML

nXML mode for GNU Emacs provides a powerful environment for creating valid XML documents.

If you've been editing XML from within GNU Emacs using PSGML, here's a tip: get rid of it. That's right, tear it out, dump it, make it disappear—because there's a much better tool available: nXML. (Grab the latest *nxml-mode-200nnnnn.tar.gz* file from *http://www.thaiopensource.com/download/*.)

nXML was developed by James Clark, the man who brought us groff, expat, sgmls, SP, and Jade, as well as being a driving force behind the development of XPath, XSLT (and before that, DSSSL), and, along with Murata Makoto, RELAX NG (*http://www.relaxng.org/*).

Which brings us back to what nXML is all about: nXML is a very clever mechanism for doing RELAX NG-driven, context-sensitive, validated editing. What's particularly clever about it is that, unlike PSGML and unlike virtually every other XML editing application available—with the exception of the Topologi Collaborative Markup Editor (*http://www.topologi.com/products/tme/*)—it provides real-time, automatic visual identification of validity errors.

This hack assumes that you are familiar with Emacs. The *README* file that comes with nXML states that you must use Emacs version 21.*x* (preferably 21.3 or later) in order to use nXML. To get nXML to run in Emacs, you must first load the *rng-auto.el* file. In Emacs, type:

```
M-x load-file
```

Then load the file *rng-auto.el* from the location where you downloaded and extracted the latest version of nXML. This file defines the autoloads for nXML. Now open an XML document (C-x C-f) and enter:

```
M-x nxml-mode
```

You are good to go! For help, type:

```
C-h m
```

Spotting Validity Errors in Real Time

What "automatic visual identification of validity errors" means is that if you create and edit documents using nXML, you never need to manually run a separate validation step to determine whether a document is valid; i.e., if a document contains a validity error, you will know instantly as you edit the document because it will be visually flagged. Here's how it works. As you're editing a document:

- nXML incrementally reparses and revalidates the document in the background during idle periods between the times when you are actually typing in content. You can wait for nXML to finish validating the entire document (which usually takes only a matter of seconds), or if you're working with a large document, you don't need to wait: the moment you start typing in content, nXML will stop its background parsing and validating until you're idle once again.

- nXML describes the current validity state in the mode line at the bottom of the Emacs interface; at any point while you're editing a document, the mode line will say either Valid, Invalid, or Validated nn%, where nn is a number indicating what percentage of the document has been validated so far.

- nXML visually highlights all instances of invalidity it finds in the part of the document it has validated so far (by default, the value of the Emacs face it uses is a red underline, but the highlighting can be changed by customizing that face).

If you mouse over or move your cursor over one of the points that nXML has highlighted as invalid, text appears describing the validity error, either as popup text or in the minibuffer echo area at the bottom of the Emacs interface. Figure 2-2 shows a validity error in DocBook **[Hack #62]**. You can use the keyboard combination C-c C-n to step through all validity errors in a document.

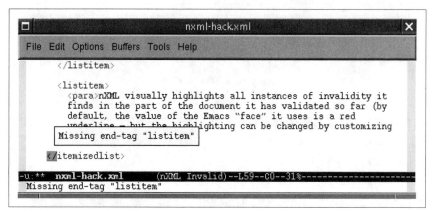

Figure 2-2. nXML validation error message

Getting Help with nXML

To get oriented with the basics of editing within nXML:

- Type C-h (or M-x describe-mode) for quick help with nXML commands and key bindings.

- For more extensive documentation, access the nXML manual (in texinfo format) by typing M-x info.

- Make sure to read the NEWS file in the nXML distribution; it probably contains some late information that hasn't yet made its way into the nXML manual.

Using Context-Sensitive Completion

The nXML mechanism for doing context-sensitive insertion/completion of markup is similar to the mechanism that PSGML provides. With nXML, you:

1. Place your cursor at some point in a document.

2. Type a keyboard combination (in the nXML case, C-Return) to do context-sensitive checking to see what markup (elements, attributes, or enumerated attribute values) is valid at that point in the document; Emacs then opens up a completion buffer containing a list of the valid markup choices.

3. Either use your mouse to select one of the choices from the completion buffer, or type the first few letters of one of the choices and then tab to cause Emacs to do completion on that name or value. Figure 2-3 shows context-sensitive completion using DocBook.

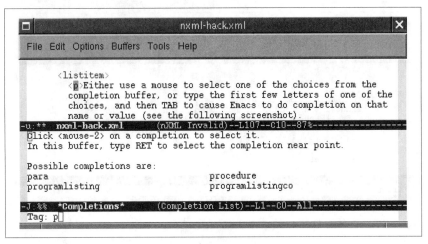

Figure 2-3. nXML context-sensitive completion

Making nXML Work Your Way

To fine-tune the behavior of nXML:

- Explore nXML's extensive, well-documented set of customization options by typing M-x customize-group nXML.

- Even if you change no other nXML option, try setting the value of the Nxml Sexp Element Flag option (nxml-sexp-element-flag variable) to on (non-nil). The default value (nil) means that Emacs sexp commands— for example, C-M-k (kill-sexp)—operate on tags. What you probably want instead is for them to operate on elements, which is what turning on the Nxml Sexp Element Flag option will do for you.

- Spend some time experimenting with the syntax-highlighting options; nXML provides what must be by far the best and most configurable syntax-highlighting capabilities of any XML editing application currently available. Over 30 customizable Emacs faces enable you to independently control color and character formatting of everything from the level of element and attribute names down to the level of different types of markup delimiters (e.g., angle-bracket tag delimiters, the quote marks around attribute values, etc.).

Entering and Displaying Special Characters

Another area where nXML is very clever is the way in which it enables you to enter and display special characters. To enter a special character, such as a copyright sign:

1. Type C-c C-u. nXML then prompts you for the name of the character to enter.

2. Type the first few letters of the character name and then hit tab. nXML then does completion, presenting you with a list of all character names that start with the letters you type in. For example, if you enter *cop*, nXML will present you with a list of several character names that starts with *COPTIC*, along with the name of the character that's probably the one you're looking for: *COPYRIGHT SIGN*.

3. Either use your mouse to select one of the choices from the completion buffer, or type more letters then tab again to narrow down the choices to the character you need. Or, if you just type *copy* to begin with, you'll get straight to the copyright sign (because it's the only character name that begins with *COPY*).

Note that, by default, nXML inserts the hexadecimal character entity reference, not the actual character; e.g., for the copyright sign, nXML inserts the character reference ©. This ensures that you will be able to interpret what the character is if it is displayed by software that does not understand Unicode.

But this is where things get interesting: even though nXML writes only the numeric character reference to the file, it displays the glyph for the character (along with the character reference itself). And if you mouse over the character reference, nXML displays the full name of the character, either as pop-up text or in the minibuffer echo area at the bottom of the Emacs interface (Figure 2-4).

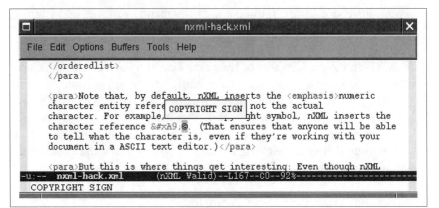

Figure 2-4. nXML display of special characters

As far as special characters go, nXML lets you have your cake and eat it too. You get:

- An easy way to enter special characters as character references, without needing to memorize or look up their numeric values or ISO entity names.

- The ability to see glyphs and full names for all the character references in your documents, while still being able to distribute them to others as ASCII-encoded files (so you're not depending on others having editors that support Unicode or some other encoding).

To enter special characters in other ways:

- Instead of typing C-c C-u to get prompted for a character name, type C-u C-c C-u. You'll go through the same completion process to enter the name, but when you're done, nXML will insert the character directly, instead of inserting the character reference. GNU Emacs 21.x or later supports display of Unicode and many other encodings (as long as you have the fonts), so you don't have to avoid inserting characters directly unless you need to share your source documents with others who might not have Unicode-enabled editors.

- Try Norm Walsh's XML Unicode Lisp package (*http://nwalsh.com/ emacs/xmlchars/*). Among other things, it automatically inserts "smart" quotes in just the same way that most word-processing applications do, along with a smart em-dash/en-dash feature. It also provides a menu-driven mechanism for entering special characters, so you don't need to type and do completion; instead, you just select a character name from a menu. Compatibility with nXML's native character-insertion mechanism isn't a problem—the two coexist with one another quite happily.

See Also

- *Learning GNU Emacs* by Debra Cameron, Bill Rosenblatt, and Eric S. Raymond (O'Reilly)
- The nXML mailing list is the first place to go if you have questions or run into problems: *http://groups.yahoo.com/group/emacs-nxml-mode/*

—Michael Smith

HACK #13 Edit XML with Vim

With some special configuration, Vim can become a powerful XML editor.

So you want to edit XML, but Vim is your favorite editor? The good news is that you don't need an XML-specific editor! If you're mortal, you'll soon discover that editing raw XML can become tedious even in Vim (with its default configuration). But Vim is highly customizable and extensible. After a little tailoring, Vim performs excellently as an XML editor, with syntax highlighting, automatic indentation, navigational aids, and automation.

Basic Configuration

I will assume you have Vim set up the way you like it already on a Unix system, so we won't fiddle much with your *.vimrc* file. Example 2-1 shows the bare minimum of what you need to make the rest of the hack work properly.

Example 2-1. Minimum .vimrc file

```
" $HOME/.vimrc
" Don't pretend to be vi
set nocompatible
" Turn on syntax highlighting
syntax on
" Indicate that we want to detect filetypes and want to run filetype
" plugins.
filetype plugin on
```

Everything else will go in a `filetype` plug-in. Vim will source this file when it detects that you are editing an XML file (i.e., when the file ends with the *.xml* suffix or if it has a proper XML declaration). Example 2-2 is a good starter `ftplugin`. Save it to your home directory as *.vim/after/ftplugin/xml.vim*. (The file *xml.vim* is in the book's file archive.) The `after` segment of the path means that it will be sourced after all the normal scripts, plug-ins, and so on are sourced, which allows you to override defaults and other plug-ins without changing the original scripts. That makes upgrading those scripts easier.

Example 2-2. The ftplugin xml.vim

```
" $VIMRUNTIME/after/ftplugin/xml.vim
" Turn on auto-indentation

set autoindent

" Let's use a 2-character indent

set shiftwidth=2

" With smarttab set, we can press tab at the beginning
" of a line and get shiftwidth indent even though
" tabstop is something else (e.g. the default 8)

set smarttab

" A lot of XML looks really bad and gets really confusing if
" screen-wrapped. I prefer to turn off wrapping.

set nowrap
```

On Windows, your *vimrc* file is *$VIM\_vimrc* (default *C:\vim\_vimrc*). Consider *$VIMRUNTIME* by default to be *C:\vim\vimfiles*. So, for example, you should install the *ftplugin* in *C:\vim\vimfiles\after\ftplugin*. See :help doslocations for more details.

Syntax Highlighting

All XML files can benefit from the generic XML syntax highlighting included with Vim. But not all XML is created equal. Imagine you came up with a nifty XML format for your data and now you want certain items to be emphasized to make editing and reading easier. That probably wasn't too hard to imagine, was it?

There are two steps to customized syntax highlighting. The first step is telling Vim how to differentiate your special XML from regular XML. The second step is to define how your special syntax highlighting differs.

We'll work with a simple RSS 2.0 file [Hack #83] as our example, called *frodo. rss* (Example 2-3). Figure 2-5 shows *frodo.rss* in gVim, a GUI version of Vim (*ftp://ftp.vim.org/pub/vim/pc/gvim63.zip*), on Debian (GTK2 in Grand Canyon theme).

Example 2-3. frodo.rss

```
<?xml version="1.0"?>
<rss version="2.0">
  <channel>
    <title>The Gondor Times</title>
    <link>http://www.gondortimes.com/</link>
```

Example 2-3. frodo.rss (continued)

```
    <description>News for the race of men.</description>
    <item>
      <title>Sauron defeated!</title>
      <category>Middle Earth</category>
      <description>Now comes the story of Nine-fingered Frodo and the
          Ring of Doom.</description>
      <guid>http://www.gondortimes.com/middleearth/3/25</guid>
    </item>
  </channel>
</rss>
```

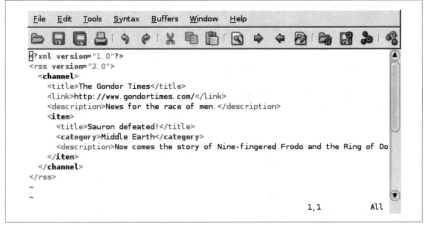

Figure 2-5. frodo.rss in gVim

In order for Vim to treat an XML vocabulary specially, it needs to differentiate it from normal XML. The easiest way to do this is by using a different file extension. Setting up a new `filetype` with a unique extension is straightforward (see `:help new-filetype`). Let's define a `filetype` for RSS 2.0 files with *.vim/filetype.vim*, as shown in Example 2-4.

Example 2-4. filetype.vim

```
" my filetype file
if exists("did_load_filetypes")
    finish
endif
augroup filetypedetect
    au! BufRead,BufNewFile *.rss        set filetype=rss
augroup END
```

Now when you restart Vim and edit *frodo.rss*, you should notice that it is not being recognized as XML any longer. That means no syntax highlighting, no ftplugin, nada. Wait, don't despair! You don't need to rewrite syntax highlighting for XML.

Let's set a modest goal for ourselves: highlight the channel and item tag names in bold, and make category tag names a different color. The way to achieve this is to utilize the xmlTagHook cluster provided by the *syntax/xml.vim* author. A syntax cluster is an open-ended bag of syntax groups that can occur in certain places. That means we can define a syntax group and say that it belongs to the xmlTagHook cluster, and it will be matched only when the match would otherwise be a regular XML tag. Let's look at Example 2-5.

Example 2-5. rss.vim

```
" Vim syntax file
" Language:      RSS 2.0
" Maintainer:    Hans Fugal <hans@fugal.net>
" Last Change:   Thu, 11 Mar 2004 15:44:28 -0700

" REFERENCES:
"    1. http://blogs.law.harvard.edu/tech/rss

" Quit when a syntax file was already loaded
if exists("b:current_syntax")
    finish
endif

" Base our syntax highlighting on xml
runtime syntax/xml.vim

syn match rssElement /\<channel\>/
syn match rssElement /\<item\>/
syn match rssCategory /\<category\>/

syn cluster xmlTagHook add=rssElement,rssCategory

highlight rssElement cterm=bold gui=bold
highlight link rssCategory Statement
```

Those syn match lines define the patterns that will match the rssElement group. The \< and \> match the beginning and end of a word (tag), respectively. So we are matching the full word channel or the full word item. The syn cluster line adds our new rssElement and rssCategory groups to the xmlTagHook cluster. The highlight lines define how we want things to look. You'll want to look up the help on highlight because that's where your creativity can really flow.

syntax/xml.vim also provides these hooks:

- xmlAttribHook
- xmlNamespaceHook
- xmlTagHook

- xmlStartTagHook
- xmlRegionHook
- xmlCdataHook

See the comments in *syntax/xml.vim* from the Vim distribution for more details.

OK, so now you have syntax highlighting, but you've lost the behaviors we defined in *after/ftplugin/xml.vim*, and many more behaviors that we'll talk about shortly that you certainly won't want to miss out on. The easiest solution to this problem is to create a symbolic link from *after/ftplugin/xml.vim* to *after/ftplugin/rss.vim* (or whatever new filetype you created).

Indentation

Vim's auto-indent is OK, but smart indentation is better. Enabling smart indent for XML in Vim is as simple as putting filetype indent on in your *.vimrc* or in your *ftplugin*. If you don't like the XML smart indentation but do like filetype indent on in your *.vimrc*, then you can put let b:did_indent = 1 in your XML *ftplugin*.

Sometimes you want to clean up the formatting of the whole XML file. To do this you can either type gg=G with filetype indent on or use an external filter. The internal method is prone to messing with your whitespace in verbatim elements, while external formatters such as Paul DuBois's *xmlformat* (*http://www.kitebird.com/software/xmlformat/*) or *xmllint* with --format (see "Test XML Documents from the Command Line" [Hack #9]) can do a much better job.

To use *xmlformat* to format your XML in Vim, try the following command (assuming *xmlformat* is installed and in the path):

    :!xmlformat %

To use *xmllint*, try:

    :!xmllint --format %

Both of these commands are good candidates for mappings (see "Automation").

Folding

Folding is a new feature in Vim Version 6 and later that allows you to collapse arbitrary portions of your document down to one line, similar to collapsing and expanding trees in menus or dialog boxes. XML lends itself well to folding because of its hierarchical nature. There are several ways to do folding (see :help folding). The easiest way to fold XML is to use the syn-

tax method. To enable folding in XML documents, add the following lines
to your XML *ftplugin*:

```
set foldenable
set foldmethod=syntax
set foldlevel=1
```

The set foldlevel=1 line tells Vim to leave the top element unfolded. You
can tune this number to your liking. You can also tune it to specific files by
using a modeline at the bottom of the file; for example:

```
<!-- vim:foldlevel=5 -->
```

All fold commands start with z. zo opens a fold, zc closes one, zm increases
the number of folds (decreases foldlevel), and zr reduces the number of
folds. zM and zR fold everything and nothing, respectively. Figure 2-6 shows
an example of folding with *frodo.rss*.

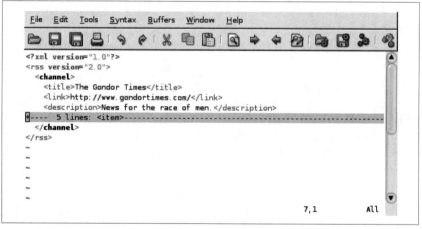

Figure 2-6. frodo.rss in gVim with folding

Automation

The biggest problem with editing XML by hand is all that typing. Vim can
help you avoid a lot of that extra typing thanks to some wonderful contributed scripts that can be found at *http://www.vim.org*.

matchit.vim
> Extends the behavior of % and includes support for XML. Pressing % will
> take you from opening tag to closing tag, and vice versa. It was written
> by Benji Fisher. See *http://www.vim.org/scripts/script.php?script_id=39*.

closetag.vim
> Closes the next open tag when you press Ctrl-_. This is a real boon when
> you get tired of typing things like </xsl:apply-templates>. It was writ-

ten by Steven Mueller. See *http://www.vim.org/scripts/script.php?script_id=13*.

EnhCommentify.vim

A handy script for commenting and uncommenting segments of your file, and supports XML very well. It was written by Meikel Brandmeyer. See *http://www.vim.org/scripts/script.php?script_id=23*.

xmledit.vim

The mother of all XML Vim scripts is *xmledit.vim*. It further enhances %, provides other navigation facilities, auto-creates closing tags, can %delete a surrounding tag, and has a dialog-driven tag creator in visual mode that will wrap a tag around whatever is selected. *xmledit.vim* makes writing XML much less tedious, and it makes well-formedness easier than ever to achieve. It was written by Devin Weaver. See *http://www.vim.org/scripts/script.php?script_id=301*.

There are many other scripts and tips available. In addition to general scripts and tips, you may find yourself with specific desires for automation. Do you create similar XML documents frequently by hand? Use a template (see :help :r). Maybe you want to map *xmlformat* to a simple keystroke (see :help key-mapping). Perhaps you type <xsl:apply-templates> far too often and would prefer to type <a-t> and watch it magically expand to <xsl:apply-templates> (see :help abbrev). Maybe an abbreviation isn't enough and you want <a-t> to expand to <xsl:apply-templates select=""> with the cursor right between the quotation marks, in which case you're in the realm of scripting (see :help vim-script-info). If you don't like Vim's scripting language, you can extend Vim with Perl, Python, Ruby, or Tcl. With Vim, the sky's the limit.

See Also

- The Vim help files: :help or online at *http://vimdoc.sourceforge.net/*
- Tobias Rief's excellent HOWTO on Vim as an XML editor: *http://www.pinkjuice.com/howto/vimxml/*
- Steve Oualline's *Vi Improved—Vim* (New Riders Press) is a must-have reference for any serious Vimmer (also available to read online at *http://vimdoc.sourceforge.net/*)
- Vim tips: *http://www.vim.org/tips/tip_search_results.php?keywords=xml&order_by=rating&direction=descending&search=search*
- Vim scripts: *http://www.vim.org/scripts/script_search_results.php?keywords=xml&script_type=&orderby=rating&direction=descending&search=search*

—Hans Fugal

HACK #14 Edit XML Documents with Microsoft Word 2003

Edit, validate, and save XML documents with Microsoft Word 2003.

Microsoft Office 2003 has the best XML support that a version of Office has offered yet. It's not perfect, but in some places it shines. Not all Office 2003 products provide direct XML support, but three of the flagship products do—Microsoft Word 2003, Excel 2003, and Access 2003. This hack will discuss how to "do XML" with Word 2003.

Sadly, not all versions of Word 2003 have full-featured XML support. In order to get the full support, you need to buy Office 2003 Professional, Office 2003 Enterprise, or Word 2003 individually. Word has its own built-in schema called WordprocessingML. If you create a regular document in Word, you can save the document as XML in WordprocessingML. All versions of Word 2003 have this capability.

Attaching Schemas to Word

In the Office 2003 Professional, Office 2003 Enterprise, and individually packaged Word 2003 versions of Word 2003, you can attach your own XML Schema [Hack #69] document to an XML document. This means that you can export Word documents as XML, and they will be structured according to your own custom schema rather than Word's obscure binary format or its own WordprocessingML. This means that you can test and validate such documents using external XML tools—in other words, you aren't landlocked if you use the professional, enterprise, or individual versions of Word to produce XML.

You can store or attach XML schema in Word's schema library, and you can validate XML documents against their schema. To add a schema to Word's library, go to Tools → Templates and Add-ins and then click the XML Schema tab. Now click the Add Schema button and navigate to the working directory where you will find the schema *time.xsd*. Click Open. You will be asked to associate a URI with the schema (any URI seems to work). Click "Validate document against attached schema" and "Allow saving as XML even if not valid," then click OK. The result will look like Figure 2-7.

Figure 2-8 shows how the XML document *time.xml* will look when edited in Word 2003. To view the XML Structure pane as shown, select an XML tag, right-click the mouse, and then choose View XML Structure. The XML Structure pane appears at the right of the window. Here you see a tree view of the elements in the document near the top of the pane, and below that, a list of elements that you can insert into the document by clicking them in

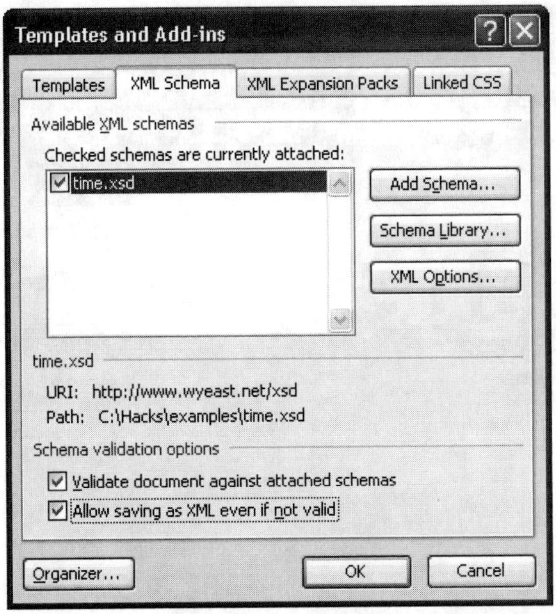

Figure 2-7. XML Schema tab of the Templates and Add-ins dialog box

the list. If you check and uncheck the box "Show XML tags in the document," it will turn the XML tags on and off.

To see attributes, click on a start tag (such as time) and then right-click and choose Attributes. You will see the assigned attributes for the tag in the Attributes dialog box as shown in Figure 2-9.

Using XSLT with Word 2003

You can also perform transformations with XSLT in Word 2003. There are several ways to do it. One way is to click Browse in the XML data views pane (at the right of the editing pane in Word 2003). Select an appropriate stylesheet for the document *time.xml*, such as *hour.xsl*. Choose an encoding such as Unicode for the output of the transformation. To return to editing *time.xml*, click "Data only;" to transform the file again, click *hour.xsl*. (See Figure 2-10.)

Another way to use XSLT is when you save a file as XML. You have a chance to select a stylesheet at that time. To see this, choose File → Save As. Near the bottom of the Save As dialog box, you'll see a checkbox "Apply transform." If checked, this means that the document will be transformed when saved. When you click Transform, you can select an XSLT stylesheet to apply when the file is saved. If you check the "Save data only" box, only the content of the elements is saved.

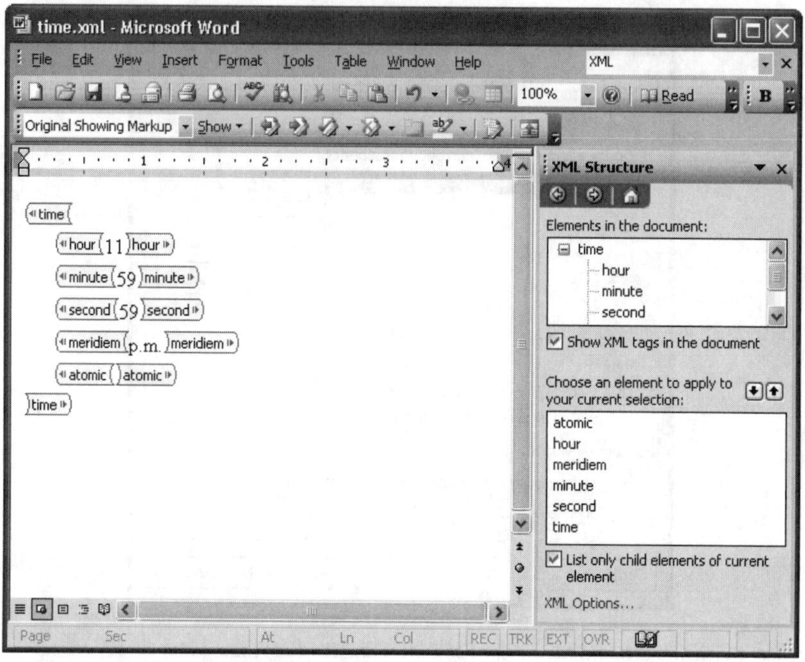

Figure 2-8. time.xml in Word 2003

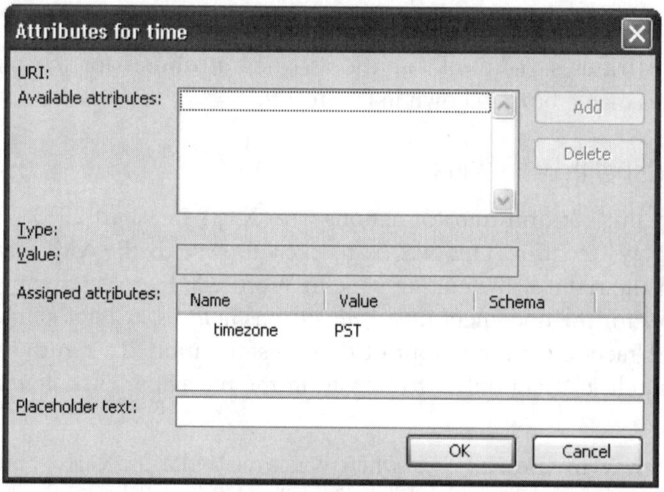

Figure 2-9. Attributes dialog box in Word 2003

You can also apply a transform when opening an XML document. Choose File → Open and then navigate to an XML document in the Open dialog

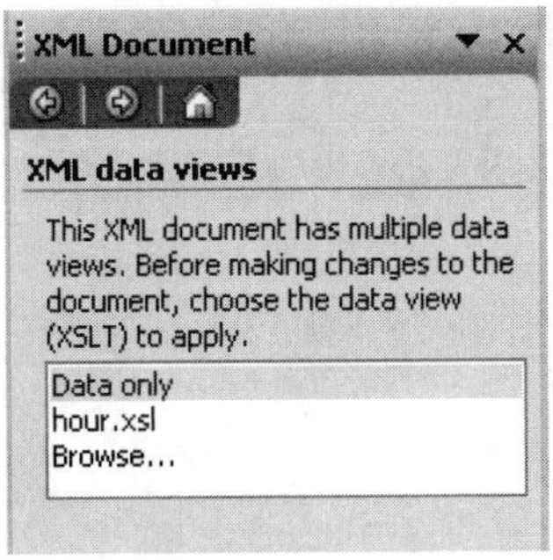

Figure 2-10. XML data views pane from Word 2003

box. Select a file, then click on the down-arrow on the Open button. There you will be able to choose Open with Transform. When you do, you will have a chance to choose an XSLT stylesheet in the Choose an XSL Transformation dialog box. Select one and click OK to perform the transformation. (Word is picky here for security reasons; if a stylesheet has scripts and is not signed, you can't use it. Also, even if a stylesheet works with another XSLT processor, it may not work with Word.)

Saving Word 2003 Files as XML

If you are working with a regular Word document, such as *time.doc* from the file archive (Figure 2-11), you can save it as XML. Choose File → Save As. In the "Save as type" pull-down menu, select XML Document. Enter a name for the file such as *Time_word.xml*. Then click Save.

This saves a long file that uses the WordprocessingML vocabulary, which stores information about the file in great detail. If you examine the file, you will find that it uses a total of 244 elements with 256 attributes. Gulp. You can bring up this file not only in Word but also in Internet Explorer with similar styling. A portion of *Time_word.xml* is shown here (I have inserted line breaks for readability):

```
<?xml version="1.0" encoding="UTF-8" standalone="yes"?>
<?mso-application progid="Word.Document"?>
<w:wordDocument xmlns:w="http://schemas.microsoft.com/office/word/2003/
wordml" xmlns:v="urn:schemas-microsoft-com:vml" xmlns:w10="urn:schemas-
microsoft-com:office:word" xmlns:sl="http://schemas.microsoft.com/
schemaLibrary/2003/core" xmlns:aml="http://schemas.microsoft.com/aml/2001/
core" xmlns:wx="http://schemas.microsoft.com/office/word/2003/auxHint"
xmlns:o="urn:schemas-microsoft-com:office:office" xmlns:dt="uuid:C2F41010-
65B3-11d1-A29F-00AA00C14882" w:macrosPresent="no" w:embeddedObjPresent="no"
w:ocxPresent="no" xml:space="preserve">
<o:DocumentProperties>
 <o:Title>Time</o:Title>
 <o:Author>Mike Fitzgerald</o:Author>
```

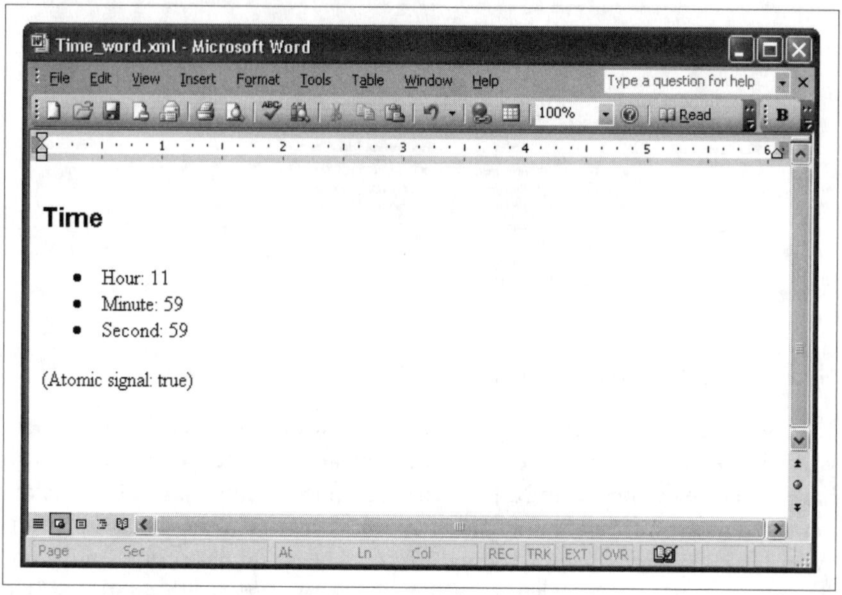

Figure 2-11. time.doc in Word 2003

```
<o:LastAuthor>Mike Fitzgerald</o:LastAuthor>
<o:Revision>2</o:Revision>
<o:TotalTime>0</o:TotalTime>
<o:Created>2004-02-11T23:07:00Z</o:Created>
<o:LastSaved>2004-02-11T23:07:00Z</o:LastSaved>
<o:Pages>1</o:Pages>
<o:Words>9</o:Words>
<o:Characters>52</o:Characters>
<o:Lines>1</o:Lines>
<o:Paragraphs>1</o:Paragraphs>
<o:CharactersWithSpaces>60</o:CharactersWithSpaces>
<o:Version>11.5604</o:Version>
</o:DocumentProperties>
<w:fonts>
 <w:defaultFonts w:ascii="Times New Roman" w:fareast="Times New Roman" w:h-
ansi="Times New Roman" w:cs="Times New Roman"/>
 <w:font w:name="Wingdings">
  <w:panose-1 w:val="05000000000000000000"/>
  <w:charset w:val="02"/>
  <w:family w:val="Auto"/>
  <w:pitch w:val="variable"/>
  <w:sig w:usb-0="00000000" w:usb-1="10000000" w:usb-2="00000000" w:usb-
3="00000000" w:csb-0="80000000" w:csb-1="00000000"/>
 </w:font>
</w:fonts>
 ...
```

See Also

- *Office 2003 XML*, by Evan Lenz, Mary McRae, and Simon St.Laurent (O'Reilly)

- WordprocessingML documentation and schema: *http://www.microsoft. com/downloads/details.aspx?FamilyID=fe118952-3547-420a-a412- 00a2662442d9&displaylang=en*

HACK #15 Work with XML in Microsoft Excel 2003

Using table-structured data or spreadsheets? Open, format, and save XML documents with Excel 2003.

Microsoft Excel 2003 offers unprecedented XML support. As with Word, full XML features are not available except with the Microsoft Office Professional Edition 2003, Enterprise Edition 2003, and the individual version. Other versions (the Standard or Small Business editions) won't have XML support except for the ability to save a file in SpreadsheetML format.

Excel 2003 allows you to open an XML document and then save or export data as XML. Choose File → Open and then navigate to the file *time.xml* in the Open dialog box. Select the file and then click Open. You can open the document in one of three ways: as an XML list, as a read-only workbook, or by using the XML Source task pane.

When you open an XML file as an XML list, Excel automatically creates an XML Schema that corresponds with the XML (it warns you of that). It also maps each of the attribute values and the content from each of the elements to a cell in the spreadsheet. The XML Source task pane lists each of the elements in the imported document in a tree view. As a cell is highlighted in the spreadsheet, the corresponding element or attribute is highlighted in the task pane.

> If the task pane does not appear automatically, choose Data → XML → XML Source.

In Figure 2-12, notice that in the XML Source pane, the hour element is highlighted; it is associated through a mapping with cell B1, which is also highlighted. If you were to select cell C1, the minute element in the XML Source pane would be highlighted.

If you open an XML document as a read-only workbook, no mappings or schema generation occurs, but cells are labeled with the names of elements and attributes automatically, with the labels resembling XPath location paths.

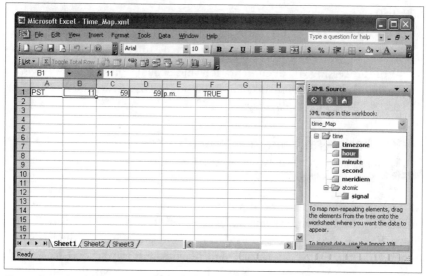

Figure 2-12. Mapping time.xml to fields in Excel 2003

When an XML document is opened by using the Use the XML Source task pane option, a schema is created, and the elements appear in a tree view. However, no data is imported into the spreadsheet and mappings between cells, and elements or attributes must be done manually, but this gives you more control over where the data winds up.

Under the Data → XML menu, you have several choices for working with XML. You can import or export data (you cannot export read-only worksheets, though), refresh XML data, adjust XML map properties, or open XML expansion packs. Expansion packs are used for converting workbooks into smart documents. Smart documents can help you complete tasks, fill in information, use boilerplates, and so forth.

If you are working with a regular Excel spreadsheet, like the loan calculator that appears in Figure 2-13, you can save it in Excel's SpreadsheetML format. (You can't save native XML documents in this format.) Choose File → Save As, and in the "Save as type" pull-down menu, select XML. Enter the filename (*loan.xml* in this example) and click the Save button. Analysis of this file yields that it has over 18,000 lines, 25,667 elements, and 28,697 attributes—by no means a small specimen. A portion of this file follows. I find SpreadsheetML files more humanly readable than the WordprocessingML format. They are nicely indented and generally eschew unnecessary element name prefixing.

```
<?xml version="1.0"?>
<?mso-application progid="Excel.Sheet"?>
<Workbook xmlns="urn:schemas-microsoft-com:office:spreadsheet"
 xmlns:o="urn:schemas-microsoft-com:office:office"
 xmlns:x="urn:schemas-microsoft-com:office:excel"
 xmlns:ss="urn:schemas-microsoft-com:office:spreadsheet"
 xmlns:html="http://www.w3.org/TR/REC-html40">
 <DocumentProperties xmlns="urn:schemas-microsoft-com:office:office">
  <Author>Microsoft Corporation</Author>
  <LastAuthor>Mike Fitzgerald</LastAuthor>
  <LastPrinted>2000-10-20T19:37:33Z</LastPrinted>
  <Created>2000-08-25T00:46:01Z</Created>
  <LastSaved>2004-02-12T01:52:34Z</LastSaved>
  <Company>Microsoft Corporation</Company>
  <Version>11.5606</Version>
 </DocumentProperties>
 <OfficeDocumentSettings xmlns="urn:schemas-microsoft-com:office:office">
  <Colors>
   <Color>
    <Index>29</Index>
    <RGB>#FFE1E2</RGB>
   </Color>
   <Color>
    <Index>30</Index>
    <RGB>#FDF1DF</RGB>
   </Color>
   <Color>
    <Index>31</Index>
    <RGB>#FFCCFF</RGB>
   </Color>
  </Colors>
 </OfficeDocumentSettings>
 <ExcelWorkbook xmlns="urn:schemas-microsoft-com:office:excel">
  <WindowHeight>8865</WindowHeight>
  <WindowWidth>13590</WindowWidth>
  <WindowTopX>0</WindowTopX>
  <WindowTopY>15</WindowTopY>
  <ProtectStructure>False</ProtectStructure>
  <ProtectWindows>False</ProtectWindows>
  <DisplayInkNotes>False</DisplayInkNotes>
 </ExcelWorkbook>
 ...
```

See Also

- *Office 2003 XML*, by Evan Lenz, Mary McRae, and Simon St.Laurent (O'Reilly)

- SpreadsheetML documentation and schema: *http://www.microsoft.com/ downloads/details.aspx?FamilyID=fe118952-3547-420a-a412- 00a2662442d9&displaylang=en*

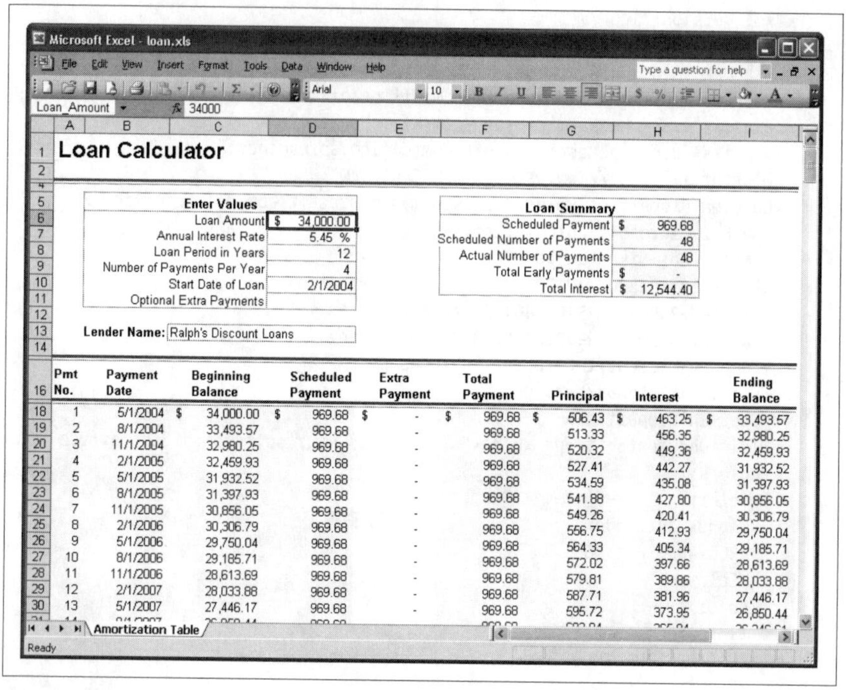

Figure 2-13. loan.xls in Excel 2003

HACK #16 Work with XML in Microsoft Access 2003

If you are a Microsoft Access user, you'll be happy to know that you can export Access 2003 data as XML.

Microsoft Access 2003 is Office's database application. You can create a table of data—an Access database—and label each field with a name you'd like to use as an XML element name. One way to get started is by importing an existing XML document into Access. Here's how to do it.

Open Access, and then select File → Get External Data → Import. In the Import dialog box, make sure it says *XML* in the "Files of type" pull-down menu. Navigate to the working directory and click on the file *time.xml*. Then click Import. Not all information is preserved, but close.

You will then see the Import XML dialog box. Click on the Options button, and the dialog will appear as it does in Figure 2-14. You can choose to import the XML structure only (i.e., only the markup) or the structure with data (i.e., the markup and content). You can also choose to append the data to an existing table; i.e., a table with the same name as the original document (in this example, *time*). If you append the data, the content of the XML document is added to a record of the database file using the same fields that are created from the element names.

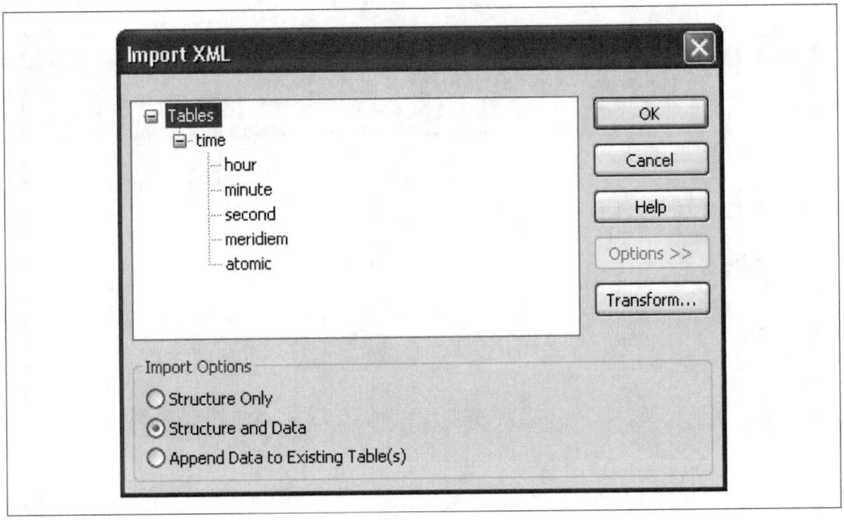

Figure 2-14. Import XML dialog box in Access 2003

After you have imported the document, you should see a database table in the navigator view of Access, as shown in Figure 2-15. Click on the table's icon to open it. In Figure 2-16, you can see that the fields are labeled with the names of elements in *time.xml*.

To save this data as an XML document, select File → Export, and the Export Table dialog box appears. In the "Save as type" pull-down menu, select XML, and enter a filename, such as *TimeTable.xml*. Then click Export All.

At this point, a few more choices are presented in the Export XML dialog (Figure 2-17). You can check one to three boxes to tell Access what you want to do. When all three boxes are checked, Access will save your database as an XML document (*TimeTable.xml*); create and save an XML Schema for the saved XML document (*TimeTable.xsd*); create and save an XSLT stylesheet that can transform the newly saved XML document as HTML (*TimeTable.xsl*); and create and save an HTML document based on this transformation (*TimeTable.htm*). Access reportedly supports only some of the XML Schema structures (*http://www.w3.org/TR/xmlschema-1/*), which will be reflected in the saved XSD file; namely, xsd:schema, xsd:element, xsd: appinfo, xsd:annotation, xsd:complexType, xsd:simpleType, xsd:restriction, xsd:choice, and xsd:all.

> As exported, *TimeTable.htm* can be displayed only in Internet Explorer because it uses a VBScript function ApplyTransform( ) to apply *TimeTable.xsl*.

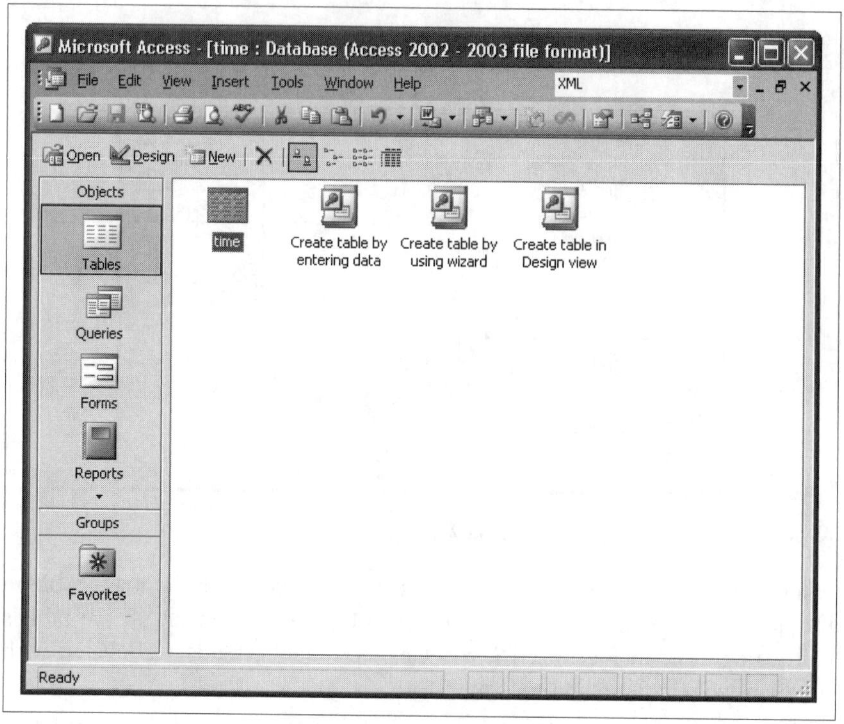

Figure 2-15. time table in Access 2003 navigator view

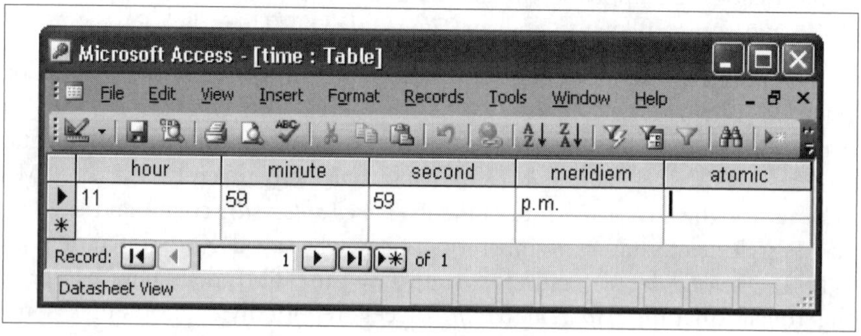

Figure 2-16. time.mdb in Access 2003

If you click the More Options button on the Export XML dialog box, you can pick more settings for the XML document, the XML Schema, or the stylesheet. Under the Data tab, you can see that you can export all records of the database or just the current one. You can select UTF-8 or UTF-16 encoding. You can also apply a transformation (an XSLT stylesheet) to be applied at the time of export. Under the Schema tab, you get to choose whether to include primary key and index information or leave it out. You

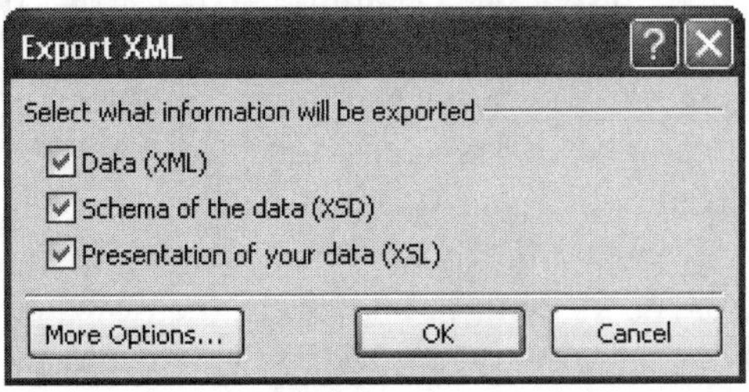

Figure 2-17. Export XML dialog box in Access 2003

can also choose whether to save the schema as a separate file or embed the schema with the XML document. The Presentation tab lets you save as an additional document in HTML or ASP format and choose whether to include images. All three tabs let you browse to a location for the saved file as well as name the file.

See Also

- *Office 2003 XML*, by Evan Lenz, Mary McRae, and Simon St.Laurent (O'Reilly)

HACK #17 Convert Microsoft Office Files, Old or New, to XML

Use OpenOffice as a tool to convert Microsoft Office files to XML.

OpenOffice (*http://www.openoffice.org/*), the free, open source, multiplatform office application suite that provides an alternative to Microsoft Office, uses a documented XML format as its native file format. Put this together with OpenOffice 1.1's ability to read Word, Excel, and PowerPoint files from Office 97, 2000, and XP, plus Word 6.0 files, Word 95 files, and Excel 4.0, 5.0, and 95 files, and you've got a simple way to convert these files to XML.

When you store a document in OpenOffice's own file format **[Hack #65]**, you'll create a ZIP file with the extension *.sxw* if you saved it with the OpenOffice Writer word processing program, *.sxc* if you saved it with the OpenOffice Calc spreadsheet program, or *.sxi* if you used the OpenOffice Impress slideshow program. The six files that you'll find in these ZIP files have self-explanatory names: *mimetype, content.xml, styles.xml, meta.xml, settings. xml*, and *manifest.xml*.

Unless you're strongly interested in the inner workings of OpenOffice, the file *content.xml* should hold the most interest. Along with file content, it stores information about the use of built-in styles, styles you defined your-self, and even on-the-fly styling information not tied to defined styles, such as bolding of text with Ctrl-B. For word-processing files, the XML also iden-tifies bulleted and numbered lists and footnotes. XML versions of spread-sheets include information about spanned cells and calculation formulas as well as results, and OpenOffice XML versions of slideshows store separate slides in separate elements, with slide notes in their own elements. (As soon as I found out about that, I wrote an XSLT stylesheet to pull slide titles and slide notes, minus slide content, into a single document that I could print and hold in my hand when giving presentations—something I'd always wanted to do when giving PowerPoint presentations, but could not.)

DocBook

The OpenOffice Writer application provides an added bonus for DocBook [Hack #62] users: a DocBook (simplified) option in the Save As menu. This saves your document with a document type of article and with each para-graph in a para element. If the document used built-in Word styles such as Heading 1 and Heading 2, OpenOffice saves them as title children of appro-priate containers such as sect1 and sect2, and it adds the container start and end tags in the right places to explicitly identify the hierarchical struc-ture that the original Word file only hinted at.

The conversion to DocBook format loses any references to defined para-graph and inline styles or on-the-fly formatting in the document, but because the conversion to DocBook is done with an XSLT stylesheet installed as part of the OpenOffice distribution, anyone familiar with XSLT can edit it—adding template rules to handle specialized cases for their own documents. From the OpenOffice Write Tools menu, select XML Filter Set-tings, and then with DocBook File highlighted, click the Edit button and pick the Transformation tab to find out the name and location of the stylesheet that creates exported DocBook files.

The formats I've listed above aren't the only formats that OpenOffice can read. If you have data dating back to the earlier days of personal computers, you may be interested in OpenOffice Calc's ability to read Lotus 1-2-3 and dBase files. So download OpenOffice—remember, it's free—and take a look at the formats it can read and the XML that it can create from these formats.

—Bob DuCharme

Create an XML Document from a Text File with xmlspy

How do you get your old stuff into XML? Legacy text files can be translated into XML with xmlspy.

Perhaps you have plain-text files that you'd like to convert to XML so that the data will interoperate with the latest applications. You can do it by hand with a text or XML editor or you can use a tool that will do it for you automatically. xmlspy (Professional or Enterprise edition) is one of those tools. It's easy to figure out xmlspy's text-to-XML interface, so that's the one I'll show you here. (I used the Enterprise edition when testing this.)

First, here is a little plain-text file, *time.txt*, that just contains data fields separated by semicolons:

```
timezone;hour;minute;second;meridiem;atomic
PST;11;59;59;p.m.;
```

The first line defines fields that will be converted to XML markup; the second line defines the content of that markup. A semicolon (;) delimits each of the fields. The second line ends with a field containing a single space, which of course you can see.

Now open xmlspy and select Convert → Import Text file. The Text import dialog box is shown in Figure 2-18. Click the Choose File button and open the file *time.txt*. Make sure that the file encoding is Unicode UTF-8, the field delimiter is Semicolon, and that "First row contains field names" is checked.

Click the symbol to the left of the timezone field name in the first row so that it becomes an equals sign. This specifies that the timezone field will be interpreted as an attribute in the output. Then click OK.

Click the Text label at the bottom of the document pane to see the result in Figure 2-19. The XML declaration and the import and row elements were inserted by xmlspy; the remaining elements were derived from *time.txt*. You could change the new document by hand to match *time.xml* (from Chapter 1), or you could apply an XSLT stylesheet to it. XSLT hacks begin in earnest in Chapter 3, but I'll use an XSLT stylesheet here (without going into detail about the stylesheet itself) to show you how to shape this document up.

Select XSL → XSL Transformation or press F10, and the dialog box in Figure 2-20 appears. Click the Browse button and open the stylesheet *time.xsl*. Then click OK. The imported text is then transformed by xmlspy's XSLT engine, according to *time.xsl*. Again click the Text label under the document

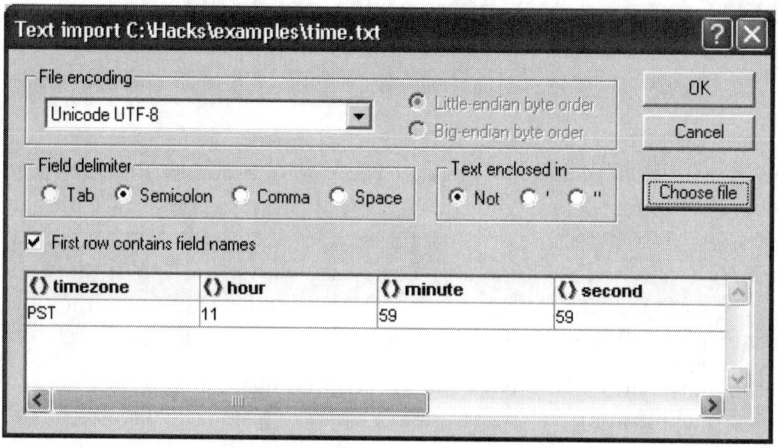

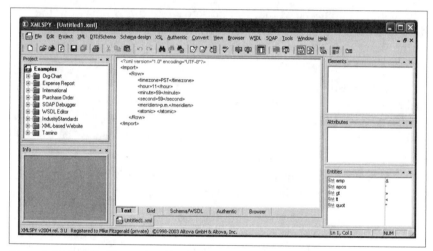

Figure 2-18. time.txt in xmlspy's Text Import dialog box

Figure 2-19. Result of importing time.txt

pane and select Edit → Pretty-Print XML Text. The final result is shown in Figure 2-21. You can save this document with File → Save.

You can also convert text files whose data fields are separated by tabs, commas, or spaces. You can also select fields whose text is enclosed in single or double quotes. I chose semicolons in the first example because they are easier to see than space and tabs. The text file *time2.txt* (Example 2-6) uses tabs as delimiters.

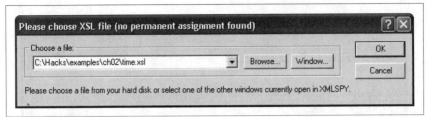

Figure 2-20. XSL file dialog box in xmlspy

Figure 2-21. Transformed and beautified text-to-XML conversion

Example 2-6. time2.txt

timezone		hour	minute	second	meridiem	atomic
PST	11	59	59	p.m.		
MST	12	59	59	a.m.		
CST	01	59	59	a.m.		
EST	02	59	59	a.m.		
AST	03	59	59	a.m.		
BST	04	59	59	a.m.		
FST	05	59	59	a.m.		
AT	06	59	59	a.m.		
UTC	07	59	59	a.m.		

Run this file through the conversion steps, making sure to select Tab as the field delimiter in the Text Import dialog box, as shown in Figure 2-22.

You can experiment with the other delimiters by changing the delimiters in *time.txt* or *time2.txt* to other kinds of delimiters and stepping through the conversion again. With some experimentation you will see that xmlspy can convert many kinds of text files.

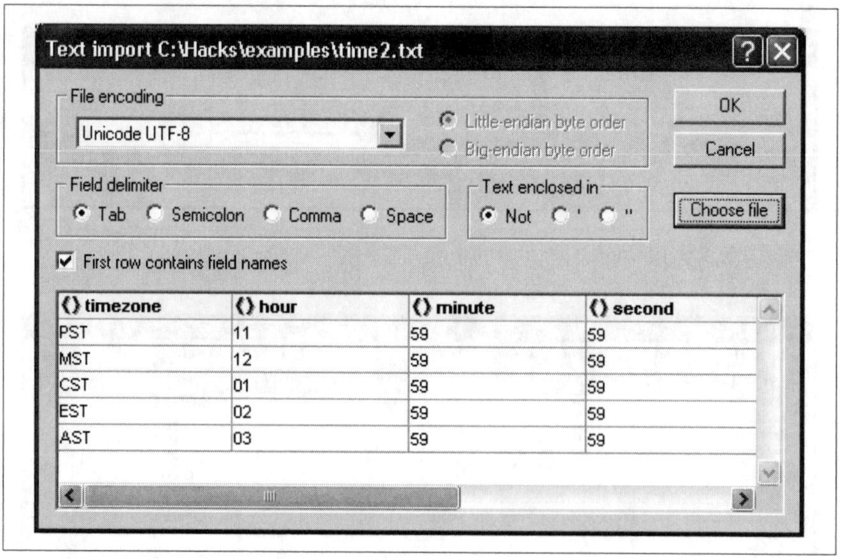

Figure 2-22. time2.txt in the Text import dialog box

See Also

- Sysonyx's xmlArchitect: *http://www.sysonyx.com/Products/xmlLinguist/features.asp*

- For heavy-duty text-to-XML conversions, a dedicated hardware solution from Xlipstream offers rackmounted appliances that do the conversions: *http://www.xlipstream.com/*

Convert Text to XML with Uphill

HACK #19

This hack is a little different. It shows you how to convert plain text to XML using Dave Pawson's Java program, Uphill. Along the way, Dave also explains how and why he developed the software, which may be helpful for those developing their own text-to-XML packages in Java.

Text without any formatting is boring and repetitive to mark up XML—just the sort of problem that a computer is good at, except that most text is not regular, which is the cost side of automation. I decided to try to create a solution in which the cost would be less for any automated solution over a by-hand conversion. That's why I wrote Uphill (*http://www.dpawson.co.uk/java/uphill/*), a Java program for converting plain text into XML.

The goal for the program was to output a new file containing the XML markup for headings, paragraphs, and acronyms (needed for Braille output). First, I prototyped a solution with Python (*http://www.python.org/*)

because Python has dictionaries that can be preloaded. I had a list of acronyms that I quickly converted into a Python structure to initialize a dictionary. The match I used was:

```
if acrs.has_key(str[i:i+4]):
```

I walked the input string, testing for four-letter, then three-letter, then two-letter acronyms. It worked, and though it was weak, it gave me enough confidence to move on.

A line from my acronym file looks like this:

```
USA:<acr>USA</acr>
```

That is, the acronym USA is marked up with the acr tag. I realized that some acronyms may be generalized. If the first two letters can be captured, any remaining uppercase letters were probably a part of the acronym. I came up with this as an entry:

```
BD:*
```

This tells me that if I spot BD, I can keep on looking for more uppercase letters, up until a terminal.

Trying It Out

Download, unzip, and install Uphill in the working directory. Type this command:

```
java -jar uphill.jar
```

You will then see this usage information:

```
No Input File available; Quitting
Uphill 1.2 from Dave Pawson
Usage: java Uphill [options] {param=value}...
Options:
   -a filename    Take Acronyms from named file
   -o filename    Send output to named file
   -i filename    Take text input from named file
   -s filename    State machine input from named file
   -t             Display version information
   -?             Display this message
```

There are sample files in Uphill's *src* directory (in the ZIP archive). One is shown below. You can use them to produce some output with this command:

```
java -jar uphill.jar -a src/acronyms.txt -i src/test.txt
-s src/state.txt -o test.xml
```

The program outputs this report:

```
ChxState: Using 1
ChxState: Using 1
```

```
ChxState: Using 0
ChxState: Using 0
ChxState: Using 2
ChxState: Using 1
ChxState: Using 2
ChxState: Using 2
ChxState: Using 0
ChxState: Using 1
ChxState: Using 0
ChxState: Using 1
Done; Output written to file
```

The resulting file should look like this:

```
<?xml version="1.0" encoding="utf-8"?>
<!-- Uphill 1.2 from Dave Pawson -->
<dtbook>
 <head>  <title>Main title</title>
  <link style="text/css" href="location.css"/>
  <meta name="dc:author" content="Uphill"/> </head>
<book>
 <frontmatter>
  <docauthor></docauthor>
  <doctitle></doctitle>

 </frontmatter>
 <bodymatter><dtbook>
<p>A starter para</p>
<p>Para &lt;  we need to talk!  I would prefer, if at all
possible to take some time out beforethe end of the year to do this
as I would want to concentrate on my new role from January (we'll
need someContinuationPara. time to go into each project in enough
detail). You also need to talk to Tony re project proioritisation.</p>
<h2>Head. this to test SHAKESPEARE <acronym>SH</acronym> <acronym>ATW
</acronym>
<acronym>ATW</acronym>xxx acronym markup Stood (stood) </h2>
<p>Para. this to test shakespeare sh atw atwxxx acronym markup</p>
<h2>Heading by itself</h2>
<h2>Testing block structure. This is a headingthis is a heading
continuation</h2>
<p>This is a paraThis is the same para continued</p>
<p>this is another para</dtbook>

</bodymatter>
</book>
</dtbook>
```

How the Code Works

The following explanations are for Java programmers who might be interested in how the code works. Uphill's acronyms class builds the hash table of acronyms from a plain-text file of the format mentioned in the previous section, and provides get( ) and test( ) methods to retrieve and test for the presence of an acronym in the table. The main method allowed easy testing of this class in isolation.

I then moved on to a quick port to Java, and new thoughts about the markup of paragraphs. I realized that the software needed to be state-aware if it was to differentiate between a paragraph and a heading. My state diagram looked something like Figure 2-23.

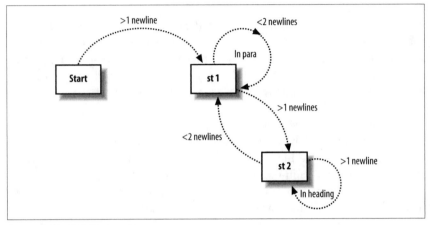

Figure 2-23. Uphill state diagram

The number of linefeed characters determines the state change I decided to use: one newline between paragraphs, and more than one newline to change state to a heading. Thus, having two successive headings would require two newline separators.

A later development enabled me to abstract this into a separate class that implements the state table. Although the trigger is hardcoded, the state is defined by an external text file, which has a format for an example input document with markup as shown below. It shouldn't be hard to generalize it even more.

```
# StateTable for 'AS you like it: Shakespeare'
# Format is
# currentState : InputCountofNewLineChars : OutPutString : NextState
# Note that no additional spaces are allowed.
# Note, output string, n represents newLine character
# para = state 1
0:1:n<p>:1
1:1:</p>n<p>:1
1:0::1
1:2:</p>n<h2>:2
# head    = state  2
2:0::2
2:1:</h2>n<p>:1
2:2:</h2>n<h2>:2
```

Comments are preceded by the # symbol. Otherwise, each line represents four colon-delimited fields: a state transition from current state; trigger conditions detected, in this case a count of newline characters (minimum); an output string; and the new state. States are represented by integer values.

In order to obtain nicely formatted XML output, I used the character n to represent a newline character. For example, the line:

```
2:2:</h2>n<h2>:2
```

represents a state change from state 2 (heading), with a trigger of two or more occurrences, the output string, and the new state (again 2). In addition to the state table, there are two other pieces used for managing state: *stateTable.java* codes the state, and *state.java* loads and implements the state transitions through the methods initStateTable and chxState.

The markup class. This class does the bulk of the work. It holds the state machine variable, which keeps track of the state. The prFile( ) method processes each line of the file one at a time, first counting newline characters (remember this is a plain-text file), and then using the prLine( ) method to process the line. The process line method, prLine( ), first replaces any characters that need escaping for XML (ampersand and less-than symbols) with their entity values. Acronyms are replaced with their markup, using the findAcrs( ) method. The state is updated and any required markup is generated using the chxState( ) method.

Support routines are needed for whitespace treatment and to replace an acronym once detected.

The uphill class. The main class is used for the command-line interface. It provides a usage method, validation for input parameters, and calls on the version class (which records the software version). The produceXML( ) method writes out the XML header and any wrappers needed. The example uses heading material for the DAISY book format (*http://www.daisy.org*) for which I developed this software.

Summary

The basic approach seems viable, and presents a tradeoff between using an XML editor to mark up bare text and reformatting plain text by inserting newline characters. I find the latter to be less work on a large file. I'm certainly gaining benefit from the acronym markup, and using the XML editor that I do, it's very easy both to add structure to the file and to change markup tags (e.g., replace paragraph tags with list tags), rather than mark up plain text within a well-formed document. This is probably a case of choosing the right XML editor, since not all editors support working with partially well-formed and occasionally invalid documents.

There are still a few things to do. The state table is too closely linked to the output text generated by a state change, but this isn't hard to uncouple. There are probably one or two areas where greater generalization is possible, but I've not found them yet, and since I'm not working with an XML-aware tool, they may prove more trouble than they are worth. I'll leave it until the need is greater.

So far, I've created a small tool that helps me do a job. I hope you've learned a little from it and maybe even found it useful, too.

See Also

- Chaperon converts structured text to XML using Java; it provides a lexical scanner, a parser generator, a parser, a tree builder, and an XML generator: *http://chaperon.sourceforge.net/*

—*Dave Pawson*

HACK #20 Create Well-Formed XML with Minimal Manual Tagging Using an SGML Parser

Convert minimal markup into XML with James Clark's SP.

The problem of converting plain text into basic, well-formed XML occurs over and over again in XML processing. As a general rule, I like to get data into XML as quickly as possible and leave it in XML for as long as possible (preferably forever). The sooner I can get data into XML, the sooner I can bring all my XML-processing tools and knowledge to bear on the data-processing challenges.

When the volume of markup to be created is small, hand-editing using one-off text editor macros is a powerful technique. For higher volumes of markup, a custom program is often the best way to go—Python, Ruby, and Perl, for example, all excel at this sort of work.

Sometimes, the quickest way to get data into XML is by combining judicious use of hand-edits and automatic addition of the markup required using an SGML parser. XML is a subset of a much larger markup technology standard known as SGML (ISO 8879:1986), which has been an international standard since 1986. SGML provides a variety of mechanisms, not found in XML, to minimize the amount of tagging required in documents. Collectively, these techniques are known as *markup minimization features*. By using an SGML parser to process text, it is possible to take advantage of the tag minimization features to automatically add markup and help create well-formed XML documents.

In these examples, we will use James Clark's SP SGML parser. You can download it from *http://www.jclark.com/sp/*. The examples in this hack assume that SP has been installed in the working directory for the book's files.

From HTML to XML

You may already be familiar with some of SGML's tag minimization capabilities, as they are used extensively in HTML. (HTML is an example of an SGML application—by far the most successful SGML application in the world.)

The most common tag minimization technique from SGML used in HTML is known as tag omission. Here is a small HTML document, *min.html*, which, thanks to SGML's tag omission features, is valid per the HTML DTD:

```
<!DOCTYPE HTML PUBLIC "-//IETF//DTD HTML Strict//EN">
<title>Hello World</title>
<p>Hello World
```

Note that numerous HTML tags that you normally see have been omitted from the document: there is no head element, no body element, and no html element. The end tag of the p element has also been omitted.

Using the *nsgmls* command-line application that ships with SP, we can parse this document against the HTML DTD on Windows using this command:

```
nsgmls -c pubtext/html.soc min.html >nul
```

Or on Unix by using this:

```
nsgmls -c pubtext/html.soc min.html >/dev/null
```

The -c command-line option is used to tell the parser where to find the HTML DTDs. These are shipped in the *pubtext* subdirectory of SP, which came with the archive of files for the book. I have redirected normal output to the null device in the examples. The fact that no errors are displayed on the screen tells us that, from an SGML perspective, the document is both well-formed and valid per the HTML DTD.

SP also ships with *sx*, a utility for converting documents from SGML to XML. Using the *sx* utility, we can now automatically add all the tags needed to make *min.html* a valid XML document. Run it on Windows or Unix like this:

```
sx -c pubtext/html.soc -xno-nl-in-tag min.html >min.xml
```

The -x command-line option tells the *sx* application not to add newlines into the tags it creates. This is an option provided by *sx* for situations where you might wish to avoid the creation of very long lines of XML output. For a complete list of *sx* options, see *doc/sx.htm* in the SP distribution.

The resultant file, *min.xml*, is shown in Example 2-7 and is indented for clarity.

Example 2-7. min.xml

```
<?xml version="1.0"?>
<HTML VERSION="-//IETF//DTD HTML 2.0 Strict//EN" SDAFORM="Book">
 <HEAD>
  <TITLE SDAFORM="Ti">Hello World</TITLE>
 </HEAD>
 <BODY>
  <P SDAFORM="Para">Hello World</P>
 </BODY>
</HTML>
```

There are a total of ten tags in this document, of which *sx* has added seven automatically, while we only contributed three manually—a 70 percent savings on manual markup!

In addition to adding start and end tags as required, *sx* has also added attributes called SDAFORM and VERSION. These are examples of defaulted attribute values. Defaulting attribute values is a form of markup minimization that, unlike SGML's tag minimization, is included in the XML standard.

Marking Up the Names of People

A common problem in XML data processing is dealing with the names of people. Many applications require that people's names be split into two parts—a family name and a given name. In the general case, doing this across all languages and cultures is very complex at best and impossible at worst. Even within a limited set of languages/cultures, the complexity of the problem rapidly manifests itself. Consider the following text file (*names.txt*), which contains the names of three people:

```
Asmar Hohsen  Mickey Joe Mac Entaggart   Javier Ausas Lopez de Castro
```

Splitting these names into their given name and surname component parts requires the application of complex rules, rules that are very difficult to explain to a computer. We can take advantage of our human ability to outguess machines to get this data into an XML form quickly by using an SGML parser. The critical human interventions we need to make are:

- Split the list into separate names using the whitespace information and our best guess as to where the boundaries lie.
- Mark the point where the surname begins, changing the order of given name and surname, as needed.

Here is an SGML document created with the minimal amount of markup added. A Name tag is used to mark the start of each name, and an S tag is used to mark the point where a surname starts (*names.sgml*):

```
<!DOCTYPE Names SYSTEM "names.dtd">
<Name>Hohsen  <S>Asmar <Name>Mickey Joe <S>MacEntaggart
<Name>Javier <S>Ausas Lopez de Castro
```

Now we need to create a DTD to describe the Names document type. In XML, it would look like this (*namex.dtd*):

```
<!ELEMENT Names (Name*)>
<!ELEMENT Name (F,S)>
<!ELEMENT F (#PCDATA)>
<!ELEMENT S (#PCDATA)>
```

To make it SGML compatible, we need to make a minor alteration (*names.dtd*):

```
<!ELEMENT Names o o (Name*)>
<!ELEMENT Name o o (F,S)>
<!ELEMENT F o o (#PCDATA)>
<!ELEMENT S o o (#PCDATA)>
```

Note the pair of lowercase o's (o o) between the element type name and the content model of each element type declaration. The o stands for *omissable* and indicates that documents may omit the start tag (first o) and end tag (second o).

Now we can parse the document with the *nsgmls* utility to check for errors. On Windows, the command is:

```
nsgmls names.sgml >nul
```

On Unix, the command is:

```
nsgmls names.sgml >/dev/null
```

The fact that no error messages appear on the screen tells us that the document is well-formed and valid per *names.dtd*. Now we can proceed to use the *sx* utility to generate fully marked-up XML from this document. On Windows or Unix, the command is:

```
sx -x no-nl-in-tag -x lower names.sgml >names.xml
```

Note the addition of another -x switch with lower. This will produce tag names in lowercase. The resultant XML file is *names.xml*, which is indented for clarity (Example 2-8).

Example 2-8. names.xml

```
<?xml version="1.0"?>
<names>
 <name>
  <f>Agmar</f>
  <s>Hohsen </s>
 </name>
 <name>
  <f>Mickey Joe </f>
  <s>MacEntaggart    </s>
 </name>
 <name>
  <f>Javier </f>
  <s>Ausas Lopez de Castro</s>
 </name>
</names>
```

You can't do that with just plain old XML!

See Also

* "From Wiki to XML, Through SGML" **[Hack #94]**
* *PARSEME.1st: SGML for Software Developers*, by Sean McGrath (Prentice Hall)

—*Sean McGrath*

HACK
#21

Create an XML Document from a CSV File

Want to go from CSV to XML? Use Dave Pawson's CSVToXML tool to convert CSV files to XML with Java.

Dave Pawson's CSVToXML translator converts comma-separated value (CSV) files to XML. CSV is a reliable, plain-text file format for the storing the output of a spreadsheet or database.

Suppose you are running Excel 2000 and you want to convert a file, *inventory.xls*, to XML (see Figure 2-24). Unfortunately, you haven't been able to talk your boss into buying Excel 2003 yet, which could easily output the spreadsheet as XML. Luckily, there is a workaround.

Save the file as CSV by choosing File → Save As and selecting a CSV file format in the "Save as type" pull-down box. Navigate to the working directory where the other files from this book are, enter the name *inventory.csv* in the File name text box, and then click the Save button. The CSV file will appear as follows:

```
line,desc,quan,date
1,Oak chairs,6,31-Dec-04
```

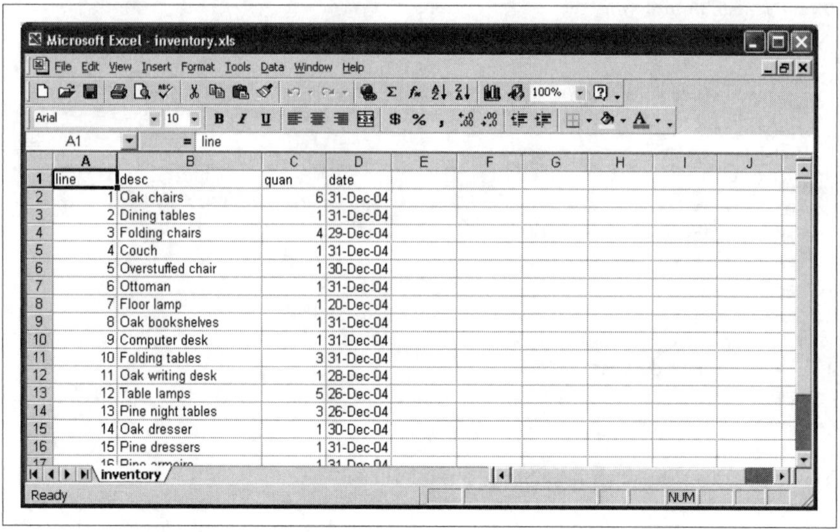

Figure 2-24. inventory.xls in Excel 2000

```
2,Dining tables,1,31-Dec-04
3,Folding chairs,4,29-Dec-04
4,Couch,1,31-Dec-04
5,Overstuffed chair,1,30-Dec-04
6,Ottoman,1,31-Dec-04
7,Floor lamp,1,20-Dec-04
8,Oak bookshelves,1,31-Dec-04
9,Computer desk,1,31-Dec-04
10,Folding tables,3,31-Dec-04
11,Oak writing desk,1,28-Dec-04
12,Table lamps,5,26-Dec-04
13,Pine night tables,3,26-Dec-04
14,Oak dresser,1,30-Dec-04
15,Pine dressers,1,31-Dec-04
16,Pine armoire,1,31-Dec-04
```

Download the latest version of CSVToXML from *http://www.dpawson.co.uk/ java/index.html* and extract the JAR file *CVSToXML.jar* from the ZIP archive and place it in the working directory. Enter this command:

```
java -jar CSVToXML.jar
```

If you see this output, you are ready to roll:

```
No property File available; Quitting
CSVToXML 1.0 from Dave Pawson
Usage: java CSVToXML [options] {param=value}...
Options:
    -p filename     Take properties from named file
    -o filename     Send output to named file
    -i filename     Take CSV input from named file
    -t              Display version and timing information
    -?              Display this message
```

CSVToXML relies on a properties file to determine how it will output XML. In the working directory, you will find an example properties file, *props.txt*, shown in Example 2-9.

Example 2-9. props.txt

```
1   [head]
2   comment=Generated using Dave Pawson's CSVToXML
3   fielddelimiter=,
4   rowdelimiter=\n
5   rootname=Inventory
6   recordname=Line
7   fields=4
8
9   [fields]
10  field0=ItemNumber
11  field1=Description
12  field2=Quantity
13  field3=Date
```

Lines 1 through 7 provide head properties that will affect the entire file. The comment header (line 2) creates an XML comment at the beginning of the file. Line 3 specifies that a comma will separate the values in the source, and line 4 indicates that a row is delimited by a newline. Line 5 gives the document element for the XML document, and line 6 is a name for a parent element to each line of CSV. Line 7 specifies the number of fields the processor can expect. Lines 9 through 13 define the XML element names for each of the four fields (lines 10 through 13).

Now you're ready to put CSVToXML to work. Type the following line at a command prompt (the -p switch is for specifying a properties file, the -i option is for denoting the input file, and -o gives the output file):

```
java -jar CSVToXML.jar -p props.txt -i inventory.csv -o inventory.xml
```

The XML output is not indented and so is not very readable. However, you can apply an identity transform to it **[Hack #38]** and make it more attractive. Here is a portion of what *inventory.xml* looks like after applying the pretty-print hack:

```
<?xml version="1.0" encoding="ISO-8859-1"?>
<!-- Generated using Dave Pawson's CSVToXML -->
<Inventory>
 <Line>
  <ItemNumber>line</ItemNumber>
  <Description>desc</Description>
  <Quantity>quan</Quantity>
  <Date>date</Date>
 </Line>
 <Line>
```

```
 <ItemNumber>1</ItemNumber>
 <Description>Oak chairs</Description>
 <Quantity>6</Quantity>
 <Date>31 Dec 2004</Date>
</Line>
<Line>
 <ItemNumber>2</ItemNumber>
 <Description>Dining tables</Description>
 <Quantity>1</Quantity>
 <Date>31 Dec 2004</Date>
</Line>
<Line>
 <ItemNumber>3</ItemNumber>
 <Description>Folding chairs</Description>
 <Quantity>4</Quantity>
 <Date>29 Dec 2004</Date>
</Line>
<Line>
...
```

You can use the XSLT stylesheet *inventory.xsl* from the book's file archive to format the output of CSVToXML as an HTML table. See "Transform an XML Document with a Command-Line Processor" [Hack #32] and "Transform an XML Document Within a Graphical Editor" [Hack #33].

See Also

- Danny Ayers's Java code CSVtoXML: *http://www.dannyayers.com/old/code/CSVtoXML.htm*

HACK #22   Convert an HTML Document to XHTML with HTML Tidy

HTML Tidy was initially developed as a tool to clean up HTML, but it is an XML tool, too. This hack shows you how to use HTML Tidy to make your HTML into XHTML.

HTML Tidy was initially developed at the W3C by Dave Raggett (*http://www.w3.org/People/Raggett/#tidy*). Essentially, it's an open source HTML parser with the stated purpose of cleaning up and pretty-printing HTML, XHTML, and even XML. It is now hosted on Sourceforge (*http://tidy.sourceforge.net*). You can download versions of Tidy for a variety of platforms there.

Example 2-10 shows an HTML document, *goodold.html*, which we will run through HTML Tidy.

Example 2-10. goodold.html

```
<HTML>
<HEAD><TITLE>Time</TITLE></HEAD>
<BODY style="font-family:sans-serif">
<H1>Time</H1>
<TABLE style="font-size:14pt" cellpadding="10">
<TR>
 <TH>Timezone</TH>
 <TH>Hour</TH>
 <TH>Minute</TH>
 <TH>Second</TH>
 <TH>Meridiem</TH>
 <TH>Atomic</TH>
</TR>
<TR>
 <TD>PST</TD>
 <TD>11</TD>
 <TD>59</TD>
 <TD>59</TD>
 <TD>p.m.</TD>
 <TD>true</TD>
</TR>
</TABLE>
</BODY>
</HTML>
```

Assuming that Tidy is properly installed, you can issue the following command to convert *goodold.html* to the XHTML document *goodnew.html* using the -asxhtml switch:

```
tidy -indent -o goodnew.html -asxhtml goodold.html
```

The -indent switch indents the output, and the -o switch names the output file. Tidy will issue warnings if necessary, and provide tips that encourage accessibility. The new file *goodnew.html* looks like Example 2-11.

Example 2-11. goodnew.html

```
<!DOCTYPE html PUBLIC "-//W3C//DTD XHTML 1.0 Strict//EN"
    "http://www.w3.org/TR/xhtml1/DTD/xhtml1-strict.dtd">
<html xmlns="http://www.w3.org/1999/xhtml">
<head>
  <meta name="generator" content=
  "HTML Tidy for Windows (vers 1st January 2004), see www.w3.org" />

  <title>Time</title>
</head>

<body style="font-family:sans-serif">
  <h1>Time</h1>
```

Example 2-11. goodnew.html (continued)

```
<table style="font-size:14pt" cellpadding="10">
  <tr>
    <th>Timezone</th>

    <th>Hour</th>

    <th>Minute</th>

    <th>Second</th>

    <th>Meridiem</th>

    <th>Atomic</th>
  </tr>

  <tr>
    <td>PST</td>

    <td>11</td>

    <td>59</td>

    <td>59</td>

    <td>p.m.</td>

    <td>true</td>
  </tr>
</table>
</body>
</html>
```

What was once HTML is now well-formed, indented XHTML 1.0, an XML-ized version of HTML [Hack #61]. A document type declaration was added that references the strict XHTML 1.0 DTD, as well as a namespace declaration (http://www.w3.org/1999/xhtml), and all of the tag names were changed to lowercase. Other than a meta tag in the head section, the rest of the document remains similar to the original HTML.

There's a lot more possible with Tidy; for example, it gives you considerable control over character encodings with switches like -ascii, -utf8, and -utf16; allows you to replace the deprecated elements FONT, NOBR, and CENTER with CSS equivalents using the -clean or -c switch; lets you accept XML as input with -xml; and even converts XHTML back to HTML (-ashtml).

Transform Documents with XQuery

XQuery is a new language under development by the W3C that's designed to query collections of XML data. XQuery provides a mechanism to efficiently and easily extract data from XML documents or from any data source that can be viewed as XML, such as relational databases.

XQuery (*http://www.w3.org/XML/Query*) provides a powerful mechanism to pull XML content from multiple sources and dynamically generate new content using a programmer-friendly declarative language. The XQuery code in Example 2-12 (*shakes.xqy*) formats in XHTML a list of unique speakers in each act of Shakespeare's play *Hamlet*. The *hamlet.xml* file can be found at *http://www.oasis-open.org/cover/bosakShakespeare200.html*.

Example 2-12. A simple XQuery to search Shakespeare (shakes.xqy)

```
<html><head/><body>
{
  for $act in doc("hamlet.xml")//ACT
  let $speakers := distinct-values($act//SPEAKER)
  return
    <span>
      <h1>{ $act/TITLE/text( ) }</h1>
      <ul>
      {
        for $speaker in $speakers
        return <li>{ $speaker }</li>
      }
      </ul>
    </span>
}
</body></html>
```

This example demonstrates a XQuery FLWOR (pronounced *flower*) expression. The name comes from the five possible clauses of the expression: for, let, where, order by, and return. Example 2-12 says that for every ACT element appearing at any level in the *hamlet.xml* file, let the $speakers variable equal the distinct values of all the SPEAKER elements found under that instance of ACT. Then for every $act and $speakers value, return the $act's TITLE text using an h1 element followed by a ul listing of every speaker in an li element.

XML is a native data type of XQuery and can be used in queries directly without quoted strings, objects, or other tricks. You separate XML elements from enclosed expressions using curly braces. Example 2-13 shows the query result (using ellipses to shorten the output).

Example 2-13. Shakespeare speakers

```
<html>
  <span>
    <h1>ACT I</h1>
    <ul>
      <li>BERNARDO</li><li>FRANCISCO</li><li>HORATIO</li> ...
    </ul>
  </span><span>
    <h1>ACT II</h1>
    <ul>
      <li>LORD POLONIUS</li><li>REYNALDO</li><li>OPHELIA</li> ...
    </ul>
  </span><span>
    <h1>ACT III</h1>
    <ul>
      <li>KING CLAUDIUS</li><li>ROSENCRANTZ</li><li>GUILDENSTERN</li> ...
    </ul>
  </span><span>
    <h1>ACT IV</h1>
    <ul>
      <li>KING CLAUDIUS</li><li>QUEEN GERTRUDE</li><li>HAMLET</li> ...
    </ul>
  </span><span>
    <h1>ACT V</h1>
    <ul>
      <li>First Clown</li><li>Second Clown</li><li>HAMLET</li> ...
    </ul>
  </span>
</html>
```

Example 2-14 (*speakers.xqy*) demonstrates a more advanced form of the query. This longer query pulls content from multiple source documents and beautifies the speaker names so that they're always printed in standard case (capitalized first letters only).

Example 2-14. An XQuery with multiple inputs and beautified output

```
declare function local:singleWordCase($name as xs:string)
    as xs:string {
  if ($name = "") then "" else
  let $first := substring($name, 1, 1)
  let $rest := substring($name, 2)
  let $firstUpper := upper-case($first)
  let $restLower := lower-case($rest)
  return concat($firstUpper, $restLower)
};

declare function local:multiWordCase($name as xs:string)
    as xs:string {
  string-join(
    let $words := tokenize($name, "\s+")
    for $word in $words
```

Example 2-14. An XQuery with multiple inputs and beautified output (continued)

```
    return local:singleWordCase($word)
  , " ")
};

<html><head/><body>
{
  for $file in ("all_well.xml", "dream.xml", "hamlet.xml", "lear.xml",
                "macbeth.xml", "merchant.xml", "much_ado.xml",
                "r_and_j.xml")
  let $play := doc($file)
  let $speakers := distinct-values($play//SPEAKER)
  order by $play/PLAY/TITLE/text()
  return
    <span>
      <h1>{ $play/PLAY/TITLE/text() }</h1>
      <ul>
      {
        for $speaker in $speakers
        let $speakerPretty := local:multiWordCase($speaker)
        order by $speakerPretty
        return
        <li>{ $speakerPretty }</li>
      }
      </ul>
    </span>
}
</body></html>
```

The top portion of the query defines two functions to handle the conversion of names to standard case. The first function, singleWordCase() placed in the special local namespace, takes an xs:string source name and returns an xs:string that is the input parameter converted to standard case. Typing is optional in XQuery. When used, typing is based on XML Schema types (*http://www.w3.org/TR/xquery/#id-types*).

The first line of the function short-circuits so that if the $name is empty, then the expression evaluates to empty; otherwise, the second half of the expression gets evaluated. Assuming $name is non-empty, we assign $first to its first character and $rest to the remainder, uppercase the $first, lowercase the $rest, and return the concatenation. The return keyword is not used to return a value but rather as a clause of a FLWOR expression. A better name for it might have been do.

The second function, multiWordCase(), tokenizes the input string based on whitespace characters (\s is the regular-expression pattern for a whitespace character and the + modifier means "one or more"). Then for every word returned by that tokenization, it executes singleWordCase() with the result joined together with the string-join() function, which adds a space between each reformatted word.

XQuery Expressions

XQuery is a functional language consisting entirely of expressions. There are no statements, even though some of the keywords imply statement-like behaviors. To execute a function, the expression within the body gets evaluated and its value returned. Thus, to write a function to double an input value, you simply write:

```
declare function local:doubler($x) { $x * 2 }
```

To write a full query that says Hello World, you write the expression:

```
"Hello World"
```

That's probably the simplest Hello World program you've ever seen.

The query body executes against eight plays that have been named explicitly. For every $file in the list we assign the $play variable to be the document node associated with that document name. Then we use distinct-values() to calculate the unique speakers in the $play. The order by clause of the FLWOR expression orders the *tuples* (ordered sequence of values) coming out of the for and let clauses so that the tuples are sorted alphabetically by the play's title text. The return clause is evaluated once for each tuple and prints the play title followed by the list of unique speakers in the play, beautified and sorted alphabetically. The result appears in Example 2-15.

Example 2-15. More Shakespeare speakers

```
<html>
  <span>
    <h1>A Midsummer Night's Dream</h1>
    <ul>
      <li>All</li><li>Bottom</li><li>Cobweb</li><li>Demetrius</li> ...
    </ul>
  </span><span>
    <h1>All's Well That Ends Well</h1>
    <ul>
      <li>All</li><li>Bertram</li><li>Both</li><li>Both</li>
<li>Clown</li> ...
    </ul>
  </span><span>
    <h1>Much Ado about Nothing</h1>
    <ul>
      <li>Antonio</li><li>Balthasar</li><li>Beatrice</li>
<li>Benedick</li> ...
    </ul>
  </span><span>
```

Example 2-15. More Shakespeare speakers (continued)

```
  <h1>The Merchant of Venice</h1>
  <ul>
    <li>All</li><li>Antonio</li><li>Arragon</li>
<li>Balthasar</li> ...
  </ul>
 </span><span>
  <h1>The Tragedy of Hamlet, Prince of Denmark</h1>
  <ul>
    <li>All</li><li>Bernardo</li><li>Captain</li>
<li>Cornelius</li> ...
  </ul>
 </span><span>
  <h1>The Tragedy of King Lear</h1>
  <ul>
    <li>Albany</li><li>Burgundy</li><li>Captain</li>
<li>Cordelia</li> ...
  </ul>
 </span><span>
  <h1>The Tragedy of Macbeth</h1>
  <ul>
    <li>All</li><li>Angus</li><li>Attendant</li>
<li>Banquo</li> ...
  </ul>
 </span><span>
  <h1>The Tragedy of Romeo and Juliet</h1>
  <ul>
    <li/><li>Abraham</li><li>Apothecary</li>
<li>Balthasar</li> ...
  </ul>
 </span>
</html>
```

Development of XQuery 1.0 is not yet complete. As of this writing, the W3C specification documents are in Last Call (*http://www.w3.org/XML/ Query#specs*). It looks like there will be a second Last Call before the specifications proceed to candidate recommendation (with two more formal stages after that). The example code shown here was written against the Last Call draft from November 2003.

See Also

- You can find pointers to the XQuery specifications, online articles, mailing lists, and a community Wiki at *http://www.xquery.com*

—Jason Hunter

Execute an XQuery with Saxon

#24 So you know how to write an XQuery? Great! But can you execute an XQuery? This hack shows you how.

When executing XQuery you have a wide range of options. Nearly every vendor—from the well-known old guard (IBM, Oracle, BEA, and Microsoft) to the plucky upstarts (Mark Logic, X-Hive/DB, and Qizx/open) to the open source projects led by individuals (Saxon and Qexo)—has expressed their support for XQuery and have XQuery implementations to offer. The implementations vary widely in purpose as well as in performance and scalability.

XQuery implementations tend to fall into one of three camps. First, there's the streaming transformation model. In this fairly simple application, XQuery defines the mapping from one file format to another. XQuery as a language has certain optional features (such as reverse axes) not needed for implementations doing simple streaming transformations where you can forget nodes right after you read them. In this use XQuery is similar to XSLT, but XQuery adds data typing and static type-analysis. Letting you statically verify your XQuery code will always generate a properly constructed document conformant to a specific schema. A good example of the streaming engine is BEA's WebLogic Integration product (*http://www.bea.com/framework.jsp?CNT=index.htm&FP=/content/products/integrate*).

Second, XQuery can be used as a meta query language executing against one or more relational databases. In this scenario, XQuery accesses the relational stores as if their tables were XML documents, pushing query predicates to the database as SQL for optimized execution and then merging and manipulating the results within the XQuery code as XML. Theoretically any data store, not just relational data, can be made accessible to the XQuery environment. Here XQuery becomes a lingua franca query language, the X standing more for "plug your data format in here" than for XML. XQuery also can be used to query columns containing XML typed data. A good example of the relational approach is BEA's Liquid Data for WebLogic product (*http://www.bea.com/framework.jsp?CNT=index.htm&FP=/content/products/liquid_data*) or Microsoft's upcoming version of SQL Server code-named Yukon (*http://www.microsoft.com/sql/yukon/productinfo/*).

Third, there's the pure-play XQuery implementation where instead of mapping XQuery to another query language, it's used directly against a content database designed from the ground up for XQuery. This approach works well for managing data that hasn't yet been put into a database or that doesn't fit neatly into the rectangular boxes imposed by relational databases; for example, medical records, textbook content, office documents, and web pages. In this model, you store the documents directly into the

XQuery database—possibly going through a conversion to XML, but without any complicated shredding to a relational format needed. Then you query the documents to extract the bits and pieces deemed important. Personally, I'm most interested in the pure-play approach because it's the most likely to change the world, as they say. A good example of this is Mark Logic's Content Interaction Server (*http://www.marklogic.com/prod.html*). Most open source products are also following this model, but without the real database backing.

The mechanism to execute an XQuery depends on which of these camps your product falls into. Streaming XQuery engines may be triggered by web service requests (a convenient XML input) and typically generate web service responses. Relational XQuery engines may include XQuery in their SQL calls or in lieu of SQL calls. And pure-play implementations can execute from files, via Java interfaces, or over networks.

Executing XQuery from a File Using Saxon

Executing XQuery from a file can be the easiest way to get started. Many engines allow file-based execution. One of the best open source engines for this is Saxon, written by Michael Kay and available at *http://saxon. sourceforge.net*. In its current 8.0 release, it exposes the following command-line interface (with *saxon8.jar* explicitly in the classpath):

```
java -cp saxon8.jar net.sf.saxon.Query [options] queryfile
    [params...]
```

It uses the files in the filesystem as its backend data store. (The data is naturally unindexed so the scalability isn't comparable to an XQuery engine running as a database, but it works great for learning.) By placing the Shakespeare files from **[Hack #23]** (available at *http://www.oasis-open.org/cover/ bosakShakespeare200.html*) in the current directory and using the file *speakers.xqy*, we can run the example against Saxon like this:

```
java -cp saxon8.jar net.sf.saxon.Query speakers.xqy
```

Piping Queries to Saxon

A neat trick is to pipe XQuery expressions to Saxon via the command line using a hyphen as the query filename to indicate reading from standard input.

Of course, you can also pipe the results of your XQuery to another program, here counting the characters in the title:

```
echo "doc('hamlet.xml')/PLAY/TITLE/text()" | java -cp
    saxon8.jar net.sf.saxon.Query - | wc -c
```

Let your mind work on that one for a minute. The possibilities are interesting.

Executing XQuery from Java Using XQJ

XQuery vendors often provide custom Java interfaces to their products. Right now every vendor has a different API, but there's an effort underway in the Java Community Process to standardize the Java interface to an XQuery engine. The effort is called XQJ (XQuery API for Java) and is led by Oracle and IBM under JSR 225 (*http://www.jcp.org/en/jsr/detail?id=225*). It's expected that XQJ will be to XQuery what JDBC is to SQL. Example 2-16 demonstrates how to use XQJ to execute a simple XQuery expression from Java (this is not a complete Java program).

Example 2-16. Using XQJ to portably access an XQuery engine

```
...

XQConnection conn = null;
XQExpression expr = null;
XQResultSequence result = null;

try {
  // Use JNDI to get an initial XQDataSource to build Connections
  InitialContext initCtx = new InitialContext();
  XQDataSource source =
    (XQDataSource) initCtx.lookup("java:comp/env/xqj/primary");

  // XQDataSource to XQConnection to XQExpression to XQResultSequence
  conn = source.getConnection();
  expr = conn.createExpression();

  String query =
    "declare function prime($i as xs:integer) as xs:boolean {" +
    "  $i = 2 or not(some $denom in (2 to $i - 1) satisfies $i mod
                    $denom = 0)" +
    "}; " +
    "for $i in (1 to 100)" +
    "return" +
    "  if (prime($i)) then $i else ()";

  result = expr.executeQuery(query);

  // Iterate over the result sequence pulling answers one at a time
  while (result.next()) {
    int prime = result.getInt();
    System.out.println("Prime: " + prime);
  }
}
catch (XQException e) {
  e.printStackTrace();
}
// Free the resources whether or not there was an exception
finally {
```

Example 2-16. Using XQJ to portably access an XQuery engine (continued)

```
  if (conn != null) {
    try { conn.close( ); } catch (XQException ignored) { }
  }
}
```

As demonstrated in the first line of the `try` block, JNDI provides the standard mechanism to get an initial `XQDataSource`. The `XQDataSource` heads the chain of objects that goes from a connection to an expression to an executed query. The query here manually calculates prime numbers between 1 and 100. Java gets the result as an `XQResultSequence` that can be iterated over, fetching each returned value in the result.

Note that XQJ, like XQuery, is still under active development. The code shown here is based on the May 2004 early draft release. Details are highly likely to change before final release.

Executing XQuery on the Web

One final and interesting way to execute XQuery is by placing it directly on the Web. Some vendors, such as Mark Logic and Qexo, let you place a query script file directly under an HTTP server document root. When a client requests the query file with its special extension (such as *http://example.com/request.xqy*), the server executes the query file content and returns the result. It's basically CGI for XQuery. And because XQuery so easily constructs dynamic XHTML output, it's an amazingly quick development and deployment model. There's no need to use Java classes in processing the result.

The recipe:

1. Write an XQuery program that outputs XHTML.

2. Save it under the server's document root with a special file extension.

3. Have clients request the file, causing the query to run.

For vendors without built-in support, it's possible to write a servlet that handles the *.xqy* file pattern and uses XQJ to execute the file's contents, streaming the results back to the client.

See Also

- X-Hive/DB, a native XML database with XQuery support: *http://www.x-hive.com/products/db/*

- Qizx/open, an open source Java implementation of XQuery: *http://www.xfra.net/qizxopen/*
- Qexo, the GNU Kawa implementation of XQuery: *http://www.gnu.org/software/qexo/*

—*Jason Hunter*

HACK #25 Include Text and Documents with Entities

You can insert external text and even documents into XML documents by using external entities.

XML comes with a native mechanism for including text from both internal and external sources. The mechanism is called *entities* (*http://www.w3.org/TR/REC-xml.html/#sec-physical-struct*). This feature allows you to make XML documents modular. Entities can be declared and stored internally in a document, in an external file, and even across a network. Entities are declared in DTDs and can contain just small bits of non-XML text, XML markup, or even large amounts of text.

XML has a concept of a *document entity*, which is a starting point for an XML processor. A document entity, from one standpoint, may exist in a file with an associated name. However, from the standpoint of the XML spec, a document entity does not have a name and might be an input stream that has no means of identification at all.

The rather minimal XML document *entity.xml* declares one internal entity (line 3) and two external entities (lines 4 and 5), as shown in Example 2-17.

Example 2-17. entity.xml

```
1   <?xml version="1.0" encoding="UTF-8"?>
2   <!DOCTYPE time [
3   <!ENTITY tm "59">
4   <!ENTITY tme SYSTEM "tm.ent">
5   <!ENTITY rmt SYSTEM "http://www.wyeast.net/rmt.ent">
6   ]>
7
8   <!-- a time instant -->
9   <time timezone="PST">
10    <hour>11</hour>
11    <minute>&tm;</minute>
12    <second>&tme;</second>
13    <meridiem>p.m.</meridiem>
14    &rmt;
15  </time>
```

This kind of DTD is called the *internal subset* because it is internal to the XML document itself. You can have an internal subset, an external subset, or both at the same time (see "Validate an XML Document with a DTD" [Hack #68]).

> The XML 1.0 spec allows for validating and non-validating processors. Validating processors care about DTDs, but non-validating processors do not. A non-validating processor is *not* required to resolve external entities. See *http://www.w3.org/TR/2004/REC-xml-20040204/#proc-types*.

Line 3 contains a declaration for an internal, parsed entity. tm is the *entity name* and the text in quotes (59) is *replacement text*. A reference to this entity [Hack #4] is on line 11, &tm;. Entity references begin with an ampersand (&) and end with a semicolon (;), with the entity name sandwiched in between (tm). When processed with entity replacement "turned on," the reference on line 11 will be replaced by the replacement text 59.

The entity declared on line 4 is an external, parsed entity. Its replacement text is found in the external local file *tme.ent*. (The suffix *.ent* is certainly not required—it's just a convention that some folks use for naming entity files.) When processed, the reference &tme; on line 12 will be replaced by the little fragment of text found in the file *tme.ent*:

```
<?xml encoding="UTF-8"?>59
```

Right before the text 59 is a *text declaration* (*http://www.w3.org/TR/REC-xml.html/#sec-TextDecl*). It looks like an XML declaration [Hack #1] minus the version information. The version information is allowed here, but unlike the XML declaration, it is not required. Text declarations allow you to explicitly assign an encoding to an external entity file. If a text declaration is present, it must have an encoding declaration and must appear at the beginning of the entity.

The final entity, declared on line 5, is also an external, parsed entity, like the one defined on the line before it. The difference is that this entity's replacement text comes from an external file out on the Web, *http://www.wyeast.net/rmt.ent*. The contents of *rmt.ent* contains markup and looks like this:

```
<?xml encoding="UTF-8"?><atomic signal="true"/>
```

A reference to *rmt.ent* turns up on line 14 of *entity.xml* (&rmt;). When processed, the reference is replaced with the missing markup in *entity.xml*.

You can process this document at the command line to expand the entities using a tool like *rxp* or *xmllint*. Here's an example for *xmllint* using the --noent switch, which turns entity processing on:

```
xmllint --noent entity.xml
```

xmllint will yield the output shown in Example 2-18, provided that you have a connection to the Internet at runtime.

Example 2-18. xmllint output from entity.xml

```
 1   <?xml version="1.0" encoding="UTF-8"?>
 2   <!DOCTYPE time [
 3   <!ENTITY tm "59">
 4   <!ENTITY tme SYSTEM "tm.ent">
 5   <!ENTITY rmt SYSTEM "http://www.wyeast.net/rmt.ent">
 6   ]>
 7   <!-- a time instant -->
 8   <time timezone="PST">
 9    <hour>11</hour>
10    <minute>59</minute>
11    <second>59
12   </second>
13    <meridiem>p.m.</meridiem>
14    <atomic signal="true"/>
15   </time>
```

The entity references are gone, replaced by the declared replacement text, including the empty element tag on line 14. Microsoft Internet Explorer (IE) can process these entities as well. Figure 2-25 shows *entity.xml* as displayed in IE.

Unparsed Entities and Notations

XML also supports *unparsed entities*. The XML specification states that:

> "An unparsed entity is a resource whose contents may or may not be text, and if text, may be other than XML. Each unparsed entity has an associated notation, identified by name. Beyond a requirement that an XML processor make the identifiers for the entity and notation available to the application, XML places no constraints on the contents of unparsed entities." (See *http://www.w3.org/TR/2004/REC-xml-20040204/#dt-unparsed.*)

Unparsed entities are declared in DTDs together with *notations*. A notation identifies the name of an unparsed entity. To see how unparsed entities and notations work together, see "Validate an XML Document with a DTD" **[Hack #68]**.

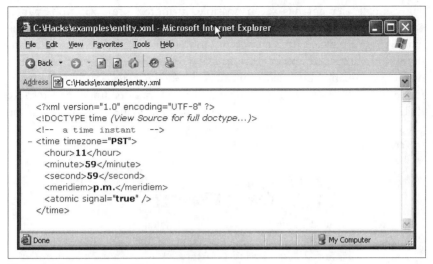

Figure 2-25. entity.xml in IE

Include External Documents with XInclude

Beyond entity inclusion, there is another mechanism for including external text and documents. It's called XInclude.

XML Inclusions, or XInclude, is still a working draft specification at W3C (*http://www.w3.org/TR/xinclude/*), but it is being implemented with reasonable confidence as a step up from external entities. XInclude allows on-the-spot replacement of text or markup, without a DTD or entity reference. It also has a fallback mechanism in case something goes haywire.

The main feature of XInclude is the include element. The namespace name for XInclude is http://www.w3.org/2003/XInclude, and the common prefix is xi.

This hack is based on the November 2003 working draft of XInclude (*http://www.w3.org/TR/2003/WD-xinclude-20031110/*). The candidate recommendation for XInclude was issued in April 2004, just as I was finishing this book. The candidate rec specifies a previous namespace name, http://www.w3.org/2001/XInclude. I am using the older namespace URI so that it works with the software I'm using here, but it's likely that the software will catch up with the current version of the specification soon, and you'll have to change the namespace URI to get it to work.

The include element has seven possible attributes: href, xpointer, parse, encoding, accept, accept-charset, and accept-language. The href attribute is mandatory unless xpointer is present (and vice versa), because you have to point to the included text or markup using one or the other. href retrieves a whole document, but xpointer (based on *http://www.w3.org/TR/xptr-framework/*) can supposedly pinpoint a location in a document and retrieve it. The parse attribute can have one of two possible values: text or xml. If the value is text, the included resource must be made up of characters; if xml, the resource must be well-formed XML.

What Is XPointer?

The XML Pointer Language (XPointer) is a language for creating fragment identifiers for URI references to XML documents (the media types text/xml and application/xml). It is specified in three W3C recommendations: the XPointer Framework (*http://www.w3.org/TR/xptr-framework/*), the XPointer element( ) scheme (*http://www.w3.org/TR/xptr-element/*), and the XPointer xmlns( ) scheme (*http://www.w3.org/TR/xptr-xmlns/*). Beyond element( ) and xmlns( ), XPointer also has an xpointer( ) scheme; however, xpointer( ), which is based on XPath, is not yet fully developed. In other words, XPointer is not quite ready for prime time. However, Mozilla currently offers partial XPointer support, with additional non-W3C schemes (*http://www.mozilla.org/newlayout/xml/#linking*).

The encoding attribute may be used only when the value of parse is text. It is intended to help an XInclude processor figure out the character encoding of the included text. Legal values are encoding="UTF-8", encoding="UTF-16", and others as specified by *http://www.w3.org/TR/REC-xml.html/#charencoding*.

The last three attributes, accept, accept-charset, and accept-language, are used for content negotiation when the resource is transported over HTTP (see Section 14 of *http://www.ietf.org/rfc/rfc2616.txt*). Each of these attribute names match HTTP message header names; i.e., Accept, Accept-Charset, and Accept-Language. If any of these attributes is used, and a matching header exists in the HTTP request, the value of the attribute should match that of the header field value. For example, if accept-language="de" is on the include element, then the HTTP message header in the request should be Accept-Language: de.

include may have one and only one possible element child, fallback, which provides the fallback or fail-safe mechanism mentioned earlier. If the resource include is trying to reach is unavailable for some reason, the content of the `fallback` element is used instead. If the `fallback` element is empty, `include` is simply ignored in the output.

libxml2's (*http://xmlsoft.org*) utility *xmllint* (*http://xmlsoft.org/xmllint.html*) offers preliminary support for XInclude. Take the document *include.xml* (Example 2-19), part of the file archive that came with the book (note emphasis):

Example 2-19. include.xml

```
<?xml version="1.0" encoding="UTF-8"?>

<!-- a time instant -->
<time timezone="PST">
 <hour>11</hour>
 <minute>59</minute>
 <second>59</second>
 <meridiem>59</meridiem>
 <xi:include xmlns:xi="http://www.w3.org/2003/XInclude"
     parse="xml" href="http://www.wyeast.net/rmt.ent">
  <xi:fallback>Oops!</xi:fallback>
 </xi:include>
</time>
```

The properly namespaced `include` element is looking for a piece of well-formed XML at `http://www.wyeast.net/rmt.ent`. If it doesn't find it, the word "Oops!" is written at the point of inclusion in the result. Let's test it with *xmllint* using the `--xinclude` option:

```
xmllint --xinclude include.xml
```

If everything goes all right, the result should look like Example 2-20.

Example 2-20. xmllint output with XInclude processing

```
<?xml version="1.0" encoding="UTF-8"?>
<!-- a time instant -->
<time timezone="PST">
 <hour>11</hour>
 <minute>59</minute>
 <second>59</second>
 <meridiem>59</meridiem>
 <atomic signal="true" xml:base="http://www.wyeast.net/rmt.ent"/>
</time>
```

The base URI **[Hack #28]** for the atomic element is not changed by the XInclude processor, so it is stated explicitly with the `xml:base` attribute (see *http://www.w3.org/TR/xinclude/#base*). For fun, change *rmt.ent* in the `href` attribute on the `include` element to *rmt.xml* (which does not exist) to see what happens. You could also make the `fallback` element empty to see what result you'll get.

See Also

- The XMLmind XML Editor has XInclude support: *http://www.xmlmind. com/xmleditor/*

- Apache's Xerces v2.6.1 and above now support XInclude: *http://xml. apache.org/news.html#xerces-j-2.6.1*

- Elliotte Rusty Harold's Java XML Object Model (XOM) offers XInclude support with its XIncluder class: *http://cafeconleche.org/XOM/*

- W3C's list of XInclude implementations: *http://www.w3.org/XML/2002/ 09/xinclude-implementation*

HACK #27   Encode XML Documents

Character encoding is quite important, especially as XML documents cross international boundaries. This hack will help you understand and use character encoding in XML.

To understand XML, you need to understand the characters that can make up XML documents. XML 1.0 supports the UCS standard, officially ISO/ IEC 10646-1:1993 Information technology—Universal Multiple-Octet Coded Character Set (UCS)—Part 1: Architecture and Basic Multilingual Plane, and its seven amendments (search for 10646 on *http://www.iso.ch*). Since the time that XML became a recommendation at the W3C, UCS has advanced to ISO/IEC 10646-1:2000. In addition, Unicode is a parallel standard to UCS (see *http://www.unicode.org*). XML 1.0 supports Unicode Version 2.0, but Unicode has advanced to Version 4.0 at this time, so there are differences in what XML 1.0 supports and in what the latest versions of UCS and Unicode support.

Both ISO/IEC 10646-1 UCS and Unicode assign the same values and descriptions for each character; however, Unicode defines some semantics for the characters that ISO/IEC 10646-1 does not.

> Mike Brown's XML tutorial at *http://www.skew.org/xml/ tutorial* is good background reading on Unicode and character sets. To look up general character charts, see Kosta Kostis's charts at *http://www.kostis.net/charsets/*. For Unicode character charts, go to *http://www.unicode.org/charts/*.

Each character in Unicode is represented by a unique, hexadecimal (base-16) number. The first 128 characters in Unicode are the same characters in US-ASCII or Latin 1 (ISO-8859-1), which surely makes the transition to Unicode easier. The numbers that represent these characters are called *code points*.

An XML document, whether in a file or in a stream, is really just a series of bytes. A *byte* is a chunk of *bits* (ones and zeros), usually eight per chunk (an *octet*). When you assign a character encoding to a document, you express an intent for the processing software to transform the bytes in the document into a sequence of characters that another processor, such as a word processor, can recognize.

Character encoding is the mapping of binary values to code points or character positions. Let me explain what code points are and why it's important to understand them. Back in the 1960s, the standards organization ANSI created the ASCII or US-ASCII character encoding format. (ASCII is an acronym for American Standard Code for Information Interchange.) US-ASCII represents only 128 characters, numbered in decimal 0–127, with each numbered position representing a code point. In their binary forms, every US-ASCII character is represented by only seven bits—a 7-bit byte rather than an 8-bit byte (octet). Other 7-bit encoding forms were created in other parts of the world at this time as well, not just in the United States.

Character sets map numeric values to graphic character representations; for example, the US-ASCII character set maps the integer 65 to the character A. The uppercase letter A in US-ASCII is represented by the seven bits 1000001 and is mapped to the code point 65 in decimal (integer form) or 41 in hexadecimal.

Seven bits can represent only 128 distinct values (the highest 7-bit binary number, 1111111, equals the decimal equivalent 127), but in human writing systems there are millions of characters beyond the provincial 128 characters of US-ASCII. So if you want more characters, such as 256 rather than 128, you need to at least bump up your binary numbers from seven bits to eight bits. The ISO 8859 standards do just that.

ISO/IEC 8859

The ISO-8859-1 character set, commonly called Latin-1, represents 256 Western European characters, numbered 0–255, using 8-bit bytes or octets. It was originally specified by the European Computer Manufacturers Association (ECMA) in the 1980s, and is currently defined there as ECMA-94 (see *http://www.ecma-international.org*). This standard was also endorsed by ISO and is specified in ISO/IEC 8859-1:1998 Information technology—8-bit single-byte graphic character sets—Part 1: Latin alphabet No. 1 (see *http://www.iso.ch*). ISO-8859-1 is only the beginning of a series: there are actually 15 characters sets in this family. These character sets helped to unify earlier 7-bit efforts. All 15 of these 8-bit character sets are specified by ISO and are listed in Table 2-1.

Table 2-1. ISO 8859 specifications

ISO standard	Description	Character set name
ISO/IEC 8859-1:1998	Part1 1, Latin 1	ISO-8859-1
ISO/IEC 8859-2:1999	Part 2, Latin 2	ISO-8859-2
ISO/IEC 8859-3:1999	Part 3, Latin 3	ISO-8859-3
ISO/IEC 8859-4:1998	Part 4, Latin 4	ISO-8859-4
ISO/IEC 8859-5:1998	Part 5, Cyrillic	ISO-8859-5
ISO/IEC 8859-6:1996	Part 6, Arabic	ISO-8859-6
ISO 8859-7:1987	Part 7, Greek	ISO-8859-7
ISO/IEC 8859-8:1999	Part 8, Hebrew	ISO-8859-8
ISO/IEC 8859-9:1999	Part 9, Latin 5	ISO-8859-9
ISO/IEC 8859-10:1998	Part 10, Latin 6	ISO-8859-10
ISO/IEC 8859-11:2001	Part 11, Thai	ISO-8859-11
ISO/IEC 8859-13:1998	Part 13, Latin 7	ISO-8859-13
ISO/IEC 8859-14:1998	Part 14, Latin 8 (Celtic)	ISO-8859-14
ISO/IEC 8859-15:1999	Part 15, Latin 9	ISO-8859-15
ISO/IEC 8859-16:2001	Part 16, Latin 10	ISO-8859-16

Using octets rather than 7-bit bytes to represent single characters expands the limit from 128 to 256 characters. The ISO 8859 character sets reuse the code points 0–255 for each part, though the characters assigned to those code points can differ. For example, Part 1 assigns the small Latin letter ÿ (y with dieresis) to code point 255 but the same code point 255 is assigned to the —ü (Cyrillic small letter *dzhe*) in Part 5.

Unicode avoids the code point conflicts seen in the ISO 8859 specs by assigning a unique number to each character, and it accomplishes this by not limiting character definitions to a single octet. Two of the most common applications of Unicode are the UTF-8 and UTF-16 character encodings.

UTF-8 and UTF-16

XML processors are required to support both UTF-8 and UTF-16 character encodings. These encodings provide different ways of representing Unicode characters in binary form. UTF stands for UCS Transformation Format.

UTF-8 is not limited to a fixed-length character encoding, but can use between one and six octets to represent Unicode characters. Unicode code points in the range 0–255 are represented with one octet, while those in the range 256–2047 are represented with two octets, the range 2048–65535 with three octets, and so forth. UTF-8 uses a special encoding scheme to get the most out of the least bits, using the first octet of a sequence of more than one octet to indicate how many octets are in the sequence. (See *http://www.ietf.org/rfc/rfc2279.txt*.)

UTF-16 uses a minimum of two octets to represent characters; if the character cannot be represented with two octets, it uses four octets. It also uses a special encoding scheme (see *http://www.ietf.org/rfc/rfc2279.txt*), but if you are using only Latin characters, UTF-16 characters can take up more space than necessary. For example, the letter A would only take one octet in UTF-8 but would take two octets in UTF-16. On the other hand, a character in the higher ranges that might take six octets in UTF-8 would take at most four octets in UTF-16. UTF-8 is a good choice for Latin alphabets, and UTF-16 is good for Chinese, Japanese, and Korean characters.

The Byte Order Mark. A Byte Order Mark (BOM) is a special space character—the Unicode character FEFF—that is used only as an encoding signature. If an XML document is UTF-16, it must begin with a BOM. In the absence of an XML declaration, an XML processor can read the BOM and guess that the document is UTF-16. (If it is UTF-8, it may or may not begin with a BOM.) If the document is not UTF-8 or UTF-16, then the character encoding *must* be declared explicitly in the XML declaration. (See Section 4.3.3 of the XML specification.)

XML processors may support other encodings such as US-ASCII, ISO-8859-1, or Shift_JIS (Japanese). The Internet Assigned Numbers Authority (IANA) keeps track of encoding names and publishes them at *http://www.iana.org/assignments/character-sets*. You can use your own private encoding name if you start it with x-, but you would have to write your own code to process it.

What if you have a document that has an encoding declared but is really stored in another encoding? Such is the case with the file *oops.xml*, which looks identical to *time.xml* but is stored as UTF-16 even though the encoding declaration says UTF-8. If you check *oops.xml* for well-formedness with *rxp*:

```
rxp oops.xml
```

you will get this report:

```
Error: Declared encoding UTF-8 is incompatible with UTF-16 which was used
to read it in unnamed entity at line 1 char 37 of
file:///C:/Hacks/examples/oops.xml
```

There are a number of ways to fix this problem. I'll share a couple. One tool you should have on your shelf is Sharmahd Computing's SC UniPad, a

Windows Unicode text editor available for download from *http://www. unipad.org/download/*. This editor has many helpful features for creating and editing Unicode documents, one of which is changing a document's character encoding.

Figure 2-26 shows *oops.xml* in SC UniPad. The XML declaration in the file says that the encoding is UTF-8, but the status bar at the bottom of the editor window reports that the file is in UTF-16(L) (*L* is for little endian) and that the BOM is present. To fix that, choose Options → Current Options, and the Current Options dialog box appears. In the File tab, select the UTF-8 format (encoding) and then click OK. This changes the encoding. Save the file with File → Save. If you process this file with *rxp* again, you won't get the incompatible encoding error you saw earlier.

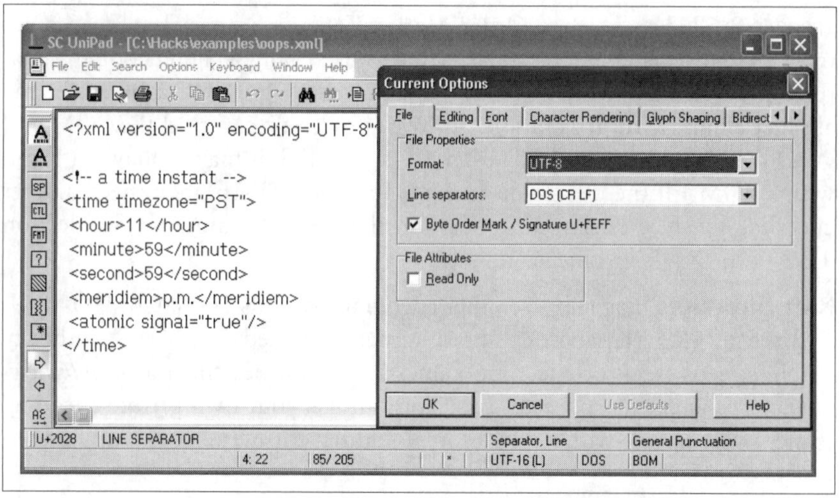

Figure 2-26. Changing the character encoding of oops.xml with SC UniPad

Another way to do this is with the -utf8 option of HTML Tidy [Hack #22]. This command:

```
tidy -utf8 -xml -o noops.xml oops.xml
```

will save *oops.xml* in UTF-8 as *noops.xml*. The -xml option indicates that the input is well-formed XML.

See Also

- HTML Tidy offers a variety of command-line options to change the encoding of a document: "Convert an HTML Document to XHTML with HTML Tidy" [Hack #22]

- The command *xxd*, available on Cygwin and Unix systems, dumps a file, giving a hexadecimal representation of each character; try xxd -g 1 time.xml
- Simon St.Laurent's Gorille is a Java tool that tests the characters, names, and content of XML documents: *http://gorille.sourceforge.net/*

HACK #28 Explore XLink and XML

XLink and XML Base are implemented or partially implemented by Mozilla. This hack explores these technologies, using Mozilla as a platform.

The XML Linking Language or XLink (*http://www.w3.org/TR/xlink/*) defines a vocabulary for creating hyperlinks to resources using XML syntax. XLink goes beyond the simple linking in HTML and XHTML by adding concrete semantics and extended links that can link to more than one resource. XLink hasn't really taken off yet, but Mozilla supports simple links in XLink, though not extended links (*http://www.mozilla.org/newlayout/xml/ #linking*). Use of XLink is growing, if slowly—see, for example, the use of XLink in the OpenOffice specification (*http://www.oasis-open.org/ committees/download.php/6037/office-spec-1.0-cd-1.pdf*).

XML Base (*http://www.w3.org/TR/xmlbase/*) consists of a single XML attribute, xml:base, that acts like the base element from HTML and XHTML; i.e., it explicitly sets the base URI for a document. A base URI is often understood implicitly by a program such as a Web browser by the location of a resource, such as a location on the web or the location of a file in a directory or file structure. In HTML or XHTML, this base URI could be set directly with the base element, as shown in this fragment of XHTML markup (note bold):

```
<html xmlns="http://www.w3.org/1999/xhtml" xml:lang="en">
<head>
 <title>Links</title>
 <base href="http://www.xml.com"/>
</head>
<body>
 ...
```

You set a base URI explicitly using xml:base, as shown in the example document *base.xml* (Example 2-21). It is also displayed in Mozilla Firefox in Figure 2-27.

Example 2-21. base.xml

```
1 <?xml version="1.0" encoding="UTF-8"?>
2 <?xml-stylesheet href="base.css" type="text/css"?>
3
```

Example 2-21. base.xml (continued)

```
 4  <links xml:base="http://www.xml.com/"
 5    xmlns:xlink="http://www.w3.org/1999/xlink">
 6  <heading>Resources on XML.com.</heading>
 7  <block>Start here:
 8   <link xlink:type="simple" xlink:href="index.csp">Home</link></block>
 9  <block>Topics:
10   <link xlink:type="simple" xlink:href="/programming/">Programming
     articles</link> :
11   <link xlink:type="simple" xlink:href="/schemas/">Schema articles </link> :
12   <link xlink:type="simple" xlink:href="/style/">Style articles</link>
13  </block>
14  <block xml:base="/images/">Logo for XML.com:
15   <link xlink:type="simple" xlink:href="logo_tagline.jpg">logo</link>
16  </block>
17  </links>
```

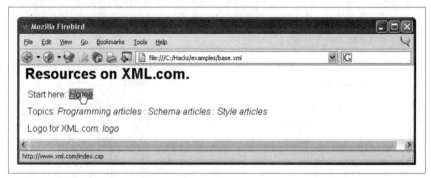

Figure 2-27. base.xml in Firefox

XML Base

The base URI is set to http://www.xml.com with xml:base on line 4. This setting is inherited by the children of links. The XLink to *index.csp* on line 8,
therefore, is able to resolve to *http://www.xml.com/index.csp* because *index.
csp* is relative to *http://www.xml.com*.

The xml:base attribute on line 14 adds the *images* directory to the base URI
so that it becomes http://www.xml.com/images/, changing the earlier setting
on line 4. This is in effect only for the children of the block where it is set.
Hence, the XLink on line 15 can find the JPEG image of the XML.com logo
with only the filename *logo_tagline.jpg*.

XLink

The namespace for XLink is declared on line 5 and is associated with the
xlink prefix (xmlns:xlink="http://www.w3.org/1999/xlink"). The xlink prefix is customary, and Mozilla won't work without it.

The namespace declaration allows the link elements on lines 8, 10, 11, 12, and 15 to use the XLink attributes xlink:type and xlink:href. The value of xlink:type states the type of XLink (simple in Example 2-21). Other possible values are extended, locator, arc, resource, title, or none, but because Mozilla supports only simple links, I only used simple. The xlink:href attribute contains a URI that identifies the resource that the link can traverse, similar to the href attribute on the a element in HTML or XHTML.

When the mouse pointer hovers over the XLinks in *base.xml* in the browser, the background changes according to the CSS styling defined in *base.css*, which is referenced by the XML stylesheet PI on line 2.

Other XLink Functionality

Three other XLink attributes merit some discussion: xlink:actuate, xlink:show, and xlink:label. Unlike xlink:type and xlink:href, these attributes have not been implemented in Mozilla. In fact, they apparently have not been implemented in software that can be easily demonstrated on the Web, so unfortunately I can't show you any practical examples of them. Nevertheless, it would be good for you to at least get familiar with the intended functionality of these XLink attributes, should they ever reach the masses.

The xlink:actuate attribute indicates when or how a link is to be traversed. The value of xlink:actuate can be onRequest, onLoad, none, or other. onRequest means the link is actuated when it is clicked or triggered in some way. onLoad means that the link is actuated when the page or resource is loaded by an application such as a browser. A value of none essentially turns off the behavior, and a value of other allows for application-specific behavior.

The xlink:show attribute can have these values and behaviors:

new
> Load the ending resource in a new window.

replace
> Load the resource in the same window, frame, pane, or what have you.

embed
> Load the resource at the place where the link is actuated.

other
> Application-specific behavior.

none
> Essentially "don't do anything," though behavior is not specified by the spec.

The xlink:label attribute contains a label that identifies an element holding a link to a resource. Then the xlink:from and xlink:to attributes can contain values that match values in xlink:label attributes (see Example 2-23).

Extended links. Extended links (*http://www.w3.org/TR/xlink/#extended-link*) are hard to explain. There is no simple way to demonstrate them because browsers don't support them. The fact that they are complicated is perhaps one reason why they are not widely implemented. But they are worthy of a few passing remarks, as they hold potential.

We are used to simple links that go in one direction from one resource to another. Extended links can point to more than one resource at a time. This is done by using the xlink:type="locator" attribute/value pair on an element, in combination with xlink:href. You can provide some advisory text with xlink:title. xlink:role can contain a URI value that annotates the link, but doesn't actually link to a resource. An extended link using all these attributes would look something like Example 2-22.

Example 2-22. Extended link example

```
<link xml:base="http://www.ri.gov/living/" xlink:type="extended">
 <country>United States</country>
 <state>Rhode Island</state>
 <city xlink:type="locator" xlink:title="Bristol"
   xlink:href="/towns/town.php?town=Bristol">Bristol</city>
 <city xlink:type="locator" xlink:title="Newport"
   xlink:href="/towns/town.php?town=Newport">Newport</city>
</link>
```

XLink linkbases. An XLink link database or *linkbase* (*http://www.w3.org/TR/xlink/#xlg*) is an XML document that contains one or more inbound and third-party links. Linkbases are a little hard to grasp, especially because, once again, you can't really demonstrate them.

An *arc* provides information about how to traverse a pair of resources, including direction and perhaps some information about how an application may act. An arc is said to be *outbound* if it starts at a local resource and ends at a remote resource. An arc is *inbound* if it starts at a remote resource and lands in a local one. An arc is a *third-party arc* if it neither starts nor ends at a local resource. In other words, a third-party arc is one for which you do not or cannot create the link at either the starting or ending resource.

The following XML fragment (Example 2-23) indicates that when *exterior. xml* is loaded, the *linkbase.xml* document should be loaded. On the load element, the xlink:actuate attribute specifies load behavior, and using the labels in the link and linkbase elements (defined by xlink:label), load also establishes a traversal from ext to lb using the xlink:to and xlink:from attributes.

Example 2-23. Linkbase example

```
<block>
  <link xlink:label="ext" xlink:href="exterior.xml" />
  <linkbase xlink:label="linkbase" xlink:href="linkbase.xml" />
  <load xlink:from="ext" xlink:to="lb" xlink:actuate="onLoad" />
</block>
```

See Also

- For more insight into XLink: *http://www.xml.com/pub/a/2002/09/25/linkoffering.html*

HACK #29 What's the Diff? Diff XML Documents

If you are handling many XML documents, sometimes you need to check the differences between two or more documents. You can perform diffs of XML documents with online and command-line tools.

When you manage a lot of XML documents, it is likely that you will have similar files with different content. Also, it is likely that you will need to keep track of changes on files within a given project. There are online tools—one from DecisionSoft (*http://www.decisionsoft.com*) and another from DeltaXML (*http://www.deltaxml.com*)—that can help you quickly compare XML files to see how different they are. There are also several command-line tools available, such as IBM's XML Diff and Merge Tool (*http://www.alphaworks.ibm.com/tech/xmldiffmerge*). This hack will walk you through the steps of using these tools.

DecisionSoft's xmldiff

You can diff local XML files on your computer online with DecisionSoft's *xmldiff. xmldiff* makes line-by-line comparisons of XML documents, and therefore is helpful for comparing similar documents that use the same structure and vocabulary.

To compare two similar documents, follow these steps:

1. In a web browser, go to *http://tools.decisionsoft.com/xmldiff.html* (see Figure 2-28).

2. Click the first Browse button, and the File Upload dialog box appears. Find the file *time.xml* in the working directory and click the Open button.

3. Click the second Browse button and find *time2.xml*, and then click Open.

4. Select the "Split attributes" checkbox.

5. Click the "Show differences" button. The results are shown in Figure 2-29.

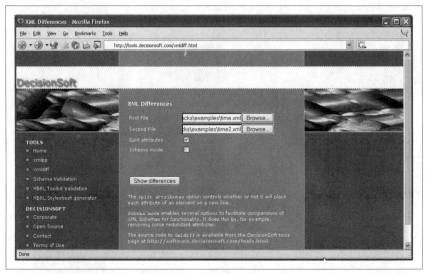

Figure 2-28. DecisionSoft's xmldiff

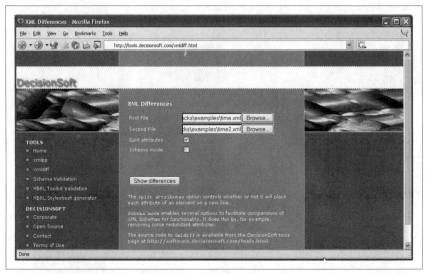

Figure 2-29. Results from xmldiff

If lines are the same, they are shown in gray. If the same lines in both files differ, the differences are highlighted by different colors: the line from the first file is highlighted in red and the line from the second file is shown in green. Because you selected the "Split attributes" checkbox, the attributes are each listed on separate lines, making them easier to read.

> Currently, *xmldiff* works only on local files. You cannot access remote files with URLs.

DeltaXML's XML Comparator

You can also diff local XML files online by using DeltaXML's comparator utility, available at *http://compare.deltaxml.com/*. Like *xmldiff*, this utility makes line-by-line comparisons of XML documents, and so is likewise helpful for comparing similar documents using the same structure and vocabulary. It is also possible to paste XML documents into the two paste boxes provided on the DeltaXML comparator page (Figure 2-30).

To compare two similar documents using DeltaXML, follow these steps:

1. In a web browser, go to *http://compare.deltaxml.com/* (see Figure 2-30).
2. Select all three checkboxes in the Options area.
3. Click the first Browse button, and the File Upload dialog box appears. Find the file *time.xml* in the working directory and click the Open button.
4. Click the second Browse button, find *time2.xml*, and then click Open.
5. Click the Compare Files button. The results are displayed in the browser window (see Figure 2-31).

Changed lines are highlighted in blue italics. Unchanged lines are shown in plain text. The differences between the first and second files are shown by striking through the item from the first file in red and by underlining the item from the second file in green. I found the output of DeltaXML's utility more grokable than that of *xmldiff*.

IBM's XML Diff and Merge Tool

Download and install IBM's XML Diff and Merge Tool from *http://www. alphaworks.ibm.com/tech/xmldiffmerge* (you will be required to register on the IBM alphaWorks site). In the *bin* directory under the installation directory *xmldiff*, you will find a Windows batch file called *xmldiff2.bat* as well as a shell script called *xmldiff2.sh*. Edit the appropriate script file, depending

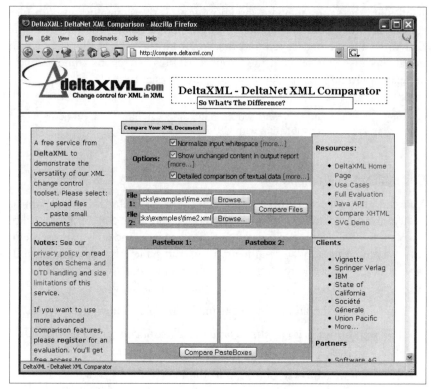

Figure 2-30. DeltaXML's XML Comparator

on your environment, by setting or exporting environment variables for the location of Java and the *xmldiff* directory. After you complete these steps, you should be able to run this command at a prompt:

```
xmldiff2 time.xml time2.xml
```

This command will give you the following results indicating what lines have changed in the second file:

```
java -DIVB_HOME="C:\temp\xmldiff" -Xnoclassgc -Xmx255m -Xms30m
  com.ibm.ivb.xmldiff.XMLDiffLauncher time.xml time2.xml
 Parsing time.xml ...
 Parsing time2.xml ...
Comparing ...
  <time timezone="PST"> --- CHANGED
    <hour> --- CHANGED
    </hour>
    <minute>
    </minute>
    <second>
    </second>
```

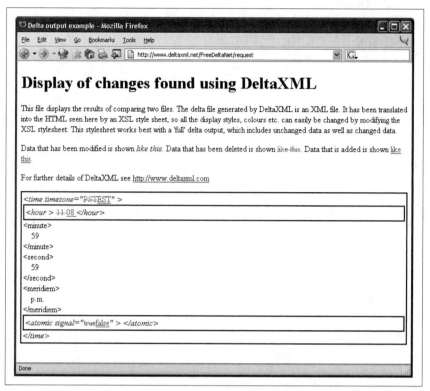

Figure 2-31. Results from DeltaXML

```
        <meridiem>
        </meridiem>
        <atomic signal="true"/> --- CHANGED
      </time>
```

See Also

- xmlspy 2004 Professional and Enterprise Editions have diff capabilities: *http://www.xmlspy.com* and *http://www.altova.com/matrix.html*
- Microsoft's XML Diff and Patch: *http://apps.gotdotnet.com/xmltools/xmldiff/*
- Logilab's xmldiff, written in Python: *http://www.logilab.org/projects/xmldiff/*
- Advanced Software's Docucomp: *http://www.docucomp.com/*

Look at XML Documents Through the Lens of the XML Information Set

If you get a grip on the XML Information Set, you'll know you don't have to worry about it too much.

The XML Information Set or Infoset (*http://www.w3.org/TR/xml-infoset*) is a recommendation from the W3C that describes an abstract data set whose definitions can be used to describe well-formed XML documents (documents don't have to be valid). These definitions are set forth so that other W3C specs can use the same terminology and not trip over each other's shoelaces.

An *infoset* is supposed to describe the result of parsing an XML document; it can also be constructed by other means, such as in a Document Object Model (DOM) tree (*http://www.w3.org/TR/xml-infoset/#intro.synthetic*). Normally, you don't hear folks talk about structures in XML documents using the terms defined in this spec.

The infoset consists of a set of 11 information items, each with a set of properties. The following list briefly outlines these information items and their associated properties:

Document information item
    Properties: all declarations processed, base URI, character encoding scheme, children, document element, notations, standalone, unparsed entities, version

Element information item
    Properties: attributes, base URI, children, in-scope namespaces, local name, namespace attributes, namespace name, parent, prefix

Attribute information item
    Properties: attribute type, local name, namespace name, normalized value, owner element, prefix, references, specified

Processing instruction information item
    Properties: base URI, content, notation, parent, target

Unexpanded entity reference information item
    Properties: declaration base URI, name, parent, public identifier, system identifier

Character information item
    Properties: character code, element content whitespace, parent

Comment information item
    Properties: content, parent

Document type declaration information item
    Properties: children, parent, public identifier, system identifier

Unparsed entity information item
    Properties: declaration base URI, name, notation, notation name, public identifier, system identifier

Notation information item
    Properties: declaration base URI, name, public identifier, system identifier

Namespace information item
    Properties: namespace name, prefix

> If you need help understanding the meanings behind the individual information items and properties, consult the spec. There isn't enough space in this little hack to explain them all here. Applying the stylesheet *infoset.xsl* should help you understand better what the infoset describes.

To help you understand the infoset better, the file archive includes *infoset.xsl*, an XSLT 2.0 stylesheet. The reason I used XSLT 2.0 is that it has more facilities for creating an infoset implementation than XSLT 1.0. *infoset.xsl* is only a partial XSLT implementation of the reporting infoset.

To use the stylesheet, you need an XSLT 2.0 processor, such as Saxon 8.0 or later (*http://saxon.sourceforge.net*). Saxon 8.0 isn't a complete XSLT 2.0/XPath 2.0 implementation, but it's getting closer. Download and unzip Saxon, and place *saxon8.jar* in the working directory where you installed the archive of files that came with the book. You'll need Java Version 1.4 or later, too.

You can apply this stylesheet to any XML document, as demonstrated here:

```
java -jar saxon8.jar prefix.xml infoset.xsl
```

Your results will be as follows:

```
Comment information item (1)
[content]:  a time instant
[parent]: /

Document information item
[document element]: time
[base URI]: file:/C:/Hacks/examples/115959p.m.

Element information item (document element)
[namespace]: http://www.wyeast.net/time
[local name]: time
[prefix]: tz
```

```
[children]:
[attributes]: timezone
[base URI]: file:/C:/Hacks/examples/115959p.m.

Element information item (1)
[namespace]: http://www.wyeast.net/time
[local name]: hour
[prefix]: tz
[children]: 11
[attributes]:
[parent]: tz:time
[base URI]: file:/C:/Hacks/examples/11

Element information item (2)
[namespace]: http://www.wyeast.net/time
[local name]: minute
[prefix]: tz
[children]: 59
[attributes]:
[parent]: tz:time
[base URI]: file:/C:/Hacks/examples/59

Element information item (3)
[namespace]: http://www.wyeast.net/time
[local name]: second
[prefix]: tz
[children]: 59
[attributes]:
[parent]: tz:time
[base URI]: file:/C:/Hacks/examples/59

Element information item (4)
[namespace]: http://www.wyeast.net/time
[local name]: meridiem
[prefix]: tz
[children]: p.m.
[attributes]:
[parent]: tz:time
[base URI]: file:/C:/Hacks/examples/p.m.

Element information item (5)
[namespace]: http://www.wyeast.net/time
[local name]: atomic
[prefix]: tz
[children]:
[attributes]: signal
[parent]: tz:time
[base URI]: file:/C:/Hacks/examples/
```

## CHAPTER THREE

Transforming XML Documents
Hacks 31–58

Extensible Stylesheet Language, or XSLT (*http://www.w3.org/TR/xslt*) is a declarative language for transforming XML (including XHTML) into new XML, XHTML, HTML, or text documents. It works along with a companion spec called XML Path Language, or XPath for short (*http://www.w3.org/TR/xpath*). XSLT munges the markup while XPath locates the nodes. This chapter covers a range of hacks that deal with XSLT and XPath. This is the longest chapter and it contains many hacks; here are some of the highlights.

We start out with an introductory hack for XSLT [Hack #31]. Later you will get up to speed with the XPath 1.0 data model using the TreeViewer stylesheets [Hack #34]. You'll transform XML into CSV [Hack #41] and transform into HTML an iTunes library file [Hack #44].

You'll pull information out of a MySQL database in XML form [Hack #46] and learn the basics of XSL-FO [Hack #48]. You'll also learn how to process HTML as if it were XML with TagSoup [Hack #49] and you'll create dithered scatter-plots using SVG [Hack #55]. There are also a few hacks that use XSLT 2.0 ([Hack #45] and [Hack #57]).

The example files mentioned in this chapter are available from a file archive that can be downloaded from *http://www.oreilly.com/catalog/xmlhks/*.

Understand the Anatomy of an XSLT Stylesheet
#31

Get acquainted with the basic elements of an XSLT stylesheet.

You had a close brush with XSLT in the hack that discussed converting text to XML [Hack #18], but you didn't see much more than the stylesheet's name. Here is the complete stylesheet, *time.xsl*:

```
1  <xsl:stylesheet version="1.0"
     xmlns:xsl="http://www.w3.org/1999/XSL/Transform">
2
3  <xsl:template match="Import">
4    <xsl:apply-templates select="Row"/>
5  </xsl:template>
6
7  <xsl:template match="Row">
8    <time timezone="{@timezone}">
9      <xsl:copy-of select="hour|minute|second"/>
10     <xsl:apply-templates select="atomic"/>
11   </time>
12 </xsl:template>
13
14 <xsl:template match="atomic">
15   <xsl:copy>
16     <xsl:attribute name="signal">true</xsl:attribute>
17   </xsl:copy>
18 </xsl:template>
19
20 </xsl:stylesheet>
```

The Document Element

An XSLT stylesheet has two possible document elements, stylesheet and transform (see line 1). Both have identical attributes; in fact, the only difference between the two is that they have different names, but stylesheet seems more popular with developers than transform.

The version attribute is required. Some XSLT processors support a value of 1.1 or 2.0, in support of those versions of the XSLT specs, but 1.0 is the most commonly used value. (Version 1.1 of XSLT is not and will never be a W3C recommendation, so any support for it is processor-dependent.) The namespace declaration is also required if you want an XSLT processor to recognize the XSLT markup. The namespace name for XSLT 1.0 is http://www.w3.org/1999/XSL/Transform. The prefix xsl is conventional: you can't get very far with XSLT without using a namespace prefix. Believe me, I've tried.

Templates

Templates are at the heart of what XSLT does. Templates match nodes in the document being processed, and when a node is matched, the content of the template is instantiated or executed. Nodes are the building blocks of an XML document. According to the XPath 1.0 data model (*http://www.w3.org/TR/xpath#data-model*), seven nodes are identifiable within an XML document: root, element, attribute, text, comment, processing instruction, and namespace nodes.

XSLT has some built-in templates that are instantiated in the absence of matched templates. In other words, if nodes are matched but no templates are found for a processed document, built-in templates will automatically be instantiated, returning text nodes, among other things.

Using apply-templates. This stylesheet has three templates (lines 3, 7, and 14). The first template matches the element Import, the document element of a converted text document in xmlspy (see **[Hack #18]**). When an apply-templates element is encountered, it processes all the children of the matched node. If apply-templates has a select attribute, it processes only the selected nodes. The apply-templates element on line 4 attempts to find other templates in the stylesheet that match the Row element, the child of Import.

A literal result element. The template beginning on line 7 matches the Row element. When found, the template is instantiated: a literal result element time is output to the result tree, with a timezone attribute taking its value from an attribute in the source tree. A literal result element is output literally (appearing directly in the result), and is subject to a well-formedness check by the processor, as is the entire stylesheet.

The attribute value template. The braces on line 8 hold something called an *attribute value template*. This is sort of a template within a template. When the XSLT processor encounters a timezone attribute in the source tree, it grabs the value held by the attribute and places it in the value of the attribute represented in the stylesheet.

The copy-of and copy elements. Line 9 contains a copy-of element that makes copies of the hour, minute, and second nodes in the result tree. apply-templates (line 10) searches for a template matching atomic elements. copy-of makes deep copies of elements, copying attributes if present.

When the template on line 14 matches an atomic element, it makes a copy of the element with the copy element, adding a signal attribute (line 16) to it in the output using an attribute instruction element (there are instruction elements for elements, attributes, comments, and more). copy makes a shallow copy of a node, leaving attribute nodes behind.

HACK #32 Transform an XML Document with a Command-Line Processor

Perform XSLT transformations at the command line.

A good number of free XSLT processors are available for transforming XML on the command line. I'll introduce some possible choices here: Michael

Kay's Saxon written in Java (*http://saxon.sourceforge.net*), Apache's Xalan written in C++ (*http://xml.apache.org/xalan-c/*), and Microsoft's MSXSL, also written in C++ (search for MSXSL on *http://msdn.microsoft.com*). Xalan is written in both Java (*http://xml.apache.org/xalan-j/*) and C++, but I'll be covering only the C++ version.

Saxon

You can use Saxon in the regular Java version (*saxon8.jar*) or as Instant Saxon, which is a Windows executable (*saxon.exe*).. Both are available at *http://saxon.sourceforge.net*. The latest (and probably last) release of Instant Saxon is Version 6.5.3, which came out in August 2003. The latest release of the regular Saxon is Version 8.0. It is likely that a more recent version of Saxon will be available after this book goes to print, as Saxon's development is keeping up with drafts of XSLT 2.0 and XPath 2.0. Both Instant Saxon and Saxon are free, and Saxon is open source, although you can also now purchase a commercial version from Saxonica.

Saxon was the first spec-compliant XSLT 1.0 processor and was released 17 days after the XSLT 1.0 and XPath 1.0 recommendations were published in 1999. Saxon's creator, Michael Kay, is the editor of the XSLT 2.0 specification and one of the editors for XPath 2.0.

Instant Saxon. Download Instant Saxon from *http://saxon.sourceforge.net* (*instant-saxon6_5_3.zip*), unzip and install it, and place *saxon.exe* in your path. You can then display usage information for Instant Saxon by typing the following at a Windows command prompt:

```
saxon
```

You should see the usage information as shown in Example 3-1.

Example 3-1. Saxon 6.5.3 usage information

```
No source file name
SAXON 6.5.3 from Michael Kay
Usage: saxon [options] source-doc style-doc {param=value}...
Options:
  -a             Use xml-stylesheet PI, not style-doc argument
  -ds            Use standard tree data structure
  -dt            Use tinytree data structure (default)
  -o filename    Send output to named file or directory
  -m classname   Use specified Emitter class for xsl:message output
  -r classname   Use specified URIResolver class
  -t             Display version and timing information
  -T             Set standard TraceListener
  -TL classname  Set a specific TraceListener
  -u             Names are URLs not filenames
```

Example 3-1. Saxon 6.5.3 usage information (continued)

```
-w0             Recover silently from recoverable errors
-w1             Report recoverable errors and continue (default)
-w2             Treat recoverable errors as fatal
-x classname    Use specified SAX parser for source file
-y classname    Use specified SAX parser for stylesheet
-?              Display this message
```

Instant Saxon expects the name of the source document followed by the name of the stylesheet as parameters, as shown:

```
saxon time.xml clock.xsl
```

You will get this output:

```
11:59:59 p.m.
```

To direct Instant Saxon's output to a file, use the -o switch:

```
saxon -o time.out time.xml clock.xsl
```

You can transform a document that has an XML stylesheet PI [Hack #3] by using the -a option:

```
saxon -a clock.xml
```

For verbose output, use the -t option:

```
saxon -t time.xml clock.xsl
```

Full Java version of Saxon. A stable version of Saxon for XSLT 1.0 is 6.5.3. The latest version at the time of writing is 8.0. Saxon progressively supports the working drafts for XSLT 2.0 and XPath 2.0. Saxon will most probably have gone beyond Version 8.0 by the time you are reading this.

You can use Saxon on any platform that supports Java. This requires you to have a JRE or Java VM installed (Version 1.4 or later). You can download the latest SDK or JRE from *http://sun.java.com*.

Download Saxon 8.0 (or later) from *http://saxon.sourceforge.net* and install it. You can place the *saxon8.jar* in your classpath [Hack #10]. The following examples assume that the JAR is in your current directory.

For usage information, enter this line at a command or shell prompt:

```
java -jar saxon8.jar
```

The output shown in Example 3-2 will appear.

Example 3-2. Saxon 8.0 usage information

```
No source file name
SAXON 8.0 from Saxonica
Usage:  java net.sf.saxon.Transform [options] source-doc
```

Example 3-2. Saxon 8.0 usage information (continued)

```
        style-doc {param=value}...
Options:
  -a              Use xml-stylesheet PI, not style-doc argument
  -c              Indicates that style-doc is a compiled stylesheet
  -ds             Use standard tree data structure
  -dt             Use tinytree data structure (default)
  -im modename    Start transformation in specified mode
  -m template     Start transformation by calling named template
  -l              Retain line numbers in source doucment tree
  -o filename     Send output to named file or directory
  -m classname    Use specified Emitter class for xsl:message output
  -r classname    Use specified URIResolver class
  -t              Display version and timing information
  -T              Set standard TraceListener
  -TJ             Trace calls to external Java functions
  -TL classname   Set a specific TraceListener
  -u              Names are URLs not filenames
  -v              Validate source documents using DTD
  -w0             Recover silently from recoverable errors
  -w1             Report recoverable errors and continue (default)
  -w2             Treat recoverable errors as fatal
  -x classname    Use specified SAX parser for source file
  -y classname    Use specified SAX parser for stylesheet
  -?              Display this message
  param=value     Set stylesheet string parameter
  +param=file     Set stylesheet document parameter
  !option=value   Set serialization option
```

Now transform *time.xml* with *clock.xsl* by typing the following:

```
java -jar saxon8.jar time.xml clock.xsl
```

Send output to a file with the -o command-line option:

```
java -jar saxon8.jar -o time.out time.xml clock.xsl
```

An XML stylesheet PI [Hack #3] in an XML document allows you to transform using the -a switch like this:

```
java -jar saxon8.jar -a clock.xml
```

Use the -t option for verbose output:

```
java -jar saxon8.jar -t test.xml test.xsl
```

If the XML source document has a DTD with a document type declaration [Hack #68], you can validate it with the -v switch:

```
java -jar saxon8.jar -v valid.xml clock.xsl
```

Instant Saxon does not have the -v option.

Xalan

Xalan is an open source XSLT processor developed by Apache. To use Xalan C++, you must install the C++ version of Apache's XML parser, Xerces. Both Xalan C++ and Xerces C++ are available at Apache's XML site (*http://xml.apache.org*). At the time of writing, Xalan C++ is at Version 1.8.0 and Xerces C++ is at Version 2.5.0.

Download and install both Xerces and Xalan, and then add the executables to your path. Both run on Windows and various flavors of Unix. After you have installed Xalan and Xerces, you can enter the following at a command prompt or in a shell:

```
xalan
```

You will then get the output shown in Example 3-3.

Example 3-3. Xalan 1.8.0 usage information

```
Xalan version 1.8.0
Xerces version 2.5.0
Usage: Xalan [options] source stylesheet
Options:
  -a                   Use xml-stylesheet PI, not the
                       'stylesheet' argument
  -e encoding          Force the specified encoding for the
                       output.
  -i integer           Indent the specified amount.
  -m                   Omit the META tag in HTML output.
  -o filename          Write output to the specified file.
  -p name expression   Sets a stylesheet parameter.
  -u                   Disable escaping of URLs in HTML output.
  -?                   Display this message.
  -v                   Validates source documents.
  -                    A dash as the 'source' argument reads
                       from stdin. ('-' cannot be used for both arguments.)
```

Transform a document with Xalan using this command:

```
xalan time.xml clock.xsl
```

To direct the result tree from the processor to a file, use the -o option:

```
xalan -o time.out time.xml clock.xsl
```

The result of the transformation is redirected to the file named *time.out*.

Process a document with an XML stylesheet PI **[Hack #3]** using Xalan's -a like this:

```
xalan -a clock.xml
```

If an XML source document uses a DTD [Hack #68], Xalan can validate it using the -v switch:

```
xalan -v valid.xml clock.xsl
```

MSXSL

MSXSL is a free Win32 executable XSLT processor from Microsoft. To get it, go to *http://msdn.microsoft.com/downloads/* and search for "MSXSL." The latest version of MSXSL also requires MSXML 4.0, which you can download from the same location (search for "MSXML 4.0 Service Pack 2"). MSXSL is small (about 25 KB) and fast. You can download the source code, too.

MSXSL uses UTF-16 output by default, which doesn't produce very attractive output in a console window. You have to use the encoding attribute on an output element [Hack #43] in a stylesheet to override this, as *clock.xsl* does.

After downloading MSXSL, place the executable *msxsl.exe* in your path. To display usage information for MSXSL, type the following line at a Windows command prompt:

```
msxsl -?
```

You will see this usage information (Example 3-4).

Example 3-4. MSXSL 4.0 usage information

```
Microsoft (R) XSLT Processor Version 4.0

Usage: MSXSL source stylesheet [options] [param=value...] [xmlns:prefix=uri...]

Options:
    -?          Show this message
    -o filename Write output to named file
    -m startMode Start the transform in this mode
    -xw         Strip non-significant whitespace from source
                and stylesheet
    -xe         Do not resolve external definitions during
                parse phase
    -v          Validate documents during parse phase
    -t          Show load and transformation timings
    -pi         Get stylesheet URL from xml-stylesheet PI in
                source document
    -u version  Use a specific version of MSXML: '2.6', '3.0',
                '4.0'
    -           Dash used as source argument loads XML from
                stdin
    -           Dash used as stylesheet argument loads XSL
                from stdin
```

To transform a document using MSXSL, type:

```
msxsl time.xml clock.xsl
```

To direct output from MSXSL to a file, use the -o switch:

```
msxsl -o time.out time.xml clock.xsl
```

To transform an XML document that contains an XML stylesheet PI [Hack #3], use the -pi option:

```
msxsl -pi clock.xml
```

For timing information, use the -t switch:

```
msxsl -t time.xml clock.xsl
```

If the source document uses a DTD [Hack #68], you can validate it by using the -v option:

```
msxsl -v valid.xml clock.xsl
```

HACK #33 Transform an XML Document Within a Graphical Editor

Transform XML documents with XSLT in a graphical environment.

Graphical XML editors almost universally offer built-in XSLT transformations now. This hack will show you how to transform XML documents with XSLT in xmlspy, xRay2, and <oXygen/>.

xmlspy

Altova's xmlspy 2004 is a Windows-only graphical XML editor, which you can download from *http://www.xmlspy.com*. As you install xmlspy, you can get a free license for the Home Edition. Assuming that you have downloaded and installed xmlspy, follow these steps to transform *time.xml* with *clock.xsl* (you saw a brief example of this in the hack that discussed creating an XML Document from a text file [Hack #18]):

1. Launch xmlspy.
2. Open the file *time.xml* with File → Open from the working directory (the directory where you extracted the file archive for the book).
3. Choose View → Text view.
4. Open the file *clock.xsl* with File → Open, also in the same working directory as *time.xml*.
5. Choose View → Text view again. At this point, xmlspy should appear as it does in Figure 3-1.

6. Click on the *time.xml* window to give it focus.

7. Press F10 or choose XSL → XSL Transformation, and the "Please choose XSL file" dialog box appears, as shown in Figure 3-2.

8. Click the Browse button, select *clock.xsl*, and click OK.

9. Another window appears showing you the result of the transformation. Choose View → View text. The result appears in Figure 3-3.

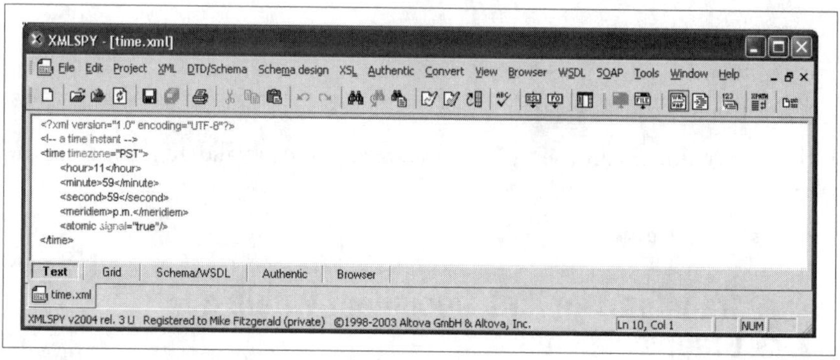

Figure 3-1. time.xml in xmlspy

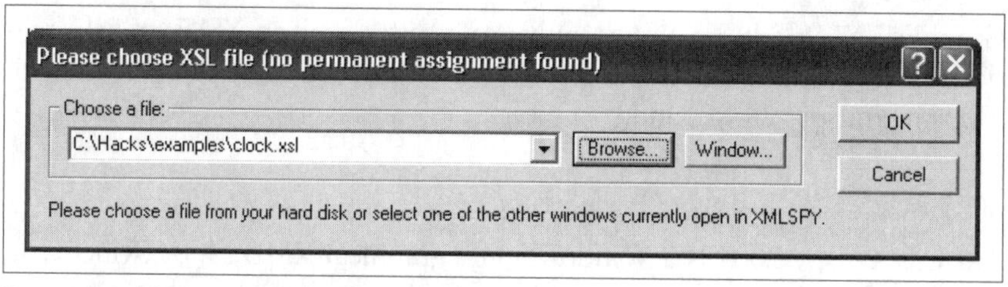

Figure 3-2. Choosing an XSL file in xmlspy

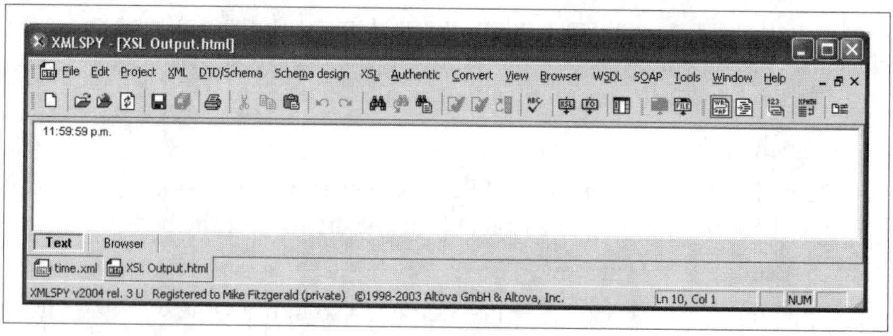

Figure 3-3. Result of transforming time.xml with clock.xsl

xRay2

Architag's xRay2 is a free, graphical XML editor that runs only on the Windows platform. Like xmlspy, it has XSLT processing capability. You can download it from *http://www.architag.com/xray*.

After you have successfully downloaded and installed it, follow these steps to perform a transformation with xRay2.

1. Launch xRay2.
2. Open *time.xml* with File → Open from the working directory.
3. Open *clock.xsl* with File → Open in the same location.
4. Choose File → New XSLT Transform.
5. In the XML Document pull-down menu, select *time.xml* (see Figure 3-4).
6. In the XSLT Program pull-down menu, select *clock.xsl* (see Figure 3-5).
7. If it's not checked, check Auto-update.
8. The result appears in the transform window as shown in Figure 3-6.

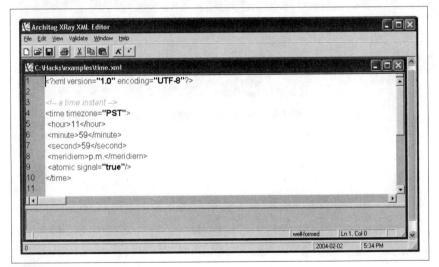

Figure 3-4. time.xml in xRay2

SyncRO Soft's is a graphical XML editor that runs on the Windows, Mac, and Linux platforms. Like both xmlspy and xRay2, can process documents with XSLT. You can download a trial copy from *http://www.oxygenxml.com/download.html/*.

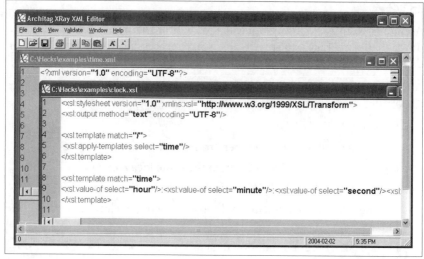

Figure 3-5. clock.xsl in xRay2

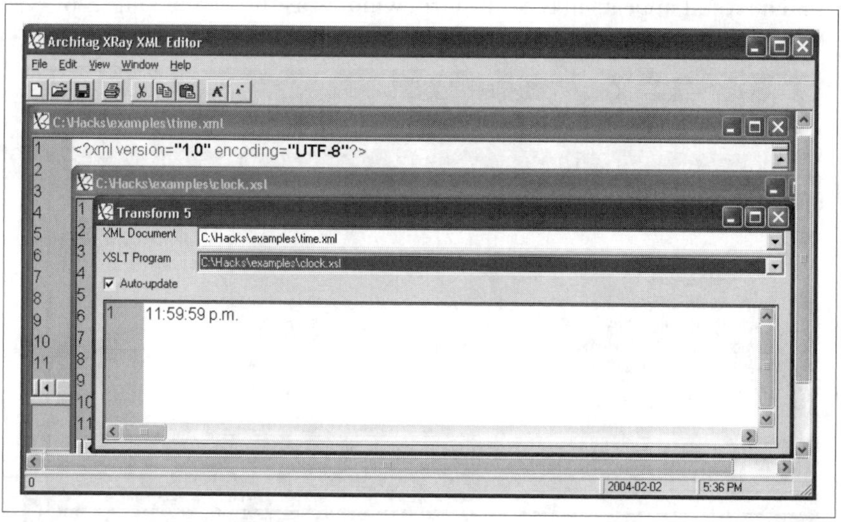

Figure 3-6. Result of transforming time.xml with clock.xsl in xRay2

After you have downloaded and installed <oXygen/>, follow these steps:

1. Launch <oXygen/>.

2. Open *time.xml* with File → Open from the working directory (see Figure 3-7).

3. Choose Xml → Configure transformation scenario, then click New. The Edit scenario dialog box appears.

4. Name the scenario "Time," click the browse button, and open *clock.xsl* (see Figure 3-8). Click OK.

5. In the Configure transformation scenario dialog box, click Transform now. The result appears in a tabbed pane at the bottom of the <oXygen/> window (see Figure 3-9).

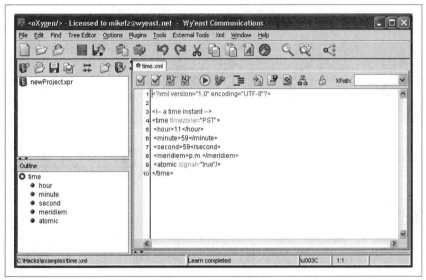

Figure 3-7. time.xml in <oXygen/>

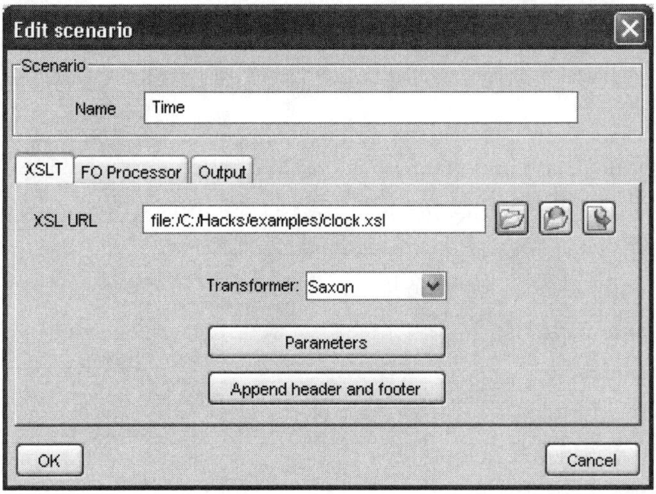

Figure 3-8. Edit scenario dialog box in <oXygen/>

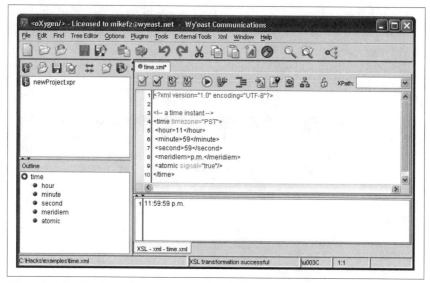

Figure 3-9. Result of transforming time.xml with clock.xsl in <oXygen/>

See Also

- Marrowsoft's <Xselerator> is an XSLT editor and debugger: *http://www. marrowsoft.com/Products.htm*

- Sonic Software's Stylus Studio includes an XSLT editor, debugger, and mapper: *http://www.stylusstudio.com/*

 ### HACK #34   Analyze Nodes with TreeViewer

View nodes in an XML document according to the XPath 1.0 data model.

The XPath 1.0 data model (*http://www.w3.org/TR/xpath#data-model*) views XML documents as containing seven possible node types:

- Root nodes (called the *document nodes* in the XPath 2.0 data model; see *http://www.w3.org/TR/xpath-datamodel/#DocumentNode*)

- Element nodes

- Attribute nodes

- Text nodes

- Comment nodes

- Processing instruction nodes

- Namespace nodes

Mike Brown and Jeni Tennison have created several stylesheets, available at *http://skew.org/xml/stylesheets/treeview/*, that visually represent all seven of the XPath node types. Such tools can be useful when trying to uncover less obvious nodes (namespace or whitespace-only text nodes) or when just learning about the XPath model. These stylesheets allow you to view an XML tree either in ASCII (*ascii-treeview.xsl*) or in HTML (*tree-view.xml* with *tree-view.css*). All three are available in the working directory where you extracted the file archive for the book.

When you apply *ascii-treeview.xsl* to *time.xml* using an XSLT processor such as Xalan by using this command:

```
xalan time.xml ascii-treeview.xsl
```

it will produce the text tree view of *time.xml* shown in Example 3-5.

Example 3-5. Output from ascii-treeview.xsl

```
root
   |___comment ' a time instant '
   |___element 'time'
         |  \___attribute 'timezone' = 'PST'
         |___text '\n '
         |___element 'hour'
         |     |___text '11'
         |___text '\n '
         |___element 'minute'
         |     |___text '59'
         |___text '\n '
         |___element 'second'
         |     |___text '59'
         |___text '\n '
         |___element 'meridiem'
         |     |___text 'p.m.'
         |___text '\n '
         |___element 'atomic'
         |         \___attribute 'signal' = 'true'
         |___text '\n'
```

In the result, each of the nodes in *time.xml* has a label: root, comment, element, attribute, or text. You can even see where the whitespace text nodes are (\n).

By default, namespace nodes are not shown. You can show namespace nodes with the show_ns parameter. Parameters are values that you can pass into stylesheets or templates at run time. These values can change the outcome of a transformation.

Now we'll expose a tree view of *namespace.xml*. To see the namespace nodes, pass the show_ns parameter into *ascii-treeview.xsl* using the -p switch with Xalan, as shown here:

```
saxon namespace.xml ascii-treeview.xsl show_ns=yes
```

Figure 3-10 shows the result; notice the ns and namespace labels.

```
root
  |___comment ' a time instant '
  |___element 'time' in ns 'http://www.wyeast.net/time' ('time')
  |    \___attribute 'timezone' = 'PST'
  |    \___namespace 'xml' = 'http://www.w3.org/XML/1998/namespace'
  |    \___namespace '' = 'http://www.wyeast.net/time'
  |___text '\n '
  |___element 'hour' in ns 'http://www.wyeast.net/time' ('hour')
  |    |  \___namespace 'xml' = 'http://www.w3.org/XML/1998/namespace'
  |    |  \___namespace '' = 'http://www.wyeast.net/time'
  |    |___text '11'
  |___text '\n '
  |___element 'minute' in ns 'http://www.wyeast.net/time' ('minute')
  |    |  \___namespace 'xml' = 'http://www.w3.org/XML/1998/namespace'
  |    |  \___namespace '' = 'http://www.wyeast.net/time'
  |    |___text '59'
  |___text '\n '
  |___element 'second' in ns 'http://www.wyeast.net/time' ('second')
  |    |  \___namespace 'xml' = 'http://www.w3.org/XML/1998/namespace'
  |    |  \___namespace '' = 'http://www.wyeast.net/time'
  |    |___text '59'
  |___text '\n '
  |___element 'meridiem' in ns 'http://www.wyeast.net/time' ('meridiem')
  |    |  \___namespace 'xml' = 'http://www.w3.org/XML/1998/namespace'
  |    |  \___namespace '' = 'http://www.wyeast.net/time'
  |    |___text 'p.m.'
  |___text '\n '
  |___element 'atomic' in ns 'http://www.wyeast.net/time' ('atomic')
  |       \___attribute 'signal' = 'true'
  |       \___namespace 'xml' = 'http://www.w3.org/XML/1998/namespace'
  |       \___namespace '' = 'http://www.wyeast.net/time'
  |___text '\n'
```

Figure 3-10. Output from ascii-treeview.xsl showing namespace nodes

The document *tree.xml* contains a processing instruction and has only namespace-qualified, prefixed elements (Example 3-6).

Example 3-6. tree.xml

```
<?xml version="1.0" encoding="UTF-8"?>
<?xml-stylesheet href="tree-view.xsl" type="text/xsl"?>

<!-- a time instant -->
<tz:time timezone="PST" xmlns:tz="http://www.wyeast.net/time">
 <tz:hour>11</tz:hour>
 <tz:minute>59</tz:minute>
 <tz:second>59</tz:second>
 <tz:meridiem>p.m.</tz:meridiem>
 <tz:atomic signal="true"/>
</tz:time>
```

The XML stylesheet PI near the top of the document refers to the *tree-view.xsl* stylesheet, which produces HTML using CSS (*tree-view.css*). To apply *tree-view.xsl* to *tree.xml*, open *tree.xml* in a browser that supports client-side XSLT transformations, such as IE, Mozilla, Firefox, or Netscape. Figure 3-11 shows a portion of the tree view of *tree.xml* in the Netscape browser. Each of the node labels uses a different background color, and namespace names are enclosed in braces. The names of elements and attributes use a white background.

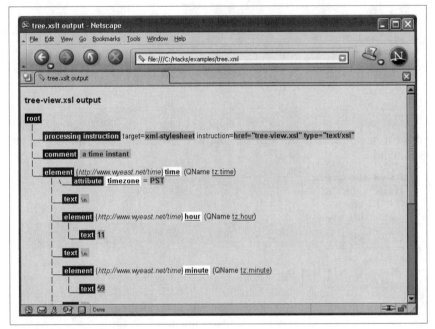

Figure 3-11. tree.xml transformed by tree-view.xsl and styled by tree-view.css

HACK #35 Explore a Document Tree with the xmllint Shell

Explore the tree structure of an XML document with *xmllint*'s shell mode.

xmllint is a command-line tool available as part of *libxml2* (*http://xmlsoft. org*). It is included in distributions such as Cygwin (*http://www.cygwin.com*) and Red Hat Linux (*http://www.redhat.com*). You can also download *xmllib2* individually from *http://xmlsoft.org*. *xmllint* has an interactive shell mode that lets you traverse an XML document's tree structure as if it were a file structure, allowing you to examine any node in the tree discretely. Provided that you have an Internet connection, this shell mode will work on remote files as well as local ones. This hack will show you how it's done.

While in the working directory, we first invoke the shell on an XML document with *xmllint* :

```
xmllint --shell time.xml
/ >
```

A prompt appears (>). The location in the tree is shown to the left of the prompt (/), but with the depth of only one node. Enter the dir command to see information about the document or root node, and follow that with the base command to see the base URI of the document being explored:

```
/ > dir
DOCUMENT
version=1.0
encoding=UTF-8
URL=time.xml
standalone=true
/ > base
time.xml
/>
```

Move to a different node with cd, followed by another dir, then by a cat command:

```
/ > cd time/atomic
atomic > dir
ELEMENT atomic
  ATTRIBUTE signal
    TEXT
      content=true
atomic > cat
<atomic signal="true"/>
atomic >
```

A dir gives you information about the node, and cat gives you the XML representation of the node. Try the validate directive:

```
atomic > validate
validity error : no DTD found!
atomic >
```

time.xml doesn't have a DTD associated with it, so load *valid.xml* (which has a document type declaration) and try validate again:

```
atomic > load valid.xml
/ > validate
/ >
```

load replaces the current document *time.xml* with *valid.xml*, so validate is successful this time (no bad news means success). Use cd to move down the tree to time, enter pwd to see the path to the current node, and then enter du to see the element names in the subtree:

```
/ > cd time
time > pwd
```

```
/time
time > du
time
  hour
  minute
  second
  meridiem
  atomic
time >
```

Save the document in a new file with the save command, and then exit the shell with bye (exit and quit work, too):

```
time > save timeagain.xml
time > bye
```

You can also invoke the shell on a remote file (follow it with base):

```
xmllint --shell http://www.wyeast.net/time.xml
/ > base
http://www.wyeast.net/time.xml
/ >
```

You will be able to use the same commands on a remote document as you did on the local file. A list of *xmllint*'s shell commands concludes this hack.

xmllint Shell Commands

Following are the shell commands available in *xmllint*'s shell mode:

base
> Display the xml:base of the node.

bye
> Leave the shell (same as exit and quit).

cat [node]
> Display the path to the node, if one is given, or the path to the current node.

cd [path]
> Change the current node to the path if given and unique, but change to the document or root node if no argument is given.

dir [path]
> Dump information about elements, attributes, namespaces, and so forth. Select the current node or node in the path, if given.

du [path]
> Show the structure of the subtree under the current node or the path, if given.

exit
> Leave the shell (same as bye and quit).

---

help
> Show help.

free
> Display memory usage.

load docname
> Load a new document with the given name.

ls [path]
> List contents of the path if given or the current directory.

pwd
> Display the path to the current node.

quit
> Leave the shell (same as bye or exit).

save [docname]
> Save the current document to the document name if given or to the original name.

validate
> Check the document for errors.

write name
> Write the current node to the given filename.

HACK #36 View Documents as Tables Using Generic CSS or XSLT

While XML documents come in all shapes and sizes, a common pattern makes it very easy to present information stored in XML as a table.

XML's structural flexibility is impressive, but many applications are well-served using only a tiny subset of its capabilities, often following a pattern of three levels of nested elements where only the child elements have content. The pattern looks roughly like this:

```
<table>
  <row>
    <cell-1>...value...</cell-1>
    <cell-2>...value...</cell-2>
    <cell-3>...value...</cell-3>
    <cell-4>...value...</cell-4>
  </row>
  <row>
    <cell-1>...value...</cell-1>
    <cell-2>...value...</cell-2>
    <cell-3>...value...</cell-3>
    <cell-4>...value...</cell-4>
```

```
    </row>
    ....
  </table>
```

where *table* is any root element, *row* is any container element, and the *cell* elements are leaf elements containing data. (The names of the elements and whether or not they use namespaces don't matter, provided that the *cell* elements stay in the same order throughout.) This pattern is common for XML vocabularies representing database tables or query results, as well as those representing data that was originally comma- or tab-separated. Looking beyond the browser for a moment, Excel 2003 **[Hack #15]** can work with this data easily, and Access 2003 **[Hack #16]** can import and export it with minimal effort.

Take, for example, the document *contracts.xml*, which represents two rows of such a table (shown in Example 3-7).

Example 3-7. contracts.xml

```
<?xml-stylesheet type="text/css" href="table.css"?>

<contracts>

<contract>
<recipient>Josiah Smith</recipient>
<signing_date>1999-06-03</signing_date>
<signing_time>09:03:22</signing_time>
<birthyear>1962</birthyear>
<birthday>--06-21</birthday>
<male>true</male>
<payment_amount>0004002.00200</payment_amount>
<years_to_pay>26</years_to_pay>
</contract>


<contract>
<recipient>Jane Zang</recipient>
<signing_date>1999-04-03</signing_date>
<signing_time>11:04:28</signing_time>
<birthyear>1968</birthyear>
<birthday>--04-23</birthday>
<male>false</male>
<payment_amount>000401.0200</payment_amount>
<years_to_pay>2</years_to_pay>
</contract>

</contracts>
```

The PI at the top of it:

```
<?xml-stylesheet type="text/css" href="table.css"?>
```

will apply the stylesheet *table.css* in Example 3-8 to it.

Example 3-8. table.css

```
:root {display:table;}
:root * {display:table-row;}
:root * * {display:table-cell; padding:5px; border-style:inset;}
```

Open it in Mozilla, and you'll see a table like that shown in Figure 3-12 (with a different filename).

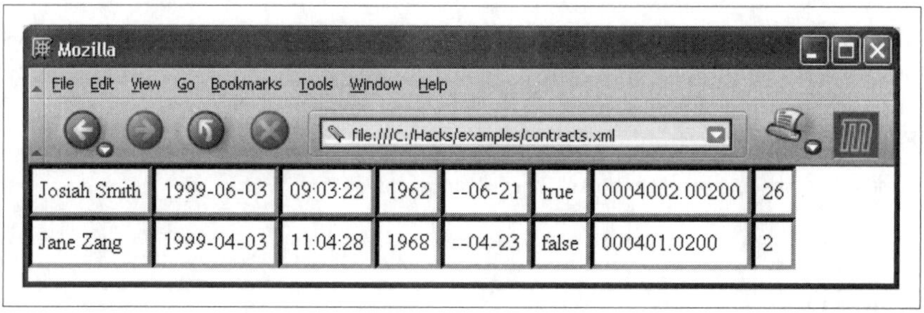

Figure 3-12. A table created with CSS, viewed in Mozilla

It also works nicely in Apple's Safari browser, as shown in Figure 3-13 (under a different name).

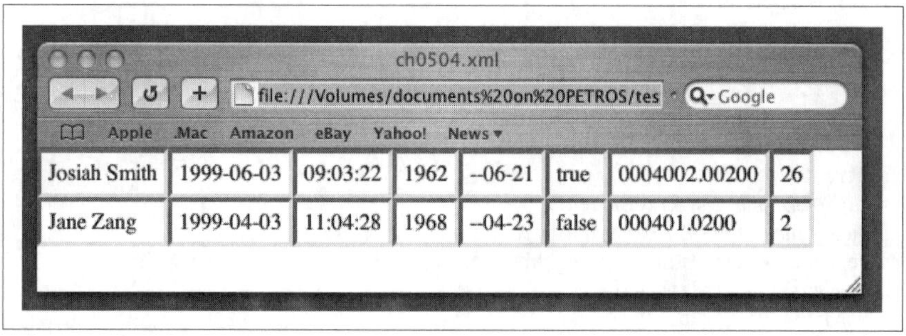

Figure 3-13. A table created with CSS, viewed in Safari

The results in Internet Explorer 6, as shown in Figure 3-14, are less enticing, as Microsoft has never updated Internet Explorer to support display:table and related table properties (from CSS2, *http://www.w3.org/TR/1998/REC-CSS2-19980512*) nor the :root selector (from CSS3, see *http://www.w3.org/Style/CSS/current-work*).

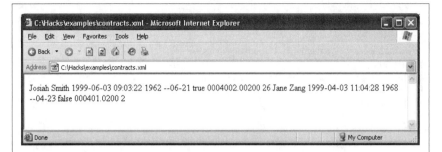

Figure 3-14. An attempt to create a table with CSS, which doesn't work in Internet Explorer

You can, of course, create a similarly generic stylesheet in XSLT (*table.xsl* shown in Example 3-9), though it's much longer than the CSS equivalent.

Example 3-9. table.xsl

```
<xsl:stylesheet version="1.0" xmlns:xsl="http://www.w3.org/1999/XSL/Transform">
  <xsl:output method="html" />

  <xsl:template match="*">
    <html>
      <head><title>Auto-generated table</title></head>
      <body>
        <table border="1">
          <xsl:for-each select="*">
            <tr>
              <xsl:for-each select="*">
                <td>
                 <xsl:value-of select="."/>
                </td>
              </xsl:for-each>
            </tr>
          </xsl:for-each>
        </table>
      </body>
    </html>
  </xsl:template>
</xsl:stylesheet>
```

This stylesheet generates an HTML table from *contracts.xml*. Applied with Xalan C++:

```
xalan -o table.html contracts.xml table.xsl
```

it produces *table.html*, shown in Example 3-10.

Example 3-10. table.html

```
<html>
<head>
<META http-equiv="Content-Type" content="text/html;
    charset=UTF-16">
<title>Auto-generated table</title></head>
<body>
<table border="1">
<tr>
<td>Josiah Smith</td>
<td>1999-06-03</td>
<td>09:03:22</td>
<td>1962</td>
<td>--06-21</td>
<td>true</td>
<td>0004002.00200</td>
<td>26</td>
</tr>
<tr>
<td>Jane Zang</td>
<td>1999-04-03</td>
<td>11:04:28</td>
<td>1968</td>
<td>--04-23</td>
<td>false</td>
<td>000401.0200</td>
<td>2</td>
</tr>
</table>
</body>
</html>
```

To use the XSLT stylesheet directly rather than the CSS stylesheet to display a table, change the XML stylesheet processing instruction in *contracts.xml* to look like:

```
<?xml-stylesheet type="text/xsl" href="table.xsl"?>
```

Opening the document *table.html* (or *contracts.xml* with the processing instruction change) will produce the result shown in Figure 3-15 in Mozilla, and Figure 3-16 in Internet Explorer 6.

Unfortunately, Safari (as of Version 1.2) doesn't support client-side XSLT, so it produces the unhappy result shown in Figure 3-17 (under a different name, again). The Opera browser (as of Version 7) also doesn't support XSLT.

Because of cross-browser considerations, you'll probably want to use these hacks only when you control which browser will be used, but they're still very handy tools for exploring data quickly.

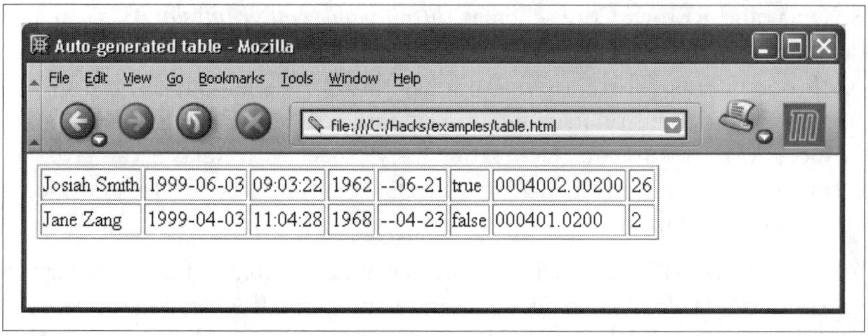

Figure 3-15. A table created with generic XSLT, viewed in Mozilla

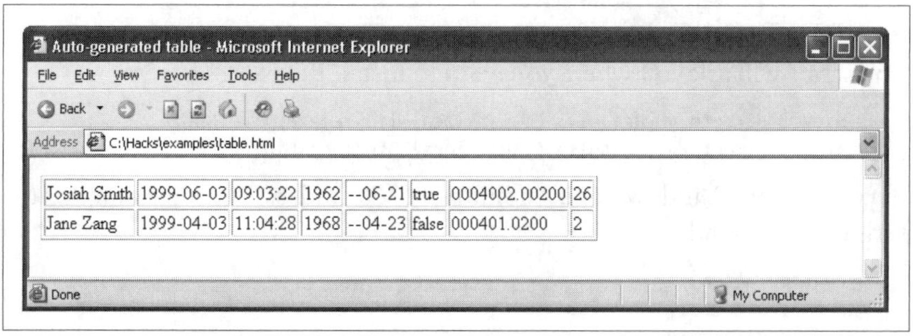

Figure 3-16. A table created with generic XSLT, viewed in Internet Explorer 6

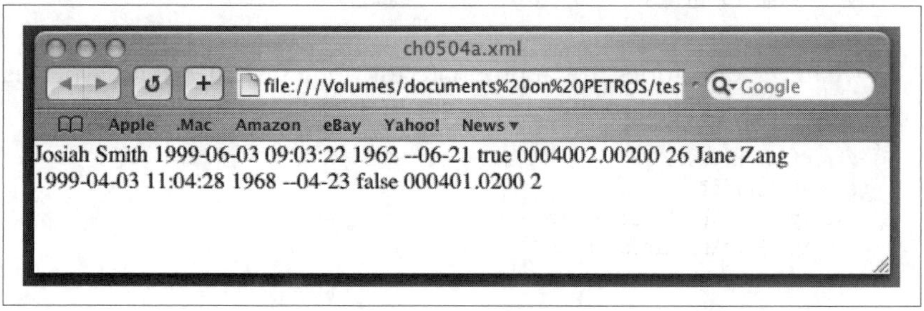

Figure 3-17. An attempt to create a table with generic XSLT, which doesn't work in Safari

—Simon St.Laurent

HACK #37 Generate an XSLT Identity Stylesheet with Relaxer

Quickly generate XSLT stylesheets with Asami Tomoharu's Relaxer.

Relaxer (*http://www.relaxer.org*) is a Java schema compiler for XML. Relaxer can generate Java classes [Hack #99] based on RELAX NG, DTDs, XML

Schema, and RELAX Core schemas (*http://www.xml.gr.jp/relax/*). It can also generate schemas (see [Hack #73], [Hack #74], and [Hack #75]) from one or more XML documents. There are many other things Relaxer can do, but in this hack I want to focus on its ability to generate XSLT stylesheets based on one or more XML documents. Generating a stylesheet with Relaxer can give you a start for designing your own stylesheets. It's quite easy to use and merits some of our attention.

You can download Version 1.0 of Relaxer (*relaxer-1.0.zip*) from *http://www. relaxer.org/download/index.html*. After downloading the file, you can run the installation script by typing this line, assuming of course that you have Java on your system:

```
java -jar relaxer-1.0.zip
```

The script will ask you where you want to install Relaxer:

```
Install directory [default: C:\usr\local\lib\relaxer]: c:\lib
Command directory [default: C:\usr\local\bin]: c:\bin
```

If you are on Windows and submitted *c:\lib* and *c:\bin*, for example, the script will respond:

```
[Configuration]
Install directory = c:\lib
Command directory = c:\bin

Type "yes" to install, "no" to re-enter, "exit" to exit
>
```

Use whatever directories are appropriate for your system. If you type yes here, you will see this report:

```
Extract archives...
Generate script...
  script = c:\bin\relaxer.bat
  script = c:\bin\relaxer
Done.
```

Now check the Relaxer version:

```
relaxer -version
```

This should yield:

```
Copyright(c) 2000-2003 ASAMI,Tomoharu. All rights reserved.
Relaxer Version 1.0 (20031224) by asami@relaxer.org
```

Now you're ready to generate an XSLT stylesheet with Relaxer. You'll use a file called *gen.xml*, which is identical to *time.xml* (Example 3-11).

Example 3-11. gen.xml

```
<?xml version="1.0" encoding="UTF-8"?>

<!-- a time instant -->
<time timezone="PST">
 <hour>11</hour>
 <minute>59</minute>
 <second>59</second>
 <meridiem>p.m.</meridiem>
 <atomic signal="true"/>
</time>
```

Use the -xslt switch to generate the stylesheet, and the -verbose switch to see what Relaxer's doing during processing time:

```
relaxer -verbose -xslt gen.xml
```

You should see this:

```
Copyright(c) 2000-2003 ASAMI,Tomoharu. All rights reserved.
Relaxer Version 1.0 (20031224) by asami@relaxer.org
Source file    : file:/C:/Hacks/examples/gen.xml
       artifact = gen.xsl
```

Relaxer generated the artifact *gen.xsl*. It's a simple stylesheet that mirrors *gen.xml* and can perform an identity transform on *gen.xml* (Example 3-12).

Example 3-12. gen.xsl

```
<?xml version='1.0'?>
<xsl:stylesheet version="1.0" xmlns:xsl="http://www.w3.org/1999/XSL/Transform">
  <xsl:output indent="yes" method="xml"/>
  <xsl:template match="minute">
    <minute>
      <xsl:apply-templates/>
    </minute>
  </xsl:template>
  <xsl:template match="atomic">
    <atomic>
      <xsl:attribute name="signal">
        <xsl:value-of select="@signal"/>
      </xsl:attribute>
      <xsl:apply-templates/>
    </atomic>
  </xsl:template>
  <xsl:template match="meridiem">
    <meridiem>
      <xsl:apply-templates/>
    </meridiem>
  </xsl:template>
  <xsl:template match="second">
    <second>
      <xsl:apply-templates/>
```

Example 3-12. gen.xsl (continued)

```
    </second>
  </xsl:template>
  <xsl:template match="time[hour and minute and second and
    meridiem and atomic]">
    <time>
      <xsl:attribute name="timezone">
        <xsl:value-of select="@timezone"/>
      </xsl:attribute>
      <xsl:apply-templates/>
    </time>
  </xsl:template>
  <xsl:template match="hour">
    <hour>
      <xsl:apply-templates/>
    </hour>
  </xsl:template>
</xsl:stylesheet>
```

Apply this stylesheet to *gen.xml*:

```
xalan gen.xml gen.xsl
```

and you'll get a close copy of the original:

```
<?xml version="1.0" encoding="UTF-8"?>
<time timezone="PST">
  <hour>11</hour>
  <minute>59</minute>
  <second>59</second>
  <meridiem>p.m.</meridiem>
  <atomic signal="true"/>
</time>
```

Generating stylesheets is quick and easy to do with Relaxer. It will provide you with a ready-made stylesheet that you can then edit for your own purposes. You could also use Relaxer to programmatically generate a series of stylesheets based on one or more instance documents.

Pretty-Print XML Using a Generic Identity Stylesheet and Xalan

Sometimes your XML output from various programs is less than attractive. Spruce it up in a hurry with Xalan C++ and an identity transform.

In earlier hacks ("Edit XML Documents with Microsoft Word 2003" **[Hack #14]** and "Create an XML Document from a CSV File" **[Hack #21]**), you saw the unsightly XML output from Word 2003 and CSVToXML. The reason why this XML is unsightly is that it is output on only one or two lines. If you want this XML to be human-readable, here is a quick hack that pretty-prints the XML by properly indenting it.

In the working directory for this book you will find *identity.xsl* (Example 3-13), a very simple identity stylesheet that effectively copies all nodes from source to the result as XML.

Example 3-13. identity.xsl

```
<xsl:stylesheet version="1.0" xmlns:xsl="http://www.w3.org/1999/XSL/Transform">
<xsl:output method="xml" indent="yes" encoding="ISO-8859-1"/>

<xsl:template match="@*|node( )">
 <xsl:copy>
  <xsl:apply-templates select="@*|node( )"/>
 </xsl:copy>
</xsl:template>

</xsl:stylesheet>
```

The template matches all nodes (node( )), including all attributes (@*), and copies them using the copy instruction, repeatedly applying templates until all nodes are processed. The indent attribute on the output element indents the output using a processor-dependent number of spaces. If you apply this stylesheet using Xalan C++ on the command line, you can use the -i switch to specify the number of spaces to indent the output. If you use Saxon, you can use the Saxon extension saxon:indent-spaces on output, and you can set the number of spaces used in indentation (use the namespace xmlns: saxon="http://saxon.sf.net/"). This makes it possible to turn *Time_word. xml*, the WordprocessingML output of Word 2003, into something more readable.

Assuming that you have Xalan C++ downloaded and installed (from *http:// xml.apache.org/xalan-c*), run this command at a shell prompt:

```
xalan -i 1 -o pretty.xml Time_word.xml identity.xsl
```

A sampling of *pretty.xml* is shown here, and it is much more readable than the original. It went from 2 long lines to 325 lines (Example 3-14).

Example 3-14. pretty.xml

```
<?xml version="1.0" encoding="ISO-8859-1"?>
<?mso-application progid="Word.Document"?>

<w:wordDocument xmlns:w="http://schemas.microsoft.com/office/word/2003/wordml"
xmlns:v="urn:schemas-microsoft-com:vml" xmlns:w10="urn:schemas-
```

Example 3-14. pretty.xml (continued)

```
microsoft-com:office:word" xmlns:sl="http://schemas.microsoft.com/schemaLibrary/
2003/core" xmlns:aml="http://schemas.microsoft.com/aml/2001/core" xmlns:wx="http:
//schemas.microsoft.com/office/word/2003/auxHint" xmlns:o="urn:schemas-microsoft-
com:office:office"
xmlns:dt="uuid:C2F41010-65B3-11d1-A29F-00AA00C14882"
w:macrosPresent="no" w:embeddedObjPresent="no" w:ocxPresent="no" xml:
space="preserve">
 <o:DocumentProperties>
  <o:Title>Time</o:Title>
  <o:Author>Mike Fitzgerald</o:Author>
  <o:LastAuthor>Mike Fitzgerald</o:LastAuthor>
  <o:Revision>2</o:Revision>
  <o:TotalTime>0</o:TotalTime>
  <o:Created>2004-02-11T23:07:00Z</o:Created>
  <o:LastSaved>2004-02-11T23:07:00Z</o:LastSaved>
  <o:Pages>1</o:Pages>
  <o:Words>9</o:Words>
  <o:Characters>52</o:Characters>
  <o:Lines>1</o:Lines>
  <o:Paragraphs>1</o:Paragraphs>
  <o:CharactersWithSpaces>60</o:CharactersWithSpaces>
  <o:Version>11.5604</o:Version>
 </o:DocumentProperties>
 <w:fonts>
  <w:defaultFonts w:ascii="Times New Roman" w:fareast="Times
New Roman" w:h-ansi="Times New Roman" w:cs="Times New Roman"/>
  <w:font w:name="Wingdings">
   <w:panose-1 w:val="05000000000000000000"/>
   <w:charset w:val="02"/>
   <w:family w:val="Auto"/>
   <w:pitch w:val="variable"/>
   <w:sig w:usb-0="00000000" w:usb-1="10000000"
w:usb-2="00000000" w:usb-3="00000000" w:csb-0="80000000"
w:csb-1="00000000"/>
  </w:font>
 </w:fonts>
```

HACK #39 Create a Text File from an XML Document

Use this stylesheet to extract only the text from any XML document.

Sometimes you just want to leave the XML behind and keep only the text found in a document. The stylesheet *text.xsl* can do that for you. (There's an even easier way; see "Built-in Templates" following). It can be applied to any XML document, which includes XHTML. It is shown in Example 3-15.

Example 3-15. text.xsl

```
<xsl:stylesheet version="1.0"
<xsl:output method="text"/>
```

Example 3-15. text.xsl (continued)

```
      xmlns:xsl="http://www.w3.org/1999/XSL/Transform">

<xsl:template match="/">
 <xsl:apply-templates select="*"/>
</xsl:template>

</xsl:stylesheet>
```

This stylesheet finds the root node and then selects all element children (*) for processing. To test, apply this stylesheet to the XHTML document *magnacarta.html*, the pact between King John and the barony in England that was first signed at Runnymede on June 15, 1215 (see *http://www.cs. indiana.edu/statecraft/magna-carta.html*):

```
    xalan magnacarta.html text.xsl
```

A small portion of the output is shown in Example 3-16. The result is shown in IE in Figure 3-18.

Example 3-16. A portion of the Magna Carta

```
Magna Carta

The Magna Carta
JOHN, by the grace of God King of England, Lord of Ireland,
Duke of Normandy and Aquitaine, and Count of Anjou, to his
archbishops, bishops, abbots, earls, barons, justices,
foresters, sheriffs, stewards, servants, and to all his
officials and loyal subjects, Greeting.

KNOW THAT BEFORE GOD, for the health of our soul and those of
our ancestors and heirs, to the honour of God, the exaltation
of the holy Church, and the better ordering of our kingdom, at
the advice of our reverend fathers Stephen, archbishop of
Canterbury, primate of all England, and cardinal of the holy
Roman Church, Henry archbishop of Dublin, William bishop of
London, Peter bishop of Winchester, Jocelin bishop of Bath and
Glastonbury, Hugh bishop of Lincoln, Walter Bishop of Worcester,
William bishop of Coventry, Benedict bishop of Rochester, Master
Pandulf subdeacon and member of the papal household, Brother
Aymeric master of the knighthood of the Temple in England,
William Marshal earl of Pembroke, William earl of Salisbury,
William earl of Warren, William earl of Arundel, Alan de
Galloway constable of Scotland, Warin Fitz Gerald, Peter Fitz
Herbert, Hubert de Burgh seneschal of Poitou, Hugh de Neville,
Matthew Fitz Herbert, Thomas Basset, Alan Basset, Philip Daubeny,
Robert de Roppeley, John Marshal, John Fitz Hugh, and other loyal
subjects:
```

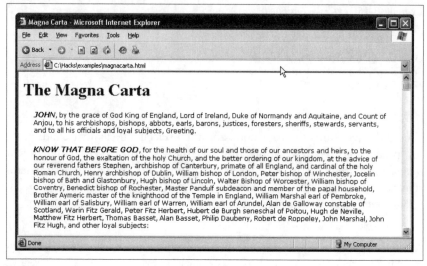

Figure 3-18. The Magna Carta (magnacarta.html) in IE

Built-in Templates

You can also extract text from a document just by relying on XSLT's built-in templates. A stylesheet as simple as this single line:

```
<xsl:stylesheet version="1.0"
    xmlns:xsl="http://www.w3.org/1999/XSL/Transform"/>
```

will invoke the built-in templates because there is no explicit template for any nodes that might be found in the source document. The built-in templates process all the children of the root and all elements, and copies text through for attributes and text nodes (the built-in templates do nothing for comment, processing-instruction, or namespace nodes). The benefit of using *text.xsl* over built-in templates is that *text.xsl* gives you a framework to exercise some control over the output (e.g., through additions of templates). However, adding templates to *text.xsl* won't make any difference, unless those templates match the document element more precisely (and therefore have higher priority than the template matching *). An empty stylesheet is the simplest one to start from if you want to add more precise templates.

HACK #40 Convert Attributes to Elements and Elements to Attributes

Transform elements into attributes and back the other way with XSLT.

You're sitting in a conference room, leaning back in your chair. Opinions are flying back and forth across the room about whether to represent the XML data from a new application in either element or attribute form.

One engineer says, combing his beard with his fingers, "You don't want to use attributes at all. What if down the line you need more than one attribute with the same name. You can't do that in XML. You can only use one attribute with a given name."

"Attributes contain metadata *about* elements," another barks. "You don't store metadata in element content. Period. That's where the real data goes."

You rock forward in your chair. "Excuse me," you say with a chuckle, "but none of these arguments matter." The room goes silent. Your project manager's nostrils flare. "You better explain yourself," she says, taking the last swig of her spring water.

"Gladly," you say. "I've got a pair of XSLT stylesheets that can transform the data easily between element and attribute forms in seconds. Walk with me to my cubicle and I'll give you a demo."

In reference to the element-or-attribute debate, Michael Kay has wisely said: "Beginners always ask this question. Those with a little experience express their opinions passionately. Experts tell you there is no right answer" (*http://lists.xml.org/archives/xml-dev/200006/msg00285.html*). This hack will allow you to keep changing your mind.

Element-to-Attribute Conversion

XML document design does matter, and it's worthwhile to consider some questions when deciding between elements and attributes:

- Are you dealing with data or metadata (data about data)? Elements are generally a good fit for data, and attributes are a good fit for metadata.
- Is there a possibility of name conflicts when labeling data? If so, remember that you can have only one attribute with a given name per element.
- Should the data be structured (i.e., does it have a logical relationship with nearby markup)? You can't use XML to structure attribute values.

It's nice to come away from a meeting like that sounding and looking like a genius. That's one reason why this book contains a hack on how to use

XSLT to convert XML elements to attributes or attributes to elements. You'll recall our tried and true *time.xml* document:

```
<?xml version="1.0" encoding="UTF-8"?>

<!-- a time instant -->
<time timezone="PST">
 <hour>11</hour>
 <minute>59</minute>
 <second>59</second>
 <meridiem>p.m.</meridiem>
 <atomic signal="true"/>
 </time>
```

Let's say you want to convert the elements hour, minute, second, and so forth into attributes. You can do it with the stylesheet *elem2attr.xsl* shown in Example 3-17.

Example 3-17. elem2attr.xsl

```
1  <xsl:stylesheet version="1.0" xmlns:xsl="http://www.w3.org/1999/XSL/Transform">
2  <xsl:output method="xml" encoding="UTF-8" indent="yes"/>
3
4  <xsl:template match="time">
5   <xsl:copy>
6    <xsl:copy-of select="@timezone">
7       <xsl:for-each select="*">
8    <xsl:attribute name="{name(.)}">
9     <xsl:value-of select="."/>
10     <xsl:value-of select="@signal"/>
11    </xsl:attribute>
12    </xsl:for-each>
13   </xsl:copy>
14  </xsl:template>
15
16  </xsl:stylesheet>
```

This stylesheet could be adapted to match the needs of your XML data. On line 4, the single template in this stylesheet matches the document element time (a built-in template first matches the root node, though this is not evident from the markup). The stylesheet copies the time element (line 5), and the copy-of on line 6 copies over the timezone attribute (line 6). Then the for-each element marches through all the child elements (select="*") of time (line 7). For each element found, an attribute is created (line 8), using the element names as attribute names (that's what the name( ) function does). The element content is retrieved with value-of (line 9), as well as the value of the signal attribute (using @signal on line 10).

Apply this stylesheet to *time.xml* using Xalan with this command:

```
xalan -o attr.xml time.xml elem2attr.xsl
```

You can see in *attr.xml* that all the element names and content have been converted to attribute names and values (plus the timezone attribute has been carried over):

```
<?xml version="1.0" encoding="UTF-8"?>
<time timezone="PST" hour="11" minute="59" second="59"
meridiem="p.m." atomic="true"/>
```

A little information is lost in the transformation: the signal attribute's value of true is assigned to the new attribute atomic. This information is restored with the next stylesheet, *attr2elem.xsl*.

Attribute-to-Element Conversion

Now let's take it back in the other direction with *attr2elem.xsl*, shown in Example 3-18.

Example 3-18. attr2elem.xsl

```
1   <xsl:stylesheet version="1.0" xmlns:xsl="http://www.w3.org/1999/XSL/Transform">
2   <xsl:output method="xml" encoding="UTF-8" indent="yes"/>
3
4   <xsl:template match="time">
5    <xsl:comment> a time instant </xsl:comment>
6    <xsl:copy>
7     <xsl:copy-of select="@timezone"/>
8
9     <xsl:apply-templates select="@*"/>
10   </xsl:copy>
11  </xsl:template>
12
13  <xsl:template match="@*">
14   <xsl:element name="{name(.)}">
15    <xsl:value-of select="."/>
16   </xsl:element>
17  </xsl:template>
18
19  <xsl:template match="@timezone"/>
20
21  <xsl:template match="@atomic">
22   <xsl:element name="{name(.)}">
23    <xsl:attribute name="signal"><xsl:value-of select="."/> </xsl:attribute>
24   </xsl:element>
25  </xsl:template>
26
27  </xsl:stylesheet>
```

As with the previous stylesheet in this hack, adapt this one to your needs. The first template matches time (line 4). A comment is created (line 5), the time element is copied into the result tree (line 6), and the timezone attribute is re-created on time (line 7). Then apply-templates selects all attributes associated with time (@* on line 9).

The template on line 13 matches all attributes and creates an element for each one found using name(.). When apply-templates on line 9 selects @timezone, it finds another template for the timezone attribute (line 19), more specific than the one on line 13, which just no-ops. This is done because the stylesheet already re-created the timezone attribute on line 7. (The timezone attribute must be re-created before any elements are created, which is why the stylesheet deals with it explicitly rather than leaving it to the templates that follow.)

When apply-templates selects @atomic, the template on line 21 is instantiated, which creates an atomic element with a signal attribute, just as in *time.xml*.

Apply this to *attr.xml* using:

```
xalan -i 1 attr.xml attr2elem.xsl
```

and you will get the following result, which looks an awful lot like *time.xml*:

```
<?xml version="1.0" encoding="UTF-8"?>
<!-- a time instant -->
<time timezone="PST">
 <hour>11</hour>
 <minute>59</minute>
 <second>59</second>
 <meridiem>p.m.</meridiem>
 <atomic signal="true"/>
</time>
```

See Also

- Sal Mangano's *XSLT Cookbook* (O'Reilly), pages 202–206, which inspired this hack

- Peter Flynn's XML FAQ, "Which should I use in my DTD, attributes or elements?": *http://www.ucc.ie/xml/#attriborelem*

- Robin Cover's CoverPages "Using Elements and Attributes": *http://xml.coverpages.org/elementsAndAttrs.html*

- Uche Ogbuji's IBM developerWorks article "When to Use Elements Versus Attributes": *http://www-106.ibm.com/developerworks/xml/library/x-eleatt.html*

HACK #41 Convert XML to CSV

Turn your XML into CSV for use by applications that don't support XML.

In "Create an XML Document from a CSV File" [Hack #21], you saw how to convert a comma-separated values (CSV) file to XML. This hack does the reverse, turning XML into CSV. This could be useful to you if you want to read XML data into an application that does not directly support XML but does support CSV, such as Excel 2000.

Let's go back to the output of CSVToXML, the file *inventory.xml*, after it has been cleaned up by "Pretty-Print XML Using a Generic Identity Stylesheet and Xalan" [Hack #38]. Here is a portion of it (Example 3-19).

Example 3-19. A portion of inventory.xml

```xml
<?xml version="1.0" encoding="ISO-8859-1"?>
<!-- Generated using Dave Pawson's CSVToXML -->
<Inventory>
 <Line>
  <ItemNumber>line</ItemNumber>
  <Description>desc</Description>
  <Quantity>quan</Quantity>
  <Date>date</Date>
 </Line>
 <Line>
  <ItemNumber>1</ItemNumber>
  <Description>Oak chairs</Description>
  <Quantity>6</Quantity>
  <Date>31 Dec 2004</Date>
 </Line>
 <Line>
  <ItemNumber>2</ItemNumber>
  <Description>Dining tables</Description>
  <Quantity>1</Quantity>
  <Date>31 Dec 2004</Date>
 </Line>
 <Line>
  <ItemNumber>3</ItemNumber>
  <Description>Folding chairs</Description>
  <Quantity>4</Quantity>
  <Date>29 Dec 2004</Date>
 </Line>
 <Line>
  <ItemNumber>4</ItemNumber>
  <Description>Couch</Description>
  <Quantity>1</Quantity>
  <Date>31 Dec 2004</Date>
 </Line>
 ...
```

You can transform this file with the stylesheet *csv.xsl*, shown in Example 3-20.

Example 3-20. csv.xsl

```
1  <xsl:stylesheet version="1.0" xmlns:xsl="http://www.w3.org/1999/XSL/Transform">
2  <xsl:output method="text"/>
3
4  <xsl:template match="Inventory">
5   <xsl:apply-templates select="Line"/>
6  </xsl:template>
7
8  <xsl:template match="Line">
9   <xsl:for-each select="*">
10   <xsl:value-of select="."/>
11   <xsl:if test="position() != last()">
12    <xsl:value-of select="','"/>
13   </xsl:if>
14  </xsl:for-each>
15  <xsl:text>&#10;</xsl:text>
16 </xsl:template>
17
18 </xsl:stylesheet>
```

The output of this stylesheet is text (line 2). The template starting on line 8 matches all the Line elements in *inventory.xml* and processes its element children. The for-each element (line 9) works like a template within a template, instantiating its template for all the element nodes (*) it processes. value-of retrieves the string value of these nodes (line 10).

The if instruction (line 11) tests to see if the node is the last node by using the Boolean position() != last(). The position() function returns an integer representing the position of the current node, and last() returns an integer representing the position of the last node. If the node is not (!=) the last node, value-of places a comma in the result. If it is the last node, this step is skipped.

After all the element node children of a given Line element are processed, the text element (line 15) outputs a newline. When the template matching Line exhausts its search, the transform is complete.

Apply *csv.xsl* to *inventory.xml* with this command:

```
xalan -o newinventory.csv inventory.xml csv.xsl
```

You have now round-tripped the data back to the original, as the output file *newinventory.csv* (Example 3-21) is identical to *inventory.csv*.

Example 3-21. newinventory.csv

```
line,desc,quan,date
1,Oak chairs,6,31 Dec 2004
2,Dining tables,1,31 Dec 2004
3,Folding chairs,4,29 Dec 2004
4,Couch,1,31 Dec 2004
5,Overstuffed chair,1,30 Dec 2004
6,Ottoman,1,31 Dec 2004
7,Floor lamp,1,20 Dec 2004
8,Oak bookshelves,1,31 Dec 2004
9,Computer desk,1,31 Dec 2004
10,Folding tables,3,31 Dec 2004
11,Oak writing desk,1,28 Dec 2004
12,Table lamps,5,26 Dec 2004
13,Pine night tables,3,26 Dec 2004
14,Oak dresser,1,30 Dec 2004
15,Pine dressers,1,31 Dec 2004
16,Pine armoire,1,31 Dec 2004
```

You can now display *inventory.csv* in Excel 2000 (Figure 3-19) or another application that can handle CSV files.

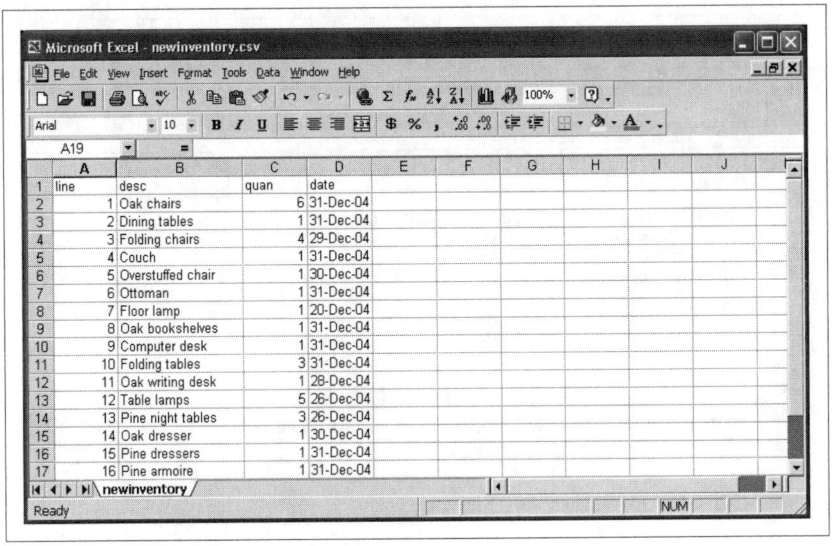

Figure 3-19. newinventory.csv in Excel 2000

See Also

- *XSLT Cookbook*, by Sal Mangano (O'Reilly), pages 155-170.
- Danny Ayers' Java code XMLToCSV: *http://www.dannyayers.com/old/code/CSVtoXML.htm*

Create and Process SpreadsheetML

HACK
#42

Since Excel XP, Excel has included an XML export option. SpreadsheetML
provides an XML representation of your spreadsheets, complete with
formatting and formula information.

Although there are several ways to read and write Excel spreadsheet files
without using Excel, one of the easiest options is to import and export XML
files that use Microsoft's SpreadsheetML vocabulary. SpreadsheetML isn't
complete—most notably, charts and VBA code are omitted—but it does
represent the core components of a spreadsheet, including formulas, named
ranges, and formatting.

This hack uses Excel features that are available only in Excel XP and Excel
2003 on Windows. Earlier versions of Excel do not support this, and neither do current or announced Macintosh versions of Excel.

The easiest way to get started with SpreadsheetML is to save a spreadsheet
as XML. The spreadsheet shown in Figure 3-20 includes data, formulas,
named ranges and cells, and some simple formatting.

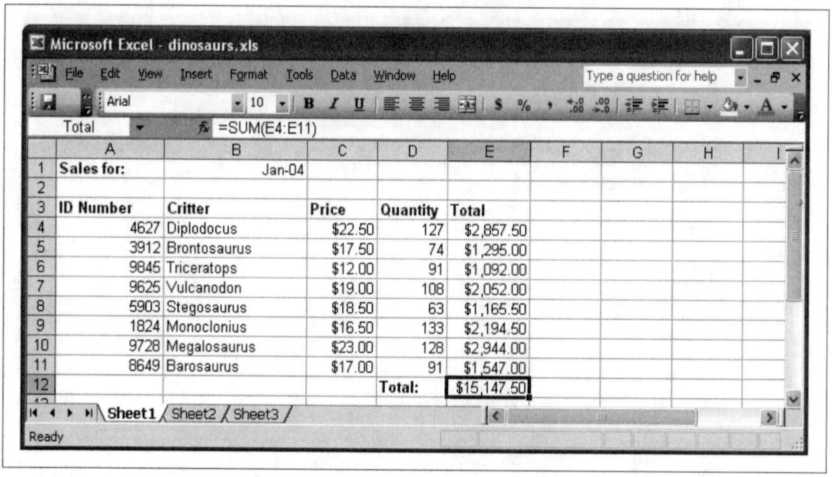

Figure 3-20. A test spreadsheet for SpreadsheetML

If you save the spreadsheet using the XML Spreadsheet (*.xml*) format,
which you can access by selecting File → Save As, you'll get an XML document named *SpreadsheetML.xml* containing the markup shown in
Example 3-22. Key portions are highlighted in bold.

Example 3-22. A SpreadsheetML document

```
<?xml version="1.0"?>
<?mso-application progid="Excel.Sheet"?>
```

Example 3-22. A SpreadsheetML document (continued)

```xml
<Workbook xmlns="urn:schemas-microsoft-com:office:spreadsheet"
 xmlns:o="urn:schemas-microsoft-com:office:office"
 xmlns:x="urn:schemas-microsoft-com:office:excel"
 xmlns:ss="urn:schemas-microsoft-com:office:spreadsheet"
 xmlns:html="http://www.w3.org/TR/REC-html40">
 <DocumentProperties xmlns="urn:schemas-microsoft-com:office:office">
  <Author>Simon St.Laurent</Author>
  <LastAuthor>Simon St.Laurent</LastAuthor>
  <Created>2003-12-03T15:48:38Z</Created>
  <LastSaved>2004-01-26T21:04:14Z</LastSaved>
  <Company>O'Reilly &amp; Associates</Company>
  <Version>11.5703</Version>
 </DocumentProperties>
 <ExcelWorkbook xmlns="urn:schemas-microsoft-com:office:excel">
  <WindowHeight>6150</WindowHeight>
  <WindowWidth>8475</WindowWidth>
  <WindowTopX>120</WindowTopX>
  <WindowTopY>30</WindowTopY>
  <ProtectStructure>False</ProtectStructure>
  <ProtectWindows>False</ProtectWindows>
 </ExcelWorkbook>
 <Styles>
  <Style ss:ID="Default" ss:Name="Normal">
   <Alignment ss:Vertical="Bottom"/>
   <Borders/>
   <Font/>
   <Interior/>
   <NumberFormat/>
   <Protection/>
  </Style>
  <Style ss:ID="s21">
   <NumberFormat ss:Format="mmm\-yy"/>
  </Style>
  <Style ss:ID="s22">
   <NumberFormat ss:Format="&quot;$&quot;#,##0.00"/>
  </Style>
  <Style ss:ID="s23">
   <Font x:Family="Swiss" ss:Bold="1"/>
  </Style>
 </Styles>
 <Names>
  <NamedRange ss:Name="Critters"
              ss:RefersTo="=Sheet1!R4C2:R11C2"/>
  <NamedRange ss:Name="Date" ss:RefersTo="=Sheet1!R1C2"/>
  <NamedRange ss:Name="ID" ss:RefersTo="=Sheet1!R4C1:R11C1"/>
  <NamedRange ss:Name="Price"
              ss:RefersTo="=Sheet1!R4C3:R11C3"/>
  <NamedRange ss:Name="Quantity"
              ss:RefersTo="=Sheet1!R4C4:R11C4"/>
  <NamedRange ss:Name="Total" ss:RefersTo="=Sheet1!R12C5"/>
 </Names>
```

Example 3-22. A SpreadsheetML document (continued)

```
<Worksheet ss:Name="Sheet1">
 <Table ss:ExpandedColumnCount="5" ss:ExpandedRowCount="12"
        x:FullColumns="1" x:FullRows="1">
  <Column ss:AutoFitWidth="0" ss:Width="73.5"/>
  <Column ss:AutoFitWidth="0" ss:Width="96.75"/>
  <Column ss:Index="5" ss:AutoFitWidth="0" ss:Width="56.25"/>
  <Row>
   <Cell ss:StyleID="s23"><Data ss:Type="String">Sales
    for:</Data></Cell>
   <Cell ss:StyleID="s21"><Data ss:Type="DateTime">
    2004-01-01T00:00:00.000</Data><NamedCell
    ss:Name="Date"/></Cell>
  </Row>
  <Row ss:Index="3" ss:StyleID="s23">
   <Cell><Data ss:Type="String">ID Number</Data></Cell>
   <Cell><Data ss:Type="String">Critter</Data></Cell>
   <Cell><Data ss:Type="String">Price</Data></Cell>
   <Cell><Data ss:Type="String">Quantity</Data></Cell>
   <Cell><Data ss:Type="String">Total</Data></Cell>
  </Row>
  <Row>
   <Cell><Data ss:Type="Number">4627</Data><NamedCell
    ss:Name="ID"/></Cell>
   <Cell><Data ss:Type="String">Diplodocus</Data><NamedCell
    ss:Name="Critters"/></Cell>
   <Cell ss:StyleID="s22"><Data ss:Type="Number">22.5</Data>
    <NamedCell ss:Name="Price"/></Cell>
   <Cell><Data ss:Type="Number">127</Data><NamedCell
    ss:Name="Quantity"/></Cell>
   <Cell ss:StyleID="s22" ss:Formula="=RC[-2]*RC[-1]"><Data
    ss:Type="Number">2857.5</Data></Cell>
  </Row>
  <Row>
   <Cell><Data ss:Type="Number">3912</Data><NamedCell
    ss:Name="ID"/></Cell>
   <Cell><Data ss:Type="String">Brontosaurus</Data><NamedCell
    ss:Name="Critters"/></Cell>
   <Cell ss:StyleID="s22"><Data ss:Type="Number">17.5</Data>
    <NamedCell ss:Name="Price"/></Cell>
   <Cell><Data ss:Type="Number">74</Data><NamedCell
    ss:Name="Quantity"/></Cell>
   <Cell ss:StyleID="s22" ss:Formula="=RC[-2]*RC[-1]"><Data
    ss:Type="Number">1295</Data></Cell>
  </Row>
  <Row>
   <Cell><Data ss:Type="Number">9845</Data><NamedCell
    ss:Name="ID"/></Cell>
   <Cell><Data ss:Type="String">Triceratops</Data><NamedCell
    ss:Name="Critters"/></Cell>
   <Cell ss:StyleID="s22"><Data ss:Type="Number">12</Data>
    <NamedCell ss:Name="Price"/></Cell>
```

Example 3-22. A SpreadsheetML document (continued)

```
<Cell><Data ss:Type="Number">91</Data><NamedCell
 ss:Name="Quantity"/></Cell>
<Cell ss:StyleID="s22" ss:Formula="=RC[-2]*RC[-1]"><Data
 ss:Type="Number">1092</Data></Cell>
</Row>
<Row>
 <Cell><Data ss:Type="Number">9625</Data><NamedCell
  ss:Name="ID"/></Cell>
 <Cell><Data ss:Type="String">Vulcanodon</Data><NamedCell
  ss:Name="Critters"/></Cell>
 <Cell ss:StyleID="s22"><Data ss:Type="Number">19</Data>
  <NamedCell ss:Name="Price"/></Cell>
 <Cell><Data ss:Type="Number">108</Data><NamedCell
  ss:Name="Quantity"/></Cell>
 <Cell ss:StyleID="s22" ss:Formula="=RC[-2]*RC[-1]"><Data
  ss:Type="Number">2052</Data></Cell>
</Row>
<Row>
 <Cell><Data ss:Type="Number">5903</Data><NamedCell
  ss:Name="ID"/></Cell>
 <Cell><Data ss:Type="String">Stegosaurus</Data><NamedCell
  ss:Name="Critters"/></Cell>
 <Cell ss:StyleID="s22"><Data ss:Type="Number">18.5</Data>
  <NamedCell ss:Name="Price"/></Cell>
 <Cell><Data ss:Type="Number">63</Data><NamedCell
  ss:Name="Quantity"/></Cell>
 <Cell ss:StyleID="s22" ss:Formula="=RC[-2]*RC[-1]"><Data
  ss:Type="Number">1165.5</Data></Cell>
</Row>
<Row>
 <Cell><Data ss:Type="Number">1824</Data><NamedCell
  ss:Name="ID"/></Cell>
 <Cell><Data ss:Type="String">Monoclonius</Data><NamedCell
  ss:Name="Critters"/></Cell>
 <Cell ss:StyleID="s22"><Data
  ss:Type="Number">16.5</Data><NamedCell
  ss:Name="Price"/></Cell>
 <Cell><Data ss:Type="Number">133</Data><NamedCell
  ss:Name="Quantity"/></Cell>
 <Cell ss:StyleID="s22" ss:Formula="=RC[-2]*RC[-1]"><Data
  ss:Type="Number">2194.5</Data></Cell>
</Row>
<Row>
 <Cell><Data ss:Type="Number">9728</Data><NamedCell
  ss:Name="ID"/></Cell>
 <Cell><Data ss:Type="String">Megalosaurus</Data><NamedCell
  ss:Name="Critters"/></Cell>
 <Cell ss:StyleID="s22"><Data
  ss:Type="Number">23</Data><NamedCell
  ss:Name="Price"/></Cell>
 <Cell><Data ss:Type="Number">128</Data><NamedCell
```

Example 3-22. A SpreadsheetML document (continued)

```
     ss:Name="Quantity"/></Cell>
    <Cell ss:StyleID="s22" ss:Formula="=RC[-2]*RC[-1]"><Data
     ss:Type="Number">2944</Data></Cell>
   </Row>
   <Row>
    <Cell><Data ss:Type="Number">8649</Data><NamedCell
     ss:Name="ID"/></Cell>
    <Cell><Data ss:Type="String">Barosaurus</Data><NamedCell
     ss:Name="Critters"/></Cell>
    <Cell ss:StyleID="s22"><Data
     ss:Type="Number">17</Data><NamedCell
     ss:Name="Price"/></Cell>
    <Cell><Data ss:Type="Number">91</Data><NamedCell
     ss:Name="Quantity"/></Cell>
    <Cell ss:StyleID="s22" ss:Formula="=RC[-2]*RC[-1]"><Data
     ss:Type="Number">1547</Data></Cell>
   </Row>
   <Row>
    <Cell ss:Index="4" ss:StyleID="s23"><Data
     ss:Type="String">Total:</Data></Cell>
    <Cell ss:StyleID="s22" ss:Formula="=SUM(R[-8]C:R[-1]C)">
     <Data ss:Type="Number">15147.5</Data><NamedCell
     ss:Name="Total"/></Cell>
   </Row>
  </Table>
  <WorksheetOptions xmlns="urn:schemas-microsoft-com:office:excel">
   <Print>
    <ValidPrinterInfo/>
    <HorizontalResolution>600</HorizontalResolution>
    <VerticalResolution>600</VerticalResolution>
   </Print>
   <Selected/>
   <Panes>
    <Pane>
     <Number>3</Number>
     <ActiveRow>11</ActiveRow>
     <ActiveCol>4</ActiveCol>
    </Pane>
   </Panes>
   <ProtectObjects>False</ProtectObjects>
   <ProtectScenarios>False</ProtectScenarios>
  </WorksheetOptions>
 </Worksheet>
 <Worksheet ss:Name="Sheet2">
  <WorksheetOptions xmlns="urn:schemas-microsoft-com:office:excel">
   <ProtectObjects>False</ProtectObjects>
   <ProtectScenarios>False</ProtectScenarios>
  </WorksheetOptions>
 </Worksheet>
 <Worksheet ss:Name="Sheet3">
  <WorksheetOptions xmlns="urn:schemas-microsoft-com:office:excel">
```

Example 3-22. A SpreadsheetML document (continued)

```
    <ProtectObjects>False</ProtectObjects>
    <ProtectScenarios>False</ProtectScenarios>
   </WorksheetOptions>
  </Worksheet>
 </Workbook>
```

The first highlighted line, `<?mso-application progid="Excel.Sheet"?>`, is an XML processing instruction that tells Windows (actually, a component Office 2003 adds to Windows) that this XML document is, in fact, an Excel spreadsheet. When Windows displays the file, it will have an Excel logo on it, and double-clicking it will open it in Excel.

The root element of the document, `Worksheet`, appears immediately after the processing instruction. Its attributes define namespaces used for various pieces of SpreadsheetML. The next few lines comprise mostly metadata, window presentation, and formatting information, and it isn't until you get to the `Names` and `Worksheet` elements that there's much worth examining closely.

The `Names` element identifies the named ranges and cells in the document. These two `NamedRange` elements define the Quantity named range—which extends from row 4, column 4, to row 11, column 4—and the Total named range, which is just the cell in row 12 of column 5:

```
    <NamedRange ss:Name="Quantity" ss:RefersTo="=Sheet1!R4C4:R11C4"/>
    <NamedRange ss:Name="Total" ss:RefersTo="=Sheet1!R12C5"/>
```

The meat of the spreadsheet is in the `Worksheet` element. It starts by defining how large the actual table of data is:

```
    <Worksheet ss:Name="Sheet1">
    <Table ss:ExpandedColumnCount="5" ss:ExpandedRowCount="12"
    x:FullColumns="1" x:FullRows="1">
```

This sheet, named Sheet1, used 5 columns and 12 rows. (The `x:FullColumns` and `x:FullRows` attributes are in another namespace that Excel won't use for layout.) The actual information in the table is stored in `Row` and `Cell` elements:

```
    <Row>
     <Cell ss:StyleID="s23"><Data ss:Type="String">Sales
       for:</Data></Cell>
     <Cell ss:StyleID="s21"><Data
       ss:Type="DateTime">2004-01-01T00:00:00.000</Data>
       <NamedCell ss:Name="Date"/></Cell>
    </Row>
    <Row ss:Index="3" ss:StyleID="s23">
     <Cell><Data ss:Type="String">ID Number</Data></Cell>
```

This Row, the first in the spreadsheet, contains two Cell elements. The first, formatted as s23 (bold, in this spreadsheet) and using the datatype String, contains the text "Sales for:". The second cell is formatted as s21 (plain), and uses the datatype DateTime. Its contents are given in a verbose ISO 8601 format. This cell also is part of a named range, in this case, Date.

Most of the other Row elements follow similar patterns, but there are a few items worth extra attention. The second Row element has an extra attribute on it, ss:Index:

```
<Row ss:Index="3" ss:StyleID="s23">
```

Excel doesn't represent empty rows or empty columns with empty Row or Cell elements. It just adds an ss:Index attribute to the next Row or Cell with content to tell you where you are. This requires programs that process this XML to pay a little more attention when assembling their tables. The other thing to watch is formulas:

```
<Cell ss:StyleID="s22" ss:Formula="=SUM(R[-8]C:R[-1]C)">
    <Data ss:Type="Number">15147.5</Data><NamedCell
    ss:Name="Total"/></Cell>
```

In Figure 3-19 this cell had a name of Total, a value of $15,147.50, and a formula of =SUM(E4:E11). All of those parts are here. But you must assemble them from the style of s22 (defined earlier in the document as a monetary number format), the value 15147.5, and a formula that uses relative references to say "the sum of the values in the same column as this one from 8 rows up to 1 row up."

This might not seem like much fun to process, but it's actually not that hard to do once you have an XML toolkit. You can use C#, Java, Perl, Python, VB, or your favorite XML-enabled programming language to extract the information, but we'll use XSLT to demonstrate.

The stylesheet in Example 3-23, *SpreadsheetML.xsl*, run against the XML in Example 3-22, will produce the much simpler XML in Example 3-24.

Example 3-23. An XSLT stylesheet for extracting content from the SpreadsheetML in Example 3-22

```
<xsl:stylesheet version="1.0"
  xmlns:xsl="http://www.w3.org/1999/XSL/Transform"
  xmlns="http://simonstl.com/ns/dinosaurs/"
  xmlns:ss="urn:schemas-microsoft-com:office:spreadsheet"
>

<xsl:output method="xml" omit-xml-declaration="yes"
    indent="yes" encoding="US-ASCII"/>

<xsl:template match="/">
```

Example 3-23. An XSLT stylesheet for extracting content from the SpreadsheetML in Example 3-22 (continued)

```
  <xsl:apply-templates select="ss:Workbook"/>
</xsl:template>

<xsl:template match="ss:Workbook">
  <dinosaurs>
      <xsl:apply-templates
          select="ss:Worksheet[@ss:Name = 'Sheet1']"/>
  </dinosaurs>
</xsl:template>

<xsl:template match="ss:Worksheet">
   <date><xsl:value-of
          select="ss:Table/ss:Row/ss:Cell[@ss:StyleID =
            's21']" />
   </date>
   <xsl:apply-templates select="ss:Table" />
</xsl:template>

<xsl:template match="ss:Table">
   <xsl:apply-templates select="ss:Row[position( ) &gt; 2]" />
<!--Note that because Excel skips the blank row,
the third row is in position 2-->
</xsl:template>

<xsl:template match="ss:Row[ss:Cell[4]]">
<sale>
   <IDnum><xsl:apply-templates select="ss:Cell[1]" /></IDnum>
   <critter><xsl:apply-templates select="ss:Cell[2]"
     /></critter>
   <price><xsl:apply-templates select="ss:Cell[3]" /></price>
   <quantity><xsl:apply-templates select="ss:Cell[4]"
     /></quantity>
   <total><xsl:apply-templates select="ss:Cell[5]" /></total>
</sale>
</xsl:template>

<xsl:template match="ss:Row">
<total><xsl:apply-templates select="ss:Cell[2]" /></total>
</xsl:template>

</xsl:stylesheet>
```

The heart of the stylesheet is the template that matches all rows with four or more child cell elements. It extracts the information from the cells and puts it into XML elements that reflect the data, producing the result shown in Example 3-24, *dinosaurs.xml*.

Example 3-24. From SpreadsheetML to a custom XML vocabulary

```
<dinosaurs xmlns="http://simonstl.com/ns/dinosaurs/" xmlns:ss="urn:schemas-
microsoft-com:office:spreadsheet">
<date>2004-01-01T00:00:00.000</date>
<sale>
<IDnum>4627</IDnum>
<critter>Diplodocus</critter>
<price>22.5</price>
<quantity>127</quantity>
<total>2857.5</total>
</sale>
<sale>
<IDnum>3912</IDnum>
<critter>Brontosaurus</critter>
<price>17.5</price>
<quantity>74</quantity>
<total>1295</total>
</sale>
<sale>
<IDnum>9845</IDnum>
<critter>Triceratops</critter>
<price>12</price>
<quantity>91</quantity>
<total>1092</total>
</sale>
<sale>
<IDnum>9625</IDnum>
<critter>Vulcanodon</critter>
<price>19</price>
<quantity>108</quantity>
<total>2052</total>
</sale>
<sale>
<IDnum>5903</IDnum>
<critter>Stegosaurus</critter>
<price>18.5</price>
<quantity>63</quantity>
<total>1165.5</total>
</sale>
<sale>
<IDnum>1824</IDnum>
<critter>Monoclonius</critter>
<price>16.5</price>
<quantity>133</quantity>
<total>2194.5</total>
</sale>
<sale>
<IDnum>9728</IDnum>
<critter>Megalosaurus</critter>
<price>23</price>
<quantity>128</quantity>
<total>2944</total>
```

Example 3-24. From SpreadsheetML to a custom XML vocabulary (continued)

```
</sale>
<sale>
<IDnum>8649</IDnum>
<critter>Barosaurus</critter>
<price>17</price>
<quantity>91</quantity>
<total>1547</total>
</sale>
<total>15147.5</total>
</dinosaurs>
```

It's the same data, but in a very different form. The formula information has been discarded in this case, but because Excel provides the values as well as the formulas, this particular application didn't need to understand the formulas.

It's also possible to round-trip this data back into Excel, again using XSLT. The stylesheet in Example 3-25, *toSpreadsheetML.xsl*, uses the original spreadsheet as a template, and will produce XML similar to the SpreadsheetML you saved from Excel originally. I've left out some formatting so that there's a visible difference.

Example 3-25. An XSLT stylesheet for converting the custom XML vocabulary back to SpreadsheetML

```
<xsl:stylesheet version="1.0"
  xmlns:xsl="http://www.w3.org/1999/XSL/Transform"
  xmlns:d="http://simonstl.com/ns/dinosaurs/"
  xmlns:ss="urn:schemas-microsoft-com:office:spreadsheet"
  xmlns="urn:schemas-microsoft-com:office:spreadsheet"
 >

<xsl:output method="xml" omit-xml-declaration="no" indent="yes" encoding="US-ASCII"/>

<xsl:template match="/">
  <xsl:apply-templates select="d:dinosaurs" />
</xsl:template>

<xsl:template match="d:dinosaurs">

<xsl:processing-instruction name="mso-application">progid="Excel.Sheet"</xsl:processing-instruction>
<Workbook xmlns="urn:schemas-microsoft-com:office:spreadsheet"
  xmlns:o="urn:schemas-microsoft-com:office:office"
  xmlns:x="urn:schemas-microsoft-com:office:excel"
  xmlns:ss="urn:schemas-microsoft-com:office:spreadsheet"
  xmlns:html="http://www.w3.org/TR/REC-html40">
  <DocumentProperties xmlns="urn:schemas-microsoft-com:office:office">
   <Author>Simon St.Laurent</Author>
```

Example 3-25. An XSLT stylesheet for converting the custom XML vocabulary back to SpreadsheetML (continued)

```
<LastAuthor>Simon St.Laurent</LastAuthor>
<Created>2003-12-03T15:48:38Z</Created>
<LastSaved>2003-12-03T15:57:46Z</LastSaved>
<Company>O'Reilly &amp; Associates</Company>
<Version>11.5606</Version>
</DocumentProperties>
<ExcelWorkbook xmlns="urn:schemas-microsoft-com:office:excel">
 <WindowHeight>6150</WindowHeight>
 <WindowWidth>8475</WindowWidth>
 <WindowTopX>120</WindowTopX>
 <WindowTopY>30</WindowTopY>
 <ProtectStructure>False</ProtectStructure>
 <ProtectWindows>False</ProtectWindows>
</ExcelWorkbook>
<Styles>
 <Style ss:ID="Default" ss:Name="Normal">
  <Alignment ss:Vertical="Bottom"/>
  <Borders/>
  <Font/>
  <Interior/>
  <NumberFormat/>
  <Protection/>
 </Style>
 <Style ss:ID="s21">
  <NumberFormat ss:Format="mmm\-yy"/>
 </Style>
 <Style ss:ID="s22">
  <NumberFormat ss:Format="&quot;$&quot;#,##0.00"/>
 </Style>
</Styles>
<Worksheet ss:Name="Sheet1">
 <Table ss:ExpandedColumnCount="5" ss:ExpandedRowCount="{count(d:sale)+4}" x:
FullColumns="1"
  x:FullRows="1">
  <Column ss:AutoFitWidth="0" ss:Width="73.5"/>
  <Column ss:AutoFitWidth="0" ss:Width="96.75"/>
  <Column ss:Index="5" ss:AutoFitWidth="0" ss:Width="56.25"/>
  <Row>
   <Cell><Data ss:Type="String">Sales for:</Data></Cell>
   <Cell ss:StyleID="s21"><Data ss:Type="DateTime">
     <xsl:value-of select="d:date"/></Data></Cell>
  </Row>
  <Row ss:Index="3">
   <Cell><Data ss:Type="String">ID Number</Data></Cell>
   <Cell><Data ss:Type="String">Critter</Data></Cell>
   <Cell><Data ss:Type="String">Price</Data></Cell>
   <Cell><Data ss:Type="String">Quantity</Data></Cell>
   <Cell><Data ss:Type="String">Total</Data></Cell>
  </Row>
```

*Example 3-25. An XSLT stylesheet for converting the custom XML vocabulary back to
SpreadsheetML (continued)*

```
<xsl:apply-templates select="d:sale" />

  <Row>
   <Cell ss:Index="4"><Data ss:Type="String">Total:</Data></Cell>
   <Cell ss:StyleID="s22" ss:Formula="=SUM(R[-{count(d:sale)}]C:R[-1]C)"><Data
ss:Type="Number"></Data></Cell>
  </Row>
 </Table>
 <WorksheetOptions xmlns="urn:schemas-microsoft-com:office:excel">
  <Print>
   <ValidPrinterInfo/>
   <HorizontalResolution>600</HorizontalResolution>
   <VerticalResolution>600</VerticalResolution>
  </Print>
  <Selected/>
  <Panes>
   <Pane>
    <Number>3</Number>
    <ActiveRow>12</ActiveRow>
    <ActiveCol>1</ActiveCol>
   </Pane>
  </Panes>
  <ProtectObjects>False</ProtectObjects>
  <ProtectScenarios>False</ProtectScenarios>
 </WorksheetOptions>
</Worksheet>
<Worksheet ss:Name="Sheet2">
 <WorksheetOptions xmlns="urn:schemas-microsoft-com:office:excel">
  <ProtectObjects>False</ProtectObjects>
  <ProtectScenarios>False</ProtectScenarios>
 </WorksheetOptions>
</Worksheet>
<Worksheet ss:Name="Sheet3">
 <WorksheetOptions xmlns="urn:schemas-microsoft-com:office:excel">
  <ProtectObjects>False</ProtectObjects>
  <ProtectScenarios>False</ProtectScenarios>
 </WorksheetOptions>
</Worksheet>
</Workbook>
</xsl:template>

<xsl:template match="d:sale">
   <Row>
    <Cell><Data ss:Type="Number"><xsl:value-of select="d:IDnum" /></Data>
<NamedCell ss:Name="ID"/></Cell>
    <Cell><Data ss:Type="String"><xsl:value-of select="d:critter" /></Data>
<NamedCell ss:Name="Critters"/></Cell>
    <Cell ss:StyleID="s22"><Data ss:Type="Number"><xsl:value-of select="d:price"
/></Data><NamedCell
     ss:Name="Price"/></Cell>
```

Example 3-25. An XSLT stylesheet for converting the custom XML vocabulary back to SpreadsheetML (continued)

```
    <Cell><Data ss:Type="Number"><xsl:value-of select="d:quantity" /></Data>
<NamedCell ss:Name="Quantity"/></Cell>
    <Cell ss:StyleID="s22" ss:Formula="=RC[-2]*RC[-1]"><Data ss:Type="Number">
<xsl:value-of select="d:total" /></Data></Cell>
    </Row>
</xsl:template>

<xsl:template match="d:date" />
<xsl:template match="d:total" />

</xsl:stylesheet>
```

A few pieces of this example are worth special attention. First, note that the SpreadsheetML is wrapped in XSLT; the SpreadsheetML becomes part of the stylesheet. There's one piece of the SpreadsheetML you can't re-create with this method: the processing instruction noted earlier that tells Windows that this is an Excel spreadsheet. For that, you have to manually insert the following:

```
<xsl:processing-instruction name="mso-application">progid="Excel.Sheet"</
xsl:processing-instruction>
```

Because XPath 1.0 won't allow you to use the default namespace (no prefix) to refer to content that has a namespace, all the references to content in the source document now have the prefix d:, such as d:sale, d:date, etc.

Also, because the named ranges will vary depending on the number of sale elements in the original, this stylesheet won't generate the Names element and its contents. Excel will re-create the named ranges from the NamedCell elements in any case. The heart of this stylesheet is again the part that generates the Row and Cell elements, as shown in the following:

```
<xsl:template match="d:sale">
    <Row>
    <Cell><Data ss:Type="Number"><xsl:value-of select="d:IDnum" /></Data>
<NamedCell ss:Name="ID"/></Cell>
```

The xsl:template element will collect every sale element in the original and produce a Row element that contains Cell elements matching its contents. If you open in Excel the SpreadsheetML that this stylesheet produces (which looks much like that in Example 3-22, minus named ranges and some formatting), you get the result shown in Figure 3-21.

This process might not look very beautiful, but there are lots of reasons you might want to follow it. For one, saving as SpreadsheetML gives you better access to the XML map information described in **[Hack #15]** than Excel's GUI offers at present. More importantly in the long run, SpreadsheetML is porta-

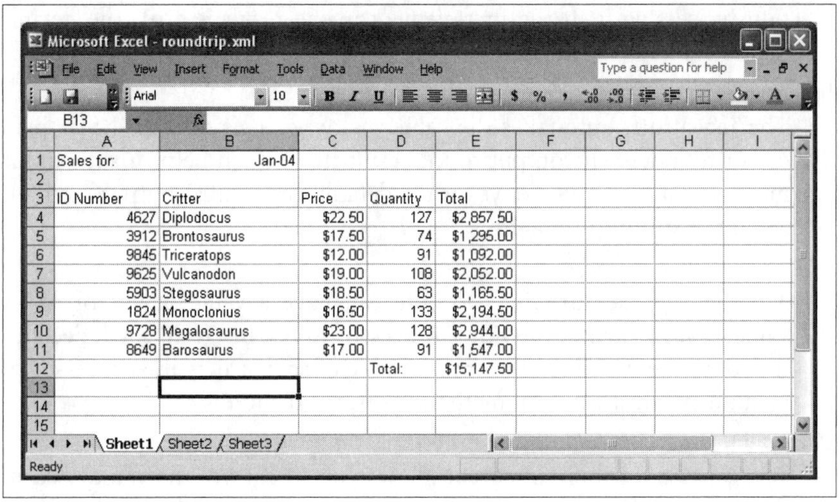

Figure 3-21. The test spreadsheet after its data has gone from SpreadsheetML to another vocabulary and back again

ble, and you can process it and generate it on virtually any computer that has basic XML facilities.

—Simon St.Laurent

HACK #43 Choose Your Output Format in XSLT

Take control of the output of an XSLT stylesheet.

The output element in XSLT has 10 attributes, each controlling a different aspect of XSLT output. This hack lists each of these attributes and shows you how to use them. All of output's attributes are optional.

An XSLT stylesheet can have more than one output element, and the values found in the attributes of those elements are combined. However, if a given attribute occurs on more than one output element, the last occurrence trumps all previous occurrences. Nevertheless, it is technically an error if an attribute (aside from cdata-section-elements) occurs on more than one output element in the stylesheet; however, processors can recover by choosing the value from the last output in the stylesheet.

Output method

The method attribute can have the value xml, html, or text for XML, HTML, and text output, respectively. XSLT 2.0 will support a value of xhtml for XHTML support. The method attribute can also have a QName as a value, but the QName must be recognized by the application processing it. If the first element in the result is html, the default method is html; xml if otherwise.

Indentation

The indent attribute takes the value yes or no. This tells the XSLT processor to indent the output to the result tree, which helps make output more readable. A value of yes is the default for the html output method, no for the xml output method.

XML declaration

The omit-xml-declaration attribute can have a value of yes or no. A value of yes instructs the XSLT processor to not insert an XML declaration onto the first line of output; a value of no instructs the processor to include one. If the output method is xml, the default is no.

Version information

The version attribute of output allows you to control the value used in the version information of the XML declaration; by default, it's 1.0 for the xml output method, 4.0 for the html method. With XML 1.1 now here (*http://www.w3.org/TR/xml11/*), it's good to know that you can control this value; for example, version="1.1".

Encoding declaration

The encoding attribute lets you specify a value for the encoding declaration on an XML declaration. Possible values include UTF-8, UTF-16, ISO-8859-1, and Shift_JIS. A hack in the previous chapter ("Encode XML Documents" **[Hack #27]**) covers encoding.

Standalone declaration

The standalone attribute can have a value of yes or no. This will then appear on the XML declaration. A value of yes means there are no external markup declarations in a DTD upon which the document depends, no if otherwise. Don't worry about this too much, as explained in an earlier hack on the XML document **[Hack #1]**.

CDATA sections

The cdata-section-elements attribute can contain one or more QNames for the elements in the result tree that should output the text content of such an element in a CDATA section **[Hack #1]**. A CDATA section, which is formed like <![CDATA[Barnes & Noble]]>, hides characters such as the ampersand (&) from the processor. Use of this attribute is relatively rare.

Document type declarations

You can insert a document type declaration **[Hack #7]** for the output XML document by using the doctype-public attribute for inserting a public identifier, such as in <!DOCTYPE html PUBLIC "-//W3C//DTD XHTML 1.0

String//EN">, or the doctype-system attribute for inserting a system identifier, such as a simple filename (<!DOCTYPE time SYSTEM "time. dtd">).

Media type

The media-type attribute lets you specify a media (MIME) type explicitly, though you won't see such a type show up in the XSLT output. It is ostensibly for internal consumption, such as for the Content-Type header of an HTTP header. (I've never seen this attribute have a practical impact in downstream processing.) The default value is text/xml for the xml output method, text/html for the html method, and text/plain for the text method.

The following snippet shows a pair of output elements in an XSLT stylesheet. The values in both elements are used.

```
<xsl:output method="xml" indent="yes" omit-xml-declaration="yes"/>
<xsl:output encoding="UTF-8" standalone="yes"/>
```

HACK #44 Transform Your iTunes Library File

Grab data out of your iTunes library file and transform it into HTML.

Apple's iTunes (*http://www.apple.com/itunes/*) is a nifty application that allows you to purchase, store, organize, and play media on either the Mac or Windows. You can buy and download individual songs or whole albums from the iTunes Music Store, and then store them on your hard drive, burn them to CD, or load them into an iPod digital music player (*http://www. apple.com/ipod/*). Figure 3-22 shows the iTunes Music Store in the iTunes application in Windows.

One XML feature of iTunes is that you can save information about your music library in an XML file using the File → Export Library command. This file is an example of the Apple Property List (plist) file format, common on Mac OS X systems. For example, the file *~/.MacOSX/environment.plist* is a plist file in which a user's environment variables are stored and that can be edited with the *PropertyListEditor.app* (see *http://developer.apple.com/qa/ qa2001/qa1067.html* for an example).

In raw form, plist files can be long and hard to decipher. That's where XSLT can help. This hack will show you how to transform your *Library.xml* plist file into HTML. A few lines of an instance of *Library.xml* (Version 4.2.0.72) are shown in Example 3-26.

Figure 3-22. iTunes Music Store

Example 3-26. Library.xml

```
<?xml version="1.0" encoding="UTF-8"?>
<!DOCTYPE plist PUBLIC "-//Apple Computer//DTD PLIST 1.0//EN" "http://www.apple.
com/DTDs/PropertyList-1.0.dtd">
<plist version="1.0">
<dict>
    <key>Major Version</key><integer>1</integer>
    <key>Minor Version</key><integer>1</integer>
    <key>Application Version</key><string>4.2</string>
    <key>Music Folder</key><string>file://localhost/C:/
Documents%20and%20Settings/xxxxxx/Documents/My%20Music/iTunes/iTunes%20Music/</
string>
    <key>Tracks</key>
    <dict>
        <key>33</key>
        <dict>
            <key>Track ID</key><integer>33</integer>
            <key>Name</key><string>A Thousand Years</string>
            <key>Artist</key><string>Sting</string>
            <key>Album</key><string>Brand New Day</string>
            <key>Genre</key><string>Rock</string>
            <key>Kind</key><string>Protected AAC audio
                file</string>
            <key>Size</key><integer>5912496</integer>
            <key>Total Time</key><integer>358144</integer>
            <key>Disc Number</key><integer>1</integer>
            <key>Disc Count</key><integer>1</integer>
            <key>Track Number</key><integer>1</integer>
            <key>Track Count</key><integer>10</integer>
            <key>Year</key><integer>1999</integer>
            <key>Date Modified</key><date>2004-02-04T02:12:06Z</date>
            <key>Date Added</key><date>2004-02-04T02:10:11Z</date>
```

Example 3-26. Library.xml (continued)

```
<key>Bit Rate</key><integer>128</integer>
<key>Sample Rate</key><integer>44100</integer>
<key>Play Count</key><integer>5</integer>
<key>Play Date</key><integer>-1136265306</integer>
<key>Play Date UTC</key><date>2004-02-04T08:13:10Z</date>
<key>Normalization</key><integer>1202</integer>
```

The fields that represent tracks are stored in key elements, followed by string, integer, or date elements.

Having previously saved your *Library.xml* file to the XSLT working directory (where the archive files are stored), you can now transform it with *Library.xsl*, shown in Example 3-27.

Example 3-27. Library.xsl

```
<xsl:stylesheet version="1.0" xmlns:xsl="http://www.w3.org/1999/XSL/Transform">
<xsl:output method="html" indent="yes"/>

<!-- Stylesheet for tracks in Apple iTunes library export file -->

<xsl:template match="plist">
 <html>
 <head>
 <title>My iTunes</title>
 <style type="text/css">
 body {font-family:sans-serif}
 h1 {text-align:center}
 table {margin-left:auto;margin-right:auto;}
 thead {background-color:black;color:white}
 td,th {padding: 7px 7px 7px 7px;font-size:15px}
 </style>
 </head>
 <body>
 <h1>My iTunes</h1>
 <xsl:apply-templates select="dict"/>
 </body>
 </html>
</xsl:template>

<xsl:template match="dict">
 <table border="1" rules="all">
 <thead>
  <tr>
   <!--th>Track ID</th-->
   <th>Name</th>
   <th>Artist</th>
   <th>Album</th>
   <th>Genre</th>
   <!--th>Kind</th-->
   <!--th>Size</th-->
```

Example 3-27. Library.xsl (continued)

```
  <!--th>Total Time</th-->
  <!--th>Disc Number</th-->
  <!--th>Disc Count</th-->
  <!--th>Track Number</th-->
  <!--th>Track Count</th-->
  <th>Year</th>
  <!--th>Date Modified</th-->
  <th>Date Added</th>
  <!--th>Bit Rate</th-->
  <!--th>Sample Rate</th-->
  <!--th>Play Count</th-->
  <!--th>Play Date</th-->
  <!--th>Play Date UTC</th-->
  <!--th>Normalization</th-->
  <!--th>Location</th-->
  <!--th>File Folder Count</th-->
  <!--th>Library Folder Count</th-->
  </tr>
 </thead>
 <xsl:apply-templates select="dict/dict"/>
 </table>
</xsl:template>

<xsl:template match="dict/dict">
 <tr>
 <!--td style="text-align:center"><xsl:value-of select="key[.='Track ID']/
following-sibling::integer"/></td-->
 <td><xsl:value-of select="key[.='Name']/following-sibling::string"/></td>
 <td><xsl:value-of select="key[.='Artist']/following-sibling::string"/></td>
 <td><xsl:value-of select="key[.='Album']/following-sibling::string"/></td>
 <td><xsl:value-of select="key[.='Genre']/following-sibling::string"/></td>
 <!--td><xsl:value-of select="key[.='Kind']/following-sibling::string"/></td-->
 <!--td style="text-align:center"><xsl:value-of select="key[.='Size']/following-
sibling::integer"/></td-->
 <!--td style="text-align:center"><xsl:value-of select="key[.='Total Time']/
following-sibling::integer"/></td-->
 <!--td style="text-align:center"><xsl:value-of select="key[.='Disc Number']/
following-sibling::integer"/></td-->
 <!--td style="text-align:center"><xsl:value-of select="key[.='Disc Count']/
following-sibling::integer"/></td-->
 <!--td style="text-align:center"><xsl:value-of select="key[.='Track Number']/
following-sibling::integer"/></td-->
 <!--td style="text-align:center"><xsl:value-of select="key[.='Track Count']/
following-sibling::integer"/></td-->
 <td style="text-align:center"><xsl:value-of select="key[.='Year']/following-
sibling::integer"/></td>
 <!--td><xsl:value-of select="substring(key[.='Date Modified']/following-sibling:
:date, 1, 10)"/></td-->
 <td><xsl:value-of select="substring(key[.='Date Added']/following-sibling::date,
1, 10)"/></td>
```

Example 3-27. Library.xsl (continued)

```
<!--td style="text-align:center"><xsl:value-of select="key[.='Bit Rate']/
following-sibling::integer"/></td-->
<!--td style="text-align:center"><xsl:value-of select="key[.='Sample Rate']/
following-sibling::integer"/></td-->
<!--td style="text-align:center"><xsl:value-of select="key[.='Play Count']/
following-sibling::integer"/></td-->
<!--td><xsl:value-of select="key[.='Play Date']/following-sibling::integer"/>
</td-->
<!--td><xsl:value-of select="substring(key[.='Play Date UTC']/following-sibling:
:date, 1, 10)"/></td-->
<!--td><xsl:value-of select="key[.='Normalization']/following-sibling::integer"/>
</td-->
<!--td><xsl:value-of select="key[.='Location']/following-sibling::string"/>
</td-->
<!--td style="text-align:center"><xsl:value-of select="key[.='File Folder
Count']/following-sibling::integer"/></td-->
<!--td style="text-align:center"><xsl:value-of select="key[.='Library Folder
Count']/following-sibling::integer"/></td-->
</tr>
</xsl:template>

</xsl:stylesheet>
```

This stylesheet produces HTML output. (It's just one approach to the problem—there are plenty of other possibilities that could work, too.) Though most of the lines are commented out, each of the track's fields are represented. Only those lines that are uncommented will capture nodes from *Library.xml*. Currently, the stylesheet grabs the Name, Artist, Album, Genre, Year, and Date Added fields. This is done through the use of predicates or filters in square brackets (such as key[.='Name']), which identify the content of key elements. The following-sibling axis (such as following-sibling::string) helps find nodes that follow and are siblings of the selected node.

If you'd like, you can uncomment other fields, but you must do so in two places for each field: first, where the track name is stored in a th element near the top of the stylesheet; and second, in a complementary td element later in the stylesheet.

Now transform *Library.xml* with *Library.xsl*, saving it in an HTML file such as *Library.html*. I'll use Xalan to do the job, with this line:

```
xalan -o Library.html Library.xml Library.xsl
```

Next, display *Library.html* in a browser. You should see something that looks like Figure 3-23.

Figure 3-23. Library.html in Mozilla Firebird

HACK #45   Generate Multiple Output Documents with XSLT 2.0

Unlike XSLT 1.0, XSLT 2.0 allows you to produce more than one result tree from a single transformation.

XSLT 2.0 has added the functionality to serialize more than one result tree when performing a single transformation with the new `result-document` element. The stylesheet in this hack will show you how to produce four result documents from one source document.

The *result-document.xsl* stylesheet produces four result trees based on *time.xml*. The default result tree is output as text, and the remaining three are output as XML, HTML, and XHTML, respectively. The stylesheet is listed in Example 3-28.

Example 3-28. result-document.xsl

```
1  <xsl:stylesheet version="2.0" xmlns:xsl="http://www.w3.org/1999/XSL/Transform">
2  <xsl:output method="text"/>
3  <xsl:output name="xml" method="xml" indent="yes"/>
4  <xsl:output name="html" method="html" indent="yes"/>
5  <xsl:output name="xhtml" method="xhtml" indent="yes"/>
6  <xsl:param name="dir">file:///C:/Hacks/examples/</xsl:param>
7
8  <xsl:template match="/">
9
10   <xsl:apply-templates select="time" mode="text"/>
11
12   <xsl:result-document format="xml" href="{$dir}/rd.xml">
13     <time>
14       <xsl:message terminate="no">Printing XML result tree in rd.xml...</xsl:
    message>
15       <xsl:apply-templates select="time" mode="xml"/>
```

Example 3-28. result-document.xsl (continued)

```
16   </time>
17   </xsl:result-document>
18
19   <xsl:result-document format="html" href="{$dir}/rd.html">
20     <xsl:message terminate="no">Printing HTML result tree in rd.html...
     </xsl:message>
21     <html>
22     <body>
23     <h2>Time</h2>
24     <ul>
25       <xsl:apply-templates select="time" mode="html"/>
26     </ul>
27     </body>
28     </html>
29     </xsl:result-document>
30
31     <xsl:result-document format="xhtml" href="{$dir}/rd-x.html">
32       <xsl:message terminate="no">Printing XHTML result tree in rd-x.html...
     </xsl:message>
33       <html xmlns="http://www.w3.org/1999/xhtml">
34       <body>
35       <h2>Time</h2>
36       <ul>
37         <xsl:apply-templates select="time" mode="xhtml"/>
38       </ul>
39       </body>
40       </html>
41     </xsl:result-document>
42     <xsl:message terminate="no">Printing text result tree...</xsl:message>
43   </xsl:template>
44
45   <xsl:template match="time" mode="text">
46     <xsl:value-of select="hour"/>:<xsl:value-of select="minute"/>:<xsl:value-of
     select="second"/><xsl:text> </xsl:text><xsl:value-of select="meridiem"/>
47   </xsl:template>
48
49   <xsl:template match="time" mode="xml">
50     <hr><xsl:value-of select="hour"/></hr>
51     <min><xsl:value-of select="minute"/></min>
52     <sec><xsl:value-of select="second"/></sec>
53     <mer><xsl:value-of select="meridiem"/></mer>
54   </xsl:template>
55
56   <xsl:template match="time" mode="html">
57     <li><xsl:value-of select="hour"/></li>
58     <li><xsl:value-of select="minute"/></li>
59     <li><xsl:value-of select="second"/></li>
60     <li><xsl:value-of select="meridiem"/></li>
61   </xsl:template>
62
63   <xsl:template match="time" mode="xhtml">
```

Example 3-28. result-document.xsl (continued)

```
64    <li xmlns="http://www.w3.org/1999/xhtml"><xsl:value-of select="hour"/></li>
65    <li xmlns="http://www.w3.org/1999/xhtml"><xsl:value-of select="minute"/></li>
66    <li xmlns="http://www.w3.org/1999/xhtml"><xsl:value-of select="second"/></li>
67    <li xmlns="http://www.w3.org/1999/xhtml"><xsl:value-of select="meridiem"/></li>
68    </xsl:template>
69
70    </xsl:stylesheet>
```

The version attribute on the stylesheet element (line 1) has a value of 2.0 because it's a 2.0 stylesheet. On lines 2–5 are four output elements, three of them named. This is so that a result-document element can reference an output element by name.

The global parameter dir declared on line 6 stores the name of the directory where the three result trees are to be written as files. The attribute value template {$dir} in the href attributes (on lines 12, 19, and 31) passes in a value for the dir parameter. If you want to change where the output files are written, you can edit the content of the param element on line 6.

The template matching / creates a text result tree. Each of the other three result trees are inside result-document elements, and each creates a message using the message element. Each result tree also applies templates to time elements, each in a different mode (text, xml, html, and xhtml). The different modes for each result help create an appropriate tree for each of the given formats.

You need to use the Java version of Saxon, preferably Version 8.0 or later, to get this to work. Saxon 8.0 is available from *http://saxon.sourceforge.net*. Once everything is installed, you can type this command:

```
java -jar saxon8.jar time.xml result-document.xsl
```

You get the following messages:

```
Printing XML result tree in rd.xml...
Printing HTML result tree in rd.html...
Printing XHTML result tree in rd-x.html...
Printing text result tree...
11:59:59 p.m.
```

The last line shows the text output of the transformation. The files that the three result-document elements produced contain the other result trees. The first one is *rd.xml*:

```
<?xml version="1.0" encoding="UTF-8"?>
<time>
    <hr>11</hr>
    <min>59</min>
    <sec>59</sec>
    <mer>p.m.</mer>
</time>
```

The second one is *rd.html*, which contains simple HTML:

```html
<html>
    <body>
        <h2>Time</h2>
        <ul>
            <li>11</li>
            <li>59</li>
            <li>59</li>
            <li>p.m.</li>
        </ul>
    </body>
</html>
```

And the final document is *rd-x.html*, a simple XHTML document:

```html
<html xmlns="http://www.w3.org/1999/xhtml">
    <body>
        <h2>Time</h2>
        <ul>
            <li>11</li>
            <li>59</li>
            <li>59</li>
            <li>p.m.</li>
        </ul>
    </body>
</html>
```

If you're still using XSLT 1.0, you can probably produce multiple result documents, but it will be through extension features that vary from processor to processor.

HACK #46 Generate XML from MySQL

Using MySQL and want to use the data stored there elsewhere? Dump XML out of a MySQL database and then transform it with XSLT.

MySQL (*http://www.mysql.com*) is a popular, nearly ubiquitous, multiplatform database engine, available under both open source and commercial licenses. It is commonly used as a data store for web sites. This hack shows you how to examine a MySQL database, dump its contents as XML, and then use XSLT to transform and refine the result.

You can download MySQL from *http://www.mysql.com/downloads/*. It has versions for Windows, Linux, FreeBSD, NetBSD, Solaris, SCO, and even OS/2. For information on installing MySQL, see *http://www.mysql.com/documentation/mysql/bychapter/manual_Installing.html*. If you are unfamiliar with MySQL, you can get up to speed quickly by reading the tutorial at *http://www.mysql.com/documentation/mysql/bychapter/manual_Tutorial.html*.

Here we have a database horses containing the table horse. The table has five fields: id, name, owner, age, and breed. First we invoke the command-line tool *mysql*, and then issue some Structured Query Language (SQL) commands, shown in Example 3-29.

Example 3-29. SQL commands

```
C:\Hacks\examples>mysql
Welcome to the MySQL monitor.  Commands end with ; or \g.
Your MySQL connection id is 12 to server version: 3.23.54-max-nt

Type 'help;' or '\h' for help. Type '\c' to clear the buffer.

mysql> show databases;
+----------+
| Database |
+----------+
| horses   |
+----------+
1 row in set (0.00 sec)

mysql> use horses;
Database changed
mysql> show tables;
+------------------+
| Tables_in_horses |
+------------------+
| horse            |
+------------------+
1 row in set (0.00 sec)

mysql> describe horse;
+-------+-------------+------+-----+---------+-------+
| Field | Type        | Null | Key | Default | Extra |
+-------+-------------+------+-----+---------+-------+
| id    | tinyint(4)  |      | PRI | 0       |       |
| name  | varchar(20) |      |     |         |       |
| owner | varchar(20) |      |     |         |       |
| age   | tinyint(2)  |      |     | 0       |       |
| breed | varchar(30) |      |     |         |       |
+-------+-------------+------+-----+---------+-------+
5 rows in set (0.00 sec)

mysql> select * from horse;
+----+---------+--------+-----+---------------+
| id | name    | owner  | age | breed         |
+----+---------+--------+-----+---------------+
|  1 | Babes   | Tom    |  12 | Quarter       |
|  2 | Stanley | Mike   |  13 | Quarter       |
|  3 | Sassy   | Aubrey |  16 | Welsh-Hackney |
|  4 | Sissy   | Cristi |  10 | Quarter-Arab  |
|  5 | Gypsy   | Margie |   7 | Albino        |
```

Example 3-29. SQL commands (continued)

```
|  6 | Jubal   | Kathy   |   4 | Pinto         |
+----+---------+--------+-----+---------------+
6 rows in set (0.00 sec)

mysql> quit
Bye
```

You will not have this database in the downloaded files; however, you will have
the files produced in the following exercise (i.e., *horses.xml* and *mysql.xsl*). It's
now time to dump the data out of the database as XML. We'll do that with the
mysqldump tool. At a command prompt, type this line:

```
mysqldump --xml horses > horses.xml
```

The tool extracts the information in the database horses and redirects it into
the file *horses.xml*, which looks like this (Example 3-30).

Example 3-30. horses.xml

```xml
<?xml version="1.0"?>
<mysqldump>
<database name="horses">
        <table name="horse">
        <row>
                <field name="id">1</field>
                <field name="name">Babes</field>
                <field name="owner">Tom</field>
                <field name="age">12</field>
                <field name="breed">Quarter</field>
        </row>
        <row>
                <field name="id">2</field>
                <field name="name">Stanley</field>
                <field name="owner">Mike</field>
                <field name="age">13</field>
                <field name="breed">Quarter</field>
        </row>
        <row>
                <field name="id">3</field>
                <field name="name">Sassy</field>
                <field name="owner">Aubrey</field>
                <field name="age">16</field>
                <field name="breed">Welsh-Hackney</field>
        </row>
        <row>
                <field name="id">4</field>
                <field name="name">Sissy</field>
                <field name="owner">Cristi</field>
                <field name="age">10</field>
                <field name="breed">Quarter-Arab</field>
        </row>
```

Example 3-30. horses.xml (continued)

```
        <row>
                <field name="id">5</field>
                <field name="name">Gypsy</field>
                <field name="owner">Margie</field>
                <field name="age">7</field>
                <field name="breed">Albino</field>
        </row>
        <row>
                <field name="id">6</field>
                <field name="name">Jubal</field>
                <field name="owner">Kathy</field>
                <field name="age">4</field>
                <field name="breed">Pinto</field>
        </row>
        </table>
</database>
</mysqldump>
```

The elements in this XML document—mysqldump, database, table, row, and
field—are consistent. That's why you will be able to use the following
stylesheet, *mysqldump.xsl* (Example 3-31), with most any *mysqldump* XML.

Example 3-31. mysqldump.xsl

```
<xsl:stylesheet version="1.0" xmlns:xsl="http://www.w3.org/1999/XSL/Transform">
<xsl:output method="xml" encoding="UTF-8"/>

<xsl:template match="mysqldump">
 <xsl:apply-templates select="database"/>
</xsl:template>

<xsl:template match="database">
 <xsl:element name="{@name}">
  <xsl:apply-templates select="table"/>
 </xsl:element>
</xsl:template>

<xsl:template match="table">
  <xsl:apply-templates select="row"/>
</xsl:template>

<xsl:template match="row">
 <xsl:element name="{../@name}">
  <xsl:apply-templates select="field"/>
 </xsl:element>
</xsl:template>

<xsl:template match="field">
 <xsl:element name="{@name}">
  <xsl:value-of select="."/>
 </xsl:element>
```

Example 3-31. mysqldump.xsl (continued)

```
</xsl:template>

</xsl:stylesheet>
```

The stylesheet finds each of the common element names in the *mysqldump* output, and creates new elements based on the values of the name attributes. Process it with this command using Xalan C++:

```
xalan -i 2 horses.xml mysqldump.xsl
```

The -i option followed by 2 means that the output will be indented by two spaces at each level in the structure. Xalan will produce the output in Example 3-32.

Example 3-32. Output from mysqldump.xsl

```
<?xml version="1.0" encoding="UTF-8"?>
<horses>
  <horse>
    <id>1</id>
    <name>Babes</name>
    <owner>Tom</owner>
    <age>12</age>
    <breed>Quarter</breed>
  </horse>
  <horse>
    <id>2</id>
    <name>Stanley</name>
    <owner>Mike</owner>
    <age>13</age>
    <breed>Quarter</breed>
  </horse>
  <horse>
    <id>3</id>
    <name>Sassy</name>
    <owner>Aubrey</owner>
    <age>16</age>
    <breed>Welsh-Hackney</breed>
  </horse>
  <horse>
    <id>4</id>
    <name>Sissy</name>
    <owner>Cristi</owner>
    <age>10</age>
    <breed>Quarter-Arab</breed>
  </horse>
  <horse>
    <id>5</id>
    <name>Gypsy</name>
    <owner>Margie</owner>
    <age>7</age>
```

Example 3-32. Output from mysqldump.xsl (continued)

```
      <breed>Albino</breed>
   </horse>
   <horse>
      <id>6</id>
      <name>Jubal</name>
      <owner>Kathy</owner>
      <age>4</age>
      <breed>Pinto</breed>
   </horse>
</horses>
```

Generate PDF Documents from XML and CSS

#47

Produce PDF documents for XML documents styled with CSS using YesLogic Prince.

YesLogic (*http://yeslogic.com/*) of Melbourne, Australia offers an extremely simple little tool for converting XML documents styled with CSS into Portable Document Format (PDF) or PostScript (PS). It's called Prince and it's now at Version 3.1. It runs on Windows or Red Hat Linux (Versions 7.3 and 8.0). Prince comes with a set of examples, default stylesheets, and DTDs. This hack demonstrates Version 3.0, which is similar to 3.1.

You can download a free version (personal license) from *http://yeslogic.com/ prince/demo/*. This demo is fully featured, but outputs a link on output pages.

After downloading and installing Prince, open the application and follow these steps:

1. Choose Documents → Add and then select the document *time.xml* from the directory of working examples.

2. Choose Stylesheets → Add and select *time.css* from the same location.

3. Select the Output menu and click on PDF if it isn't already checked.

4. Click Go, and Prince produces a PDF based on *time.xml* combined with *time.css*. The application should look like Figure 3-24.

5. Select *time.pdf* in the lower-left pane and right-click on it. If Adobe Reader (Version 6.0 or greater) is installed on your computer, you should be able to open *time.pdf* with it. If it is not installed, get a free copy from *http:// www.adobe.com/products/acrobat/readstep2.html*. Figure 3-25 shows you *time.pdf* in Adobe Reader Version 6.0.

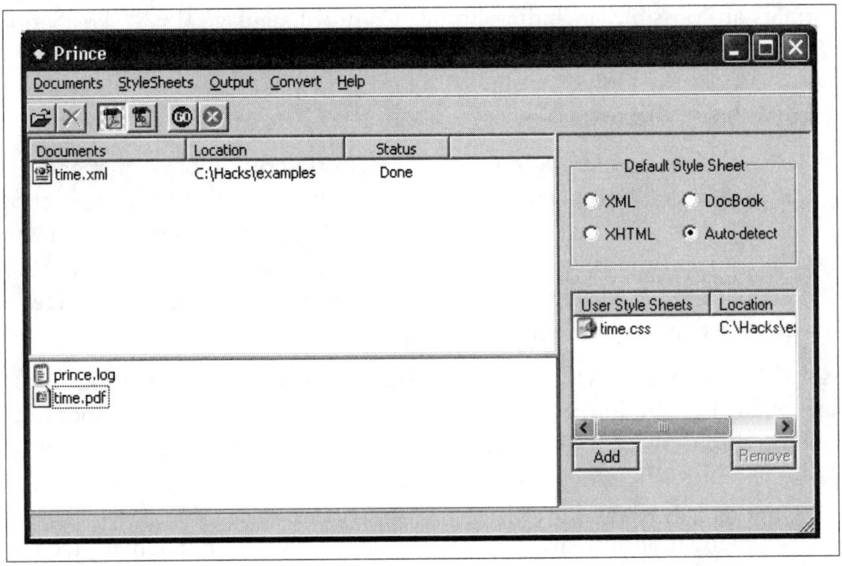

Figure 3-24. YesLogic Prince after converting time.xml styled with time.css into time.pdf

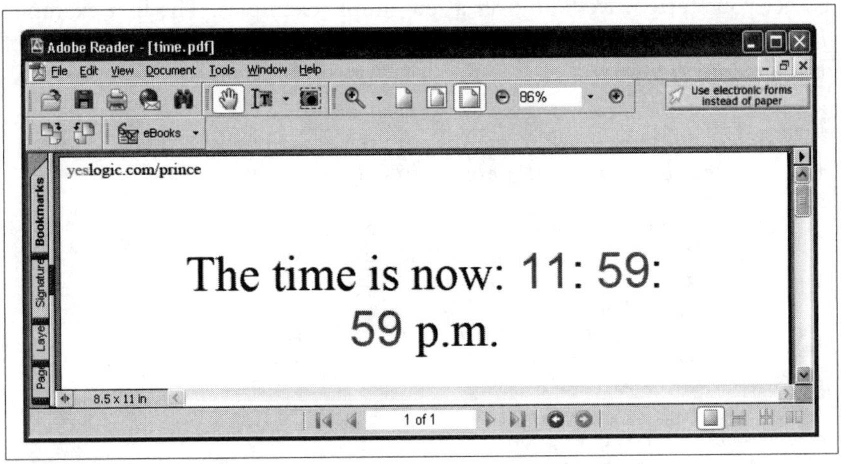

Figure 3-25. time.pdf in Adobe Reader 6

Process XML Documents with XSL-FO and FOP

HACK
#48

Use Apache's FOP engine together with XSL-FO to generate PDF output.

Apache's FOP or Formatting Objects Processor (*http://xml.apache.org/fop/*) is an open source Java application that reads an XSL-FO (*http://www.w3. org/TR/xsl/*) tree and renders the result primarily as PDF. However, other formats are possible, including Printer Control Language (PCL), PostScript (PS), Scalable Vector Graphics (SVG), an area tree representation of XML, Java Abstract Windows Toolkit (AWT), FrameMaker's Maker Interchange Format (MIF), and text.

XSL-FO defines *formatting objects* that help describe blocks, paragraphs, pages, tables, and so on. These formatting objects are aided by a large set of *formatting properties* that control fonts, text alignment, spacing, etc., many of which match the properties used in CSS (*http://www.w3.org/Style/CSS/*). XSL-FO's formatting objects and properties provide a framework for creating attractive, printable pages.

XSL-FO is a huge, richly detailed XML vocabulary for formatting documents for presentation. XSL-FO is the common name for the XSL specification produced by the W3C. The spec is nearly 400 pages long. At one time, XSL-FO and XSLT (whose finished spec is less than 100 pages) were part of the same specification, but split into two specs in April 1999. XSLT became a recommendation in November 1999, but XSL-FO did not achieve recommendation status until October 2001.

To get you started, we'll go over a few simple examples. The first example, *time.fo* (Example 3-33), is an XSL-FO document that formats the contents of the elements in *time.xml*.

Example 3-33. time.fo

```
<fo:root xmlns:fo="http://www.w3.org/1999/XSL/Format">
 <fo:layout-master-set>
  <fo:simple-page-master master-reference="Time"
      page-height="11in" page-width="8.5in" margin-top="1in"
      margin-bottom="1in" margin-left="1in"
      margin-right="1in">
   <fo:region-body margin-top=".5in"/>
   <fo:region-before extent="1.5in"/>
   <fo:region-after extent="1.5in"/>
  </fo:simple-page-master>
 </fo:layout-master-set>
 <fo:page-sequence master-name="Time">
  <fo:flow flow-name="xsl-region-body">

  <!-- Heading -->
  <fo:block font-size="24px" font-family="sans-serif"
    line-height="26px" space-after.optimum="20px"
    text-align="center" font-weight="bold"
    color="#0050B2">Time</fo:block>

  <!-- Blocks for hour/minute/second/atomic status -->
  <fo:block font-size="12px" font-family="sans-serif"
    line-height="16px"
```

Example 3-33. time.fo (continued)

```
     space-after.optimum="10px" text-align="start">Hour: 11 </fo:block>
   <fo:block font-size="12px" font-family="sans-serif"
     line-height="16px"
     space-after.optimum="10px" text-align="start">Minute: 59</fo:block>
   <fo:block font-size="12px" font-family="sans-serif"
     line-height="16px"
     space-after.optimum="10px" text-align="start">Second: 59</fo:block>
   <fo:block font-size="12px" font-family="sans-serif"
     line-height="16px"
     space-after.optimum="10px" text-align="start">Meridiem: p. m.</fo:block>
   <fo:block font-size="12px" font-family="sans-serif"
     line-height="16px"
     space-after.optimum="10px" text-align="start">Atomic? true</fo:block>

   </fo:flow>
   </fo:page-sequence>
 </fo:root>
```

XSL-FO Basics

The root element of an XSL-FO document is (surprise) root. The namespace name is http://www.w3.org/1999/XSL/Format, and the conventional prefix is fo. Following root is the layout-master-set element where basic page layout is defined. The simple-page-master element holds a few formatting properties such as page-width and page-height, and some margin settings (you could use page-sequence-master for more complex page layout, in place of simple-page-master). The region-related elements such as region-body are used to lay out underlying regions of a simple page master. The master-reference attribute links with the master-name attribute on the page-sequence element.

The page-sequence element contains a flow element that essentially contains the flow of text that will appear on the page. Following that is a series of block elements, each of which has properties for the text it contains (blocks are used for formatting things like headings, paragraphs, and figure captions). Properties specify formatting such as the font size, font family, text alignment, and so forth.

Generating a PDF

FOP is pretty easy to use. To generate a PDF from this XSL-FO file, download and install FOP from *http://xml.apache.org/fop/download.html*. At the time of this writing, FOP is at Version 20.5. In the main directory, you'll find a *fop.bat* file for Windows or a *fop.sh* file for Unix. You can run FOP using these scripts.

To create a PDF from *time.fo*, enter this command:

```
fop time.fo time-fo.pdf
```

time.fo is the input file and *time-fo.pdf* is the output file. FOP will let you know of its progress with a report like this:

```
[INFO] Using org.apache.xerces.parsers.SAXParser as SAX2 Parser
[INFO] FOP 0.20.5
[INFO] Using org.apache.xerces.parsers.SAXParser as SAX2 Parser
[INFO] building formatting object tree
[INFO] setting up fonts
[INFO] [1]
[INFO] Parsing of document complete, stopping renderer
```

The result of formatting *time.fo* with FOP can be seen in Adobe Reader in Figure 3-26.

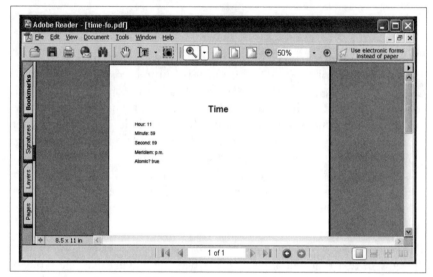

Figure 3-26. time-fo.pdf in Adobe Reader 6

You can also incorporate XSL-FO markup into an XSLT stylesheet, then transform and format a document with just one FOP command. Example 3-34 shows a stylesheet (*time-fo.xsl*) that incorporates XSL-FO.

Example 3-34. time-fo.xsl

```
<xsl:stylesheet version="1.0" xmlns:xsl="http://www.w3.org/1999/XSL/Transform"
xmlns:fo="http://www.w3.org/1999/XSL/Format">
<xsl:output method="xml" encoding="utf-8" indent="yes"/>

<xsl:template match="/">
<fo:root>
```

Example 3-34. time-fo.xsl (continued)

```
<fo:layout-master-set>
 <fo:simple-page-master master-reference="Time"
     page-height="11in" page-width="8.5in" margin-top="1in"
     margin-bottom="1in" margin-left="1in"
     margin-right="1in">
  <fo:region-body margin-top=".5in"/>
  <fo:region-before extent="1.5in"/>
  <fo:region-after extent="1.5in"/>
 </fo:simple-page-master>
</fo:layout-master-set>
<fo:page-sequence master-name="Time">
 <fo:flow flow-name="xsl-region-body">
  <xsl:apply-templates select="time"/>
 </fo:flow>
</fo:page-sequence>
</fo:root>
</xsl:template>

<xsl:template match="time">
 <!-- Heading -->
 <fo:block font-size="24px" font-family="sans-serif"
     line-height="26px" space-after.optimum="20px"
     text-align="center" font-weight="bold" color="#0050B2">
     Time
 </fo:block>

 <!-- Blocks for hour/minute/second/atomic status -->
 <fo:block font-size="12px" font-family="sans-serif"
     line-height="16px"
     space-after.optimum="10px" text-align="start">
     Hour: <xsl:value-of select="hour"/>
 </fo:block>
 <fo:block font-size="12px" font-family="sans-serif"
     line-height="16px"
     space-after.optimum="10px" text-align="start">
     Minute: <xsl:value-of select="minute"/>
 </fo:block>
 <fo:block font-size="12px" font-family="sans-serif"
     line-height="16px"
     space-after.optimum="10px" text-align="start">
     Second: <xsl:value-of select="second"/>
 </fo:block>
 <fo:block font-size="12px" font-family="sans-serif"
     line-height="16px"
     space-after.optimum="10px" text-align="start">
     Meridiem: <xsl:value-of select="meridiem"/>
 </fo:block>
 <fo:block font-size="12px" font-family="sans-serif"
     line-height="16px"
     space-after.optimum="10px" text-align="start">
     Atomic? <xsl:value-of select="atomic/@signal"/>
```

Example 3-34. time-fo.xsl (continued)

```
  </fo:block>
</xsl:template>

</xsl:stylesheet>
```

The same XSL-FO markup that you saw in *time.fo* is interspersed with templates and instructions that transform *time.xml*. Now, with this command, you can generate a PDF like the one that you generated with *time.fo*:

```
fop -xsl time-fo.xsl -xml time.xml -pdf time-fo.pdf
```

See Also

- *XSL-FO*, by Dave Pawson (O'Reilly)

HACK #49 Process HTML with XSLT Using TagSoup

Use TSaxon, a variant of Saxon, and TagSoup to help transform HTML.

Stylesheets written in XSLT are the standard method of taking XML documents in one format and transforming them into HTML, XML documents in a different format, XHTML, or plain-text documents.

There are many XSLT processors. Michael Kay's Saxon Version 6.5.3 (*http://saxon.sourceforge.net/#F6.5.3*) is a particularly mature and successful implementation for XSLT 1.0 and XPath 1.0. It is packaged as a Java JAR file called *saxon.jar*. You can download this JAR with the 6.5.3 distribution from the Saxon site on Sourceforge.

Now suppose, for example, that we want to extract just the header elements (h1, h2, h3, etc.) from an XHTML document and display them as progressively indented plain text (i.e., each h1 element is unindented, each h2 element is indented by a single space, h2 by two spaces, etc.).

The XSLT stylesheet *outline.xsl* does exactly what we want. It specifies an output method of text, and matches the h1 through h6 elements in the XHTML input, taking the content of each one and prepending the correct number of spaces. The textual content of other elements is suppressed.

The following command, executed in your working directory, will process *outline.xsl* and the XHTML document *outline.xhtml* using Saxon and will display the resulting indented plain text:

```
java -jar saxon.jar outline.xhtml outline.xsl
```

It so happens that *outline.html* contains only h1, h2, and h3 elements (borrowed from the XML specification) for the sake of brevity, but if you add other elements to it, you will see that the content of those elements is not displayed by this command.

Using TagSoup and TSaxon

The great bulk of documents on the Web are not well-formed XHTML, but are HTML, so unmodified XSLT processors cannot be applied to them. For example, the HTML document *outline.html* is similar to *outline.xhtml*, but the end tags for the h1, h2, and h3 elements are missing. If you try to apply Saxon to *outline.html*, you will get no output except an error message saying the document is not well-formed.

In this situation, you can use TSaxon instead of Saxon. TSaxon (*http://www. ccil.org/~cowan/XML/tagsoup/tsaxon*) is a variant of Saxon 6.5.3 with an HTML parser called TagSoup packaged in it. It behaves exactly like Saxon unless you give it the -H (HTML) switch, which causes it to substitute the TagSoup parser for the standard XML parser packaged with Saxon.

You can download the latest version of TSaxon from the web site, or just use the version that came in the file archive. TSaxon's version of *saxon.jar* exists in the file archive under the subdirectory *TSaxon*. In the *TSaxon* subdirectory, issuing the following command will process *outline.html* using the TSaxon and the TagSoup parser and the stylesheet:

```
java -jar saxon.jar -H outline.html outline.xsl
```

The reason that TSaxon is also packaged as the file *saxon.jar* is that it is completely backward-compatible and can be used as a drop-in replacement for Saxon. Saxon is stable, but TSaxon is not yet stable, because TagSoup (*http://www.ccil.org/~cowan/XML/tagsoup*) is still under active development. Nevertheless, TSaxon is still quite useful with even very messy HTML: less than one percent of a sample of over a thousand HTML files (downloaded from the Web at random) could not be correctly processed with the current version.

—John Cowan

HACK #50 Build Results with Literal Result and Instruction Elements

Use literal result elements, literal text, and instruction elements in an XSLT stylesheet.

This is a hack for XSLT beginners. If you are adding or changing markup in a result tree with XSLT, this hack will help you do it. You will learn how to use literal result elements (along with literal text) and XSLT instruction elements to build your output with new or additional markup.

Literal Result Elements and Literal Text

A literal result element in XSLT is an XML element written literally in a template. Literal result elements can include attributes and must produce well-formed output. Literal text appears as plain, literal text in templates, for stylesheets that have text output.

The stylesheet *timedate.xsl*, shown in Example 3-35, augments *time.xml* with additional markup using literal result elements.

Example 3-35. timedate.xsl

```
1  <xsl:stylesheet version="1.0" xmlns:xsl="http://www.w3.org/1999/XSL/Transform">
2  <xsl:output method="xml" encoding="ISO-8859-1" indent="yes"/>
3
4  <xsl:template match="/">
5   <instant>
6    <xsl:apply-templates select="time"/>
7    <date>
8     <year>2004</year>
9     <month>-06</month>
10    <day>-30</day>
11   </date>
12  </instant>
13 </xsl:template>
14
15 <xsl:template match="time">
16  <xsl:copy>
17   <xsl:attribute name="timezone">
18    <xsl:value-of select="@timezone"/>
19   </xsl:attribute>
20   <xsl:copy-of select="hour|minute|second|atomic"/>
21  </xsl:copy>
22 </xsl:template>
23
24 </xsl:stylesheet>
```

On line 2, the output is encoded as Latin1 or ISO-8859-1 (*http://en.wikipedia.org/wiki/ISO_8859-1*). The template starting on line 4 uses the literal result element instant (see lines 5 and 12) to wrap a new document element around the output. Lines 7 through 11 add new markup as well—the date element with children year, month, and day.

Apply *timedate.xsl* to *time.xml* with Xalan C++ or another XSLT processor of your choice. I like Xalan C++ (*http://xml.apache.org/xalan-c/*) because it's fast and, among other things, allows fine-grained control over indentation with the -i option (follow -i with the number of spaces you want to indent at each level of depth in the structure):

```
xalan -i 2 time.xml timedate.xsl
```

You will see this output with new markup highlighted in bold (Example 3-36).

Example 3-36. Output of timedate.xsl

```
<?xml version="1.0" encoding="ISO-8859-1"?>
<instant>
  <time timezone="PST">
    <hour>11</hour>
    <minute>59</minute>
    <second>59</second>
    <atomic signal="true"/>
  </time>
  <date>
    <year>2004</year>
    <month>-06</month>
    <day>-30</day>
  </date>
</instant>
```

timetext.xsl in Example 3-37 uses literal text in its template, shown in bold:

Example 3-37. timetext.xsl

```
<xsl:stylesheet version="1.0" xmlns:xsl="http://www.w3.org/1999/XSL/Transform">
<xsl:output method="text"/>

<xsl:template match="time">Time: <xsl:value-of select="hour"/>:<xsl:value-of
select="minute"/>:<xsl:value-of select="second"/><xsl:text> </xsl:text>
<xsl:value-of select="meridiem"/>
</xsl:template>

</xsl:stylesheet>
```

The literal text Time: and the two colons (:) will appear in the output along with the other computed values. Apply the stylesheet:

```
xalan time.xml timetext.xsl
```

Here is the result:

```
Time: 11:59:59 p.m.
```

The text element is an example of an XSLT instruction element. In *timetext. xsl*, the text element inserts a single space in the output. A discussion on instruction elements follows.

Instruction Elements

We'll discuss the XSLT instruction elements shown in Table 3-1 in this section.

Table 3-1. XSLT instruction elements

Instruction element	Description
element	Writes an element node to the result tree
text	Writes a text node to the result tree
attribute	Writes an attribute node to the result tree
attribute-set	Creates a reusable set of sets that may be used with the use-attribute-sets attribute
comment	Writes a comment to the result tree
processing-instruction	Writes a processing instruction to the result tree

The stylesheet *instruct.xsl*, shown in Example 3-38, uses all these instruction elements.

Example 3-38. instruct.xsl

```
1  <xsl:stylesheet version="1.0" xmlns:xsl="http://www.w3.org/1999/XSL/Transform">
2  <xsl:output method="xml" encoding="UTF-8" indent="yes"/>
3  <xsl:attribute-set name="att">
4   <xsl:attribute name="signal">
5    <xsl:value-of select="/time/atomic/@signal"/>
6   </xsl:attribute>
7   <xsl:attribute name="location">Ft. Collins</xsl:attribute>
8  </xsl:attribute-set>
9
10 <xsl:template match="time">
11 <xsl:processing-instruction name="xml-stylesheet"> href="time.xsl" type="text/
xsl" </xsl:processing-instruction>
12
13 <xsl:comment> a time instant </xsl:comment>
14
15 <xsl:element name="{name( )}" namespace="urn:wyeast-net:xslt">
16  <xsl:attribute name="timezone">
17   <xsl:value-of select="@timezone"/>
18  </xsl:attribute>
19  <xsl:element name="hour" xmlns="urn:wyeast-net:xslt">
20   <xsl:value-of select="hour"/>
21  </xsl:element>
22  <xsl:element name="minute" xmlns="urn:wyeast-net:xslt">
23   <xsl:value-of select="minute"/>
24  </xsl:element>
25  <xsl:element name="second" xmlns="urn:wyeast-net:xslt">
26   <xsl:value-of select="second"/>
27  </xsl:element>
28  <xsl:element name="meridiem" xmlns="urn:wyeast-net:xslt">
```

Example 3-38. instruct.xsl (continued)

```
29   <xsl:value-of select="meridiem"/>
30   </xsl:element>
31   <xsl:element name="atomic" xmlns="urn:wyeast-net:xslt" use-attribute-sets="att"/
>
32   </xsl:element>
33   </xsl:template>
34
35   </xsl:stylesheet>
```

Early on, this stylesheet generates an XML stylesheet processing instruction (line 11) and a comment (line 13). The document element for the result tree is generated based on the name of the matched time element ({name( )} in the name attribute is an attribute value template). An attribute, timezone, is created (line 16) with its value derived from time's timezone attribute.

The namespace attribute states that the new time element will be in a default namespace named with a URN (*http://www.ietf.org/rfc/rfc2141.txt*), urn:wyeast-net:xslt. Child elements will also be in this namespace (see lines 19–31). Each of these child elements derives its content from corresponding elements in the source document *time.xml*.

The atomic element uses the attribute set att, defined on lines 3–8. attribute-set is a top-level element, meaning that it must be a child of the stylesheet element. This attribute set has two attributes, signal and location, which will be added to atomic in the result tree.

Apply this stylesheet using this line:

```
xalan -i 1 time.xml instruct.xsl
```

The result will look like Example 3-39.

Example 3-39. Output of result.xsl

```
<?xml version="1.0" encoding="UTF-8"?>
<?xml-stylesheet href="time.xsl" type="text/xsl" ?>

<!-- a time instant -->
<time xmlns="urn:wyeast-net:xslt" timezone="PST">
 <hour>11</hour>
 <minute>59</minute>
 <second>59</second>
 <meridiem>p.m.</meridiem>
 <atomic signal="true" location="Ft. Collins"/>
</time>
```

Write Push and Pull Stylesheets

HACK #51

Understand the difference between push and pull XSLT stylesheets, and when to use which.

If you spend any time with XSLT, you will often hear or read about *push stylesheets* and *pull stylesheets*. This hack explains what push and pull stylesheets are and how to use them.

A pull stylesheet is one that usually has only one template, and it uses XSLT instructions like `value-of` or `for-each` to pull nodes from the source document it is processing. It then arranges the pulled nodes in the order presented in the template. The *timetext.xsl* stylesheet **[Hack #50]** is an example of a pull stylesheet. It has only one template, whose content uses four `value-of` instructions to arrange the nodes in a result tree (Example 3-40).

Example 3-40. timetext.xsl

```
<xsl:stylesheet version="1.0" xmlns:xsl="http://www.w3.org/1999/XSL/Transform">
<xsl:output method="text"/>

<xsl:template match="time">Time: <xsl:value-of select="hour"/>:<xsl:value-of
select="minute"/>:<xsl:value-of select="second"/>
<xsl:text> </xsl:text><xsl:value-of select="meridiem"/>
</xsl:template>

</xsl:stylesheet>
```

A pull stylesheet is appropriate when you are fairly certain of what your source document will look like. It's also a good idea if the structure of the result drives the processing; i.e., if you just want to pick certain information out of the source document and place it in the result.

A push stylesheet takes a different approach. Push stylesheets have any number of templates that contain `apply-templates` instructions. The order of nodes in the output is determined by the order in which they are discovered in the source. *mysqldump.xsl* is an example of a push stylesheet **[Hack #46]**. This stylesheet (shown in Example 3-41) has a template for every element node it may encounter in the source document dumped from a MySQL database using *mysqldump* (for example *horses.xml*).

Example 3-41. mysqldump.xsl

```
<xsl:stylesheet version="1.0" xmlns:xsl="http://www.w3.org/1999/XSL/Transform">
<xsl:output method="xml" encoding="UTF-8"/>

<xsl:template match="mysqldump">
 <xsl:apply-templates select="database"/>
</xsl:template>
```

Example 3-41. mysqldump.xsl (continued)

```
<xsl:template match="database">
 <xsl:element name="{@name}">
  <xsl:apply-templates select="table"/>
 </xsl:element>
</xsl:template>

<xsl:template match="table">
  <xsl:apply-templates select="row"/>
</xsl:template>

<xsl:template match="row">
 <xsl:element name="{../@name}">
  <xsl:apply-templates select="field"/>
 </xsl:element>
</xsl:template>

<xsl:template match="field">
 <xsl:element name="{@name}">
  <xsl:value-of select="."/>
 </xsl:element>
</xsl:template>

</xsl:stylesheet>
```

A stylesheet may have a template for nodes that it does not encounter in a source document with little consequence—that is, nothing happens and the XSLT processor just keeps rolling along. Push stylesheets may be most appropriate when you are not exactly sure if all the anticipated elements will be in your source document.

HACK #52 Perform Math with XSLT

XPath 1.0 offers a number of math operations that can be performed within expressions.

With the help of XPath, XSLT can perform a number of math operations within expressions. Expressions can occur within the value of a select attribute. You can perform addition, subtraction, multiplication, division, and modulo operations. There are also a number of XPath functions that perform math, such as count( ), ceiling( ), floor( ), number( ), round( ), and sum( ).

Consider the following XML representation of a spreadsheet, *worksheet.xml*, with numbers arranged in columns and rows (Example 3-42).

Example 3-42. worksheet.xml

```xml
<?xml version="1.0" encoding="UTF-8"?>

<worksheet>
 <column>
  <row>12</row>
  <row>199</row>
  <row>72</row>
  <row>29</row>
 </column>
 <column>
  <row>5</row>
  <row>783</row>
  <row>43</row>
  <row>1432</row>
 </column>
 <column>
  <row>2</row>
  <row>429</row>
  <row>598</row>
  <row>56</row>
 </column>
</worksheet>
```

Using simple addition, the stylesheet *sums.xsl* (Example 3-43) sums the values in *worksheet.xml* first by rows, then by columns.

Example 3-43. sums.xsl

```xml
<xsl:stylesheet version="1.0" xmlns:xsl="http://www.w3.org/1999/XSL/Transform">
<xsl:output method="xml" encoding="UTF-8" indent="yes"/>

<xsl:template match="worksheet">
<sums>
 <sum>
  <row1>
<xsl:value-of select="column[1]/row[1] + column[2]/row[1] + column[3]/row[1]"/>
  </row1>
  <row2>
<xsl:value-of select="column[1]/row[2] + column[2]/row[2] + column[3]/row[2]"/>
  </row2>
  <row3>
<xsl:value-of select="column[1]/row[3] + column[2]/row[3] + column[3]/row[3]"/>
  </row3>
  <row4>
<xsl:value-of select="column[1]/row[4] + column[2]/row[4] + column[3]/row[4]"/>
  </row4>
 </sum>
 <sum>
 <column1>
<xsl:value-of select="column[1]/row[1] + column[1]/row[2] + column[1]/row[3] +
column[1]/row[4]"/>
```

Example 3-43. sums.xsl (continued)

```
</column1>
<column2>
<xsl:value-of select="column[2]/row[1] + column[2]/row[2] + column[2]/row[3] +
column[2]/row[4]"/>
</column2>
<column3>
<xsl:value-of select="column[3]/row[1] + column[3]/row[2] + column[3]/row[3] +
column[3]/row[4]"/>
</column3>
</sum>
</sums>
</xsl:template>

</xsl:stylesheet>
```

Apply this stylesheet to *worksheet.xml*, directing the output to a file:

```
xalan -i 1 -o sum.xml worksheet.xml sums.xsl
```

sum.xml will look just like this:

```
<?xml version="1.0" encoding="UTF-8"?>
<sums>
 <sum>
  <row1>19</row1>
  <row2>1411</row2>
  <row3>713</row3>
  <row4>1517</row4>
 </sum>
 <sum>
  <column1>312</column1>
  <column2>2263</column2>
  <column3>1085</column3>
 </sum>
</sums>
```

Now take another step by applying this little stylesheet, *sum.xsl*, to the output of the previous stylesheet. It uses the sum( ) function to check the sums of the rows and columns (Example 3-44).

Example 3-44. sum.xsl

```
<xsl:stylesheet version="1.0" xmlns:xsl="http://www.w3.org/1999/XSL/Transform">
<xsl:output method="text"/>

<xsl:template match="sums">
<xsl:value-of select="sum(sum[1]/*)"/> rows total
<xsl:value-of select="sum(sum[2]/*)"/> columns total
----
<xsl:value-of select="sum(sum/*)"/> rows + columns total
[<xsl:value-of select="sum(sum/*) div 2"/> divide by 2 check]
</xsl:template>
```

Example 3-44. sum.xsl (continued)

```
</xsl:stylesheet>
```

This is the command to transform it:

```
xalan sum.xml sum.xsl
```

Here is the output:

```
3660 rows total
3660 columns total
----
7320 rows + columns total
[3660 divide by 2 check]
```

XSLT 1.0 itself doesn't have much math capability, but if you want to do more, explore XSLT 2.0 or EXSLT's math extensions (*http://www.exslt.org/math/index.html*), described in [Hack #58].

Transform XML Documents with grep and sed

#53

Use *grep* and *sed* to transform XML instead of XSLT.

You can use a pair of good old Unix utilities, *grep* and *sed*, to transform XML. Both of these utilities allow you to search based on regular expressions, a powerful though sometimes complex language for searching sets of strings. This hack will provide some examples of how you can use regular expressions to transform XML documents.

> This hack discusses regular expressions only as far as the examples given, but is not a tutorial on regular expressions.

grep

grep is a Unix utility, but it also runs on other platforms. If you have a Linux distribution, such as Red Hat (*http://www.redhat.com*), or if you have Cygwin on Windows (*http://www.cygwin.com*), *grep* is already available to you at the shell. You can also get the GNU distribution of *grep* from *http://www.gnu.org*, but you'll have to compile the C code to get it to work. This hack uses Version 2.5 of *grep*.

Say, for example, you wanted to grab part of an XML document and create a new one; instead of using XSLT, you could use *grep* and regular expressions in some circumstances. If you are familiar with regular expressions, using *grep* to do such things may come easily to you. Take a look at *time.xml*:

```
<?xml version="1.0" encoding="UTF-8"?>

<!-- a time instant -->
<time timezone="PST">
 <hour>11</hour>
 <minute>59</minute>
 <second>59</second>
 <meridiem>p.m.</meridiem>
 <atomic signal="true"/>
</time>
```

If you just want to extract the XML declaration, the document element, and the hour element, try:

```
grep "<?\|<time\|hour\|<\/time" time.xml
```

The quotes are essential for *grep* to interpret the entire regular expression as one. The regular expression in quotes will find matches in *time.xml* for the following: the XML declaration using <? (which would also find a processing instruction, if present); the time start tag using \|<time (the backslash \ escapes the vertical bar |); the hour element; and the time end tag (<\/time). The vertical bar (|) means alternation. In other words, the regular expression will match <? or <time or hour or </time>.

Extended *grep* (*egrep*) uses extended regular expressions, so an extended regular expression like this is possible (the -E switch is for extended expressions):

```
grep -E "(<\?|<time|hour|</time)" time.xml
```

Or:

```
egrep "(<\?|<time|hour|</time)" time.xml
```

Note the parentheses. Inside them, the vertical bars and the slash don't need to be escaped, but the question mark needs to be escaped because *egrep* interprets it as a repetition operator for zero or one.

If you run any of these commands, here is what you'll get:

```
<?xml version="1.0" encoding="UTF-8"?>
<time timezone="PST">
 <hour>11</hour>
</time>
```

A slight variation is:

```
grep "<?\|time\|hour" time.xml
```

or:

```
grep -E "(<\?|time|hour)" time.xml
```

Either of which produces:

```
<?xml version="1.0" encoding="UTF-8"?>
<!-- a time instant -->
<time timezone="PST">
 <hour>11</hour>
</time>
```

Without < or <\/ in the regular expression, *grep* picks up both time tags, plus the comment that contains the word *time*.

Another approach you can take is to invert the match; that is, to print whatever does not match the regular expression. If you wanted to remove the atomic and meridiem elements from *time.xml*, you could use either the -v switch or the --invert-match switch, which have identical meaning:

```
grep -v "meridiem\|atomic" time.xml
```

or:

```
grep -v -E "meridiem|atomic" time.xml
```

These commands would yield all but the meridiem and atomic elements:

```
<?xml version="1.0" encoding="UTF-8"?>

<!-- a time instant -->
<time timezone="PST">
 <hour>11</hour>
 <minute>59</minute>
 <second>59</second>
</time>
```

Yet another approach you can take is contextual matching. Several *grep* switches allow you to display lines near a match. Take the file *sum.xml*:

```
<?xml version="1.0" encoding="UTF-8"?>
<sums>
 <sum>
  <row1>19</row1>
  <row2>1411</row2>
  <row3>713</row3>
  <row4>1517</row4>
 </sum>
 <sum>
  <column1>312</column1>
  <column2>2263</column2>
  <column3>1085</column3>
 </sum>
</sums>
```

Suppose you wanted to grab the content of the second and last sum element. You can do that with the context switch -C:

```
grep -C 2 2263 sum.xml
```

The -C switch followed by 2 and the expression 2263 means "grab the line that matches 2263 plus two lines above it and two lines below it." The result of this command would be:

```
<sum>
 <column1>312</column1>
 <column2>2263</column2>
 <column3>1085</column3>
</sum>
```

The following example uses the -B (before) and -A (after) switches. Look at *worksheet.xml*:

```
<?xml version="1.0" encoding="UTF-8"?>

<worksheet>
 <column>
  <row>12</row>
  <row>199</row>
  <row>72</row>
  <row>29</row>
 </column>
 <column>
  <row>5</row>
  <row>783</row>
  <row>43</row>
  <row>1432</row>
 </column>
 <column>
  <row>2</row>
  <row>429</row>
  <row>598</row>
  <row>56</row>
 </column>
</worksheet>
```

Suppose you wanted to get only the first column element and its children. You could use this command:

```
grep -B 2 -A 3 199 worksheet.xml > column.xml
```

This means "get two lines before and three lines after 199." This command redirects the output to the file *column.xml*:

```
<column>
 <row>12</row>
 <row>199</row>
 <row>72</row>
 <row>29</row>
</column>
```

This has been just a sampling—a starting point—for the kinds of transformations you can apply to XML documents using *grep*. Now we will try a few tricks with *sed*.

sed

sed is a streaming editor that can apply *ed* commands to a stream of input, which includes a file. *grep* can only match content that already exists in a document, but *sed* can search and replace the content of a document. *sed* can also perform simple transformations using *ed* commands. Like *grep*, *sed* is readily available on Unix, Linus, or Cygwin, or you can download it from *http://www.gnu.org*. This hack uses Version 4.0.8 of *sed*. For example, try this command:

```
sed '2,3d;6,9d' time.xml
```

The editor command says "delete lines 2, 3, and 6 through 9." You'll get this result:

```
<?xml version="1.0" encoding="UTF-8"?>
<time timezone="PST">
 <hour>11</hour>
</time>
```

A simple search and replace script can change the name of an element. For example, the s (search) command in this line:

```
sed -e s/meridiem/am-pm/g time.xml
```

will replace the meridiem element name with am-pm:

```
<?xml version="1.0" encoding="UTF-8"?>

<!-- a time instant -->
<time timezone="PST">
 <hour>11</hour>
 <minute>59</minute>
 <second>59</second>
 <am-pm>p.m.</am-pm>
 <atomic signal="true"/>
</time>
```

You can store all your scripts in a file, such as those stored in *translate.sed*:

```
3d
8d
s/timezone/Zeitzone/g
s/PST/CET/g
s/time/Zeit/g
s/hour/Uhr/g
s/minute/Minute/g
s/second/Sekundant/g
s/atomic/atomar/g
s/signal/Signal/g
s/true/treu/g
```

These scripts will translate into German all the tag names, attribute names, and attribute values in *time.xml*, plus drop the comment. Use the -f switch to use the scripts in the file:

```
sed -f translate.sed time.xml
```

This will produce the following output:

```
<?xml version="1.0" encoding="UTF-8"?>

<Zeit Zeitzone="CET">
 <Uhr>11</Uhr>
 <Minute>59</Minute>
 <Sekundant>59</Sekundant>
 <atomar Signal="treu"/>
</Zeit>
```

The -i command-line option produces in-place changes (i.e., the changes are written to the file that is edited). To start with, the file *neue.xml* is identical to *time.xml*. The following command performs the edits in place:

```
sed -f translate.sed -i.backup neue.xml
```

The suffix *.backup* will be appended to the name of a backup file (*neue.xml.backup*). After the edits, *neue.xml* will look like this:

```
<?xml version="1.0" encoding="UTF-8"?>

<Zeit Zeitzone="CET">
 <Uhr>11</Uhr>
 <Minute>59</Minute>
 <Sekundant>59</Sekundant>
 <atomar Signal="treu"/>
</Zeit>
```

neue.xml.backup contains the original file before editing took place.

See Also

- Regular Expression Library: *http://regexlib.com/*
- *sed & awk* by Dale Dougherty and Arnold Robbins (O'Reilly).
- *Mastering Regular Expressions* by Jeffrey E. F. Friedl (O'Reilly).

HACK #54 Generate SVG with XSLT

With XSLT, you can create and alter SVG documents on the fly.

Scalable Vector Graphics [Hack #66] provides an interoperable framework for creating graphics that, as XML documents, can be easily stored, transported, displayed in a web browser, and integrated into web pages and other applications. Two-dimensional line art, charts, and art of all kinds are possible with SVG. This hack will walk you through a simple business application using SVG and XSLT.

SVG isn't always simple markup, but using XSLT you can use simple markup, separate from SVG, that can be transformed or merged into more complex SVG markup. For example, let's say that your company regularly produces charts that reflect quarterly sales figures. You can keep the sales data in a small XML document and then integrate it into SVG with XSLT.

sales-2004Q2.xml (Example 3-45) is a brief document that expresses sales figures for the Eastern United States as a percentage of a $100,000 USD target.

Example 3-45. sales-2004Q2.xml

```
<?xml version="1.0" encoding="UTF-8"?>

<sales>
 <region>
  <title>Eastern Region Quarterly Sales (Second/'04)</title>
  <key1 area="New York Area">.95</key1>
  <key2 area="Virginia Area">.89</key2>
  <key3 area="Maryland Area">.67</key3>
  <key4 area="Connecticut Area">.65</key4>
  <key5 area="Delaware Area">.45</key5>
 </region>
</sales>
```

With XSLT, you can merge this data with an SVG document that produces a bar graph using the stylesheet *bar.xsl* (Example 3-46).

Example 3-46. bar.xsl

```
1  <xsl:stylesheet version="1.0" xmlns:xsl="http://www.w3.org/1999/XSL/Transform">
2  <xsl:output method="xml" indent="yes"/>
3
4  <xsl:template match="sales">
5  <svg width="650" height="500">
6   <g id="axis" transform="translate(0 500) scale(1 -1)">
7    <line id="axis-y" x1="30" y1="20" x2="30" y2="450"
8     style="fill:none;stroke:rgb(0,0,0);stroke-width:2"/>
9    <line id="axis-x" x1="30" y1="20" x2="460" y2="20"
10    style="fill:none;stroke:rgb(0,0,0);stroke-width:2"/>
11  </g>
12
13   <xsl:apply-templates select="region"/>
14
15 </svg>
16 </xsl:template>
17
```

Example 3-46. bar.xsl (continued)

```
18  <xsl:template match="region">
19  <g id="bars" transform="translate(30 479) scale(1 -430)">
20    <rect x="30" y="0" width="50" height="{key1}"
21     style="fill:rgb(255,0,0);stroke:rgb(0,0,0);stroke-width:0"/>
22    <rect x="100" y="0" width="50" height="{key2}"
23     style="fill:rgb(0,255,0);stroke:rgb(0,0,0);stroke-width:0"/>
24    <rect x="170" y="0" width="50" height="{key3}"
25     style="fill:rgb(255,255,0);stroke:rgb(0,0,0);stroke-width:0"/>
26    <rect x="240" y="0" width="50" height="{key4}"
27     style="fill:rgb(0,255,255);stroke:rgb(0,0,0);stroke-width:0"/>
28    <rect x="310" y="0" width="50" height="{key5}"
29     style="fill:rgb(0,0,255);stroke:rgb(0,0,0);stroke-width:0"/>
30  </g>
31  <g id="scale" transform="translate(29 60)">
32    <text id="scale1" x="0px" y="320px"
33     style="text-anchor:end;fill:rgb(0,0,0);font-size:10;font-family:Arial">$25K
    </text>
34    <text id="scale2" x="0px" y="215px"
35     style="text-anchor:end;fill:rgb(0,0,0);font-size:10;font-family:Arial">$50K
    </text>
36    <text id="scale3" x="0px" y="107.5px"
37     style="text-anchor:end;fill:rgb(0,0,0);font-size:10;font-family:Arial">$75K
    </text>
38    <text id="scale4" x="0px" y="0px"
39     style="text-anchor:end;fill:rgb(0,0,0);font-size:10;font-family:Arial">$100K
    </text>
40  </g>
41  <g id="key">
42    <rect id="key1" x="430" y="80" width="25" height="15"
43     style="fill:rgb(255,0,0);stroke:rgb(0,0,0);stroke-width:1"/>
44    <rect id="key2" x="430" y="100" width="25" height="15"
45     style="fill:rgb(0,255,0);stroke:rgb(0,0,0);stroke-width:1"/>
46    <rect id="key3" x="430" y="120" width="25" height="15"
47     style="fill:rgb(255,255,0);stroke:rgb(0,0,0);stroke-width:1"/>
48    <rect id="key5" x="430" y="140" width="25" height="15"
49     style="fill:rgb(0,255,255);stroke:rgb(0,0,0);stroke-width:1"/>
50    <rect id="key4" x="430" y="160" width="25" height="15"
51     style="fill:rgb(0,0,255);stroke:rgb(0,0,0);stroke-width:1"/>
52  </g>
53    <text id="key1-text" x="465px" y="92px"
54     style="fill:rgb(0,0,0);font-size:18;font-family:Arial">
55     <xsl:value-of select="key1/@area"/>
56    </text>
57    <text id="key2-text" x="465px" y="112px"
58     style="fill:rgb(0,0,0);font-size:18;font-family:Arial">
59     <xsl:value-of select="key2/@area"/>
60    </text>
61    <text id="key3-text" x="465px" y="132px"
62     style="fill:rgb(0,0,0);font-size:18;font-family:Arial">
```

Example 3-46. bar.xsl (continued)

```
63    <xsl:value-of select="key3/@area"/>
64    </text>
65    <text id="key4-text" x="465px" y="152px"
66      style="fill:rgb(0,0,0);font-size:18;font-family:Arial">
67      <xsl:value-of select="key4/@area"/>
68    </text>
69    <text id="key5-text" x="465px" y="172px"
70      style="fill:rgb(0,0,0);font-size:18;font-family:Arial">
71      <xsl:value-of select="key5/@area"/>
72    </text>
73  <g id="title">
74    <text x="325px" y="20px"
75      style="text-anchor:middle;fill:rgb(0,0,0);font-size:24;font-family:Arial">
76      <xsl:value-of select="title"/>
77    </text>
78  </g>
79  </xsl:template>
80
81  </xsl:stylesheet>
```

The template on line 4 matching sales sets up the SVG document, and the template on line 18 matching region fills it out. Lines 20, 22, 24, 26, and 28 use attribute value templates to include the content of the key1, key2, key3, key4, and key5 elements in *sales-2004Q2.xml* to set the height of the bars. The fill property, along with rgb( ), controls the colors used. Play with the triplets in rgb( ) to change colors.

The value-of elements on lines 55, 59, 63, 67, and 71 grab the area attribute values on the key elements, placing this information on the right of the bars. The value-of on line 76 takes the content of the title element of the source and places it over the top of the bars.

Transform *sales-2004Q2.xml* with *bar.xsl*, saving the output to the file *sales-2004Q2.svg*, like this:

```
xalan -o sales-2004Q2.svg sales-2004Q2.svg bar.xsl
```

To see the result, open *sales-2004Q2.svg* in Netscape 7.1 with the Corel SVG plug-in installed (*http://www.corel.com/svgviewer/*), as shown in Figure 3-27.

See Also

- Inspired by Sal Mangano's *XSLT Cookbook* (O'Reilly), pages 324–332.

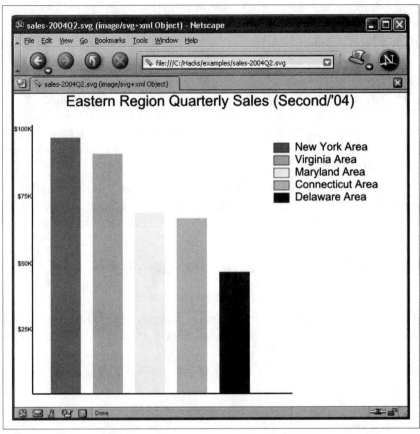

Figure 3-27. sales-2004Q2.svg in Netscape 7.1 with Corel's SVG Viewer

HACK #55 Dither Scatterplots with XSLT and SVG

Use XSLT and SVG to offset points in X-Y scatterplots so they do not plot on top of each other.

If you need to create an X-Y scatterplot from XML data, XSLT and SVG make a winning combination. But sometimes several points have the same X,Y coordinates and fall on top of each other. You can't tell that there is more than one. This is most likely to happen with so-called *categorical* data, in which the categories get translated to integer values, as in this example:

```
Unsatisfied          = 0
Slightly satisfied   = 1
Moderately satisfied = 2
Satisfied            = 3
```

A time-honored way for handling this problem is to *dither* the points by adding small random offsets to their X and Y positions. But XSLT 1.0 does not provide a random function, so how can you get the random values to add to the points?

Dimitre Novatchev has created an elegant method for generating random sequences based on his functional programming templates for XSLT. (See his work at *http://fxsl.sourceforge.net/articles/Random/ Casting%20the%20Dice%20with%20FXSL-htm.htm*.) Dimitre's approach is elegant but complex. There is a simpler way, a real hack in the best sense of the word.

In the XSLT stylesheet that will turn your source data into SVG, insert two random strings of digits, one for the X-axis offset and one for the Y-axis. This fragment of an XSLT stylesheet shows what they might look like:

```
<!--======= Random digits for the X- and Y- axes  ========-->
<xsl:variable name='ditherx'
    select='3702854522015844305808889564635884085342'/>
<xsl:variable name='dithery'
    select='5818255782986735059479247335208010636341'/>
```

You can just copy random strings from the fragment shown here, or you can use most any standard programming language to create the random strings. With Python, you can use this code:

```
import random
result = ''
for n in range(40):
    result = result + str(random.randrange(10))
print result
```

Now you just index into the string to get a random digit.

The source data looks like this in XML (*dither_data.xml*):

```
<data>
  <point x="1" y="1"/>
  <point x="1" y="2"/>
  <point x="1" y="2"/>
  <!-- ... more points ... -->
</data>
```

The stylesheet sets up the SVG definitions, such as the gridlines and the shape of the points. Then it extracts the data, scales it, gets the offsets and adds them, and finally creates the SVG elements to display the points (*dither2svg.xsl* in Example 3-47).

Example 3-47. dither2svg.xsl

```
<?xml version="1.0" encoding='utf-8'?>
<!--============================================================
    dither2svg.xsl
```

Example 3-47. dither2svg.xsl (continued)

```
    Purpose:
        Prevent points of a scatterplot that have the same
        values from falling exactly on top of each other.
    Author: Thomas B Passin
    Creation date: 7 March 2004
============================================================-->


<xsl:stylesheet version="1.0"
    xmlns:xsl="http://www.w3.org/1999/XSL/Transform"
    xmlns="http://www.w3.org/2000/svg"
    xmlns:xlink="http://www.w3.org/1999/xlink">

<!--
    NOTE - indent='yes' is just there to make the
    output more readable.  It is not necessary
    for the functionality.
-->
<xsl:output encoding='utf-8' indent='yes'/>

<!--======= Random digits for the X- and Y- axes  ========-->
<xsl:variable name='ditherx'
    select='37028545220158443058088895646358840085342'/>
<xsl:variable name='dithery'
    select='58182557829867350594792473352080106363341'/>
<!--============================================================-->


<!--============== Root template ==============-->
<xsl:template match='/data'>
<svg xmlns="http://www.w3.org/2000/svg"
    height='500' width='500'
    xmlns:xlink="http://www.w3.org/1999/xlink">

    <!--
        All the SVG setup is done by the svg-defs template.
    -->
    <xsl:call-template name='svg-defs'/>

    <!--
        Our graph should grow upwards from the lower left,
        but SVG coordinates grow downwards from the upper
        left.  So we scale the y-axis by -1 to invert it, and
        shift the whole curve down to the lower left.
    -->
    <g transform='translate(50,450) scale(1,-1)'>
        <use xlink:href='#axis'/>
        <use xlink:href='#gridlines'/>
        <xsl:apply-templates select='point'/>
    </g>
</svg>
</xsl:template>
<!--============================================-->
```

Example 3-47. dither2svg.xsl (continued)

```
<!--=========== Plot each point =================-->
<xsl:template match='point'>

    <!--
        The random digits range from 0 to 9, which is a little
        small for the desired offset, so we scale them by 2.
        A factor of 3 would also work.

        We don't want all the offsets to be in the same
        direction, so we subtract 10 (if we scaled by 3,
        we would subtract 15, and so on).

        We use the position of the point in the source
        document to index into the random strings.  There
        cannot be more points than there are digits in
        the strings! But if there are, a slight modification
        can handle it (see later commentary).
    -->
    <xsl:variable name='offsetx'
        select='2*substring($ditherx,position( ),1) - 10'/>
    <xsl:variable name='offsety'
        select='2*substring($dithery,position( ),1) - 10'/>

    <!--
        Scale the points by 100 to match our SVG drawing
        area, which is 500 by 500.
    -->
    <xsl:variable name='x' select='100*@x'/>
    <xsl:variable name='y' select='100*@y'/>

    <!--
        Here we output the SVG instruction to render
        the point.  Note the use of attribute value templates
        (in the curly braces).
    -->
    <use xlink:href="#dot"
        transform="translate({$x  + $offsetx},{$y + $offsety})"/>
</xsl:template>
<!--===============================================-->


<!--===== SVG definitions for dot shape and grid lines ===-->
<xsl:template name='svg-defs'>
    <defs>
        <circle id="dot" r="4"
        style="stroke:black; stroke-width:1; fill:none"/>

        <g id='axis'>
            <polyline points='-10,0 410,0'
              style='stroke:black;stroke-width:1'/>
            <polyline points='0,-10 0,410'
              style='stroke:black;stroke-width:1'/>
```

Example 3-47. dither2svg.xsl (continued)

```
        </g>

        <g id='xgridline'>
            <polyline points='-10,0 410,0'
              style='stroke:gray;stroke-width:0.5'/>
        </g>

        <g id='ygridline'>
            <polyline points='0,-10 0,410'
              style='stroke:gray;stroke-width:0.5'/>
        </g>

        <g id='gridlines'>
            <use xlink:href='#xgridline' x='0' y='100'/>
            <use xlink:href='#xgridline' x='0' y='200'/>
            <use xlink:href='#xgridline' x='0' y='300'/>
            <use xlink:href='#xgridline' x='0' y='400'/>

            <use xlink:href='#ygridline' x='100' y='0'/>
            <use xlink:href='#ygridline' x='200' y='0'/>
            <use xlink:href='#ygridline' x='300' y='0'/>
            <use xlink:href='#ygridline' x='400' y='0'/>
        </g>
    </defs>
</xsl:template>
<!--==========================================================
=-->

</xsl:stylesheet>
```

If there are more points than there are digits in the random strings, we have
to modify the code slightly to avoid indexing past the end of the string. We
do this by using the mod operator. If we use a different mod value for the X
and Y strings, they will not roll over at the same places. The effect is to act as
if the random strings were much longer. Here is the modified part:

```
<xsl:variable name='offsetx' select='2*substring($ditherx,1+ position() mod
39,1) - 10'/>
<xsl:variable name='offsety' select='2*substring($dithery,1+ position() mod
37,1) - 10'/>
```

It is better to use mod values that are relatively prime, as shown here. We
have to add 1 because the mod operation can return 0, but XSLT indexes into
strings starting at 1.

Prepare some source data or use the included file *dither_data.xml*. In the following, we use the Instant Saxon XSLT processor. Assuming that Saxon is
on your path and that both the data and stylesheet are in the current working directory, type the following command:

```
saxon -o dither.svg dither_data.xml dither2svg.xsl
```

The resulting file, *dither.svg*, is shown in Example 3-48, and in Figure 3-28 it
is shown in the Netscape 7.1 browser with the Corel SVG plug-in.

Example 3-48. dither.svg

```
<?xml version="1.0" encoding="iso-8859-1"?>
<svg height="500" width="500" xmlns="http://www.w3.org/2000/svg" xmlns:
xlink="http://www.w3.org/1999/xlink">
<defs>
<circle id="dot" r="4" style="stroke:black; stroke-width:1; fill:none" />
<circle id="filled-dot" r="4" style="stroke:black; stroke-width:1; fill:black" />
<g id="axis">
<polyline points="-10,0 410,0" style="stroke:black;stroke-width:1" />
<polyline points="0,-10 0,410" style="stroke:black;stroke-width:1" />
</g>
<g id="xgridline">
<polyline points="-10,0 410,0" style="stroke:gray;stroke-width:0.005%" />
</g>
<g id="ygridline">
<polyline points="0,-10 0,410" style="stroke:gray;stroke-width:0.005%" />
</g>
<g id="gridlines">
<use xlink:href="#xgridline" x="0" y="100" />
<use xlink:href="#xgridline" x="0" y="200" />
<use xlink:href="#xgridline" x="0" y="300" />
<use xlink:href="#xgridline" x="0" y="400" />
<use xlink:href="#ygridline" x="100" y="0" />
<use xlink:href="#ygridline" x="200" y="0" />
<use xlink:href="#ygridline" x="300" y="0" />
<use xlink:href="#ygridline" x="400" y="0" />
</g>
</defs>
<g transform="translate(50,450) scale(1,-1)">
<use xlink:href="#axis" />
<use xlink:href="#gridlines" />
<use xlink:href="#dot" transform="translate(4,106)" />
<use xlink:href="#dot" transform="translate(90,192)" />
<use xlink:href="#dot" transform="translate(94,206)" />
<use xlink:href="#dot" transform="translate(206,194)" />
<use xlink:href="#dot" transform="translate(300,100)" />
<use xlink:href="#dot" transform="translate(298,300)" />
<use xlink:href="#dot" transform="translate(300,304)" />
<use xlink:href="#dot" transform="translate(294,306)" />
<use xlink:href="#dot" transform="translate(194,294)" />
<use xlink:href="#dot" transform="translate(-10,108)" />
<use xlink:href="#dot" transform="translate(92,206)" />
<use xlink:href="#dot" transform="translate(100,202)" />
<use xlink:href="#dot" transform="translate(206,204)" />
<use xlink:href="#dot" transform="translate(298,96)" />
<use xlink:href="#dot" transform="translate(298,300)" />
<use xlink:href="#dot" transform="translate(290,290)" />
<use xlink:href="#dot" transform="translate(290,290)" />
```

Example 3-48. dither.svg (continued)

```
<use xlink:href="#dot" transform="translate(190,290)" />
</g>
</svg>
```

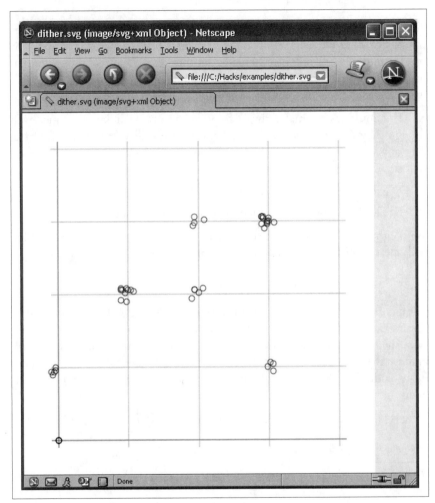

Figure 3-28. dither.svg in Netscape 7.1 with Corel's SVG Viewer

—*Tom Passin*

Use Lookup Tables with XSLT to Translate FIPS
#56 Codes

With XSLT, translate data in a source file by looking up the translation in a
lookup table, using FIPS codes as an example.

While writing XSLT transformations, sometimes you need to convert
phrases or data elements from the source file. For example, you might be
transforming data from one schema to another, and the target schema might
use different enumerated values. The source data might contain event-time,
while the target schema requires eventTime.

XSLT techniques to make these conversions are well known, and even
though they may not exactly be hacks, they are well worth including here.
The approach is to create a lookup table that pairs the input and output
phrases. There are two variations:

1. The lookup table is an external XML file.

2. The lookup table is embedded into the XSLT stylesheet.

With either, the lookup can be done with or without the help of keys, which
will often speed up access. These variations are illustrated in this hack.

The FIPS Code Example

For a concrete example, this hack translates FIPS (Federal Information Processing Standards) numerical codes into city and state names. FIPS codes are
published by the United States government. For example, the state of Indiana has the FIPS code 18, and the city of Bethel Village, which is in Indiana,
has a code of 5050. The hack changes these codes into their natural language names.

Here is part of the source document (*fips_lu_data.xml* in Example 3-49).

Example 3-49. fips_lu_data.xml

```
<places>
    <place>
        <state>17</state>
        <city>14000</city>
    </place>
    <place>
        <state>17</state>
        <city>57381</city>
    </place>
    <!-- ... -->
</places>
```

We use just a few cities and states in order to have a short example. Here is the lookup table (*fips.xml* in Example 3-50).

Example 3-50. fips.xml

```
<fips>
    <state fips="17" name="ILLINOIS">
        <city fips="57381" name="PALOS HEIGHTS"/>
        <city fips="35307" name="HINSDALE"/>
        <city fips="20149" name="DIXMOOR"/>
        <city fips="84090" name="YOUNGSDALE"/>
        <city fips="14000" name="CHICAGO"/>
        <city fips="70629" name="SOUTH CHICAGO HEIGHTS"/>
    </state>
    <state fips="18" name="INDIANA">
        <city fips="1810" name="ANTIOCH"/>
        <city fips="36000" name="INDIANAPOLIS"/>
        <city fips="5050" name="BETHEL VILLAGE"/>
        <city fips="17740" name="DENHAM"/>
    </state>
    <state fips="26" name="MICHIGAN">
        <city fips="74010" name="SIMMONS"/>
        <city fips="22000" name="DETROIT"/>
        <city fips="43180" name="KINCHELOE"/>
        <city fips="73260" name="SHERMAN TWP"/>
    </state>
</fips>
```

The easiest approach is to make the lookup table an external file, and not to use keys. The following stylesheet illustrates this variation (*fips_no_keys.xsl* in Example 3-51).

Example 3-51. fips_no_keys.xsl

```
<?xml version="1.0"?>
<!--=======================================================
        fips_no_keys.xsl
        Purpose:
                Demonstrate using a lookup table located
                in an external document.
        Author: Thomas B Passin
        Creation date: 7 March 2004

        Demonstrates using a lookup table and the use of
        document() to refer to nodes in the table.
=========================================================-->
<xsl:stylesheet version="1.0"
        xmlns:xsl="http://www.w3.org/1999/XSL/Transform">

<!--
```

Example 3-51. fips_no_keys.xsl (continued)

```
               indent='yes' is used just to try to get a more
               readable output.  It has no effect on the
               functionality of the output.
     -->
     <xsl:output encoding='utf-8' indent='yes'/>

     <!--
               It is better to declare these global variables here
               rather than to just use the expressions inline.

          The lookup table is contained in the file "fips.xml".
     -->
     <xsl:variable name='cities'
          select='document("fips.xml")/fips/state/city'/>
     <xsl:variable name='states'
          select='document("fips.xml")/fips/state'/>

     <xsl:template match='places'>
     <places>
               <xsl:apply-templates select='place'/>
     </places>
     </xsl:template>

     <!--
               This template demonstrates two methods to specify
               which part of the lookup table to use.  Note the use
               of current(), which lets us get the context-derived
               value into the lookup table predicate.  Otherwise the
               use of "city" or "state" would be taken to be elements
               in the lookup table, not in the source document.

               The variable is another way to achieve the same
               thing.
     -->
     <xsl:template match='place'>
      <xsl:variable name='city-fips' select='city'/>
      <place>
       <state><xsl:value-of
          select='$states[@fips=current()/state]/@name'/></state>
       <city><xsl:value-of
          select='$cities[@fips=$city-fips]/@name'/></city>
      </place>
     </xsl:template>

     </xsl:stylesheet>
```

Putting the Lookup Table in the Stylesheet

If the lookup table is relatively short, you can put it into the stylesheet itself.
You need to add a namespace to the top-level element of the table, and you

need to add that namespace to the stylesheet element. You refer to nodes within the stylesheet itself using document("") (note the empty string).

So change the stylesheet element to this (*fips_internal_codes.xsl* in Example 3-52).

Example 3-52. fips_internal_codes.xsl

```
<?xml version="1.0" encoding='utf-8'?>
<!--========================================================
    fips_internal_codes.xsl
    Purpose:
        Demonstrate using a lookup table located
        within the stylesheet itself.
    Author: Thomas B Passin
    Creation date: 7 March 2004

    Demonstrates inserting the lookup table using a
    namespace, and the use of document("") to refer
    to nodes in the stylesheet itself.
    =========================================================-->
<!--
    Note the use of exclude-result-prefixes to prevent
    the "lu" namespace from appearing in the output
    document (where it would be harmless but mildly
    annoying).
-->
<xsl:stylesheet version="1.0"
    xmlns:xsl="http://www.w3.org/1999/XSL/Transform"
    xmlns:lu='http://example.com/lookup'
    exclude-result-prefixes='lu'>

<!--
    indent='yes' is used just to try to get a more readable
    output.  It has no effect on the functionality of the
    output.
-->
<xsl:output encoding='utf-8' indent='yes'/>

<!--
    It is better to declare these global variables here rather
    than to just se the expressions inline.
-->
<xsl:variable name='cities' select='document("")/xsl:stylesheet/lu:fips/state/
city'/>
<xsl:variable name='states' select='document("")/xsl:stylesheet/lu:fips/state'/>

<xsl:template match='places'>
<places>
    <xsl:apply-templates select='place'/>
</places>
</xsl:template>
```

Example 3-52. fips_internal_codes.xsl (continued)

```
<!--
    This template demonstrates two methods to specify which
    part of the lookup table to use.  Note the use of
    current( ), which lets us get the context-derived value
    into the lookup table predicate.  Otherwise the use of
    "city" or "state" would be taken to be elements in the
    lookup table, not in the source document.

    The variable is another way to achieve the same
    thing.
-->
<xsl:template match='place'>
    <xsl:variable name='city-fips' select='city'/>
    <place>
        <state><xsl:value-of select='$states[@fips=current( )/state]/@name'/></
state>
        <city><xsl:value-of select='$cities[@fips=$city-fips]/@name'/></city>
    </place>
</xsl:template>

<!--
    The internal lookup table.  The exact namespace used does
    not matter as long as there is one.
-->
<lu:fips>
    <state fips="17" name="ILLINOIS">
        <city fips="57381" name="PALOS HEIGHTS"/>
        <city fips="35307" name="HINSDALE"/>
        <city fips="20149" name="DIXMOOR"/>
        <city fips="84090" name="YOUNGSDALE"/>
        <city fips="14000" name="CHICAGO"/>
        <city fips="70629" name="SOUTH CHICAGO HEIGHTS"/>
    </state>
    <state fips="18" name="INDIANA">
        <city fips="1810" name="ANTIOCH"/>
        <city fips="36000" name="INDIANAPOLIS"/>
        <city fips="5050" name="BETHEL VILLAGE"/>
        <city fips="17740" name="DENHAM"/>
    </state>
    <state fips="26" name="MICHIGAN">
        <city fips="74010" name="SIMMONS"/>
        <city fips="22000" name="DETROIT"/>
        <city fips="43180" name="KINCHELOE"/>
        <city fips="73260" name="SHERMAN TWP"/>
    </state>
</lu:fips>

</xsl:stylesheet>
```

Running the Hack

In the following, we use the Instant Saxon XSLT processor **[Hack #32]**. Assuming that Instant Saxon is on your path, and that both data and stylesheet are in the current working directory, type the following command:

```
saxon -o fips_out.xml fips_lu_data.xml fips_no_keys.xsl
```

Here the input data is in *fips_lu_data.xml*, and the external lookup table *fips. xml* is in the same directory as the stylesheet. If *fips.xml* gets moved elsewhere, you have to adjust the paths on the command line and in the document( ) call in the stylesheet. If you have a large lookup table, you can use *fips_keys.xsl* instead of *fips_no_keys.xsl* to improve performance. To use the internal lookup table, type this command:

```
saxon -o fips_out.xml fips_lu_data.xml fips_internal_codes.xsl
```

All the variations give the same results (Example 3-53).

Example 3-53. fips_out.xml

```
<?xml version="1.0" encoding="utf-8"?>
<places>
   <place>
      <state>ILLINOIS</state>
      <city>CHICAGO</city>
   </place>
   <place>
      <state>ILLINOIS</state>
      <city>PALOS HEIGHTS</city>
   </place>
   <place>
      <state>MICHIGAN</state>
      <city>DETROIT</city>
   </place>
   <place>
      <state>INDIANA</state>
      <city>BETHEL VILLAGE</city>
   </place>
</places>
```

—*Tom Passin*

Grouping in XSLT 1.0 and 2.0

HACK
#57

If your nodes are out of sorts in your source, use grouping to bring them into line.

This hack shows you several techniques for grouping nodes in the output of an XSLT processor. The first uses XSLT 1.0 and the Muenchian method, named after Steve Muench (see *http://www.oreillynet.com/pub/au/609*). The second uses XSLT 2.0, which is simpler than the XSLT 1.0 method.

Grouping with XSLT 1.0

The problem that grouping solves is that nodes may not be grouped to your liking in the source document. For example, look at *group.xml* (Example 3-54).

Example 3-54. group.xml

```
<?xml version="1.0" encoding="US-ASCII"?>
<?xml-stylesheet href="group.xsl" type="text/xsl"?>

<uscities>
 <western>
  <uscity state="Nevada">Las Vegas</uscity>
  <uscity state="Arizona">Phoenix</uscity>
  <uscity state="California">San Francisco</uscity>
  <uscity state="Nevada">Silver City</uscity>
  <uscity state="Washington">Seattle</uscity>
  <uscity state="Montana">Missoula</uscity>
  <uscity state="Washington">Spokane</uscity>
  <uscity state="California">Los Angeles</uscity>
  <uscity state="Utah">Salt Lake City</uscity>
  <uscity state="California">Sacramento</uscity>
  <uscity state="Idaho">Boise</uscity>
  <uscity state="Montana">Butte</uscity>
  <uscity state="Washington">Tacoma</uscity>
  <uscity state="Montana">Helena</uscity>
  <uscity state="Oregon">Portland</uscity>
  <uscity state="Nevada">Reno</uscity>
  <uscity state="Oregon">Salem</uscity>
  <uscity state="Oregon">Eugene</uscity>
  <uscity state="Utah">Provo</uscity>
  <uscity state="Idaho">Twin Falls</uscity>
  <uscity state="Utah">Ogden</uscity>
  <uscity state="Arizona">Flagstaff</uscity>
  <uscity state="Idaho">Idaho Falls</uscity>
  <uscity state="Arizona">Tucson</uscity>
 </western>
</uscities>
```

The uscity nodes in *group.xml* list western United States cities at random, not in an organized way as you might prefer. One feature that can help is that each uscity node has a state attribute. The XSLT grouping technique I'll show you can organize the output according to state, also listing each appropriate city with the given state. This grouping technique is popularly known as the Muenchian method.

The Muenchian method of grouping employs keys together with the generate-id( ) function. There are other grouping methods in XSLT, such as one that uses the preceding-sibling axis, but I've chosen to show you only the Muenchian method here for two reasons. First, it is the most efficient and fastest method of grouping; second, it is the most similar to the new grouping method using the XSLT 2.0 element for-each-group, which you will see in the next section.

The stylesheet *group.xsl* is shown in Example 3-55. It produces HTML output and assembles its output according to the Muenchian method.

Example 3-55. group.xsl

```
1  <xsl:stylesheet version="1.0" xmlns:xsl="http://www.w3.org/1999/XSL/Transform">
2  <xsl:output method="html"/>
3  <xsl:key name="list" match="uscity" use="@state"/>
4
5  <xsl:template match="/">
6  <html>
7  <head>
8  <title>Western State Cities</title></head>
9  <style type="text/css">
10 h2 {font-family:verdana,helvetica,sans-serif;font-size:13pt}
11 li {font-family:verdana,helvetica,sans-serif;font-size:11pt}
12 </style>
13 <body>
14 <xsl:for-each select="/uscities/western/uscity[generate-id(.)=generate-
   id(key('list', @state))]/@state">
15 <xsl:sort/>
16 <h2><xsl:value-of select="."/></h2>
17 <ul>
18  <xsl:for-each select="key('list', .)">
19   <xsl:sort/>
20   <li><xsl:value-of select="."/></li>
21  </xsl:for-each>
22 </ul>
23 </xsl:for-each>
24 </body>
25 </html>
26 </xsl:template>
27
28 </xsl:stylesheet>
```

The secret to understanding the Muenchian method lies in its use of keys and the generate-id( ) function. On line 1 of *group.xsl*, the key named list is defined. This key is used to efficiently find state attributes on uscity elements in *group.xml*.

Without getting too overwrought, the generate-id( ) function is used with the key( ) function in for-each to process the first node in a set (line 14). In this example, it finds the first node whose state attribute identifies a given state, and outputs the name of the state found in the attribute.

Following that, another for-each (line 18) processes each other node in the
document matching the previous for-each, also using key( ). The value-of
(line 20) under this for-each outputs the name of the given city. The sort
elements (lines 15 and 19) under the for-each elements sort the nodes in
alphabetical order.

It's a little complicated, but it works well. Test it with Xalan C++ **[Hack #32]**:

```
xalan -m -i 1 -o group.html group.xml group.xsl
```

You will get nicely grouped HTML output, stored in *group.html*
(Example 3-56).

Example 3-56. group.html

```
<html>
 <head>
  <title>Western State Cities</title>
 </head>
 <style type="text/css">
h2 {font-family:verdana,helvetica,sans-serif;font-size:13pt}
li {font-family:verdana,helvetica,sans-serif;font-size:11pt}
</style>
 <body>
  <h2>Arizona</h2>
  <ul>
   <li>Flagstaff</li>
   <li>Phoenix</li>
   <li>Tucson</li>
  </ul>
  <h2>California</h2>
  <ul>
   <li>Los Angeles</li>
   <li>Sacramento</li>
   <li>San Francisco</li>
  </ul>
  <h2>Idaho</h2>
  <ul>
   <li>Boise</li>
   <li>Idaho Falls</li>
   <li>Twin Falls</li>
  </ul>
  <h2>Montana</h2>
  <ul>
   <li>Butte</li>
   <li>Helena</li>
   <li>Missoula</li>
  </ul>
  <h2>Nevada</h2>
  <ul>
   <li>Las Vegas</li>
   <li>Reno</li>
   <li>Silver City</li>
```

Example 3-56. group.html (continued)

```
   </ul>
   <h2>Oregon</h2>
   <ul>
    <li>Eugene</li>
    <li>Portland</li>
    <li>Salem</li>
   </ul>
   <h2>Utah</h2>
   <ul>
    <li>Ogden</li>
    <li>Provo</li>
    <li>Salt Lake City</li>
   </ul>
   <h2>Washington</h2>
   <ul>
    <li>Seattle</li>
    <li>Spokane</li>
    <li>Tacoma</li>
   </ul>
  </body>
</html>
```

In the output, under each alphabetically listed state comes an alphabetical
list of cities. That's what grouping can do for you. Figure 3-29 shows *group.
html* in the Opera browser. Because they support client-side XSLT, you can
also open *group.xml* in Mozilla, Firefox, Netscape, or IE, which will render
the document according to *group.xsl*. Opera does not support client-side
XSLT.

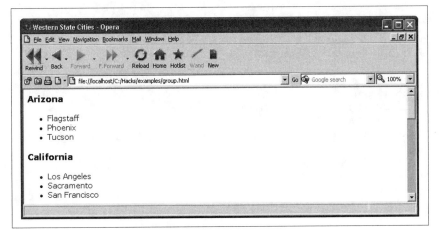

Figure 3-29. group.html in Opera

Grouping with XSLT 2.0

The design behind grouping in XSLT 2.0 probably grew out of experience with grouping in Version 1.0. Grouping in XSLT 1.0 usually brings the for-each instruction element into service. XSLT 2.0 has a new instruction element called for-each-group that makes grouping a relative snap.

Glance at *group2.xml*, which lumps XPath 2.0's context-related functions into two piles by labeling them with a type attribute (Example 3-57).

Example 3-57. group2.xml

```
<?xml version="1.0"?>

<list>
 <description>XPath 2.0 Context Functions</description>
 <date>2003-11-12</date>

 <function type="new">current-date( )</function>
 <function type="new">current-dateTime( )</function>
 <function type="new">current-time( )</function>
 <function type="new">default-collation( )</function>
 <function type="new">implicit-timezone( )</function>
 <function type="legacy">last( )</function>
 <function type="legacy">position( )</function>
</list>
```

The eight functions in this list are either legacy functions or new ones. The *group2.xsl* stylesheet (Example 3-58) groups the functions in *group2.xml* according to the content of the type attribute.

Example 3-58. group2.xsl

```
1   <xsl:stylesheet version="2.0" xmlns:xsl="http://www.w3.org/1999/XSL/Transform">
2   <xsl:output method="xml" indent="yes"/>
3
4   <xsl:template match="list">
5   <xsl:copy>
6    <xsl:for-each-group select="function" group-by="@type">
7     <functions type="{@type}">
8      <xsl:value-of select="current-group( )" separator=", "/>
9     </functions>
10    </xsl:for-each-group>
11   </xsl:copy>
12  </xsl:template>
13
14  </xsl:stylesheet>
```

The for-each-group function (line 6) selects the sequence (node-set in XSLT 1.0) to group with the select attribute; i.e., all function children of list. The group-by attribute determines the key for grouping, which in this case is the content of the type attribute in the source. The functions literal result element uses an attribute value template to reflect the value of the type attribute.

On line 8, the value-of element's select attribute uses the current-group( ) function—also a new kid on the block in XSLT 2.0—to keep track of which group is which. The separator attribute is a new addition to XSLT 2.0, too. It tells the XSLT 2.0 processor to write a comma followed by a space after each found node is sent to the result tree.

> In XSLT 1.0, value-of outputs only the first node of a returned node-set in string form; in XSLT 2.0, all nodes in a sequence can be returned, so you have to plan accordingly.

You might guess that for-each-group has several other attributes, which it does: group-adjacent, group-starting-with, group-ending-with, and collation. I'm not going to cover them here, but you can read more about for-each-group and its attributes in Section 14 of the XSLT 2.0 specification.

To get this example to work, you need the latest version of Saxon (currently 8.0, which supports XSLT 2.0 [*http://saxon.sourceforge.net*]). Use this command to transform *group2.xml*:

```
java -jar saxon8.jar group2.xml group2.xsl
```

The result is two lists of functions, grouped and comma-separated, in functions elements (Example 3-59).

Example 3-59. Output of group2.xsl

```
<?xml version="1.0" encoding="UTF-8"?>
<list>
   <functions type="new">current-date( ), current-dateTime( ), current-time( ),
default-collation( ), implicit-timezone( )</functions>
   <functions type="legacy">last( ), position( )</functions>
</list>
```

This example should give you a feel of how to group nodes in XSLT 2.0.

See Also

- *Learning XSLT*, by Michael Fitzgerald (O'Reilly), pages 206–209 and 286–288

Use EXSLT Extensions

#58

Use EXSLT extension functions to perform a variety of tasks not available in
XSLT 1.0.

Extensibility defines the ways in which a language can be extended. XSLT is
extensible, meaning that if you are a programmer, you can add your own
functionality to a processor in the form of extension elements, attributes,
and functions. The developers of XSLT realized that they couldn't please
everyone with their first shot (who can?), so they made it possible for developers to add features to their XSLT processors independently, and to share
those features with others.

Most processors offer their own internal extensions, such as Xalan and
Saxon. The EXSLT group also provides a number of extensions that can be
supported directly by a processor or by pure XSLT 1.0 processors (*http://
www.exslt.org*). EXSLT organizes its extensions into modules, such as the
math and string modules. You can even submit extensions to EXSLT.

The EXSLT effort attempts to standardize and unify all XSLT 1.0 extensions. Saxon, for example, now implements many, but not all, EXSLT extension functions. It is good practice to use EXSLT extensions when available,
if your processor supports them. It may be easier, however, to simply use a
proprietary extension offered by your processor. XSLT 2.0 and XPath 2.0
offer many more functions than their predecessors, and will likely be the
most successful at unifying previous extensions to XSLT 1.0 and XPath 1.0.

EXSLT currently offers 74 extensions, most of them functions. Many of the
functions offer a pure XSLT 1.0 solution using the `call-template` element
using `with-param` children. Table 3-2 lists a single sample from each of
EXSLT's eight modules.

Table 3-2. Sampling of EXSLT extensions

Extension	Module	Type	Description
`date:date( )`	date and time	function	Returns the current date.
`dyn:evaluate(string)`	dynamic	function	Evaluates an XPath expression.
`exsl:node-set(object)`	common	function	Returns a node-set from a result tree fragment defined in a variable.
`func:function`	functions	element	Declares an extension function.
`math:lowest(node-set)`	math	function	Returns the lowest value from a node-set.

Table 3-2. Sampling of EXSLT extensions (continued)

Extension	Module	Type	Description
regexp: test(string, string, string?)	regular expressions	function	Returns true if the string in the first argument matches the regular expression in the second argument (the third argument is an optional flag).
set: difference(node- set, node-set)	sets	function	Returns a node-set from nodes that exist in one node-set but not another.
str: tokenize(string, string?)	strings	function	Breaks a string into tokens (the second argument is an optional delimiter).

You'll get a chance to use several EXSLT extensions in the following examples.

EXSLT's date:date(), date:time(), and math:lowest() Functions

Here is a simple order for oats from a feed store represented in XML (*order. xml* in Example 3-60).

Example 3-60. order.xml

```
<?xml version="1.0"?>

<order id="TDI-983857">
 <store>Prineville</store>
 <product>feed-grade whole oats</product>
 <package>sack</package>
 <weight std="lbs.">50</weight>
 <quantity>23</quantity>
 <price cur="USD">
  <high>5.99</high>
  <regular>4.99</regular>
  <discount>3.99</discount>
 </price>
 <ship>the back of Tom's pickup</ship>
</order>
```

EXSLT extensions from the math package and the dates and times package are used in the following stylesheet, *order.xsl* (Example 3-61). They augment the information in the order.

Example 3-61. order.xsl

```
1  <xsl:stylesheet version="1.0" xmlns:xsl="http://www.w3.org/1999/XSL/Transform"
2  xmlns:date="http://exslt.org/dates-and-times" xmlns:math="http://exslt.org/math"
3  extension-element-prefixes="date math">>
4  <xsl:output method="xml" indent="yes" encoding="ISO-8859-1"/>
5  <xsl:strip-space elements="*"/>
```

Example 3-61. order.xsl (continued)

```
 6
 7  <xsl:template match="order">
 8   <xsl:copy>
 9    <xsl:attribute name="id"><xsl:value-of select="@id"/></xsl:attribute>
10    <date><xsl:value-of select="date:date()"/></date>
11    <time><xsl:value-of select="date:time()"/></time>
12    <xsl:copy-of select="product|package|weight|quantity"/>
13    <price cur="{price/@cur}"><xsl:value-of select="math:lowest(price/*)"/></price>
14    <total><xsl:value-of select="format-number(math:lowest(price/
   *)*quantity,'#,###.00')"/></total>
15    <xsl:copy-of select="ship"/>
16   </xsl:copy>
17  </xsl:template>
18
19  </xsl:stylesheet>
```

Using the date:date() and date:time() functions from the dates and times module (lines 10 and 11) and the math:lowest() function from the math module (line 14), *order.xsl* transforms and improves upon the information in the original *order.xml*. The date:date() and date:time() functions provide the system date and time to the result tree. The math:lowest() function takes a node-set as an argument. The function then selects the node having the lowest value, in this case 3.99.

The extension-element-prefixes attribute (line 3) prevents the processor from outputting prefixed namespace declarations on element nodes in the output. The format-number() function on line 14 cleans up the number produced by the lowest() function (*http://www.w3.org/TR/xslt#format-number*).

Saxon supports these EXSLT functions, so you can get results by issuing the following commands. You can get both Instant Saxon (*saxon.exe*) and Saxon JAR (*saxon8.jar*) were discussed in an earlier hack (see **[Hack #32]**).

The first example is for Instant Saxon:

```
saxon order.xml order.xsl
```

The second is for using Java directly:

```
java -jar saxon8.jar order.xml order.xsl
```

These commands will produce the following results (Example 3-62).

Example 3-62. Output of order.xsl

```
<?xml version="1.0" encoding="ISO-8859-1"?>
<order id="TDI-983857">
    <date>2004-03-05</date>
    <time>14:43:01-07:00</time>
    <product>feed-grade whole oats</product>
```

Example 3-62. Output of order.xsl (continued)

```
    <package>sack</package>
    <weight std="lbs.">50</weight>
    <quantity>23</quantity>
    <price cur="USD">3.99</price>
    <total>91.77</total>
    <ship>the back of Tom's pickup</ship>
</order>
```

EXSLT's exsl:node-set Function

EXSLT also has a function for converting result tree fragments into node-sets. In XSLT 1.0, a variable can hold a special XSLT type called a *result tree fragment*. Such a fragment can hold plain bits of text or XML nodes, but it isn't treated natively as an XML node-set. Nonetheless, with an extension function, you can cast a result tree fragment as a node-set and manipulate it as such.

EXSLT offers an extension function that treats result tree fragments as an XML node-set. It is called exsl:node-set( ). The *enode-set.xsl* stylesheet is shown in Example 3-63.

Example 3-63. encode-set.xsl

```
1  <xsl:stylesheet version="1.0" xmlns:xsl="http://www.w3.org/1999/XSL/Transform"
2  xmlns:exsl="http://exslt.org/common" extension-element-prefixes="exsl">
3  <xsl:output method="xml" indent="yes"/>
4  <xsl:variable name="frag">
5  <python>
6  <description>Python 2.3 String Escapes</description>
7  <escape purpose="ignore EOL">\</escape>
8  <escape purpose="backslash">\\</escape>
9  <escape purpose="octal value">\ddd</escape>
10  <escape purpose="hexadecimal">\xXX</escape>
11  <escape purpose="other">\other</escape>
12  <escape purpose="single quote">\'</escape>
13  <escape purpose="double quote">\"</escape>
14  </python>
15  </xsl:variable>
16
17  <xsl:template match="python">
18  <xsl:copy>
19   <xsl:copy-of select="exsl:node-set($frag)/python/*"/>
20   <xsl:apply-templates select="escape"/>
21  </xsl:copy>
22  </xsl:template>
23
24  <xsl:template match="escape">
25   <xsl:copy-of select="."/>
26  </xsl:template>
27
28  </xsl:stylesheet>
```

The EXSLT namespace is declared on line 2, and the exsl prefix is noted as an extension element prefix on line 2 as well. A variable named frag is defined on lines 4 through 15. This variable contains a result tree fragment that happens to be an XML node-set. With the node-set( ) function (line 19), the XSLT processor will treat this node-set as a chunk of XML rather than just a fragment of nondescript text.

Here is the document *escapes.xml* (Example 3-64).

Example 3-64. escapes.xml

```
<?xml version="1.0"?>

<python version="2.3">
 <escape purpose="bell">\a</escape>
 <escape purpose="backspace">\b</escape>
 <escape purpose="formfeed">\f</escape>
 <escape purpose="newline">\n</escape>
 <escape purpose="carriage return">\r</escape>
 <escape purpose="horizontal tab">\t</escape>
 <escape purpose="vertical tab">\v</escape>
</python>
```

If you apply this against *escapes.xml* with Saxon, using either:

```
saxon escapes.xml enode-set.xsl
```

or:

```
java -jar saxon8.jar escapes.xml enode-set.xsl
```

you will get the result in Example 3-65.

Example 3-65. Output of encode-set.xsl

```
<?xml version="1.0" encoding="utf-8"?>
<python>
    <description>Python 2.3 String Escapes</description>
    <escape purpose="ignore EOL">\</escape>
    <escape purpose="backslash">\\</escape>
    <escape purpose="octal value">\ddd</escape>
    <escape purpose="hexadecimal">\xXX</escape>
    <escape purpose="other">\other</escape>
    <escape purpose="single quote">\'</escape>
    <escape purpose="double quote">\"</escape>
    <escape purpose="bell">\a</escape>
    <escape purpose="backspace">\b</escape>
    <escape purpose="formfeed">\f</escape>
    <escape purpose="newline">\n</escape>
    <escape purpose="carriage return">\r</escape>
    <escape purpose="horizontal tab">\t</escape>
    <escape purpose="vertical tab">\v</escape>
</python>
```

Saxon supports many but not all EXSLT extensions; however, Saxon's documentation states that it prefers that users work with EXSLT's extensions over Saxon's (see *http://saxon.sourceforge.net/saxon6.5.3/extensions.html* or *http://www.saxonica.com/documentation/documentation.html*).

> Many EXSLT extensions are also implemented as pure XSLT 1.0, meaning that they use imported templates in tandem with call-template to implement the functionality. (Nevertheless, some extensions like node-set( ) cannot be implemented in XSLT 1.0 alone.) The call-template element acts as a function call. These pure implementations, however, are several years old, and I could not get a number of them to work as advertised. Therefore, I won't be exploring them here.

See Also

- *Learning XSLT*, by Michael Fitzgerald (O'Reilly), on pages 254–256 and 262–265.

XML Vocabularies
Hacks 59–67

This collection of hacks discusses some of the most important XML vocabularies and the technologies that support them. First off, we introduce XML namespaces [Hack #59] and RDDL [Hack #60], which helps identify resources associated with a namespace. Next we create an XHTML 1.0 document [Hack #61]. This is followed by a brief exploration of DocBook [Hack #62].

Next, we get a handle on SOAP [Hack #63] and some of its close relatives. Then it's on to a fun application of RDF called FOAF [Hack #64]. We talk about the OpenOffice file format [Hack #65], and end this foray with some experimentation with SVG [Hack #66] and XForms [Hack #67].

Example files discussed in this chapter (and all chapters) are available at *http://www.oreilly.com/catalog/xmlhks/*.

Use XML Namespaces in an XML Vocabulary

#59

Though controversial, XML namespaces are a necessity if you want to manage XML documents in the wild. This hack gets into some of the nitty-gritty of namespaces so you can more easily untangle them.

In January 1999, the W3C published its Namespaces in XML recommendation (*http://www.w3.org/TR/REC-xml-names/*), about a year after the XML recommendation arrived. There were hints of namespaces in the original XML spec, evidenced by suggestions about the use of colons, but that was about it. On the surface, namespaces appear reasonable enough, but their implications have been the subject of confusion and criticism for over five years.

Namespaces were mentioned briefly in [Hack #7]. In this hack, we'll talk about how namespaces work in more detail.

Look at the following document, *namespace.xml*, in Example 4-1.

Example 4-1. namespace.xml

```
<?xml version="1.0" encoding="UTF-8"?>

<!-- a time instant -->
<time timezone="PST" xmlns="http://www.wyeast.net/time">
 <hour>11</hour>
 <minute>59</minute>
 <second>59</second>
 <meridiem>p.m.</meridiem>
 <atomic signal="true"/>
</time>
```

This document isn't very different from *time.xml* except for the special xmlns attribute on the time element. The xmlns attribute and its value http://www.wyeast.net/time are considered a *default namespace declaration*. A default namespace declaration associates a *namespace name*—always a Uniform Resource Identifier or URI (*http://www.ietf.org/rfc/rfc2396.txt*)—with one or more elements. A local name together with its namespace name is called an *expanded name*, and is often given as {http://www.wyeast.net/time}time in descriptive text.

The default declaration in *namespace.xml* associates the namespace name http://www.wyeast.net/time with the element time and its child elements hour, minute, second, meridiem, and atomic. A default namespace declaration applies only to the element where it is declared and any of its child or descendent elements. A default declaration on the document element therefore applies to elements in the entire document. It does not apply to attributes, however. You must use a prefix in order to apply a namespace to an attribute.

Instead of a default declaration, you can also get more specific by using a prefix with a namespace. This is shown in *prefix.xml* (Example 4-2).

Example 4-2. prefix.xml

```
<?xml version="1.0" encoding="UTF-8"?>

<!-- a time instant -->
<tz:time timezone="PST" xmlns:tz="http://www.wyeast.net/time">
 <tz:hour>11</tz:hour>
 <tz:minute>59</tz:minute>
 <tz:second>59</tz:second>
 <tz:meridiem>p.m.</tz:meridiem>
 <tz:atomic tz:signal="true"/>
</tz:time>
```

In this declaration (again on the `time` element), the prefix `tz` is associated with the namespace name or URI. So any element or attribute in the document that is prefixed with `tz` will be associated with the namespace `http://www.wyeast.net/time`.

The `timezone` attribute on `time` does not have a prefix, so it is not associated with the namespace. In fact, the only way you can associate an attribute with a namespace is with a prefix. Default namespace declarations never apply to attributes.

The special namespace prefix `xml` is bound to the namespace URI `http://www.w3.org/XML/1998/namespace`, and is used with attributes such as `xml:lang` and `xml:space`. Because it is built in, it doesn't have to be declared, but you can declare it if you want. However, you are not allowed to bind `xml:` to any other namespace name, and you can't bind any other prefix to `http://www.w3.org/XML/1998/namespace`.

`xmlns` is a special attribute and can be used as a prefix (*http://www.w3.org/TR/REC-xml-names/#ns-decl*). As the result of an erratum in *http://www.w3.org/XML/xml-names-19990114-errata*, the prefix `xmlns:` was bound to the namespace name `http://www.w3.org/2000/xmlns/`. Unlike the prefix `xml:`, `xmlns` cannot be declared, and no other prefix may be bound to `http://www.w3.org/2000/xmlns/`.

The intent of namespaces was to allow different vocabularies to be mixed together in a single document and to avoid the collision of names in environments where the names might run into each other. The unfortunate and confusing part about namespaces is their use of any URI as a namespace name. The scheme or protocol name `http://` suggests that the URI identify a resource that can be retrieved using Hypertext Transfer Protocol (*http://www.ietf.org/rfc/rfc2616.txt*), just like any web resource would be retrieved. But this is not the case. The URI is just considered a name, not a guarantee of the location or existence of a resource. Fortunately, a technique that uses RDDL **[Hack #60]** can help overcome this annoyance. The nice thing about URIs, on the other hand, is that they are allocated locally; that is, you don't have to deal with a global registry to use them. However, the downside of that is you can't really police people who might use a domain name that you own as part of a URI.

A new namespace spec was created for use only with XML 1.1 (*http://www.w3.org/TR/xml-names11*). Notably, this spec allows you to undeclare a previously declared namespace; that is, with `xmlns=""` you can undeclare a default namespace declaration, and with `xmlns:tz=""` you can undeclare a namespace associated with the prefix tz. In Version 1.0 of the namespaces spec, a default namespace may be empty (as in xmlns=""), but you cannot redeclare a namespace as you can in Version 1.1.

See Also

- Section 2.4 of Simon St.Laurent's Common XML spec offers some useful tips on namespaces: *http://www.simonstl.com/articles/cxmlspec.txt*

- Joe English's reasoned "Plea for Sanity" in the use of namespaces: *http://lists.xml.org/archives/xml-dev/200204/msg00170.html*

HACK #60 Create an RDDL Document

RDDL is a XHTML language extension that can help dispel a confusion that surrounds XML namespaces, and let people find out more about your vocabularies.

The Resource Directory Description Language or RDDL (*http://www.rddl.org*) was developed by members of the xml-dev mailing list (*http://www.xml.org/xml/xmldev.shtml*) in late 2000 and early 2001; Jonathan Borden and Tim Bray were the primary developers. It was created as one possible solution to the XML namespace problem, which is basically that an URI that uses a http:// scheme suggests that the URI is pointing at a resource, such as an actual document; however, this is not necessarily the case with XML namespaces, and so it creates confusion.

RDDL provides a partial solution to this problem by providing a special document called a *resource directory* that can hold information about resources that are associated with a target namespace name. If you find XML namespaces a bit annoying, RDDL is a solution that can help. One of the main benefits of RDDL is that it's both human- and machine-readable. It uses XHTML so you can read it in a browser, and it also use XLink, whose special natures and purposes can help an application discover other resources.

RDDL essentially extends the XHTML Basic module (*http://www.w3.org/TR/xhtml-basic/*) with a resource element. This element is allowed to contain mixed content [Hack #1] but chiefly it uses XML and XLink [Hack #28] attributes. Table 4-1 describes the attributes of the resource element, based on a DTD fragment in the RDDL spec (*http://www.rddl.org/#resource*).

Table 4-1. Attributes of the RDDL resource element

RDDL attribute	Required?	Value description
id	optional	A unique identifier for the resource description.
xml:lang	optional	A language token, such as en, de, fr, or es, for the resource description.
xml:base	optional	The base URI for the resource description ("Explore XLink and XML" **[Hack #28]**).
xmlns:rddl	fixed	A namespace declaration for RDDL having a fixed value of http://www.rddl.org.
xlink:type	fixed	The XLink type. Currently a fixed value of simple.
xlink:arcrole	optional	A URI reference that is a machine-readable identifier for the purpose of this resource; for example, *http://www.rddl.org/ purposes/#schema-validation*. For a list of possible purposes, see *http://www.rddl.org/purposes/*.
xlink:role	defaulted	A URI reference that is a machine-readable identifier for the nature of this resource; defaults to http://www.rddl.org/ #resource. For a list of possible natures, see *http://www. rddl.org/natures/*.
xlink:href	optional	A URI reference to the resource related to the target.
xlink:title	optional	A short, human-readable descriptive title for the resource.
xlink:embed	fixed	Not used; value of none.
xlink:actuate	fixed	Not used; value of none.

More and more namespace names or URIs resolve to resource descriptions. For example, XML Schema's namespace URI (*http://www.w3.org/2001/ XMLSchema*) resolves to such a resource description document. The source markup for this document follows in Example 4-3, and it is displayed in Figure 4-1.

Example 4-3. xmlschema-rddl.html

```
<?xml version='1.0'?>
<!DOCTYPE html PUBLIC "-//XML-DEV//DTD XHTML RDDL 1.0//EN" "http://www.w3.org/
2001/rddl/rddl-xhtml.dtd" >
<html xmlns="http://www.w3.org/1999/xhtml" xmlns:xlink="http://www.w3.org/1999/
xlink"
xmlns:rddl="http://www.rddl.org/" xml:lang="en">
<head>
 <title>XML Schema</title>
</head>
<body>
<h1>XML Schema</h1>
<div class="head">
<p>13 February 2001<br/>[Updated 31 March 2004]</p>
</div>
<div id="toc">
```

Example 4-3. xmlschema-rddl.html (continued)

```
<h2>Table of contents</h2>
<ol>
 <li><a href="#intro">Introduction</a></li>
 <li><a href="#related.resources">Resources</a></li>
</ol>
</div>
<div id="intro">
<h2>Introduction</h2>
<p>This document describes the <a href="#xmlschemap1">XML Schema</a>
namespace. It also contains a directory of links to these
related resources, using <a href="http://www.rddl.org/">Resource
Directory Description Language</a>.</p>
</div>
<div id="related.resources">
<h2>Related Resources for XML Schema</h2>
<!-- start resource definitions -->
<h2>Schemas for XML Schema</h2>
<div class="resource" id="DTD">
<rddl:resource xlink:title="DTD for validation" xlink:arcrole="http://www.rddl.
org/purposes#validation" xlink:role="http://www.isi.edu/in-notes/iana/
assignments/media-types/application/xml-dtd" xlink:href="XMLSchema.dtd">
<h3>DTD</h3>
<p>A DTD <a href="XMLSchema.dtd">XMLSchema.dtd</a> for XML
Schema.  It incorporates an auxiliary DTD, <a href="datatypes.dtd">datatypes.
dtd</a>.</p>
</rddl:resource>
</div>
<rddl:resource id="xmlschema" xlink:title="XML Schema schema
document" xlink:role="http://www.w3.org/2001/XMLSchema" xlink:arcrole="http://
www.rddl.org/purposes#schema-validation" xlink:href="XMLSchema.xsd">
<div class="resource">
<h2>XML Schema</h2>
<p>An <a href="XMLSchema.xsd">XML Schema schema document</a>
for XML Schema schema documents. This corresponds to
<a href="http://www.w3.org/TR/2004/PER-xmlschema-1-20040318/
#normative-schemaSchema">the version published in the Proposed
Edited Recommendation</a> revision of XML Schema.</p>
</div>
</rddl:resource>
</div>
<div id="references" class="resource">
<h2>Normative References</h2>
<ol>
<li>
<rddl:resource id="xmlschemap1" xlink:title="W3C CR
XML Schema Part 1" xlink:role="http://www.w3.org/TR/html4" xlink:arcrole="http://
www.rddl.org/purposes#normative-reference" xlink:href="http://www.w3.org/TR/2004/
PER-xmlschema-1-20040318/">
<a href="http://www.w3.org/TR/2004/PER-xmlschema-1-20040318/">XML
Schema Part 1:  Structures</a> (Proposed Edited Recommendation)
</rddl:resource>
```

Example 4-3. xmlschema-rddl.html (continued)

```
</li>
</ol>
</div>
</body>
</html>
```

At the top of the document in Example 4-3, the document type declaration uses an RDDL DTD rather than an XHTML DTD. The bold portions of the XHTML markup show the resource elements prefixed with rddl, the attributes they have, and the mixed content they hold. For example, the first resource element uses the xlink:title, xlink:arcrole, xlink:role, and xlink:href attributes.

The xlink:role attribute, with a value of http://www.isi.edu/in-notes/ iana/assignments/media-types/application/xml-dtd, signifies that the document uses the application/xml-dtd media type (see *http://www.ietf.org/rfc/ rfc3023.txt*). After the start tag, the resource element contains mixed-element and text content that describes the resource in human terms.

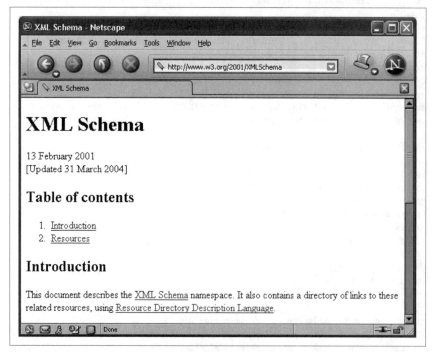

Figure 4-1. Resource description of XML Schema in Netscape

The RDDL spec also provides links for an RDDL DTD, grammars in RELAX (*http://www.xml.gr.jp/relax/*), RELAX NG (*http://www.relaxng.org*), and TREX (*http://www.thaiopensource.com/trex/*), a Schematron schema (*http://xml.ascc.net/resource/schematron/schematron.html*), and numerous other resources, including Java and C# APIs.

You can use the document *xmlschema-rddl.html* as a model for creating your own RDDL document.

See Also

- Leigh Dodds' XML.com introduction to RDDL: *http://xml.com/pub/a/2001/02/28/rddl.html*
- Elliotte Rusty Harold's "RDDL Me This: What Does a Namespace URL Locate?": *http://xml.oreilly.com/news/xmlnut2_0201.html*
- There is a proposal out for RDDL 2.0, released in early 2004, which does not include XLink attributes: *http://www.rddl.org/rddl2*

HACK #61 Create and Validate an XHTML 1.0 Document

W3C has morphed HTML into XHTML, but they still splash around in the same gene pool.

XHTML 1.0, a reformulation of HTML, appeared in 2000 as a W3C recommendation (*http://www.w3.org/TR/xhtml1/*). The simple difference between HTML and XHTML is that the tags in an HTML document are based on an SGML DTD, but the tags in an XHTML document are based on an XML DTD, and, as such, XHTML is an XML vocabulary.

An XHTML document must be well-formed XML, and may be validated against one of three official DTDs: transitional (*http://www.w3.org/TR/xhtml1/DTD/xhtml1-transitional.dtd*), strict (*http://www.w3.org/TR/xhtml1/DTD/xhtml1-strict.dtd*), and frameset (*http://www.w3.org/TR/xhtml1/DTD/xhtml1-frameset.dtd*). The transitional DTD permits some older HTML elements that have been eliminated in the strict DTD. The frameset DTD has elements for creating frames.

Here is an example of a strict XHTML document (Example 4-4).

Example 4-4. time.html

```
<?xml version="1.0" encoding="UTF-8"?>
<!DOCTYPE html PUBLIC "-//W3C//DTD XHTML 1.0 Strict//EN"
    "http://www.w3.org/TR/xhtml1/DTD/xhtml1-strict.dtd">
<html xmlns="http://www.w3.org/1999/xhtml">
<head>
```

Example 4-4. time.html (continued)

```
<title>Time</title>
</head>
<body style="font-family:sans-serif">
<h1>Time</h1>
<table style="font-size:14pt" cellpadding="10">
<tbody align="center">
<tr>
 <th>Timezone</th>
 <th>Hour</th>
 <th>Minute</th>
 <th>Second</th>
 <th>Meridiem</th>
 <th>Atomic</th>
</tr>
<tr>
 <td>PST</td>
 <td>11</td>
 <td>59</td>
 <td>59</td>
 <td>p.m.</td>
 <td>true</td>
</tr>
</tbody>
</table>
</body>
</html>
```

This document looks remarkably similar to an HTML document in text form and in a browser (see Figure 4-2). It begins with an optional XML declaration, followed by a document type declaration for the string XHTML 1.0 DTD. The XHTML 1.0 namespace (http://www.w3.org/1999/xhtml) is declared on the html element. The remaining markup is classic HTML and CSS; however, the elements are all lowercase, as mandated by XHTML 1.0.

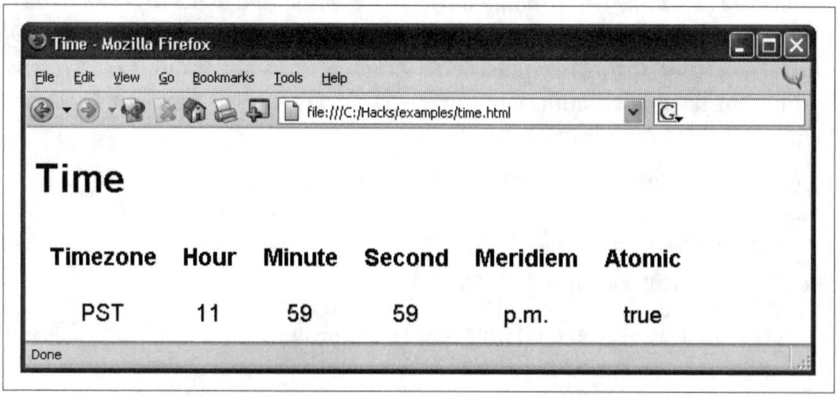

Figure 4-2. time.html in Firefox

You can validate this document using the W3C MarkUp Validation Service at *http://validator.w3.org* (see Figure 4-3). You can submit a document on the Web or upload a local document, as shown. The outcome of successfully validating this document against the strict XHTML DTD is shown in Figure 4-4.

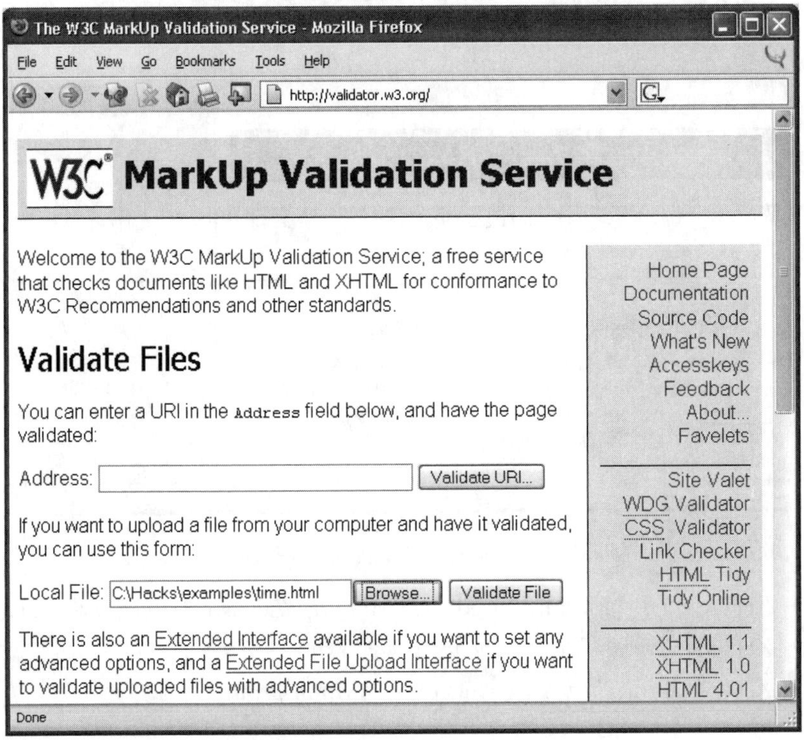

Figure 4-3. W3C MarkUp Validation Service

After XHTML 1.0, XHTML started trending toward modularization. This means that the DTDs were modularized—divided into smaller files—to facilitate use on smaller devices that don't need or want an entire XHTML DTD. Work is now underway at the W3C on XHTML 2.0 (*http://www.w3.org/TR/xhtml2/*), but there are several other XHTML-related specs sandwiched in between 1.0 and 2.0 (*http://www.w3.org/MarkUp/#recommendations*).

See Also

- XHTML Basic: *http://www.w3.org/TR/xhtml-basic*
- Modularization of XHTML: *http://www.w3.org/TR/xhtml-modularization*

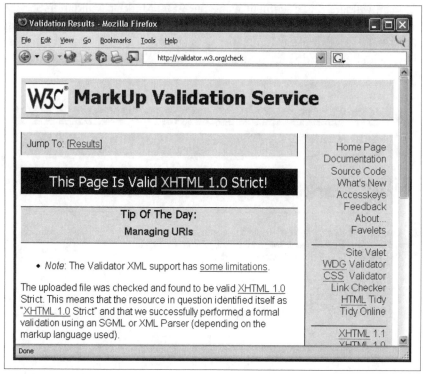

Figure 4-4. Results from the W3C MarkUp Validation Service

- XHTML 1.1—Module-based XHTML: *http://www.w3.org/TR/xhtml11*
- XHTML Events: *http://www.w3.org/TR/xml-events*
- XHTML-Print: *http://www.w3.org/TR/xhtml-print*

HACK #62 Create Books, Technical Manuals, and Papers in XML with DocBook

If you are writing a book, a manual, or a specification, DocBook provides an unsurpassed vocabulary for collecting your thoughts and words in XML form.

DocBook (*http://www.docbook.org/*) is an XML vocabulary or document type that is suited for books, technical manuals, and papers about computer hardware and software. Work on DocBook began in 1991 as a joint project of O'Reilly and HaL Computer Systems (Fujitsu). The effort evolved and was taken over by a group of technical documentation experts called the Davenport Group in 1994. In 1998, DocBook came under the control of a technical committee at OASIS (*http://www.oasis-open.org/committees/tc_home.php?wg_abbrev=docbook*). For more details on the history of DocBook, see *http://www.oasis-open.org/docbook/intro.shtml*.

Initially, DocBook was an SGML document type, but after the emergence of XML, an XML DTD was offered as well. Currently, you can download Doc-Book as an SGML DTD (*http://www.docbook.org/sgml/*), an XML DTD (*http://www.docbook.org/xml/*), a RELAX NG schema (*http://www.docbook. org/rng/*) in either XML or compact syntax, or an XML Schema (*http://www. docbook.org/xsd/*). At this point, the SGML and XML DTDs are the official versions of DocBook, and the RELAX NG and XML Schema forms should become official when DocBook reaches Version 5.

Following is a sampling of the kinds of elements you can use to mark up a document with DocBook:

- Books, manuals, articles, papers
- Tables of contents
- Chapters and sections
- Paragraphs
- Notes, cautions, and warnings
- Tables
- Images, graphics, callouts
- Code
- Author information
- Appendices
- Glossaries
- Indexes

Example 4-5 shows an article marked up with DocBook elements and called *article.xml*. It uses the DocBook 4.3 DTD and is valid with regard to it.

Example 4-5. article.xml

```
1   <?xml version="1.0" encoding="UTF-8"?>
2   <!DOCTYPE article PUBLIC "-//OASIS//DTD DocBook XML V4.2//EN"
3             "http://www.oasis-open.org/docbook/xml/4.2/docbookx.dtd">
4   <article>
5   <title>The Legend of Wy'east</title>
6    <articleinfo>
7     <author>
8      <firstname>Mike</firstname>
9      <surname>Fitzgerald</surname>
10    </author>
11    <authorinitials>mjf</authorinitials>
12    <pubdate>April 2004</pubdate>
13    <revhistory>
14     <revision>
15      <revnumber>1.0</revnumber>
16      <date>2004-04-07</date>
```

Example 4-5. article.xml (continued)

```
17    </revision>
18   </revhistory>
19  </articleinfo>
20  <para>According to local native legend, Wy'east (WHY east) was a
21  chief of the Multnomah peoples who loved a beautiful maiden named
22  Loo-wit. Klickitat, chief of the Klickitat tribe, also loved her.</para>
23  <para>Loo-wit had brought fire back to the Multnomah and Klickitat
24  peoples. The Great Spirit commanded her to light a fire on the
25  stone bridge across what we now call the Columbia River to help
26  restore warmth and light to the tribes who had fallen into a long
27  season of wrongdoing. The stone bridge was supposed to be a symbol
28  of peace between the warring peoples.</para>
29  <para>Time passed and Loo-wit could not decide which of the
30  handsome young chiefs she liked better, Wy'east or Klickitat, so
31  the two chiefs began to quarrel. The Great Spirit became angry at
32  the squabbling chiefs. He dashed the stone arch into the river, and
33  turned Wy'east into Mt. Hood in northwest Oregon and Klicktat into
34  Mt. Adams in southwest Washington. Loo-wit became Washington's Mt.
35  St. Helens. The trio are still said to be angry with one another
36  expressed by volcanic activity.</para>
37  <bibliography>
38   <bibliomixed>
39    <author><firstname>Ella E.</firstname>
40        <surname>Clark</surname></author>
41    <copyright><year>1953</year></copyright>
42    <publisher>
43     <publishername>University of California Press</publishername>
44    </publisher>
45    <title>Indian Legends of the Pacific Northwest</title>
46    <pagenums>20</pagenums>
47   </bibliomixed>
48   <bibliomixed>
49    <author>
50     <firstname>John</firstname>
51     <othername role="middle">Foeste</othername>
52     <surname>Graner</surname>
53    </author>
54    <copyright><year>1975</year></copyright>
55    <title>Mount Hood: A Complete History</title>
56    <pagenums>8</pagenums>
57   </bibliomixed>
58  </bibliography>
59  </article>
```

This document is valid with regard to the DocBook DTD shown in the document type declaration (lines 2 and 3). The document element is article (line 4), and the title is on line 5. Following that is information about the article (articleinfo on line 6), including the title, the author, when it was published, and some revision history (lines 6 through 19). The body of the article is held in para elements (lines 20, 23, and 29). At the end of the section is a bibliography (lines 37 through 58), including information about books that were referenced to write the article. You can look up reference information about any DocBook element online at *http://www.docbook.org/tdg/en/html/part2.html*.

See Also

- DocBook also offers a smaller, proper subset called Simplified Doc-Book: *http://www.docbook.org/specs/wd-docbook-simple-1.1b2.html*
- The DocBook open repository on SourceForge has all kinds of supporting files, such as XSLT stylesheets, test documents, templates for slide presentations, and more: *http://sourceforge.net/projects/docbook/*
- *DocBook: The Definitive Guide*, by Norman Walsh (O'Reilly); also available online at *http://www.docbook.org/tdg/en/html/part2.html*

HACK #63 Create a SOAP 1.2 Document

W3C's SOAP provides a way to package messages or requests in XML envelopes.

SOAP is a W3C framework or protocol for the exchange of information between "peers in a decentralized, distributed environment" (*http://www.w3.org/TR/soap12-part0/#L1153*). SOAP is managed by the W3C's XML Protocol Working Group (*http://www.w3.org/2000/xp/Group/*). Originally, SOAP was an acronym for Simple Object Access Protocol, but that interpretation has been dropped.

The original SOAP attracted a lot of interest early on, but as applications of SOAP rolled out (such as the API for Google, *http://www.google.com/apis/*), many people complained that non-SOAP interfaces were easier to use (*http://www.prescod.net/rest/googleapi/*). Amazon's Web Services developer kit offers SOAP and REST (or *Representational State Transfer*, which is basically XML plus HTTP) interfaces, but the uptake for the REST interface seems to have been greater than for SOAP. Some prefer to avoid SOAP and commercial web services solutions altogether. Nevertheless, SOAP remains an approach at least worth examining.

The main concept behind SOAP is the remote procedure call (RPC), whereby one computer on a network can send a message or command to another computer on the network. The computer that receives the call can hand such an RPC to a local program. Then, if desired, the local program can send a reply—such as a return value—back to the original machine it came from.

Doing Business with XML

SOAP is only one attempt at packaging messages or documents for web consumption. There exists an almost overwhelming number of initiatives attempting to specify vocabularies and other technologies for doing business on the Web. This sidebar is a brief roundup of some of the efforts I hear about regularly.

Web services have taken on the task of reshaping the world, and there are a gaggle of specs being developed in the space—the Web Services Interoperability Organization or WS-I is one space (*http://www.ws-i.org/*) and the Web Services technical committees of OASIS is another (*http://www.oasis-open. org*). Web Services Description Language (WSDL) is a W3C-driven initiative for a vocabulary that describes web services concisely (*http://www.w3.org/ 2002/ws/desc/*).

ebXML is a series of OASIS-sponsored specs that are intended to enable enterprises to conduct business over the Internet (*http://www.ebxml.org*). Universal Description, Discovery and Integration (UDDI) is another OASIS effort to specify a platform to help find and use web services across the Internet (*http://www.uddi.org/*). Universal Business Language (UBL) is yet another OASIS effort aimed at creating a set of common XML vocabularies for orders, invoices, and more (*http://www.oasis-open.org/committees/tc_home.php?wg_ abbrev=ubl*). Extensible Business Reporting Language (XBRL) is an XML-based language that describes financial information for businesses (*http:// www.xbrl.org/*).

SOAP is much more than just an XML vocabulary, though an XML vocabulary is an important part of it. The information in a SOAP envelope can be represented in forms other than XML across the wire. SOAP has a basic data model (*http://www.w3.org/TR/soap12-part2/#datamodel*) that represents structures as "a directed edge-labeled graph of nodes." SOAP also has a set of optional encoding rules that may be used to encode messages that conform to the SOAP data model (*http://www.w3.org/TR/soap12-part2/ #soapenc*). This hack will demonstrate what a SOAP envelope looks like in XML and some of the features that surround it.

Example 4-6 shows *soap.xml*, an XML representation of a SOAP message.

Example 4-6. soap.xml

```
<?xml version="1.0" encoding="UTF-8"?>
<env:Envelope xmlns:env="http://www.w3.org/2003/05/soap-envelope">
 <env:Header>
  <dt:instant xmlns:dt="http://www.wyeast.net/date"
```

Example 4-6. soap.xml (continued)

```
       env:role="http://www.w3.org/2003/05/soap-envelope/role/next"
       env:mustUnderstand="true">
     <dt:date year="2004" month="06" day="30"/>
   </dt:instant>
 </env:Header>
 <env:Body>
   <tz:time timezone="PST" xmlns:tz="http://www.wyeast.net/time" env:
encodingStyle="http://www.w3.org/2003/05/soap-encoding">
     <tz:hour>11</tz:hour>
     <tz:minute>59</tz:minute>
     <tz:second>59</tz:second>
     <tz:meridiem>p.m.</tz:meridiem>
     <tz:atomic signal="true"/>
   </tz:time>
 </env:Body>
</env:Envelope>
```

The document element is Envelope, the container for the SOAP message. The env: prefix is the customary prefix for SOAP envelopes using the namespace http://www.w3.org/2003/05/soap-envelope. The Envelope element has two children, Header and Body. Header is optional, but Body is not. Both of these elements contain XML elements for some other namespace.

SOAP messages are expected to be sent to at least one SOAP receiver, though there may be more. SOAP intermediaries may be included along the path of a SOAP message, and each of those intermediaries is expected to have some role in processing or handling the message.

The role attribute, with the value http://www.w3.org/2003/05/soap-envelope/role/next, indicates that the application receiving the message must look over and perhaps process the message before sending it on to the next destination. The mustUnderstand attribute with a value of true means the header block that contains it must be understood by (i.e., properly handled by) the application receiving the message.

The information contained in the Body element is considered the payload of the message. The encodingStyle attribute with a value of *http://www.w3.org/ 2003/05/soap-encoding* tells the processing application that contents of structure follow SOAP's optional encoding rules.

Finally, SOAP may be transported by a variety of protocols, most prominently HTTP. For example, you can grab SOAP messages with HTTP GET (*http://www.w3.org/TR/soap12-part0/#L26854*) or post a message with HTTP POST (*http://www.w3.org/TR/soap12-part0/#L26854*). Other transportation methods for SOAP include web architectures that identify SOAP messages with URIs (*http://www.w3.org/TR/soap12-part0/#L3677*) and email (*http://www.w3.org/TR/soap12-part0/#L26854*).

See Also

- For a more thorough introduction to SOAP, read the SOAP v1.2 primer (Part 0): *http://www.w3.org/TR/soap12-part0/*
- SOAP v1.2 messaging framework (Part 1), including information on the SOAP processing model and message constructs: *http://www.w3.org/TR/soap12-part1/*
- SOAP v1.2 adjuncts (Part 2), including information on the SOAP data model, encoding, and HTTP binding: *http://www.w3.org/TR/soap12-part2/*

HACK #64   Identify Yourself with FOAF

FOAF provides a framework for creating and publishing personal information in a machine-readable fashion. As you learn FOAF, you will also get acquainted in a practical way with RDF.

The Friend of a Friend or FOAF project (*http://www.foaf-project.org/*) is a community-driven effort to define an RDF vocabulary for expressing metadata about people and their interests, relationships, and activities. Founded by Dan Brickley and Libby Miller, the FOAF project is an open, community-led initiative that is tackling head-on a small and relatively manageable piece of the W3C's wider Semantic Web goal of creating a machine-processable web of data. Achieving this goal quickly requires a network effect that will rapidly yield a mass of data. Network effects mean people. It seems a fairly safe bet that any early Semantic Web successes are going to be riding on the back of people-centric applications. Indeed, everything interesting that we might want to describe on the Semantic Web was arguably created by or involves people in some form or another. And FOAF is all about people.

FOAF facilitates the creation of the Semantic Web equivalent of the archetypal personal homepage: my name is Leigh, this is a picture of me, I'm interested in XML, and here are some links to my friends. And just like the HTML version, FOAF documents can be linked together to form a web of data, with well-defined semantics.

Being a W3C Resource Description Framework (RDF) application (*http://www.w3.org/RDF/*) means that FOAF can claim the usual benefits of being easily harvested and aggregated. And like all RDF vocabularies, it can be easily combined with other vocabularies, allowing the capture of a very rich set of metadata. This hack introduces the basic terms of the FOAF vocabulary, illustrating them with a number of examples. The hack concludes with a brief review of the more interesting FOAF applications and considers some other uses for the data.

The FOAF Vocabulary

Like any well-behaved vocabulary, FOAF publishes both its schema and specification at its namespace URI: *http://xmlns.com/foaf/0.1*. The documentation is thorough and includes definitions of all classes and properties defined in the associated RDF schema. The schema, described using RDF Schema (*http://www.w3.org/TR/rdf-schema/*) and the Web Ontology Language, or OWL (*http://www.w3.org/TR/owl-features/*), is embedded in the specification (near the end), which is written in XHTML 1.0 (*http://www.w3.org/TR/xhtml1/*). However, it can also be accessed directly (*http://xmlns.com/foaf/0.1/index.rdf*).

Rather than cover the whole vocabulary, this hack focuses on two of the most commonly used classes it defines: Person and Image. The remaining definitions cover the description of documents, projects, groups, and organizations; consult the specification for more information. The community also has a lively mailing list (*http://rdfweb.org/mailman/listinfo/rdfweb-dev*), IRC channel (*http://www.ilrt.bris.ac.uk/discovery/chatlogs/foaf/*), and project Wiki (*http://rdfweb.org/topic/*), which serve as invaluable sources of additional information and discussion.

Personal Metadata

The Person class is the core of the FOAF vocabulary. A simple example (Example 4-7) will illustrate its basic usage.

Example 4-7. Person.rdf

```
<rdf:RDF xmlns:rdf="http://www.w3.org/1999/02/22-rdf-syntax-ns#"
         xmlns:foaf="http://xmlns.com/foaf/0.1/">
 <foaf:Person>
   <foaf:name>Peter Parker</foaf:name>
   <foaf:mbox rdf:resource="mailto:peter.parker@dailybugle.com"/>
 </foaf:Person>
</rdf:RDF>
```

In other words, *Person.rdf* says there is a person with the name "Peter Parker" who has an email address of "peter.parker@dailybugle.com".

Publishing data containing plain-text email addresses is just asking for spam; to avoid this, FOAF defines another property, foaf:mbox_sha1sum, whose value is a SHA1 encoded email address complete with the mailto: URI scheme prefix. The FOAF project Wiki has a handy reference page (*http://rdfweb.org/topic/HashPrograms*) pointing to a number of different ways of generating a SHA1 sum. The end result of applying this algorithm is a string unique to a given email address (or mailbox). The next fragment

(Example 4-8) demonstrates the use of this and several other new properties that further describe Peter Parker.

Example 4-8. Augmented Person class

```
<foaf:Person>
  <foaf:name>Peter Parker</foaf:name>
  <foaf:gender>Male</foaf:gender>
  <foaf:title>Mr</foaf:title>
  <foaf:givenname>Peter</foaf:givenname>
  <foaf:family_name>Parker</foaf:family_name>
  <foaf:mbox_sha1sum>cf2f4bd069302febd8d7c26d803f63fa7f20bd82
</foaf:mbox_sha1sum>
  <foaf:homepage rdf:resource="http://www.example.com/spidey"/>
  <foaf:weblog rdf:resource="http://www.example.com/spidey/blog/"/>
</foaf:Person>
```

This is a slightly richer description of Peter Parker, including some granularity in the markup of his name through the use of foaf:title, foaf:givenname, and foaf:family_name. We also now know that Peter Parker is male (foaf:gender) and has both a homepage (foaf:homepage) and a weblog (foaf:weblog).

Identifying Marks

Keen-eyed RDF enthusiasts will already have noticed that neither of these examples assigns a URI to the resource called Peter Parker; that is, there is no rdf:about attribute on the foaf:Person resource, as in:

```
<foaf:Person rdf:about="...uri to identify peter..."/>
```

That's because there is still some debate around both the social and technical implications of assigning URIs to people. Which URI identifies you? Who assigns these URIs? What problems are associated with having multiple URIs (assigned by different people) for the same person? Side-stepping this potential minefield, FOAF borrows the concept of an *inverse functional property* (IFP) from OWL. An inverse functional property is simply a property whose value uniquely identifies a resource.

The FOAF schema defines several inverse functional properties, including foaf:mbox, foaf:mbox_sha1sum, and foaf:homepage; consult the schema documentation for the complete list. An application harvesting FOAF data can, on encountering two resources that have the same values for an inverse functional property, safely merge the description of each and the relations of which they are part. This process, often referred to as *smushing*, must be carried out when aggregating FOAF data to ensure that data about different resources is correctly merged. As an example, consider the following RDF fragment:

```
<foaf:Person>
  <foaf:name>Peter Parker</foaf:name>
  <foaf:mbox_sha1sum>cf2f4bd069302febd8d7c26d803f63fa7f20bd82
</foaf:mbox_sha1sum>
 </foaf:Person>

<foaf:Person>
  <foaf:name>Spider-Man</foaf:name>
  <foaf:mbox_sha1sum>cf2f4bd069302febd8d7c26d803f63fa7f20bd82
</foaf:mbox_sha1sum>
 </foaf:Person>
```

Applying our knowledge that `foaf:mbox:sha1sum` is an inverse functional property, we can merge the descriptions together to discover that these statements actually describe a single person. Spider-Man is unmasked! While perfectly valid, this may not be desirable in all circumstances, and flags the importance of FOAF aggregators recording the source (provenance) of their data. This allows incorrect and potentially malicious data to be identified and isolated.

Before moving on, it's worth noting that while FOAF defines the email address properties (`foaf:mbox_sha1sum` and `foaf:mbox`) as uniquely identifying a person, this is not the same thing as saying that all email addresses are owned by a unique person. What the FOAF schema claims is that any email address used in a `foaf:mbox` (or encoded as a `foaf:mbox_sha1sum`) property uniquely identifies a person. If it doesn't, then it's not a suitable value for that property.

It's Who You Know

Having captured some basic metadata about Peter Parker, it's time to go a step further and begin describing his relationships with others. The `foaf:knows` property is used to assert that there is some relationship between two people. Precisely what this relationship is and whether it's reciprocal (if you know me, do I automatically know you?), is deliberately left undefined.

> For obvious reasons, modeling interpersonal relationships can be a tricky business. The FOAF project has therefore taken the prudent step of simply allowing a relationship to be defined without additional qualification. It is up to other communities (and vocabularies) to further define different types of relationships.

Using `foaf:knows` is simple: one `foaf:Person foaf:knows` another. The following example (*knows.rdf* in Example 4-9) shows two alternative ways of writing this using the RDF/XML syntax. The first uses a cross reference to a person defined in the same document (using the rdf:nodeID attribute), while the second describes the foaf:Person *in situ* within the foaf:knows property. The end result is the same: Peter Parker knows both Aunt May and Harry Osborn.

Example 4-9. knows.rdf

```
<rdf:RDF xmlns:rdf="http://www.w3.org/1999/02/22-rdf-syntax-ns#"
         xmlns:foaf="http://xmlns.com/foaf/0.1/"
         xmlns:rdfs="http://www.w3.org/2000/01/rdf-schema#">

  <foaf:Person rdf:nodeID="harry">
    <foaf:name>Harry Osborn</foaf:name>
    <rdfs:seeAlso rdf:resource="http://www.osborn.com/harry.rdf"/>
  </foaf:Person>

  <foaf:Person>
    <foaf:name>Peter Parker</foaf:name>

    <foaf:knows rdf:nodeID="harry"/>

    <foaf:knows>
        <foaf:Person>
          <foaf:name>Aunt May</foaf:name>
        </foaf:Person>
    </foaf:knows>
  </foaf:Person>

</rdf:RDF>
```

The other thing to notice is that, in addition to the foaf:knows relationship between Peter and Harry, a link has also been introduced to Harry's own FOAF document, using the rdfs:seeAlso property. Defined by the RDF Schema specification, the rdfs:seeAlso property indicates a resource that may contain additional information about its associated resource. In this case, it's being used to point to Harry Osborn's own FOAF description.

It is through the use of the rdfs:seeAlso property that FOAF can be used to build a web of machine-processable metadata; rdfs:seeAlso is to RDF what the anchor element is to HTML. Applications can be written to spider (or *scutter*, using the FOAF community's terminology; see *http://rdfweb.org/topic/Scutter]* these RDF hyperlinks to build a database of FOAF data.

Finer-Grained Relationships

The loose definition of foaf:knows won't fit all applications, particularly those geared to capture information about complex social and business networks. However, this doesn't mean that FOAF is unsuitable for such purposes; indeed, FOAF has the potential to be an open interchange format used by many different social networking applications.

The expectation is that additional vocabularies will be created to refine the general foaf:knows relationship to create something more specific. The correct way to achieve this is to declare new subproperties of foaf:knows. Stepping outside of FOAF for a moment, we can briefly demonstrate one example of this using the relationship schema created by Eric Vitiello and Ian Davis (*http://purl.org/vocab/relationship*).

The relationship schema defines a number of subproperties of foaf:knows, including parentOf, siblingOf, friendOf, and so on, from the namespace http://www.perceive.net/schemas/relationship/. Example 4-10 uses these properties to make some clearer statements about the relationships between Peter Parker and some of his contemporaries (*relationship.rdf*).

Example 4-10. relationship.rdf

```
<rdf:RDF xmlns:rdf="http://www.w3.org/1999/02/22-rdf-syntax-ns#"
         xmlns:foaf="http://xmlns.com/foaf/0.1/"
         xmlns:rel="http://www.perceive.net/schemas/relationship/">

  <foaf:Person rdf:ID="spiderman">
    <foaf:name>Spider-Man</foaf:name>
    <rel:enemyOf rdf:resource="#green-goblin"/>
  </foaf:Person>

  <foaf:Person rdf:ID="green-goblin">
    <foaf:name>Green Goblin</foaf:name>
    <rel:enemyOf rdf:resource="#spiderman"/>
  </foaf:Person>

  <foaf:Person rdf:ID="peter">
    <foaf:name>Peter Parker</foaf:name>
    <rel:friendOf rdf:resource="#harry"/>
  </foaf:Person>

  <foaf:Person rdf:ID="harry">
    <foaf:name>Harry Osborn</foaf:name>
    <rel:friendOf rdf:resource="#peter"/>
    <rel:childOf rdf:resource="#norman"/>
  </foaf:Person>

  <foaf:Person rdf:ID="norman">
    <foaf:name>Norman Osborn</foaf:name>
    <rel:parentOf rdf:resource="#harry"/>
  </foaf:Person>
</rdf:RDF>
```

While it is possible to model quite fine-grained relationships using this method, the most interesting applications will be those that can infer relationships between people based on other metadata. For example, have they collaborated on the same project, worked for the same company, or been pictured together in the same image? This brings us to Image, the other commonly used FOAF class.

Image Is Everything

Digital cameras being all the rage these days, it's not surprising that many people are interested in capturing metadata about their pictures. FOAF provides for this use case in several ways. First, using the foaf:depiction property we can make a statement that says "this person (resource) is shown in this image." FOAF also supports an inverse of this property (foaf:depicts) that allows us to make statements of the form "this image is a picture of this resource." Example 4-11 (*Image.rdf*) illustrates both of these properties.

Example 4-11. Image.rdf

```
<rdf:RDF xmlns:rdf="http://www.w3.org/1999/02/22-rdf-syntax-ns#"
        xmlns:foaf="http://xmlns.com/foaf/0.1/"
        xmlns:dc="http://purl.org/dc/elements/1.1/">

  <foaf:Person rdf:ID="peter">
    <foaf:name>Peter Parker</foaf:name>

    <foaf:depicts
      rdf:resource="http://www.example.com/spidey/photos/peter.jpg"/>

  </foaf:Person>

  <foaf:Person rdf:ID="spiderman">
    <foaf:name>Spider-Man</foaf:name>
  </foaf:Person>

  <foaf:Person rdf:ID="green-goblin">
    <foaf:name>Green Goblin</foaf:name>
  </foaf:Person>

  <!-- codepiction -->
  <foaf:Image rdf:about="http://www.example.com/spidey/photos/
spiderman/statue.jpg">
    <dc:title>Battle on the Statue Of Liberty</dc:title>

    <foaf:depicts rdf:resource="#spiderman"/>
    <foaf:depicts rdf:resource="#green-goblin"/>

    <foaf:maker rdf:resource="#peter"/>
```

Example 4-11. Image.rdf (continued)

```
  </foaf:Image>
</rdf:RDF>
```

This RDF instance says that the image at *http://www.example.com/spidey/ photos/peter.jpg* is a picture of Peter Parker. It also defines a `foaf:Image` resource (i.e., an image that can be found at a specific URI), which depicts both Spider-Man and the Green Goblin. Elements from the Dublin Core Metadata Initiative (*http://dublincore.org/*), such as `dc:title`, are often added to FOAF documents to title images, documents, and so forth.

Notice also that Peter Parker is defined as the author of the image using the `foaf:maker` property, which is used to relate a resource to its creator. The `dc: creator` term from Dublin Core isn't used here due to some issues with its loose definition.

Publishing FOAF Data

Having created an RDF document containing FOAF terms and copied it to the Web, the next step is to link the new information into the existing web of FOAF data. There are a few ways to do this:

- Through `foaf:knows`. Ensuring that people who know you link to your FOAF data via an `rdfs:seeAlso` link will make the data discoverable.

- Through the FOAF Bulletin Board, which is a Wiki page that links to dozens of FOAF files. FOAF harvesters generally include the RDF view of this page as one of their starting locations.

- Through auto-discovery. The FOAF project has defined a means to link to a FOAF document from an HTML page using the link element; several tools now support this mechanism.

Beyond its initial developments, FOAF has potential in many areas. For example, painful web site registrations can become a thing of the past— instead you can just indicate the location of your FOAF description, where a script can grab your personal information. Throw in the relationships, and FOAF can be used as an interchange format between social networking sites, building an open infrastructure that allows end users to retain control over their own data. Also consider e-commerce sites such as Amazon, which have become successful because of their high levels of personalization. Getting the most from these sites involves a learning process in which the sites can discover your interests either through explicit preference setting or adapting product suggestions based on a purchase history. With FOAF, there's the potential to capture this information once, in a form that can be used not by just one site, but many. The user could then move freely between systems.

See Also

- The FOAF application most immediately useful to the owner of a freshly published FOAF description is Morten Frederikson's FOAF Explorer (*http://xml.mfd-consult.dk/foaf/explorer/*), which can generate an HTML view of FOAF data, complete with referenced images and links to other data. For example look at my FOAF description at *http://xml.mfd-consult.dk/foaf/explorer/?foaf=http://www.ldodds.com/ldodds.rdf*.

- FOAF Explorer provides an effective way to browse the network of FOAF data. With the addition of a Javascript bookmarklet (see *http://www.ldodds.com/blog/archives/000026.html*) to perform auto-discovery, it's easy to jump from a blog posting to a description of that person and their interests.

- The most elegant way to browse the relationships in the network of FOAF data is by using Jim Ley's foafnaut (*http://www.foafnaut.org/*), an SVG application that provides a neat visualization of foaf:knows relationships. Here's the foafnaut view starting from my description: *http://blub.foafnaut.org/?sha1=1bca73e5c6916c738d6ec7cc0597ad0e395e7ace*

- plink is a social networking site: *http://www.plink.org/*

- foafbot (*http://usefulinc.com/foaf/foafbot*) and whwhwhwh (*http://swordfish.rdfweb.org/discovery/2003/10/whwhwhwh/*) are IRC bots that provide conversational interfaces onto FOAF data.

- Libby Miller's codepiction experiments demonstrate a novel way to explore FOAF image metadata: *http://swordfish.rdfweb.org/discovery/2001/08/codepict/*

- FOAF-a-matic tool for FOAF generation: *http://www.ldodds.com/foaf/foaf-a-matic*

—*Leigh Dodds*

Unravel the OpenOffice File Format
HACK #65

OpenOffice provides a suite of applications whose native file format consists of a set of XML files, compressed into a ZIP archive. This hack explores the basics of the OpenOffice file format.

OpenOffice (*http://www.openoffice.org*) is a suite of free, multiplatform, open source applications for the desktop, sponsored by Sun Microsystems (*http://wwws.sun.com/software/star/openoffice/*). The suite includes text-editor, spreadsheet, drawing, and presentation applications, each of which uses an XML-based file format. Table 4-2 lists the OpenOffice applications and their file extensions.

Each file is saved as a collection of XML documents and stored in a ZIP archive. (You can also save documents in other formats, such as text, Rich Text Format, or HTML. You can also export a document as PDF.) The specification of the OpenOffice XML file format is being maintained by an OASIS technical committee (*http://www.oasis-open.org/committees/tc_home. php?wg_abbrev=office*).

Table 4-2. OpenOffice applications and file extensions

OpenOffice application	File extension
Calc spreadsheet application	*.sxc
Calc templates	*.stc
Draw graphics application	*.sxd
Draw templates	*.std
Impress presentation application	*.sxi
Impress templates	*.sti
Math application	*.sxm
Master files	*.sxg
Writer text editor application	*.svw
Writer templates	*.stw

In the *OpenOffice* subdirectory of the book's file archive is a small file, *foaf. sxw*, a snippet taken from the FOAF hack **[Hack #64]**. It is shown in OpenOffice's Writer application in Figure 4-5. You can use any ZIP tool to examine or extract the XML files from this ZIP file. I'll use the *unzip* command-line tool that comes with Unix distributions such as Cygwin (*http://www.cygwin. org*).

While in the *OpenOffice* subdirectory, enter this command at a shell prompt:

```
unzip -l foaf.sxw
```

The -l option allows you to inspect the contents of the compressed file without extracting the files from it. This command produces:

```
Archive:  foaf.sxw
  Length    Date   Time   Name
 --------   ----   ----   ----
       30 04-04-04 04:51  mimetype
     4178 04-04-04 04:51  content.xml
     8062 04-04-04 04:51  styles.xml
     1174 04-04-04 04:51  meta.xml
     9180 04-04-04 04:51  settings.xml
      752 04-04-04 04:51  META-INF/manifest.xml
 --------                 -------
    23376                 6 files
```

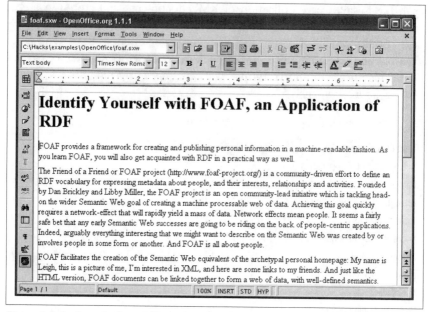

Figure 4-5. foaf.sxw in OpenOffice's Writer application

Extract these files into the *OpenOffice* subdirectory with:

```
unzip foaf.sxw
```

You'll see this:

```
Archive:  foaf.sxw
 extracting: mimetype
  inflating: content.xml
  inflating: styles.xml
 extracting: meta.xml
  inflating: settings.xml
  inflating: META-INF/manifest.xml
```

Briefly, here's what each of these files contains:

mimetype
> Contains the file's media type; e.g., `application/vnd.sun.xml.writer`.

content.xml
> Holds the text content of the file.

meta.xml
> Holds any meta information for the document. You can edit the meta information associated with this document by selecting File → Properties.

settings.xml
> Contains information about the settings of the document.

styles.xml

Stores the styles applied to the document. You can apply styles to the document by selecting Format → Stylist (or by pressing F11).

META-INF/manifest.xml

Contains a list of XML and other files that make up the default OpenOffice representation of the document.

 When you do a File → Save As, you can click the "Save with password" checkbox. If you do this, all the XML files except *meta.xml* are saved as encrypted files.

For illustration, we'll look at one of the files stored in the OpenOffice saved-file archive. Example 4-12 shows the XML markup that's inside *content.xml*. This document is nicely indented because in the Tools → Options Load/Save dialog box under General settings, I've unchecked the Size optimization for XML format (no pretty printing) checkbox. It's checked by default, meaning that normally the XML files are saved without indentation.

Example 4-12. content.xml from foaf.sxw

```
1  <?xml version="1.0" encoding="UTF-8"?>
2  <!DOCTYPE office:document-content PUBLIC
3  "-//OpenOffice.org//DTD OfficeDocument 1.0//EN" "office.dtd">
4  <office:document-content
5   xmlns:office="http://openoffice.org/2000/office"
6   xmlns:style="http://openoffice.org/2000/style"
7   xmlns:text="http://openoffice.org/2000/text"
8   xmlns:table="http://openoffice.org/2000/table"
9   xmlns:draw="http://openoffice.org/2000/drawing"
10  xmlns:fo="http://www.w3.org/1999/XSL/Format"
11  xmlns:xlink="http://www.w3.org/1999/xlink"
12  xmlns:number="http://openoffice.org/2000/datastyle"
13  xmlns:svg="http://www.w3.org/2000/svg"
14  xmlns:chart="http://openoffice.org/2000/chart"
15  xmlns:dr3d="http://openoffice.org/2000/dr3d"
16  xmlns:math="http://www.w3.org/1998/Math/MathML"
17  xmlns:form="http://openoffice.org/2000/form"
18  xmlns:script="http://openoffice.org/2000/script"
19  office:class="text" office:version="1.0">
20  <office:script/>
21  <office:font-decls>
22   <style:font-decl style:name="Tahoma1" fo:font-family="Tahoma"/>
23   <style:font-decl style:name="Lucida Sans Unicode"
24    fo:font-family="&apos;Lucida Sans Unicode&apos;"
25        style:font-pitch="variable"/>
26   <style:font-decl style:name="MS Mincho"
27        fo:font-family="&apos;MS Mincho&apos;"
28     style:font-pitch="variable"/>
```

Example 4-12. content.xml from foaf.sxw (continued)

```
29    <style:font-decl style:name="Tahoma" fo:font-family="Tahoma"
30     style:font-pitch="variable"/>
31    <style:font-decl style:name="Times New Roman"
32     fo:font-family="&apos;Times New Roman&apos;"
33        style:font-family-generic="roman"
34     style:font-pitch="variable"/>
35    <style:font-decl style:name="Arial" fo:font-family="Arial"
36     style:font-family-generic="swiss" style:font-pitch="variable"/>
37   </office:font-decls>
38   <office:automatic-styles>
39    <style:style style:name="P1" style:family="paragraph"
40     style:parent-style-name="Text body">
41     <style:properties fo:text-align="center"
42         style:justify-single-word="false"/>
43    </style:style>
44    <style:style style:name="fr1" style:family="graphics"
45     style:parent-style-name="Graphics">
46     <style:properties style:vertical-pos="top"
47         style:vertical-rel="paragraph"
48     style:horizontal-pos="center" style:horizontal-rel="paragraph"
49     style:mirror="none" fo:clip="rect(0inch 0inch 0inch 0inch)"
50        draw:luminance="0%"
51     draw:contrast="0%" draw:red="0%" draw:green="0%" draw:blue="0%"
52        draw:gamma="1"
53     draw:color-inversion="false" draw:transparency="0%"
54     draw:color-mode="standard"/>
55    </style:style>
56   </office:automatic-styles>
57   <office:body>
58    <text:sequence-decls>
59     <text:sequence-decl text:display-outline-level="0"
60         text:name="Illustration"/>
61     <text:sequence-decl text:display-outline-level="0"
62         text:name="Table"/>
63     <text:sequence-decl text:display-outline-level="0"
64         text:name="Text"/>
65     <text:sequence-decl text:display-outline-level="0"
66         text:name="Drawing"/>
67    </text:sequence-decls>
68   <text:h text:style-name="Heading 1" text:level="1">Identify Yourself with FOAF,
69   an Application of RDF</text:h><text:p text:style-name="Text body">
70   FOAF provides a framework for creating and  publishing personal information
71   in a machine-readable fashion. As you learn FOAF,  you will also
72   get acquainted with RDF in a practical way as well.</text:p>
73   <text:p text:style-name="Text body">The Friend of a Friend or FOAF project
74   (http://www.foaf-project.org/) is a community-driven effort to define an RDF
75   vocabulary for expressing metadata about people, and their interests,
76   relationships and activities. Founded by Dan Brickley and Libby Miller, the FOAF
77   project is an open community-lead initiative which is tackling head-on the wider
78   Semantic Web goal of creating a machine processable web of data. Achieving this
79   goal quickly requires a network-effect that will rapidly yield a mass of data.
```

Example 4-12. content.xml from foaf.sxw (continued)

```
80   Network effects mean people. It seems a fairly safe bet that any early Semantic
81   Web successes are going to be riding on the back of people-centric applications.
82   Indeed, arguably everything interesting that we might want to describe on the
83   Semantic Web was created by or involves people in some form or another. And FOAF
84   is all about people.</text:p><text:p text:style-name="Text body">
85    FOAF facilitates the creation of the Semantic Web equivalent of the
86   archetypal personal homepage: My name is Leigh, this is a picture of me,
87   I'm interested in XML, and here are some links to my friends. And
88   just like the HTML version, FOAF documents can be linked together to form a web
89   of data, with well-defined semantics.</text:p><text:p text:style-name=
90   "Text body"> Being a W3C Resource Description Framework or RDF application
91   (http://www.w3.org/RDF/) means that FOAF can claim the usual benefits of being
92    easily harvested and aggregated. And like all RDF vocabularies, it can be
93   easily combined with other vocabularies, allowing the capture of a very rich set
94   of metadata. This hack introduces the basic terms of the FOAF vocabulary,
95   illustrating them with a number of examples. The hack concludes with a brief
96   review of the more interesting FOAF applications and considers some other uses
97   for the data. The FOAF graphic is shown in Figure A-1.</text:p>
98   <text:p text:style-name="P1">Figure A-1: FOAFlets</text:p>
99   <text:p text:style-name="Text body"/>
100  <text:p text:style-name="Text body">
101  <draw:image draw:style-name="fr1"
102  draw:name="Graphic1" text:anchor-type="paragraph" svg:width="4.2201inch"
103  svg:height="2.4299inch" draw:z-index="0"
104  xlink:href="#Pictures/10000000000001A6000000F34FFA992C.jpg"
105  xlink:type="simple"xlink:show="embed" xlink:actuate="onLoad"/></text:p>
106  </office:body>
107  </office:document-content>
```

The XML documents in OpenOffice use DTDs [Hack #68] that come with the installed package, though XML Schema and RELAX NG schemas will be available in future versions. For example, on Windows, these files are installed by default in *C:\Program Files\OpenOffice.org1.1.1\share\dtd\ officedocument\1_0*. This document uses *office.dtd* (line 3). (These DTDs are not in the book's file archive.) On line 4, the office:document-content element is the document element with the namespace http://openoffice.org/ 2000/office. Many other namespaces are declared, along with some familiar ones, such as for SVG [Hack #66] and XSL-FO [Hack #48].

Various font declarations are stored in style:font-decl elements on lines 21 through 37. Attributes with the fo: prefix properties from XSL-FO. Lines 38 through 56 list styles that are used in the document. Lines 58 to 67 contain markup used for numeric sequencing in the document. A heading appears on line 68, followed by body text in lines 69 through 97. Lines 98 through 106 show how OpenOffice defines a reference to a graphic, including attributes from the SVG and XLink namespaces such as svg:width and xlink:href. The embedded graphic is stored in the *Pictures* subdirectory of *foaf.sxw* as the file *10000000000001A6000000F34FFA992C.jpg* (line 104).

See Also

- For details on the OpenOffice file format, see the OASIS OpenOffice specification: *http://www.oasis-open.org/committees/download.php/6037/office-spec-1.0-cd-1.pdf*
- For documentation and examples of working with OpenOffice XML, see J. David Eisenberg's *OpenOffice.org XML Essentials* (*http://books.evc-cit.info/*)

HACK #66 Render Graphics with SVG

With SVG, you can represent graphics as XML documents and render them in Internet Explorer with Adobe's SVG Viewer, in Netscape with Corel's SVG Viewer, in a branch of Mozilla that supports SVG, and in Batik's Squiggle.

Scalable Vector Graphics or SVG (*http://www.w3.org/Graphics/SVG/*) is an XML vocabulary for describing two-dimensional graphics. Using XML instead of one of a variety of proprietary graphical formats, SVG has enormous potential as a method for storing and transporting graphics. It was developed by the W3C and is currently at Version 1.1 (*http://www.w3.org/TR/SVG11/*).

SVG is popular and the number of implementations is steadily increasing. Adobe provides a popular browser plug-in, SVG Viewer 3.0, which runs on Windows and the Mac. (There is a rumor floating about that it will soon run on Linux.) Mozilla.org has a version of its browser, a branch off the main trunk of code, that supports SVG rendering natively (i.e., without a plug-in). Apache's Batik project offers an SVG browser written in Java.

Following is a simple example of an SVG document that renders some colored text, *text.svg* (Example 4-13):

Example 4-13. text.svg

```
<?xml version="1.0" encoding="UTF-8"?>
<!DOCTYPE svg PUBLIC "-//W3C//DTD SVG 1.1//EN"
        "http://www.w3.org/Graphics/SVG/1.1/DTD/svg11.dtd">

<svg xmlns="http://www.w3.org/2000/svg"
     width="600px" height="300px" font-size="150px">

<rect fill="none" stroke="black" stroke-width="3"
      x="170" y="65" width="235px" height="125px"/>

<text fill="blue" x="290" y="180">G</text>
<text fill="green" x="230" y="180">V</text>
```

Example 4-13. text.svg (continued)

```
<text fill="red" x="170" y="180">S</text>

</svg>
```

Following the XML declaration is a document type declaration for the SVG 1.1 DTD. The document element is svg, and the namespace name is http://www.w3.org/2000/svg. The width and height attributes specify the dimensions of the rendering space; font-size is an SVG property that says that the font used in the document will be 150 pixels (px) high. Though a subset, properties in SVG are intentionally the same as those used by CSS and XSL-FO (*http://www.w3.org/Style/*). For a list of all SVG properties, see *http://www.w3.org/TR/SVG/propidx.html.*

The rect element lays out a rectangle that will be drawn on the rendering canvas. The outline of the 235×125 rectangle will be black and 3 pixels wide. The upper-left corner of the rectangle will begin at the X,Y coordinate 170,65.

Following the rectangle definition are three text elements, each with a different fill color. The x and y attributes specify the text's current position. The text in each element (one character per element) overlaps the character rendered before it. Figure 4-6 shows the SVG document *text.svg* rendered in Mozilla 1.7a, which is available for download from the Mozilla SVG Project page (*http://www.mozilla.org/projects/svg/*).

> The main branch of Mozilla code, at the time of this writing, will not render SVG.

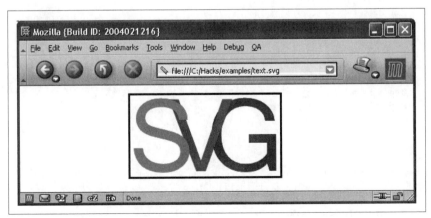

Figure 4-6. text.svg in Mozilla 1.7a

Adobe's SVG Viewer 3.0 is a browser plug-in that works with Internet Explorer 4.0 or higher on Windows (*http://www.adobe.com/svg/*). (It also reportedly works on Netscape Navigator or Communicator Versions 4.5 through 4.78 and RealPlayer 8 or higher, but I haven't tested it on any of those.) After downloading *SVGView.exe*, double-click on it, and it will install files under *WINNT\system32\Adobe\SVG Viewer 3.0* and *\Program Files\Common Files\Adobe\SVG Viewer 3.0\Plugins*. For installation and usage information, read the file *\WINNT\system32\Adobe\SVG Viewer 3.0/ ReadMe.html*.

Once the viewer is installed, you can open SVG files in IE. Mozilla doesn't support color gradients yet, but IE with SVG Viewer does. The file *grad.svg* defines gradients (Example 4-14), and is shown in Microsoft in Figure 4-7.

Example 4-14. grad.svg

```
<?xml version="1.0" encoding="UTF-8"?>
<!DOCTYPE svg PUBLIC "-//W3C//DTD SVG 1.1//EN"
        "http://www.w3.org/Graphics/SVG/1.1/DTD/svg11.dtd">

<svg xmlns="http://www.w3.org/2000/svg"
     width="600px" height="300px" font-size="150px">

<defs>

  <!-- Red gradient -->
  <linearGradient id="redgrad">
   <stop offset="5%" stop-color="white" />
   <stop offset="90%" stop-color="red" />
  </linearGradient>

  <!-- Green gradient -->
  <linearGradient id="greengrad">
   <stop offset="5%" stop-color="white" />
   <stop offset="90%" stop-color="green" />
  </linearGradient>

  <!-- Blue gradient -->
  <linearGradient id="bluegrad">
   <stop offset="5%" stop-color="white" />
   <stop offset="90%" stop-color="blue" />
  </linearGradient>

</defs>

<rect fill="none" stroke="black" stroke-width="3"
     x="170" y="65" width="235px" height="125px"/>

<text fill="url(#bluegrad)" x="290" y="180">G</text>
<text fill="url(#greengrad)" x="230" y="180">V</text>
```

Example 4-14. grad.svg (continued)

```
<text fill="url(#redgrad)" x="170" y="180">S</text>

</svg>
```

A defs element encloses three linearGradient elements. The ids on these elements each contains a name that is referenced later in the fill attributes of the three text elements (for example, the id bluegrad is referenced with fill="url(#bluegrad)").

A gradient is a smooth blend from one color to another, as shown in Figure 4-7. A linear gradient defines a transition of color from one point or stop to another. You need at least two stop elements to define a linear gradient in SVG. The stop-color properties indicate the color for a gradient stop. The offset attribute indicates the location where stop is placed, and is represented either as a percentage or as a value between 0 and 1.

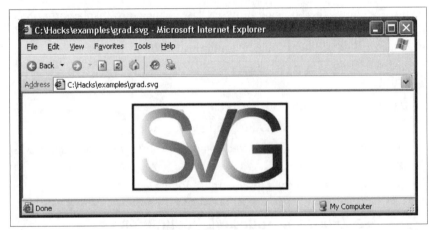

Figure 4-7. grad.svg in IE with Adobe's SVG Viewer

On Windows, you can also view SVG in IE and Netscape 7.1 with Corel's SVG Viewer (*http://www.smartgraphics.com/Viewer_prod_info.shtml*). If you install Corel's viewer, it will replace the Adobe viewer. The viewer is installed simultaneously for both IE and Netscape. Figure 4-8 shows *grad. svg* in Netscape 7.1 with the Corel viewer installed.

Apache's Batik project is a Java toolkit that can help applications render or generate SVG (*http://xml.apache.org/batik/*). After downloading and installing Batik, enter this line at a command prompt to start the Squiggle SVG browser and view the document *batikBatik.svg* from the *sample* directory:

```
java -jar batik-squiggle.jar samples/batikBatik.svg
```

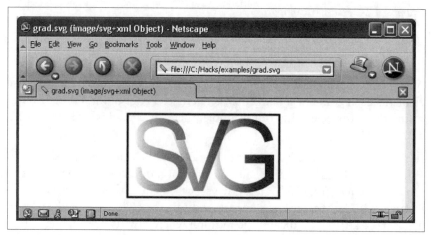

Figure 4-8. grad.svg in Netscape 7.1 with Corel's SVG Viewer

Figure 4-9 shows the Squiggle browser. Use Squiggle to display other SVG files in the *samples* directory. Looking at the SVG source for these example files in an editor will help you get familiar with SVG techniques.

See Also

- "Generate SVG with XSLT" [Hack #54]
- "Dither Scatterplots with XSLT and SVG" [Hack #55]
- Sun's Introduction to SVG: *http://wwws.sun.com/software/xml/developers/svg/*
- *SVG Essentials*, by David Eisenberg (O'Reilly)

HACK
#67 Use XForms in Your XML Documents

You may be accustomed to creating forms in HTML. XForms, an XML vocabulary, allows you to take a step up from HTML or XHTML forms.

A key advantage of most XML vocabularies is that they're more structured than, say, a Microsoft Word document. Most XML is pretty predictable, at least as far as structure goes. Likewise, forms are more structured than free-flowing documents. Taken in combination, XML and forms seem to have been made for each other. Instead of creating documents from scratch, a more fill-in-the-blanks approach becomes possible. As a bonus, this works both for creating a new XML document and for editing existing XML.

XForms (*http://www.w3.org/MarkUp/Forms/*), which became a W3C recommendation in October 2003, makes it possible to define XML form templates that can be used to create or edit other XML snippets. While a few

Figure 4-9. batikBatik.svg in Squiggle

proprietary solutions are around for creating forms data, XForms is generally a better choice because it is free to implement or use and it is open standards-based. Open standards have a proven track record of being more flexible, more compatible, and less expensive than proprietary alternatives.

XForms is also generally considered a better choice than classic HTML or XHTML forms, which tend to rely heavily on JavaScript and don't work with XML in any case. Another benefit of XForms is that it provides declarative actions for most, if not all, of the cases where JavaScript is required.

Anatomy of an XForms Document

XForms has been carefully specified as a markup module that can be reused in various host languages, such as SVG (*http://www.w3.org/Graphics/SVG/*) or more commonly XHTML (*http://www.w3.org/MarkUp/*). In fact, as of this writing, XHTML Version 2.0 (*http://www.w3.org/TR/xhtml2/*) is slated to include XForms as a core part of the document language.

Essentially, XForms documents consist of a host language sprinkled with small islands of XForms markup. One such island, called the XForms Model, contains a description of what the form is all about, without getting into details of how the form should look. This is an important design consideration, because on the whole, not every form will automatically have a specific visual component. Consider telephone and speech interfaces, Braille displays, phones, PDAs, and even universal remote controls, and you'll get an idea of the wide range of possibilities. For now, though, we'll concentrate on visual-centric forms for the desktop.

Example 4-15 is an example of an XForms Model (a fragment, really) that edits a simple purchase order vocabulary, loosely based on Universal Business Language or UBL (*http://www.oasis-open.org/committees/tc_home.php?wg_abbrev=ubl*).

Example 4-15. XForms Model with inline instance data

```
1  <model id="m1">
2   <instance>
3    <my:Invoice>
4     <my:InvoiceLine>
5      <my:Quantity unitCode="PKG">5</my:Quantity>
6       <my:Item>
7        <my:Desc>Box of Protractors; 500 count<my:Desc>
8       </my:Item>
9      </my:InvoiceLine>
10     </my:Invoice>
11   </instance>
12   <bind nodeset="my:InvoiceLine/my:Item/my:Desc" required="1"/>
13   <submission id="s" method="put" action="po.xml"/>
14  </model>
```

This model is wrapped in a model element (*http://www.w3.org/TR/xforms/index-all.html#structure-model*), followed by an instance element (*http://www.w3.org/TR/xforms/index-all.html#structure-model-instance*).   Notice that a few XML namespaces are in use here (declared elsewhere): the default namespace is that of XForms (http://www.w3.org/2002/xforms), and the instance data itself some other namespace, mapped to the prefix my:. In this example, the instance data is directly included inline (lines 3 through 10), though in many cases it's more convenient to load and save it from an external URL.

Besides the instance data, the example also shows a bind element (*http://www.w3.org/TR/xforms/index-all.html#structure-bind-element*) on line 12, which applies to all the my:Desc elements, marking them as required. The syntax of the nodeset attribute is XPath (*http://www.w3.org/TR/xpath*), another W3C language designed for selecting parts (called node-sets) of XML out of a bigger whole. Notice that the document or root element of the instance data, my:Invoice, is implied—since XML can only ever have a single root element, it's not necessary to repeat that bit of information. The required attribute simply indicates that all of the XML selected by the nodeset attribute should be flagged as required. XForms includes a number of properties, described later, that can be applied in this way across nodesets.

XForms defines several properties that can be applied to instance data using the bind element (browse the URLs to see examples):

type
>   A W3C XML Schema datatype, used to fine-tune the presentation of the form control (*http://www.w3.org/TR/xforms/index-all.html#model-prop-type*).

readonly
>   An XPath expression to control whether the form control is considered read-only (*http://www.w3.org/TR/xforms/index-all.html#model-prop-readOnly*).

required
>   An XPath expression to control whether the form control is required to be filled before submission (*http://www.w3.org/TR/xforms/index-all.html#model-xformsconstraints*).

relevant
>   An XPath expression to control whether the form control is considered relevant—non-relevant controls typically are not rendered, and the data they contain is pruned from what gets submitted (*http://www.w3.org/TR/xforms/index-all.html#model-xformsconstraints*).

calculate
>   An XPath expression that is automatically computed to provide a data value dependent on other values in the form data (*http://www.w3.org/TR/xforms/index-all.html#model-xformsconstraints*).

constraint
>   An XPath expression that must evaluate to a truth value in order for the form control to be considered valid. Whether a control is valid or not affects its rendering, which can be fine-tuned through CSS (*http://www.w3.org/TR/xforms/index-all.html#model-xformsconstraints*).

p3ptype

> A special identifier, based on the W3C recommendation Platform for Privacy Preferences 1.0 (*http://www.w3.org/TR/P3P/*), indicating the specific nature of the data collected (*http://www.w3.org/TR/xforms/index-all.html#model-xformsconstraints*).

Back to Example 4-15, the submission element (*http://www.w3.org/TR/xforms/index-all.html#structure-model-submission*) on line 13 defines the behavior of this form when it comes to submitting the data. The action attribute gives the URL to which the data is to be submitted (in this example, the relative URL *po.xml*). The method attribute, taken in combination with this URL, says that the form data is to be written back to disk (if the form is loaded from disk to begin with), or else written back to the Web through an HTTP PUT method (if the form is loaded from the Web).

A separate component of the form—the visible (or perhaps audible) part—is called the XForms User Interface, shown partially in Example 4-16.

Example 4-16. XForms User Interface repeating items

```
1   <repeat id="lineitems" nodeset="my:ItemLine">
2    <group>
3
4     <range ref="my:Quantity" incremental="true"
5               start="1" end="9" step="1">
6      <label>Quantity <output ref="."/></label>
7     </range>
8
9     <select1 ref="my:Quantity/@unitCode">
10     <item>
11      <label>Package</item>
12      <value>PKG</item>
13     </item>
14     <item>
15      <label>Unit</label>
16       <value>UNIT</value>
17     </item>
18    </select1>
19
20    <input ref="my:Item/my:Desc">
21     <label>Description</label>
22    </input>
23
24   </group>
25  </repeat>
```

This example is wrapped by a repeat element (line 1), which indicates that the contents of that element are set to repeat as many times as needed. While not shown here, simple controls can be added to dynamically add and remove repeated rows, which at the same time will add or remove elements from the instance data. The repeating contents are wrapped in a group element (line 2), useful in the context of CSS, which can be used to lay out the repeating items as needed. In fact, nearly all aspects of a form control's appearance can be conveniently styled through CSS.

The first form control is range (lines 4–7), something not present in classic XHTML forms. It represents a slider control, in this case offering a choice from 1 (start attribute) to 9 (end attribute). Every data collection control has a required label element (lines 6, 11, 15, and 21), which forces authors to think about the purpose of each control and include the needed text or markup to describe the intent behind each form control. In the case of the range control, the label contains an output element (line 6), which renders much the same as plain text but dynamically updates along with the form data. The attribute ref (line 6) contains an XPath expression pointing into the instance data, giving the location where data entered from this form control is stored—in this case, the current node (.) my:Quantity for a item line. The incremental attribute (line 4) causes data updates to happen more immediately than they otherwise might.

The second form control is select1 (line 9), which, yes, includes the digit 1 in the element name. This form control is the appropriate choice when selecting a single item from a list of possibilities. It contains several item elements (lines 10 and 14), each of which contains a label element (lines 11 and 15), indicating the human-readable label for each choice, as well as a value element (lines 12 and 16), indicating the value that gets stored in the XML. As before, the ref attribute (line 9) contains an XPath indicating where in the instance data the stored data goes. Notice the use of the @ abbreviation, which accesses the unitCode attribute of the Quantity element.

The third form control is input (line 20), indicating the intent of basic free-text entry. A real-world purchase order would have additional form controls (like the ever-important price of each line item), but this example omits them in the name of brevity.

The form controls defined in XForms (*http://www.w3.org/TR/xforms/index-all.html#controls*), chosen in such a way that the element name indicates the intent of the control, are:

input
> Entry of freeform value (*http://www.w3.org/TR/xforms/index-all.html# ui-input*).

textarea
> Entry of large amounts of freeform text (*http://www.w3.org/TR/xforms/ index-all.html#ui-textarea*).

secret

> Entry of sensitive information (*http://www.w3.org/TR/xforms/index-all. html#ui-secret*).

select1

> Choice of one and only one item from a list (*http://www.w3.org/TR/xforms/ index-all.html#ui-selectOne*).

select

> Choice of zero or more items from a list (*http://www.w3.org/TR/xforms/ index-all.html#ui-selectMany*).

range

> Selecting a value from a smooth range (*http://www.w3.org/TR/xforms/ index-all.html#ui-range*).

upload

> Selecting a data source such as file upload, scanner, microphone, and so forth (*http://www.w3.org/TR/xforms/index-all.html#ui-upload*).

trigger

> Activating a defined process or script (*http://www.w3.org/TR/xforms/ index-all.html#ui-button*).

submit

> Activating submission of the form (*http://www.w3.org/TR/xforms/index- all.html#ui-submit*).

output

> Display-only of form data (*http://www.w3.org/TR/xforms/index-all.html# ui-output*).

The quickest way to jump into some interactive examples of XForms is to point your browser at some live XForms examples, as in the next two sections.

Simple Approaches to Trying Out XForms

The web site XForms Institute (*http://xformsinstitute.com*) hosts several live examples of XForms, accomplished through a slick little Macromedia Flash applet called DENG (the Desktop Engine) that implements a large swath of XForms plus XHTML and CSS (see *http://claus.packts.net/deng*). Since XForms is still relatively new, browser support hasn't come through yet, so a Flash engine is quite a useful tool.

In addition to live examples, the site contains a view source feature and an online validator (*http://xformsinstitute.com/validator/*) for XForms documents in various host languages, and the text of O'Reilly's *XForms Essentials* (2003) under an open content license.

If you are running IE6 on Windows, another useful approach is a browser plug-in called formsPlayer, made available for free download at *http://www. formsplayer.com*. This plug-in requires a tiny bit of extra markup in documents, notably an object tag to load the necessary ActiveX bits, but otherwise turns an ordinary IE browser into a full-blown XForms solution. The formsPlayer web site also includes numerous examples, and a lively discussion group hosted at *http://groups.yahoo.com/group/formsplayer/*.

A Working Example

A fully working example, based on the UBL, can be found online at *http:// xformsinstitute.com/ubl/*. This online example shows many additional useful features of XForms, all put together in a real-world example.

What Is Universal Business Language?

Universal Business Language is a standard library of XML business documents—purchase orders, invoices, and so forth—being developed by an OASIS technical committee (*http://www.oasis-open.org/committees/tc_home. php?wg_abbrev=ubl*). The UBL effort is divided into several subcommittees that are attempting to incorporate best practices from existing libraries of XML business documents. The effort is being led by Jon Bosak (*http://www. ibiblio.org/bosak/cv.htm*), who was the chair of the W3C XML working group that produced the XML 1.0 specification (1996–1998).

See Also

- The X-Smiles browser provides XForms support: *http://www.xsmiles. org/features_xforms.html*
- Orbeon's OXF XForms/UBL example: *http://www.orbeon.com/oxf/ examples/xforms-ubl*
- W3C XForms page: *http://www.w3.org/MarkUp/Forms/*
- XForms FAQ: *http://www.w3.org/MarkUp/Forms/2003/xforms-faq.html*
- Discussion group for formsPlayer: *http://groups.yahoo.com/group/ formsplayer/*

—*Micah Dubinko*

Defining XML Vocabularies with Schema Languages

Hacks 68–79

A compliant XML processor must check that XML documents have the proper structure—called *well-formedness*—and may also check for *validity*, i.e., whether the markup in a document matches a schema definition for that document. A *schema* describes the structure and semantics an XML document must satisfy, and is usually a separate document, written in a specific language. An *instance* of a given schema is an XML document that is said to be valid or invalid with regard to that schema.

This chapter contains hacks using schema languages such as XML 1.0's native Document Type Definition or DTD [Hack #68], W3C's XML Schema [[Hack #69], OASIS' RELAX NG [Hack #72], and Academia Sinica Computing Centre's Schematron [Hack #77].

Another hack shows you how to validate multiple documents with XML Schema at one time [Hack #70], while another helps you check the integrity of an XML Schema [Hack #71]. A special, advanced hack helps you create DTD customizations with RELAX NG [[Hack #78].

You'll also see how to create a DTD from a sample XML document [Hack #73], an XML Schema file from a document [Hack #74], and a RELAX NG schema from a document [Hack #75]. If you prefer, you can develop schemas with RELAX NG and then convert them into XML Schema [Hack #76] along the way. The last hack in this group introduces a tool that lets you generate sample documents based on schemas [Hack #79].

Files mentioned in this chapter are in the book's file archive, available for downloading from *http://www.oreilly.com/catalog/xmlhks/*.

Validate an XML Document with a DTD

The Document Type Definition (DTD) is native to XML 1.0. You'll learn how to
use DTDs in this hack.

XML inherited the Document Type Definition (DTD) from SGML. It is the
native language for validating XML—though it is not itself in XML syntax—
and is interwoven into the XML 1.0 specification (*http://www.w3.org/TR/
2004/REC-xml-20040204/*). Using non-XML syntax, a DTD defines the
structure or content model of a valid XML instance. A DTD can define elements, attributes, entities, and notations, and can contain comments (just
like XML comments), conditional sections, and a structure unique to DTDs
called *parameter entities*. DTDs can be internal or external to an XML document, or both. This hack shows you how to implement all the basic structures of a DTD.

Example 5-1 shows *external.xml*, and Example 5-2 shows a DTD against
which *external.xml* is valid. The external DTD is called *order.dtd*. This is
also known as an *external subset*. This DTD is a local file in this example,
but it could also exist across a network.

Example 5-1. external.xml

```
1   <?xml version="1.0" encoding="UTF-8" standalone="no"?>
2   <!DOCTYPE order SYSTEM "order.dtd">
3
4   <order id="TDI-983857">
5   <store>Prineville</store>
6   <product>feed-grade whole oats</product>
7   <package>sack</package>
8   <weight std="lbs.">50</weight>
9   <quantity>23</quantity>
10  <price cur="USD">
11   <high>5.99</high>
12   <regular>4.99</regular>
13   <discount>3.99</discount>
14  </price>
15  <ship>the back of Tom's pickup</ship>
16  </order>
```

External Subset

The XML declaration on line 1 declares that this document does not stand
alone. That's because on line 2, *external.xml* references the DTD *order.dtd*.
The file *order.dtd* is considered an external entity and is called an external

subset. The SYSTEM keyword on line 2 indicates that the DTD will be identified by a system identifier, which for all practical purposes is a URL for a local or remote file.

In this DTD, all the valid structures found in *external.xml* are declared. The document element is order (line 4), which has child elements that describe the pieces of a purchase order, including information on the store, product, product packaging, product weight, quantity, price, and shipping method. Validate *external.xml* against its associated DTD *order.dtd* by using RXP, *xmlvalid*, or *xmllint* on the command line [Hack #9], or use RXP online, or the Brown University STG online validator [Hack #9].

Example 5-2. order.dtd

```
1   <?xml encoding="UTF-8"?>
2   <!-- Order DTD -->
3   <!ELEMENT order (store+,product,package?,weight?,quantity,price,ship*)>
4   <!-- id = part number -->
5   <!ATTLIST order id ID #REQUIRED
6                   xmlns CDATA #FIXED "http://www.wyeast.net/order"
7                   date CDATA #IMPLIED>
8   <!ELEMENT store (#PCDATA)>
9   <!ELEMENT product (#PCDATA)>
10  <!ELEMENT package (#PCDATA)>
11  <!ELEMENT weight (#PCDATA)>
12  <!ATTLIST weight std NMTOKEN #REQUIRED>
13  <!ELEMENT quantity (#PCDATA)>
14  <!ELEMENT price (high?,regular,discount?,total?)>
15  <!ATTLIST price cur (USD|CAD|AUD|EUR) "USD">
16  <!ELEMENT high (#PCDATA)>
17  <!ELEMENT regular (#PCDATA)>
18  <!ELEMENT discount (#PCDATA)>
19  <!ELEMENT ship (#PCDATA)>
```

The text declaration. A text declaration (*http://www.w3.org/TR/2004/REC-xml-20040204/#sec-TextDecl*) is similar to an XML declaration (see "The XML Declaration" in Chapter 1), except that version information (e.g., version="1.0") is optional; encoding declarations, such as encoding="UTF-8", are required; and there are no standalone declarations (e.g., standalone="no").

Element type declarations and content models. Most of the lines in this DTD contain element type declarations (*http://www.w3.org/TR/2004/REC-xml-20040204/#elemdecls*). This is one of several kinds of markup declarations (*http://www.w3.org/TR/2004/REC-xml-20040204/#dt-markupdecl*) that may appear in a DTD. The simplest, on lines 8 through 11 and lines 16 through

19, have content models for parsed character data (#PCDATA), which means that these elements must contain only text—no element children. The elements declared on lines 3 and 14 (order and price) have content models that include only child elements. The +, ?, and * symbols denote occurrence constraints, meaning that the child elements may occur only a given number of times: + means that the element may occur one or more times; ? means the element may occur zero or one time (that is, it's optional); and * means the element may occur zero or more times. When an element name in a content model is followed by a comma (,), that means that exactly one of those elements may occur.

Attribute-list declarations. The DTD *order.dtd* has three attribute-list declarations on lines 5, 12, and 15. You can declare one or more attributes at a time, hence the phrase *attribute list*. The first declares three attributes, id, xmlns, and date. XML attributes declared in DTDs must have one of 10 possible types: CDATA, ID, IDREF, IDREFS, ENTITY, ENTITIES, NMTOKEN, NMTOKENS, NOTATION, and enumeration (see *http://www.w3.org/ TR/2004/REC-xml-20040204/#sec-attribute-types* for an explanation of all the types).

The attribute id on line 5 is of type ID, which must be an XML name (*http:// www.w3.org/TR/2004/REC-xml-20040204/#NT-Name*) and must be unique (*http://www.w3.org/TR/2004/REC-xml-20040204/#id*). It is also required (#REQUIRED); that is, it must appear in any valid instance of the DTD.

Emulating Namespace Support in DTDs

DTDs do not directly support XML namespaces (*http://www.w3.org/TR/xml-names11*), but you can use a few tricks to imitate namespace support. Here is how to do it: the attribute xmlns (line 6) has a fixed value of http://www. wyeast.net/order. The #FIXED keyword means that the attribute must always have the provided default value. When an instance of this DTD is processed, for example by the command rxp -aV or xmllint --valid, it will contain the namespace declaration xmlns="http://www.wyeast.net/order". If you want to use prefixed elements, for example, change line 6 to read: xmlns:order CDATA #FIXED "http://www.wyeast.net/order". Then add the prefix order: to all the element declarations in the DTD—for example, <!ELEMENT store (#PCDATA)> becomes <!ELEMENT order:store (#PCDATA)> and so forth. Be cautious: you will want to use defaulted attributes as namespace declarations only when you are certain that your instance will use the namespace.

On line 7, the attribute date is declared. The #IMPLIED keyword means that the attribute may or may not appear in a legal instance. CDATA means that the value of date will be a string.

The std attribute for the weight element is declared on line 12. It is required (#REQUIRED) and is of type NMTOKEN. A name token is a single, atomic unit—a string with no whitespace. The attribute-list declaration on line 15 declares the cur (currency) attribute for the price element. The default value in quotes is USD (United States dollar), with possible values USD, CAD (Canadian dollar), AUD (Australian dollar), and EUR (Euro).

Internal Subset

You can also have a DTD that is internal to an XML document. This is called the *internal subset. internal.xml* is an example of an XML document that contains an internal subset (Example 5-3). The DTD is stored in the DOCTYPE declaration, which encloses markup declarations in square brackets ([ ]); see lines 2 and 21.

Example 5-3. internal.xml

```
 1  <?xml version="1.0" encoding="UTF-8" standalone="yes"?>
 2  <!DOCTYPE order [
 3  <!-- Order DTD -->
 4  <!ELEMENT order (store+,product,package?,weight?,quantity,price,ship*)>
 5  <!-- id = part number -->
 6  <!ATTLIST order id ID #REQUIRED
 7                  xmlns CDATA #FIXED "http://www.wyeast.net/order"
 8                  date CDATA #IMPLIED>
 9  <!ELEMENT store (#PCDATA)>
10  <!ELEMENT product (#PCDATA)>
11  <!ELEMENT package (#PCDATA)>
12  <!ELEMENT weight (#PCDATA)>
13  <!ATTLIST weight std NMTOKEN #REQUIRED>
14  <!ELEMENT quantity (#PCDATA)>
15  <!ELEMENT price (high?,regular,discount?,total?)>
16  <!ATTLIST price cur (USD|CAD|AUD|EUR) "USD">
17  <!ELEMENT high (#PCDATA)>
18  <!ELEMENT regular (#PCDATA)>
19  <!ELEMENT discount (#PCDATA)>
20  <!ELEMENT ship (#PCDATA)>
21  ]>
22
23  <order id="TDI-983857">
24   <store>Prineville</store>
25   <product>feed-grade whole oats</product>
26   <package>sack</package>
27   <weight std="lbs.">50</weight>
28   <quantity>23</quantity>
29   <price cur="USD">
```

Example 5-3. internal.xml (continued)

```
30    <high>5.99</high>
31    <regular>4.99</regular>
32    <discount>3.99</discount>
33    </price>
34    <ship>the back of Tom's pickup</ship>
35  </order>
```

One line 1, the document *internal.xml* is declared to be standalone; i.e., it does not depend on markup declarations in an external entity. Notice that there is no SYSTEM keyword or system identifier (URL). This is because the markup declarations are enclosed in the document type declaration, rather than in an external entity. The document type declaration (lines 2 through 21) contains the same declarations as *order.dtd*, and the document itself (lines 23 through 35) is the same as *external.xml*, except for the DOCTYPE.

Using an internal subset and an external subset together. The document *both. xml*, shown in Example 5-4, uses both an internal subset and an external subset (*both.dtd* in Example 5-5). Notice how the document type declaration uses both the SYSTEM keyword, a system identifier (*both.dtd*), and also encloses markup declarations in square brackets ([ ]). The advantage of this syntax is that DTDs can be developed and used in a modular fashion, and documents can be validated with these modules even if they exist locally or in disparate locations (across the Internet).

Example 5-4. both.xml

```
<?xml version="1.0" encoding="UTF-8" standalone="no"?>
<!DOCTYPE order SYSTEM "both.dtd" [
<!-- Order DTD -->
<!ELEMENT order (store+,product,package?,weight?,quantity,price,ship*)>
<!-- id = part number -->
<!ATTLIST order id ID #REQUIRED
                xmlns CDATA #FIXED "http://www.wyeast.net/order"
                date CDATA #IMPLIED>
<!ELEMENT store (#PCDATA)>
<!ELEMENT product (#PCDATA)>
<!ELEMENT package (#PCDATA)>
<!ELEMENT weight (#PCDATA)>
<!ATTLIST weight std NMTOKEN #REQUIRED>
<!ELEMENT quantity (#PCDATA)>
<!ELEMENT ship (#PCDATA)>
]>

<order id="TDI-983857">
 <store>Prineville</store>
 <product>feed-grade whole oats</product>
 <package>sack</package>
```

Example 5-4. both.xml (continued)

```
<weight std="lbs.">50</weight>
<quantity>23</quantity>
<price cur="USD">
 <high>5.99</high>
 <regular>4.99</regular>
 <discount>3.99</discount>
</price>
<ship>the back of Tom's pickup</ship>
</order>
```

Example 5-5. both.dtd

```
<!ELEMENT price (high?,regular,discount?,total?)>
<!ATTLIST price cur (USD|CAD|AUD|EUR) "USD">
<!ELEMENT high (#PCDATA)>
<!ELEMENT regular (#PCDATA)>
<!ELEMENT discount (#PCDATA)>
```

Parameter Entities

A parameter entity (PE) is a special entity that can be used only in a DTD. They are not allowed in XML documents. A PE provides a way to store information and then reuse that information elsewhere, multiple times. A good example of this can be found in the way the XHTML 1.0 strict DTD (*http://www.w3.org/TR/xhtml1/DTD/xhtml1-strict.dtd*) defines a set of core attributes. Here is a fragment from the DTD:

```
1  <!-- core attributes common to most elements
2     id          document-wide unique id
3     class       space separated list of classes
4     style       associated style info
5     title       advisory title/amplification
6  -->
7  <!ENTITY % coreattrs
8    "id         ID          #IMPLIED
9     class      CDATA       #IMPLIED
10    style      %StyleSheet; #IMPLIED
11    title      %Text;      #IMPLIED"
12   >
```

Lines 1 through 6 of this fragment contain a comment explaining the purpose of four attributes, id, class, style, and title. Starting on line 7, an entity is declared. The percent sign (%) is a flag to the XML processor saying that this is a parameter entity. The information in double quotes makes up part of an attribute-list declaration that is reused three times in the DTD.

Where normal entity references [Hack #4] begin with an ampersand (&), parameter entity references begin with a percent sign (%). Lines 10 and 11 show the parameter entity references %Stylesheet; and %Text;, which are defined elsewhere in the DTD as:

```
<!ENTITY % StyleSheet "CDATA">
    <!-- style sheet data -->

<!ENTITY % Text "CDATA">
    <!-- used for titles etc. -->
```

%Stylesheet; and %Text; expand to CDATA. As you can see, a parameter entity can contain a reference to another parameter entity. In fact, the attrs parameter entity in *xhtml1-strict.dtd* references coreattrs and two other parameter entities:

```
<!ENTITY % attrs "%coreattrs; %i18n; %events;">
```

attrs, in turn, is used over 60 times in the DTD, so you can see that parameter entities are a handy way to reuse information in a DTD.

Other Things That Can Go in a DTD

This section briefly covers several other things you can include in DTDs: comments, conditional sections, unparsed entities, and notations.

Comments. DTDs can contain XML-style comments [Hack #1]. For example, the pair of comments used on lines 2 and 4 in Example 5-2 are formed just as they would be in an XML document.

Conditional sections. Conditional sections allow you to include or exclude declarations in a DTD conditionally. This feature can help you develop a DTD while you are still trying out different content models. Look at this fragment from *conditional.dtd*:

```
<![INCLUDE[
<!ATTLIST price cur (USD|CAD|AUD|EUR) "USD">
]]>
<![IGNORE[
<!ATTLIST price cur (USD|EUR) "USD">
]]>
```

The structure that starts with the word INCLUDE indicates that the following declaration (which must be complete) is to be included in the DTD at validation time. The section marked IGNORE, however, is ignored. The following fragment, also in *conditional.xml*, shows how you can turn these sections on or off with parameter entities.

```
<!ENTITY % on 'INCLUDE' >
<!ENTITY % off 'IGNORE' >
...
<![%on;[
<!ELEMENT price (high?,regular,discount?,total?)>
]]>
```

```
<![[%off;[
<!ELEMENT price (regular,discount,total)>
]]>
```

Conditional sections are an interesting hack in themselves, but they are frequently considered more complicating than helpful.

Unparsed entities and notations. An unparsed entity is a resource upon which XML places no constraints. It can consist of a chunk of XML, non-XML text, a graphical file, a binary file, or any other electronic resource. An unparsed entity has a name that is associated with a system identifier or a public identifier.

For example, in DocBook **[Hack #62]**, a module of the DTD (*dbnotnx.mod*, under the subdirectory *docbook-4.3CR* in this book's file archive) is dedicated to notations. Here is a notation from that module that associates the name GIF89a with a public identifier -//CompuServe//NOTATION Graphics Interchange Format 89a//EN:

```
<!NOTATION GIF89a              PUBLIC
"-//CompuServe//NOTATION Graphics Interchange Format 89a//EN">
```

Here is another example from the same module that uses a system identifier for the name PNG:

```
<!NOTATION PNG          SYSTEM "http://www.w3.org/TR/REC-png">
```

Elsewhere in a DTD that includes this module, you could declare several entities like this:

```
<!ENTITY dbnotnx SYSTEM "dbnotnx.mod">
&dbnotnx;
...
<!ENTITY g001 SYSTEM "g001.gif" NDATA GIF89a>
<!ENTITY g002 SYSTEM "g002.png" NDATA PNG>
...
<!ELEMENT graphic EMPTY>
<!ATTLIST graphic img ENTITY #REQUIRED>
```

The entity declarations associate names with files with the names of notations. The presence of the NDATA keyword indicates an unparsed entity. Then, in an instance, you could refer to the entity in an attribute, like this:

```
<graphic img="g001"/>
...
<graphic img="g002"/>
```

The syntax for unparsed entities is the most awkward and forbidding of any syntax in XML. The use of unparsed entities is rare, and the applications that support them are even rarer. If people want to display graphics, they usually transform their XML into HTML or XHTML and use the ubiquitously supported img tag.

HACK #69 Validate an XML Document with XML Schema

XML Schema is the W3C evolution of the DTD. It is complex but powerful, in wide use but not always popular. This hack will help you start writing schema in this format.

XML Schema is a recommendation of the W3C, written in three parts. Part 0 is a nice little primer (*http://www.w3.org/TR/xmlschema-0/*) that gets you started with the language. Part 1 describes the structures of XML Schema (*http://www.w3.org/ TR/xmlschema-1/*); it is a long spec—about 200 pages long when printed—and is rather complex. Part 2 defines datatypes (*http://www.w3.org/TR/xmlschema-2/*) and has been more gladly received than Part 1, though it is considered by some to be ad hoc and not without anomalies.

XML mensch James Clark (*http://www.jclark.com*) has said of Part 1 that "it is without doubt the hardest to understand specification that I have ever read" (*http://www.imc.org/ietf-xml-use/mail-archive/msg00217.html*). Many others who have read the spec, or have attempted to read it, heartily agree with James. This is unfortunate, as it has placed many schema writers and companies in the uncomfortable position of using and supporting a difficult spec from the W3C, a widely accepted (though not always highly regarded) source. Happily, there are alternatives, such as RELAX NG **[Hack #72]** and tools such as Trang (*http://www.thaiopensource.com/relaxng/trang.html*), that can conveniently convert RELAX NG to XML Schema **[Hack #76]**.

A Quick Introduction to XML Schema

We'll start out by taking a look at the schema *time.xsd*, which was introduced but not explored in depth in "Edit XML Documents with Microsoft Word 2003" **[Hack #14]**. It is displayed in Example 5-6.

Example 5-6. time.xsd

```
1  <?xml version="1.0" encoding="UTF-8"?>
2  <xs:schema xmlns:xs="http://www.w3.org/2001/XMLSchema">
3
4  <xs:element name="time">
```

Example 5-6. time.xsd (continued)

```
5    <xs:complexType>
6     <xs:sequence>
7      <xs:element name="hour" type="xs:string"/>
8      <xs:element name="minute" type="xs:string"/>
9      <xs:element name="second" type="xs:string"/>
10     <xs:element name="meridiem" type="xs:string"/>
11     <xs:element name="atomic">
12       <xs:complexType>
13         <xs:attribute name="signal" type="xs:string" use="required"/>
14       </xs:complexType>
15     </xs:element>
16     </xs:sequence>
17     <xs:attribute name="timezone" type="xs:string" use="required"/>
18    </xs:complexType>
19   </xs:element>
20
21  </xs:schema>
```

The document element of an instance of XML Schema is always schema (line 2). The namespace name is http://www.w3.org/2001/XMLSchema and the common prefix for the namespace is xs: (also line 2). Starting on line 4, the element time is declared. This is called a *global element declaration* (*http://www. w3.org/TR/xmlschema-0/#Globals*); because it is the only global declaration in the schema, the schema will anticipate that time will be the top-level or document element in an instance.

The complexType element (line 5) indicates that its children may have complex content; that is, they can have attributes and element child content (*http://www.w3.org/TR/xmlschema-0/#DefnDeclars*). Contrariwise, elements with simple types cannot have attributes or element children. I think this terminology makes things harder to grasp than is necessary, but that's the way it is in XML Schema.

On lines 6 through 16, the sequence element specifies the order in which elements must appear in an instance. So the element declarations (lines 7 through 15) for the elements hour, minute, second, meridiem, and atomic, must appear in that order. The element names are given in the name attributes of the element, and all but the atomic element will have a string datatype (*http://www.w3.org/TR/xmlschema-2/#string*), as indicated by the type attribute.

Starting on line 11 is the declaration for the atomic element, which is different from the others. It is considered an anonymous type definition (*http:// www.w3.org/ TR/xmlschema-0/#InlineTypDefn*) because it is a complex type declaration without a name (that is, there is no name attribute on the complexType element start tag). The definition for time (starting on line 4) also is an anonymous type definition. atomic has a signal attribute (declared in the attribute element on line 13) whose type is string, and is required (hence the use attribute with a value of required).

Finally, on line 17, the required timezone attribute is declared. This declaration, way down near the bottom of the schema, applies to the time element. Its type is string, and it is also required.

Next, you need to become acquainted with the named complex type structure in XML Schema, as well as simple types. These structures can be named and reused. Example 5-7 shows a new version of our previous schema, *complex.xsd*, using these complex types and two derived simple types.

Example 5-7. complex.xsd

```
1  <?xml version="1.0" encoding="UTF-8"?>
2  <xs:schema xmlns:xs="http://www.w3.org/2001/XMLSchema">
3
4  <xs:element name="time" type="Time"/>
5
6  <xs:complexType name="Time">
7    <xs:sequence>
8     <xs:element ref="hour"/>
9     <xs:element ref="minute"/>
10    <xs:element ref="second"/>
11    <xs:element ref="meridiem"/>
12    <xs:element name="atomic" type="Atomic"/>
13   </xs:sequence>
14    <xs:attribute name="timezone" type="xs:string" use="required"/>
15 </xs:complexType>
16
17 <xs:element name="hour" type="Digits"/>
18 <xs:element name="minute" type="Digits"/>
19 <xs:element name="second" type="Digits"/>
20 <xs:element name="meridiem" type="AmPm"/>
21
22 <xs:complexType name="Atomic">
23   <xs:attribute name="signal" type="xs:string" use="required"/>
24 </xs:complexType>
25
26 <xs:simpleType name="Digits">
27  <xs:restriction base="xs:string">
28   <xs:pattern value="\d\d"/>
29  </xs:restriction>
30 </xs:simpleType>
31
32 <xs:simpleType name="AmPm">
33  <xs:restriction base="xs:string">
34   <xs:enumeration value="a.m."/>
35   <xs:enumeration value="p.m."/>
36  </xs:restriction>
```

Example 5-7. complex.xsd (continued)

```
37  </xs:simpleType>
38
39  </xs:schema>
```

When the time element is declared on line 4, rather than using a built-in type, its type is set to be the complex type named Time, which starts on line 6 (you could use time instead of Time as the name and it would not conflict with the name time used in an element declaration). Note the ref attributes on lines 8 through 11, which refer to element declarations on lines 17 through 20 (this is superfluous, but serves to illustrate how ref works). On line 12, the element atomic is of type Atomic, a complex type that contains only an attribute declaration (line 22).

The element declarations on lines 17, 18, and 19 are of type Digits, a simple type (line 26) that is a restriction of a string. The pattern facet element (line 28) restricts the content to two digits with the regular expression \d\d (*http://www.w3.org/TR/xmlschema-0/#regexAppendix*). The meridiem element is of type AmPm, an enumeration (*http://www.w3.org/TR/xmlschema-0/#CreatDt*) that can contain either of the values a.m. or p.m. (see line 33).

Validation with XML Schema Tools

Now let's validate *time.xml* against *time.xsd* or *complex.xsd*. There are a number of tools readily available to do this. We'll use three here: an online XSD Schema Validator, available from Got Dot Net (*http://www.gotdotnet.com*), and the command-line validators *xmllint* (*http://www.xmlsoft.org*) and *xsv* (*http://www.ltg.ed.ac.uk/~ht/xsv-status.html*).

XSD Schema Validator.

In a web browser, go to *http://apps.gotdotnet.com/xmltools/xsdvalidator/* (Figure 5-1). Click the Browse button next to the first text box, and the File Upload dialog box appears. Select *time.xsd* or *complex.xsd* from the working directory where the file archive was extracted, then click Open. Again, click the Browse button next to the third text box. Select *time.xml* in the File Upload dialog, and then click Open. Having selected both files, click the Submit button. Upon success, the browser will display the message "Validated OK!" and display the validated file. By selecting one or the other file alone, you can also use this service to check only an instance of an XML Schema for validity or only an XML document for well-formedness.

xmllint

The command-line tool *xmllint* was discussed and demonstrated in "Test XML Documents from the Command Line" [Hack #9]. To use this tool to vali-

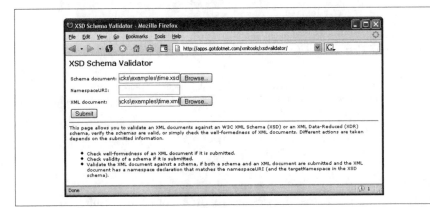

Figure 5-1. Got Dot Net's XSD Schema Validator in Firefox

date against XML Schema, all you need to do is use the --schema option. With *xmllint* installed and in the path, enter the command:

```
xmllint --schema time.xsd time.xml
```

or:

```
xmllint --schema complex.xsd time.xml
```

When successful, the validated instance is displayed, without reporting any errors. You can submit one or more XML instances at the end of the command line for validation

XSV

xsv is an XML Schema validator that is available both online and as a command-line tool (*http://www.ltg.ed.ac.uk/~ht/xsv-status.html*). It was developed by Henry S. Thompson and Richard Tobin of the University of Edinburgh. It is available for the Windows platform (*ftp://ftp.cogsci.ed.ac.uk/pub/XSV/XSV26.EXE*), in Python as an RPM (RPM Package Manager) package (*ftp://ftp.cogsci.ed.ac.uk/pub/XSV/XSV-2.6-2.noarch.rpm*), or as a tar ball (*ftp://ftp.cogsci.ed.ac.uk/pub/XSV/XSV-2.6.tar.gz*).

> We will use only the command-line version of this tool. To use the online version of this validator, go to *http://www.w3. org/2001/03/webdata/xsv*.

Once *xsv* is installed and in your path, you can use it to validate *time.xml* with *time.xsd* by typing:

```
xsv time.xml time.xsd
```

or:

```
xsv time.xml complex.xsd
```

By default, *xsv* reports its validation results with an XML document, as shown here (for *time.xsd*):

```
<?xml version='1.0'?>
<xsv xmlns="http://www.w3.org/2000/05/xsv" docElt="{None}time"
     instanceAssessed="true" instanceErrors="0" rootType="[Anonymous]"
     schemaDocs="time.xsd" schemaErrors="0"
     target="file:///C:/Hacks/examples/time.xml" validation="strict"
     version="XSV 2.6-2 of 2004/02/04 11:33:42">
  <schemaDocAttempt URI="file:///C:/Hacks/examples/time.xsd"
outcome="success" source="command line"/>
</xsv>
```

In the file archive there is a stylesheet that transforms this result into HTML; it's called *xsv.xsl*. To put it to work, use *xsv* with the -o switch for the output file and the -s switch for the XSLT stylesheet:

```
xsv -o xsvresult.xml -s xsv.xsl time.xml time.xsd
```

The -s switch places an XML stylesheet PI in the resulting file. You can then display the file in a browser that supports client-side XSLT, and it will be transformed as shown in Figure 5-2.

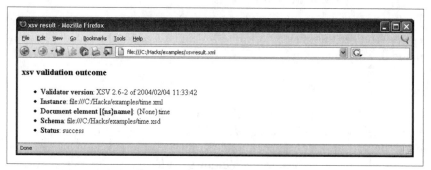

Figure 5-2. *The transformed result of xsv validation in Firefox*

Other XML Schema Features

Here are some additional interesting features from XML Schema.

choice, group, all

These three elements help you to construct content models. choice allows one of its children to appear in an instance, literally a choice of two or more options. group collects declarations into a single unit. all allows all children elements to appear once or not at all, in any order (*http://www.w3.org/TR/xmlschema-0/#groups*).

Annotations

The annotation element, with its children appInfo and documentation, can annotate and document a schema or provide information about an application (*http://www.w3.org/TR/xmlschema-0/#CommVers*).

include, import

With the include element, you can include other schemas as part of a schema definition. The import element allows you to borrow definitions from other namespaces (see *http://www.w3.org/TR/xmlschema-0/#IPO* and *http://www.w3.org/TR/xmlschema-0/#import*).

Derivation

With the restriction and extension elements, it is possible to create new types by deriving from existing types. You can, for example, add additional elements to an existing complex type or restrict or change facets in a simple type (see *http://www.w3.org/TR/xmlschema-0/#DerivExt* and *http://www.w3.org/TR/ xmlschema-0/#DerivByRestrict*).

Matching any name

You can match any element name with any and any attribute name with anyAttribute wildcards (*http://www.w3.org/TR/xmlschema-0/#any*).

Fixed and default values for elements

XML 1.0 gave us fixed and default values for attributes, and XML Schema extends that capability to elements by using the fixed and default attributes on the element declaration (*http://www.w3.org/TR/ xmlschema-0/#OccurenceConstraints*).

List and union types

A list type in XML Schema allows you to define a whitespace-separated list of values in an attribute or element. Union types allow values that are of any one of a number of simple types, such as integer and string (*http://www.w3.org/TR/xmlschema-0/#ListDt* and *http://www.w3.org/ TR/xmlschema-0/#UnionDt*).

Substitution groups

You can substitute one element for another. You can also create abstract elements. An abstract element can be the head of a substitution group, so that other elements can take its place, but it cannot be used within an XML document itself (*http://www.w3.org/TR/xmlschema-0/#SubsGroups*).

Redefinition

With the redefine element, you can redefine simple types, complex types, attribute groups, etc., from external schema files (*http://www.w3. org/TR/xmlschema-0/#Redefine*).

Identity constraints

You can use ID, IDREF, and IDREFS to constrain the identity of elements and attributes in XML Schema. You can also constrain values within a scope so that they are unique (unique), unique and present (key), or refer to a unique or key constraint (keyref) (*http://www.w3.org/TR/xmlschema-0/#specifyingUniqueness* and *http://www.w3.org/TR/xmlschema-0/#specifyingKeys&theirRefs*).

Nil values

This feature (xsi:nil in an instance and nillable="true" on an element declaration) allows you to give an element meaning to a nil value (*http://www.w3.org/tr/xmlschema-0/#Nils*).

See Also

- DecisionSoft's online schema validator: *http://tools.decisionsoft.com/schemaValidate.html*
- *XML Schema*, by Eric van der Vlist (O'Reilly)
- *Definitive XML Schema*, by Priscilla Walmsley (Prentice Hall PTR)
- xframe schema-based programming project: *http://xframe.sourceforge.net/xframe.html*
- xframe xsddoc documentation toolkit for XML Schema: *http://xframe.sourceforge.net/xsddoc.html*

HACK #70   Validate Multiple Documents Against an XML Schema at Once

A Xerces module allows you to validate more than one XML instance at a time against an XML Schema. This hack shows you how to use the Java class xni.XMLGrammarBuilder.

This book describes several online and command-line validators that let you check whether a document conforms to a W3C XML Schema definition. Some are faster than others, and some are more suitable for a particular platform. The special advantage of the Xerces Java xni.XMLGrammarBuilder sample application (which, being a Java program, runs on any platform) is its ability to validate multiple documents simultaneously. This sample application is packaged in the *xercesSamples.jar* file included with the Java Xerces distribution (*http://xml.apache.org/xerces2-j/*), which is part of the file archive that came with the book.

If you work with XML, you've probably received an email at work that says "here's the data" and included a ZIP file full of XML files—or worse, a bunch of files all attached individually to the email. Before doing anything with those files, you probably want to validate them to check whether the email's sender is passing along any problems to you. You could write a Perl script to generate a batch file that calls your favorite parser for each file, or you could enter the command to parse the first file, press your cursor-up key to retrieve that command, modify it, run it again, and repeat these steps multiple times. Or, you could use the xni.XMLGrammarBuilder utility and do it all in one command. (Because the program does this by storing a compiled version of the schema in memory and then reusing it for each document instance, the integrity checks that it does while compiling make it a useful schema development tool as well; see "Check the Integrity of a W3C Schema" [Hack #71].)

The following listings show you two short XML documents. I won't take up space showing you the *multidoc.xsd* schema that they point to; take my word for it that ZZ is not one of the valid zone values and oomph is not a valid child of the para element. Here is *multidoc1.xml*:

```
<sample zone="ZZ"
        xmlns:xsi="http://www.w3.org/2001/XMLSchema-instance"
        xsi:noNamespaceSchemaLocation="multidoc.xsd">
  <title>Peyton Place</title>
  <para>Indian summer is like a woman.</para>
</sample>
```

Here is *multidoc2.xml*:

```
<sample zone="Z1"
        xmlns:xsi="http://www.w3.org/2001/XMLSchema-instance"
        xsi:noNamespaceSchemaLocation="multidoc.xsd">
  <title>Moby Dick</title>
  <para>Call me Ishmael.</para>
  <para>I <oomph>alone</oomph> survived to tell the tale.</para>
</sample>
```

Before executing the command that follows, make sure that your classpath includes both the *xercesImpl.jar* and the *xercesSamples.jar* files (Version 2.6.2 or later) that come with the Java Xerces distribution. You can download the Xerces distribution from *http://xml.apache.org/xerces2-j/download.cgi*. In the following command line, the -a switch identifies the XSD schema and -i shows the list of documents to validate:

```
java -cp xercesImpl.jar;xercesSamples.jar xni.XMLGrammarBuilder
-a multidoc.xsd -i multidoc1.xml multidoc2.xml
```

Use a colon (:) between JAR filenames if you are working in a Unix environment. The xni.XMLGrammarBuilder lists each document's problems:

```
[Error] multidoc1.xml:3:54: cvc-enumeration-valid: Value 'ZZ' is
not facet-valid with respect to enumeration '[Z1, Z2, Z3, Z4, Z5,
Z6]'. It must be a value from the enumeration.
```

```
[Error] multidoc1.xml:3:54: cvc-attribute.3: The value 'ZZ' of
attribute 'zone' on element 'sample' is not valid with respect to
its type, 'zoneCodes'.
[Error] multidoc2.xml:6:18: cvc-complex-type.2.4.a: Invalid content
was found starting with element 'oomph'. One of '{"":emph}' is
expected.
```

The error in *multidoc1.xml* generated two error messages, and the error in *multidoc2.xml* generated one, each with information about the location and nature of the error.

Entering the following line with no parameters gives you an overview of xni. XMLGrammarBuilder's command-line options.

```
java -cp xercesImpl.jar;xercesSamples.jar xni.XMLGrammarBuilder
```

These options are shown here:

```
usage: java xni.XMLGrammarBuilder [-p config_file] -d uri ...
| [-f|-F] -a uri ... [-i uri ...]

options:
  -p config_file:  configuration to use for instance validation
  -d    grammars to preparse are DTD external subsets
  -f | -F   Turn on/off Schema full checking (default off)
  -a uri ... Provide a list of schema documents
  -i uri ... Provide a list of instance documents to validate

NOTE: both -d and -a cannot be specified!
```

See the *samples* directory and documentation that accompanies Xerces Java for more detailed documentation on xni.XMLGrammarBuilder.

—*Bob DuCharme*

Check the Integrity of a W3C Schema

HACK
#71

Use the xni.XMLGrammarBuilder class from Xerces to do some extra checking on your schemas.

Whether you create a W3C XSD Schema with the same tools you use to create other XML documents or use a specialized schema-generation tool to create one, parsing it against the schema in the Schema for Schemas appendix of the W3C Schema recommendation (*http://www.w3.org/TR/xmlschema-1/#normative-schemaSchema*) may alert you to some problems, such as whether you mistyped the name of a schema definition element or put one schema definition element inside of another where it doesn't belong. There are other potential errors that this won't catch, though; for example, what if your maxOccurs value for one element is less than the minOccurs value for the same element?

The xni.XMLGrammarBuilder class manages this multidocument validation by creating a compiled version of that schema in memory and then re-using that compiled version for each instance document passed to it. Like any compiler, it makes various integrity checks as it compiles. If you're developing an XSD schema, this round of checks can help you before you've created your first document that conforms to that schema.

Imagine that you just drafted a schema, *badschema.xsd*, which has the following problems:

- In the content model for the order element, the itemNum element has a maxOccurs value of 1 and a minOccurs value of 4. If the value must be greater than or equal to 4 or and less than or equal to 1, that doesn't leave any valid values!

- It declares the itemNum element to be of type itemTypist. While the schema does declare a type called itemType, it has no type called itemTypist, and this certainly isn't one of the primitive or derived datatypes listed in the XML Schema datatypes recommendation (*http://www.w3.org/TR/xmlschema-2/*).

- It declares the monthType type as being an integer with values between 1 and 12, inclusive. The orderMonthType is declared as an extension of monthType, but with a greater range of values allowed (0 to 12). This is illegal because a restricted type definition must restrict the allowable values, not expand them.

Here is the schema:

```xml
<xs:schema xmlns:xs="http://www.w3.org/2001/XMLSchema">

  <xs:element name="orders">
   <xs:complexType>
    <xs:sequence>
     <xs:element ref="order" maxOccurs="unbounded"/>
    </xs:sequence>
   </xs:complexType>
  </xs:element>

  <xs:element name="order">
   <xs:complexType>
    <xs:sequence>
     <xs:element name="itemNum" type="itemTypist"
                 maxOccurs="1" minOccurs="4"/> <!-- line 16 -->
     <xs:element name="orderMonth" type="orderMonthType"
                 maxOccurs="1"/>
    </xs:sequence>
   </xs:complexType>
  </xs:element>
```

```
<xs:simpleType name="itemType">
  <xs:restriction base="xs:string">
    <xs:pattern value="\d{3}-\d{4}"/>
  </xs:restriction>
</xs:simpleType>

<xs:simpleType name="monthType">
  <xs:restriction base="xs:integer">
    <xs:minInclusive value="1"/>
    <xs:maxInclusive value="12"/>
  </xs:restriction>
</xs:simpleType>

<xs:simpleType name="orderMonthType">
  <xs:restriction base="monthType">  <!-- line 37 -->
    <xs:minInclusive value="0"/>
    <xs:maxInclusive value="12"/>
  </xs:restriction>
</xs:simpleType>

</xs:schema>
```

Before trying the following command, make sure that your classpath includes both the *xercesImpl.jar* and the *xercesSamples.jar* files that come with the Java Xerces distribution (Version 2.6.2 or later). You can download the Xerces distribution from *http://xml.apache.org/xerces2-j/download.cgi*. While in the working directory, enter this command:

```
java -cp xercesImpl.jar;xercesSamples.jar xni.XMLGrammarBuilder
  -a badschema.xsd
```

Use a colon (:) between JAR filenames if you are working in a Unix environment. The xni.XMLGrammarBuilder's -a switch names the schema to parse. The error messages it outputs list the problems with the schema:

```
[Error] badschema.xsd:37:38: FacetValueFromBase: Value '0' of
facet 'minInclusive' must be from the value space of the base type.
[Error] badschema.xsd:16:46: p-props-correct.2.1: {min occurs} = '4'
must not be greater than {max occurs} = '1' for 'element'.
[Error] badschema.xsd:16:46: src-resolve: Cannot resolve the
name 'itemTypist' to a(n) type definition component.
```

I know of no other utility that lets you check XML 1.0 DTDs for correctness in this way. Previously, to check a particular DTD I'd created, I used to throw together a simple document that conformed to it and then validated that document to see if a parser would find any problem with the DTD itself on the way to parsing the document. Having done this many times, I particularly appreciate xni.XMLGrammarBuilder's ability to check schema integrity with no need for any sample documents.

—*Bob DuCharme*

Validate an XML Document with RELAX NG

Compared to the alternatives, RELAX NG schemas are easy to use and learn, and the more you use them the more you become convinced.

RELAX NG (*http://www.relaxng.org*) is a powerful schema language with a simple syntax. Originally, RELAX NG was developed in a small OASIS technical committee led by James Clark. It is based on ideas from Clark's TREX (*http://www.thaiopensource.com/trex/*) and Murata Makoto's Relax (*http://www.xml.gr.jp/relax/*), and its first committee spec was published on December 3, 2001 (*http://www.oasis-open.org/committees/relax-ng/spec.html*). A tutorial is also available (*http://www.oasis-open.org/committees/relax-ng/tutorial.html*). Recently, RELAX NG became an international standard under ISO as ISO/IEC 19757-2:2004, Information technology—Document Schema Definition Language (DSDL)—Part 2: Regular-grammar-based validation—RELAX NG (see *http://www.y12.doe.gov/sgml/ sc34/document/ 0458.htm*).

RELAX NG schemas may be written in either XML or a compact syntax. This hack demonstrates both.

XML Syntax

Recall the document *time.xml*:

```
<?xml version="1.0" encoding="UTF-8"?>

<!-- a time instant -->
<time timezone="PST">
 <hour>11</hour>
 <minute>59</minute>
 <second>59</second>
 <meridiem>p.m.</meridiem>
 <atomic signal="true"/>
</time>
```

Here is a RELAX NG schema for *time.xml* called *time.rng*:

```
<element name="time" xmlns="http://relaxng.org/ns/structure/1.0">
 <attribute name="timezone"/>
 <element name="hour"><text/></element>
 <element name="minute"><text/></element>
 <element name="second"><text/></element>
 <element name="meridiem"><text/></element>
 <element name="atomic">
  <attribute name="signal"/>
 </element>
</element>
```

At a glance, you can immediately tell how simple the syntax is. Each element is defined with an element element, and each attribute with an attribute element. The namespace URI for RELAX NG is http://relaxng. org/ns/structure/1.0. The document element in this schema happens to be element, but any element in RELAX NG that defines a pattern may be used as a document element (grammar may also be used, even though it doesn't define a pattern). Each of the elements and attributes defined in this schema has text content, as indicated by the text element for elements and by default for attributes; for example, <attribute name="signal"/> and <attribute name="signal"><text/></attribute> are equivalent.

xmllint. You can validate documents with RELAX NG using *xmllint* [Hack #9]). To validate *time.xml* against *time.rng*, type this command in a shell:

```
xmllint --relaxng time.rng time.xml
```

The response upon success will be:

```
<?xml version="1.0" encoding="UTF-8"?>
<!-- a time instant -->
<time timezone="PST">
 <hour>11</hour>
 <minute>59</minute>
 <second>59</second>
 <meridiem>p.m.</meridiem>
 <atomic signal="true"/>
</time>
time.xml validates
```

xmllint mirrors the well-formed document on standard output, plus on the last line it reports that the document validates (emphasis added). You can submit one or more XML instances at the end of the command line for validation.

Jing. You can also validate documents with RELAX NG using James Clark's Jing (*http://www.thaiopensource.com/relaxng/jing.html*). You can download the latest version from *http://www.thaiopensource.com/download/*. To validate *time.xml* against *time.rng*, use this command:

```
java -jar jing.jar time.rng time.xml
```

When Jing is silent after this command, it means that *time.xml* is valid with regard to *time.rng*. Jing, by the way, can accept one or more instance documents on the command line.

Jing also has a Windows 32 version, *jing.exe*, downloadable from the same location (*http://www.thaiopensource.com/download/*). In my tests, *jing.exe* runs faster than *jing.jar*, as you might expect.

At a Windows command prompt, run *jing.exe* like this:

```
jing time.rng time.xml
```

A more complex RELAX NG schema. Example 5-8 is a more complex, yet more precise, version of *time.rng* called *precise.rng*, which refines what is permitted in an instance.

Example 5-8. precise.rng

```
1  <grammar xmlns="http://relaxng.org/ns/structure/1.0"
2  datatypeLibrary="http://www.w3.org/2001/XMLSchema-datatypes">
3
4  <start>
5   <ref name="Time"/>
6  </start>
7
8  <define name="Time">
9  <element name="time">
10  <attribute name="timezone">
11   <ref name="Timezones"/>
12  </attribute>
13  <element name="hour">
14   <ref name="Hours"/>
15  </element>
16  <element name="minute">
17   <ref name="MinutesSeconds"/>
18  </element>
19  <element name="second">
20   <ref name="MinutesSeconds"/>
21  </element>
22  <element name="meridiem">
23   <choice>
24    <value>a.m.</value>
25    <value>p.m.</value>
26   </choice>
27  </element>
28  <element name="atomic">
29   <attribute name="signal">
30   <choice>
31    <value>true</value>
32    <value>false</value>
33   </choice>
34   </attribute>
35  </element>
36  </element>
37  </define>
38
39  <define name="Timezones">
40   <!-- http://www.timeanddate.com/library/abbreviations/timezones/ -->
41   <choice>
```

Example 5-8. precise.rng (continued)

```
42    <value>GMT</value>
43    <value>UTC</value>
44    <value>ACDT</value>
45    <value>ACST</value>
46    <value>ADT</value>
47    <value>AEDT</value>
48    <value>AEST</value>
49    <value>AKDT</value>
50    <value>AKST</value>
51    <value>AST</value>
52    <value>AWST</value>
53    <value>BST</value>
54    <value>CDT</value>
55    <value>CEST</value>
56    <value>CET</value>
57    <value>CST</value>
58    <value>CXT</value>
59    <value>EDT</value>
60    <value>EEST</value>
61    <value>EET</value>
62    <value>EST</value>
63    <value>HAA</value>
64    <value>HAC</value>
65    <value>HADT</value>
66    <value>HAE</value>
67    <value>HAP</value>
68    <value>HAR</value>
69    <value>HAST</value>
70    <value>HAT</value>
71    <value>HAY</value>
72    <value>HNA</value>
73    <value>HNC</value>
74    <value>HNE</value>
75    <value>HNP</value>
76    <value>HNR</value>
77    <value>HNT</value>
78    <value>HNY</value>
79    <value>IST</value>
80    <value>MDT</value>
81    <value>MESZ</value>
82    <value>MEZ</value>
83    <value>MST</value>
84    <value>NDT</value>
85    <value>NFT</value>
86    <value>NST</value>
87    <value>PDT</value>
88    <value>PST</value>
89    <value>WEST</value>
90    <value>WET</value>
91    <value>WST</value>
92  </choice>
```

Example 5-8. precise.rng (continued)

```
93  </define>
94
95  <define name="Hours">
96   <data type="string"><param name="pattern">[0-1][0-9]|2[0-3]</param></data>
97  </define>
98
99  <define name="MinutesSeconds">
100  <data type="integer">
101      <param name="minInclusive">0</param>
102      <param name="maxInclusive">59</param>
103     </data>
104  </define>
105
106  </grammar>
```

This schema uses the grammar document element (line 1). RELAX NG supports the XML Schema datatype library, and so it is declared on line 2. The start element (line 4) indicates where the instances will start; i.e., what the document element of the instance will be. The ref element refers to a named definition (define), which starts on line 8. There are no name conflicts between named definitions and other named structures such as element and attribute. This means that you could have a definition named time and an element named time with no conflicts. (I use Time as the name of the definition just as a personal convention.)

The possible values for the timezone attribute (line 10) are defined in the Timezones definition (line 39). The choice element (line 41) indicates the content of *one* of the 50 enumerated value elements that may be used as a value for timezone. This technique is also used for the content of the meridiem element (line 22) and the signal attribute (line 29).

The definitions for the content of the hour, minute, and second elements each refer to a definition. The hour element refers to the Hours definition (line 95). The data element points to the XML Schema type string (line 96). This string is constrained by the param element whose name is pattern (answerable to the XML Schema facet pattern). The regular expression [0-1][0-9]|2[0-3] indicates that the content of these elements must be two consecutive digits, the first in the range 00 through 19 ([0-1][0-9]) and the second in the range 20 through 23 (2[0-3]). The elements minute and second both refer to the definition MinutesSeconds (line 99). Rather than use a regular expression, this definition takes a different approach: it uses a minInclusive parameter of 0 (line 101) and a maxInclusive of 59 (line 102).

Test *precise.rng* by validating *time.xml* against it with *xmllint*:

```
xmllint --relaxng precise.rng time.xml
```

Or with Jing:

```
java -jar jing.jar -c precise.rng time.xml
```

Or with *jing.exe*:

```
jing -c precise.rng time.xml
```

Compact Syntax

RELAX NG's non-XML compact syntax is a pleasure to use (*http://www.oasis-open.org/committees/relax-ng/compact-20021121.html*). A tutorial on the compact syntax is available (*http://relaxng.org/compact-tutorial-20030326.html*). Its syntax is similar to XQuery's computed constructor syntax (*http://www.w3.org/TR/xquery/#id-computedConstructors*). Following is a compact version of *time.rng* called *time.rnc* (the *.rnc* file suffix is conventional, representing the use of compact syntax):

```
element time {
  attribute timezone { text },
  element hour { text },
  element minute { text },
  element second { text },
  element meridiem { text },
  element atomic {
    attribute signal { text }
  }
}
```

The RELAX NG namespace is assumed though not declared explicitly. The element, attribute, and text keywords define elements, attributes, and text content, respectively. Sets of braces ({ }) hold content models.

Jing with compact syntax. You cannot validate a document with *xmllint* when using compact syntax. You can validate a document using Jing and the -c switch. The command looks like:

```
java -jar jing.jar -c time.rnc time.xml
```

Or with *jing.exe* it looks like:

```
jing -c time.rnc time.xml
```

Silence is golden with Jing. In other words, if Jing reports nothing, the document is valid.

RNV. David Tolpin has developed a validator for RELAX NG's compact syntax; it is called RNV and is written in C (*http://davidashen.net/rnv.html*). It is fast and is a nice piece of work. Source is available, and you can recompile it on your platform using the make file provided or by writing your own. A

Windows 32 executable version is also available. Download the latest version of either from *http://ftp.davidashen.net/PreTI/RNV/*.

A copy of the Windows 32 executable *rnv.exe* (Version 1.6.1) is available in the file archive. Validate *time.xml* against *time.rnc* using this command:

```
rnv -p time.rnc time.xml
```

The -p option writes the file to standard output, as shown here. Without it, only the name of the validated file is displayed (see emphasis) when successful.

time.xml
```
<?xml version="1.0" encoding="UTF-8"?>

<!-- a time instant -->
<time timezone="PST">
 <hour>11</hour>
 <minute>59</minute>
 <second>59</second>
 <meridiem>p.m.</meridiem>
 <atomic signal="true"/>
</time>
```

A nice feature of RNV is that it can check a compact schema alone, without validating an instance. This is done with the -c option:

```
rnv -c time.rnc
```

As with Jing, the sound of silence means that the compact grammar is in good shape.

A more complex RELAX NG schema in compact syntax. Example 5-9 is a more complex yet more precise version of *time.rnc* called *precise.rnc*, which is only about 25 percent as long as its counterpart *precise.rng*.

Example 5-9. precise.rnc
```
1  start = Time
2  Time =
3    element time {
4      attribute timezone { Timezones },
5      element hour { Hours },
6      element minute { MinutesSeconds },
7      element second { MinutesSeconds },
8      element meridiem { "a.m." | "p.m." },
9      element atomic {
10       attribute signal { "true" | "false" }
11     }
12   }
13 Timezones =
14   # http://www.timeanddate.com/library/abbreviations/timezones/
15   "GMT" | "UTC" | "ACDT" | "ACST" | "ADT" | "AEDT" | "AEST" | "AKDT"
16   | "AKST" | "AST" | "AWST" | "BST" | "CDT" | "CEST" | "CET" | "CST"
```

Example 5-9. precise.rnc (continued)

```
17    | "CXT" | "EDT" | "EEST" | "EET" | "EST" | "HAA" | "HAC" | "HADT"
18    | "HAE" | "HAP" | "HAR" | "HAST" | "HAT" | "HAY" | "HNA" | "HNC"
19    | "HNE" | "HNP" | "HNR" | "HNT" | "HNY" | "IST" | "MDT" | "MESZ"
20    | "MEZ" | "MST" | "NDT" | "NFT" | "NST" | "PDT" | "PST" | "WEST"
21    | "WET" | "WST"
22  Hours = xsd:string { pattern = "[0-1][0-9]|2[0-3]" }
23  MinutesSeconds = xsd:integer { minInclusive = "0" maxInclusive="59"}
```

> The compact schema *precise.rnc* was generated by Trang from *precise.rng* (*http://www.thaiopensource.com/relaxng/ trang.html*).

Comparing *precise.rnc* with *precise.rng* should yield many insights into the compact syntax. The start symbol (line 1) indicates where the document element begins, as does the start element in XML syntax. The names of definitions (lines 2, 13, 22, and 23) are followed by equals signs (=), then by the patterns they represent. These definitions are referenced by name in the content models of elements or attributes (lines 1, 4, 5, 6, and 7). Choices of values are separated by a vertical bar (|) on lines 8, 10, and 15–21, and each of the values is quoted. Comments begin with # (line 14) instead of beginning with <!-- and ending with -->. The XML Schema datatype library is assumed, without being identified in the schema directly. Anything prefixed with xsd: is assumed to be a datatype from the XML Schema datatype library (xsd:string on line 22 and xsd:integer on line 23). The pattern keyword on line 22 is associated with a regular expression. The minInclusive and maxInclusive keywords are parameters (facets in XML Schema) that define an inclusive range of 0 through 59.

Test this compact schema by validating *time.xml* against it with RNV:

```
rnv precise.rnc time.xml
```

with Jing:

```
java -jar jing.jar -c precise.rnc time.xml
```

or with *jing.exe*:

```
jing -c precise.rnc time.xml
```

See Also

- Eric van der Vlist's *RELAX NG* (O'Reilly) provides a complete tutorial for RELAX NG, plus a reference
- If you run into problems, a good place to post questions is the RELAX NG user list: *http://relaxng.org/mailman/listinfo/relaxng-user*

- Sun's Multi-schema validator by Kawaguchi Kohsuke: *http://wwws.sun.com/software/xml/developers/multischema/*
- Tenuto, a C# validator for RELAX NG: *http://sourceforge.net/projects/relaxng*

Create a DTD from an Instance

#73   If you need a DTD in a hurry, create it from an XML instance using Trang, Relaxer, DTDGenerator, or xmlspy.

Several free Java tools are available that can generate a DTD based on an XML instance or instances. James Clark's Trang (*http://www.thaiopensource.com/relaxng/trang.html*) can, among other things, convert an XML document to a DTD, as can Relaxer (*http://www.relaxer.org*). Michael Kay's DTDGenerator (*http://saxon.sourceforge.net/ dtdgen.html*), once part of the Saxon project, consists of a single Java class that is dedicated to XML-to-DTD conversion. This hack walks you through the steps to generate a DTD from a simple instance using each of these tools.

Trang

You can download the current Trang JAR (*trang.jar*) from *http://www.thaiopensource.com/download/*, then place the JAR in the working directory. The Trang archive comes with a manual (*trang-manual.html*) that provides details on how to use Trang. I will cover only what is needed to create a DTD in this section. (If you need help with Java, refer to "Run Java Programs that Process XML" **[Hack #10]**.)

To create a DTD from *time.xml*, run this command:

```
java -jar trang.jar -I xml -O dtd time.xml generated.dtd
```

The -I switch indicates the type of input (XML), and -O indicates the type of output (DTD). *time.xml* is the input file and *generated.dtd* is the output file. You could simplify this command by skipping the -I and -O options, which will produce the same result:

```
java -jar trang.jar time.xml generated.dtd
```

The file *generated.dtd* looks like this:

```
<?xml encoding="UTF-8"?>

<!ELEMENT time (hour,minute,second,meridiem,atomic)>
<!ATTLIST time
  xmlns CDATA #FIXED ''
  timezone  #REQUIRED>

<!ELEMENT hour (#PCDATA)>
```

```
<!ATTLIST hour
  xmlns CDATA #FIXED ''>

<!ELEMENT minute (#PCDATA)>
<!ATTLIST minute
  xmlns CDATA #FIXED ''>

<!ELEMENT second (#PCDATA)>
<!ATTLIST second
  xmlns CDATA #FIXED ''>

<!ELEMENT meridiem (#PCDATA)>
<!ATTLIST meridiem
  xmlns CDATA #FIXED ''>

<!ELEMENT atomic EMPTY>
<!ATTLIST atomic
  xmlns CDATA #FIXED ''
  signal  #REQUIRED>
```

Trang automatically declares an xmlns attribute for every element in an effort to be namespace-friendly. Trang apparently orders the declarations it outputs according to the order in which they appear in the source.

Relaxer

With Relaxer installed [Hack #37], you can type this command to generate a DTD from *time.xml*:

```
relaxer -dir:out -dtd time.xml
```

Relaxer automatically uses the filename of the input file (*time.xml*) as the filename for the output file (*time.dtd*). So to keep from clobbering the existing *time.dtd*, Relaxer places the output file in the subdirectory *out*. If the subdirectory does not exist, Relaxer creates it. The result of this command, the file *out/time.dtd*, is shown here:

```
<!-- Generated by Relaxer 1.0 -->
<!-- Tue Mar 02 17:21:20 MST 2004 -->

<!ELEMENT hour (#PCDATA)>

<!ELEMENT time (hour, minute, second, meridiem, atomic)>
<!ATTLIST time timezone CDATA #REQUIRED>

<!ELEMENT minute (#PCDATA)>

<!ELEMENT atomic EMPTY>
<!ATTLIST atomic signal CDATA #REQUIRED>
```

```
<!ELEMENT meridiem (#PCDATA)>

<!ELEMENT second (#PCDATA)>
```

Relaxer can consider the content models of more than one XML document in order to produce a DTD. Try this:

```
relaxer -dir:out -dtd time1.xml time.xml
```

Relaxer uses the name of the first file in the list for its output filename, so the output file will be *out/time1.dtd*, which follows:

```
<!-- Generated by Relaxer 1.0 -->
<!-- Tue Mar 02 17:28:30 MST 2004 -->

<!ELEMENT hour (#PCDATA)>

<!ELEMENT time (hour, minute, second, meridiem, atomic?)>
<!ATTLIST time timezone CDATA #REQUIRED>

<!ELEMENT minute (#PCDATA)>

<!ELEMENT atomic EMPTY>
<!ATTLIST atomic signal CDATA #REQUIRED>

<!ELEMENT meridiem (#PCDATA)>

<!ELEMENT second (#PCDATA)>
```

The content for atomic is zero or one (?), as seen on the bold line. This is because atomic does not appear in *time1.xml*. Therefore, Relaxer interprets it as being an optional element rather than a required one.

DTDGenerator

The DTDGenerator JAR file came with the files for the book. To generate a DTD from *time.xml* with this utility, type the following command while in the working directory:

```
java -cp dtdgen.jar DTDGenerator time.xml
```

The result of the command is sent to standard output:

```
<!ELEMENT atomic EMPTY >
<!ATTLIST atomic signal NMTOKEN #REQUIRED >

<!ELEMENT hour ( #PCDATA ) >

<!ELEMENT meridiem ( #PCDATA ) >

<!ELEMENT minute ( #PCDATA ) >

<!ELEMENT second ( #PCDATA ) >
```

```
<!ELEMENT time ( hour, minute, second, meridiem, atomic ) >
<!ATTLIST time timezone NMTOKEN #REQUIRED >
```

It appears that DTDGenerator orders the declarations according to how they are stored on the stack. To redirect the output of DTDGenerator to a file, do this:

```
java -cp dtdgen.jar DTDGenerator time.xml > somesuch.dtd
```

xmlspy

You can also generate a DTD from an XML document with xmlspy (*http://www.xmlspy.com*). This example demonstrates how to do this in xmlspy 2004 Enterprise Edition (Release 3).

1. Start xmlspy, and use File → Open to open *time.xml* in the working directory.

2. Choose DTD/Schema → Generate DTD/Schema. The Generate DTD/ Schema dialog box appears (Figure 5-3). The DTD radio button is selected by default. Click OK.

3. You are then asked if you want to assign the generated DTD to the document. Click Yes. This adds a document type declaration to the XML document.

4. Then you are asked to save the DTD. Give it the name *spytime.dtd* and click the Save button. Overwrite *spytime.dtd* if it already exists in the working directory (it should).

5. With File → Save As, save *time.xml*—now with a document type declaration—as *spytime.xml*.

6. Choose XML → Validate or press F8 to validate *spytime.xml* against *spytime.dtd* (Figure 5-4).

If you have xmlspy available, it provides one of the quickest and easiest ways to generate a DTD for an XML document.

#74 Create an XML Schema Document from an Instance or DTD

There are several tools that can help you generate an XML Schema document from either an instance or a DTD. This hack shows you how to get the job done with little fuss.

This hack walks you through the process of creating an XML Schema document from an XML document or a DTD. The DTD2XS utility uses a DTD, but the XSD Inference, Trang, Relaxer, and xmlspy tools all rely on an

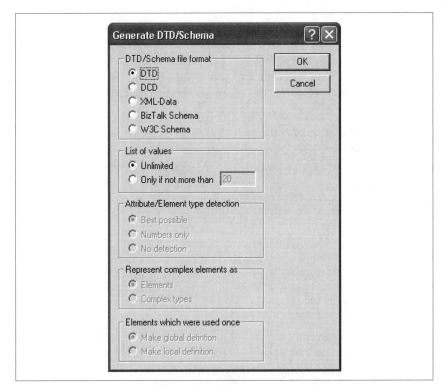

Figure 5-3. *xmlspy's Generate DTD/Schema dialog box with DTD selected*

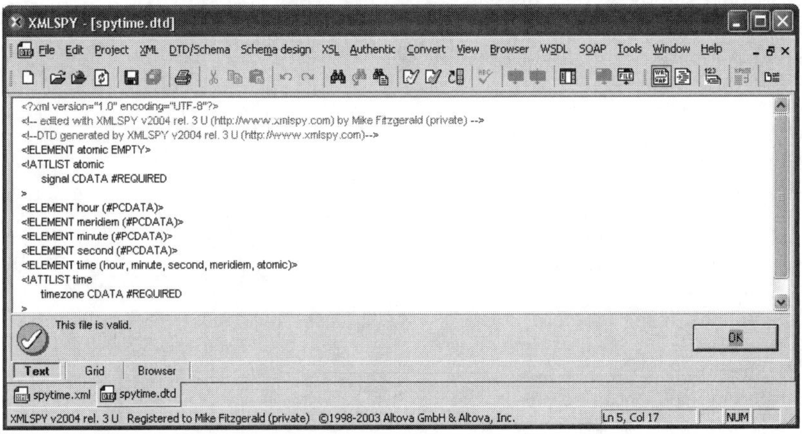

Figure 5-4. *Validating spytime.xml in xmlspy (text view)*

instance. Each of the following sections walks you through the simple steps necessary to get the job done with any of the tools.

LuMriX.net's DTD2XS

LuMriX.net (*http://www.lumrix.net*) offers a Java tool for creating an XML Schema from a DTD. Their tool is called DTD2XS (*http://sepia0.informatik. med.uni-giessen.de/ dtd2xs.php*). This tool comes with a command-line and a browser interface. We'll cover the command-line interface in this hack.

Download the tool and extract the archive. In the archive, you will find the files *dtd2xs.class*, *dtd2xsd.class*, *xurl.class*, and *complextype.xsl*. Copy these files to the working directory and type the following command (which assumes that the working directory is in the classpath):

```
java dtd2xsd time.dtd
```

The tool will generate the following output (Example 5-10).

Example 5-10. DTD2XS tool output

```
dtd2xs: dtdURI file:///C:\Hacks\examples\time.dtd
dtd2xs: resolveEntities true
dtd2xs: ignoreComments true
dtd2xs: commentLength 100
dtd2xs: commentLanguage null
dtd2xs: conceptHighlight 2
dtd2xs: conceptOccurrence 1
dtd2xs: conceptRelation element attribute
dtd2xs: load DTD ... done
dtd2xs: remove comments from DTD ... done
dtd2xs: DOM translation ...
... done
dtd2xs: complextype.xsl ... done
dtd2xs: add namespace ... done<?xml version="1.0" encoding="UTF-8"?>
<xs:schema xmlns:xs="http://www.w3.org/2001/XMLSchema">
<xs:element name="time">
<xs:complexType>
<xs:sequence>
<xs:element ref="hour"/>
<xs:element ref="minute"/>
<xs:element ref="second"/>
<xs:element ref="meridiem"/>
<xs:element ref="atomic"/>
</xs:sequence>
<xs:attribute name="timezone" type="xs:string" use="required"/>
</xs:complexType>
</xs:element>
<xs:element name="hour" type="xs:string"/>
<xs:element name="minute" type="xs:string"/>
<xs:element name="second" type="xs:string"/>
<xs:element name="meridiem" type="xs:string"/>
<xs:element name="atomic">
<xs:complexType>
<xs:attribute name="signal" type="xs:string" use="required"/>
</xs:complexType>
```

Example 5-10. DTD2XS tool output (continued)

```
</xs:element>
</xs:schema>
```

You can redirect the XML Schema to a file using >:

```
java dtd2xsd time.dtd > newtime.xsd
```

Microsoft XSD Inference 1.0

Microsoft offers a tool that infers an XML Schema document from an instance. It's called the XSD Inference 1.0 tool. It can be run online (*http://apps.gotdotnet.com/xmltools/xsdinference/*) and is also available for download (*http://apps.gotdotnet.com/xmltools/xsdinference/XSDInference.exe*). In an effort to be brief, I'll demonstrate only the online version.

The online version is shown in Internet Explorer in Figure 5-5. (For a usage overview, see *http://apps.gotdotnet.com/xmltools/xsdinference/overview.html*.) To infer a schema from an instance, click the Browse button on the form. Then search for and select *time.xml* from the "Choose file" dialog box. Click Open. Now click the Infer Schema button. (Click the Refine Schema button to refine a previously inferred schema. If you click Refine Schema without first clicking Infer Schema, the result will be the same as clicking Infer Schema.) The result is displayed in the "View the XML Schema(s) generated" text area (Figure 5-6). Any errors would be displayed in the "View the error log" text area.

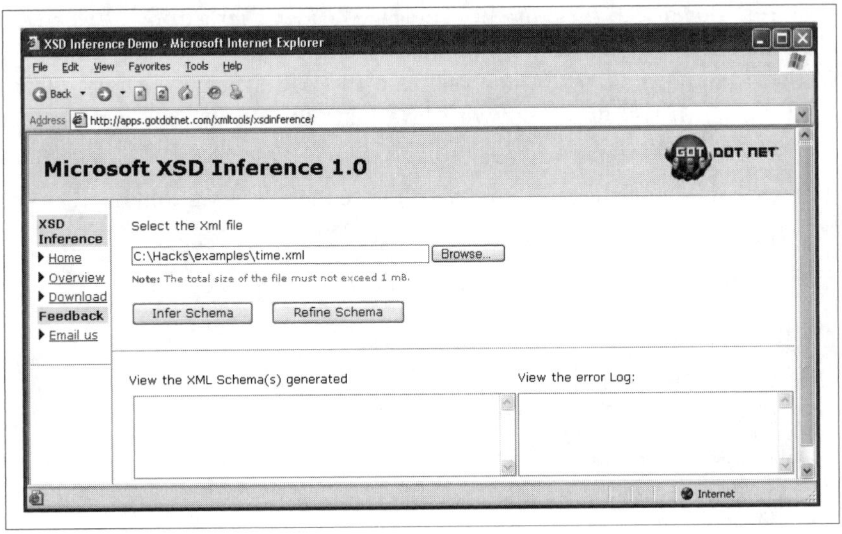

Figure 5-5. Microsoft XSD Inference tool in IE

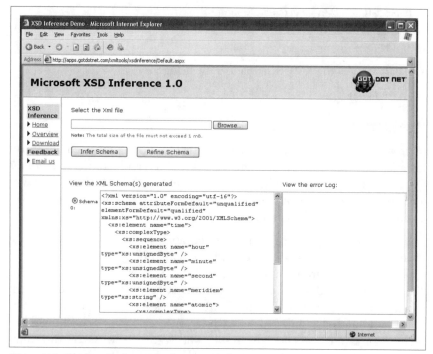

Figure 5-6. Results of inferring a schema with the XSD Inference tool in IE

Trang

You can download the current Trang JAR (*trang.jar*) from *http://www.thaiopensource.com/download/*, then place the JAR in the working directory. In this section, I will cover how to create an XML Schema document from an instance. (If you need help with Java, refer to "Run Java Programs that Process XML" **[Hack #10].**)

To create an XML Schema from *time.xml*, use the following command:

```
java -jar trang.jar time.xml generated.xsd
```

In Example 5-11, you can see what *generated.xsd* should look like.

Example 5-11. generated.xsd

```
<?xml version="1.0" encoding="UTF-8"?>
<xs:schema xmlns:xs="http://www.w3.org/2001/XMLSchema"
elementFormDefault="qualified">
  <xs:element name="time">
    <xs:complexType>
      <xs:sequence>
        <xs:element ref="hour"/>
        <xs:element ref="minute"/>
        <xs:element ref="second"/>
```

Example 5-11. generated.xsd (continued)

```
        <xs:element ref="meridiem"/>
        <xs:element ref="atomic"/>
      </xs:sequence>
      <xs:attribute name="timezone" use="required" type="xs:NCName"/>
    </xs:complexType>
  </xs:element>
  <xs:element name="hour" type="xs:integer"/>
  <xs:element name="minute" type="xs:integer"/>
  <xs:element name="second" type="xs:integer"/>
  <xs:element name="meridiem" type="xs:NCName"/>
  <xs:element name="atomic">
    <xs:complexType>
      <xs:attribute name="signal" use="required" type="xs:boolean"/>
    </xs:complexType>
  </xs:element>
</xs:schema>
```

Relaxer

Assuming that Relaxer is already installed **[Hack #37]**, you can type the following command to generate an XML Schema document from *time.xml*:

```
relaxer -dir:out -xsd time.xml
```

Because Relaxer automatically uses the filename of the input file (*time.xml*) as the filename for the output file (*time.xsd*), we use the -dir:out option so that the output file will be stored in the *out* subdirectory. (If a subdirectory does not exist, Relaxer creates it.) The result of running Relaxer with -xsd is the file *out/time.xsd*, as shown in Example 5-12.

Example 5-12. out/time.xsd

```
<?xml version="1.0" encoding="UTF-8" ?>
<xsd:schema xmlns=""
            xmlns:xsd="http://www.w3.org/2001/XMLSchema"
            targetNamespace="">
  <xsd:element name="time" type="time"/>
  <xsd:complexType name="time">
    <xsd:sequence>
      <xsd:element name="hour" type="xsd:int"/>
      <xsd:element name="minute" type="xsd:int"/>
      <xsd:element name="second" type="xsd:int"/>
      <xsd:element name="meridiem" type="xsd:token"/>
      <xsd:element name="atomic" type="atomic"/>
    </xsd:sequence>
    <xsd:attribute name="timezone" type="xsd:token"/>
  </xsd:complexType>
  <xsd:complexType name="atomic">
    <xsd:sequence/>
    <xsd:attribute name="signal" type="xsd:boolean"/>
```

Example 5-12. out/time.xsd (continued)

```
    </xsd:complexType>
</xsd:schema>
```

Relaxer can use the content models of more than one XML document at a time, each with a different content model, in order to produce an XML Schema document. Use this command:

```
relaxer -dir:out -xsd time1.xml time.xml
```

When naming the output file, Relaxer uses the name of the first file in the list, so the output file will be *out/time1.xsd*, which is listed in Example 5-13.

Example 5-13. out/time1.xsd

```
<?xml version="1.0" encoding="UTF-8" ?>
<xsd:schema xmlns=""
            xmlns:xsd="http://www.w3.org/2001/XMLSchema"
            targetNamespace="">
  <xsd:element name="time" type="time"/>
  <xsd:complexType name="time">
    <xsd:sequence>
      <xsd:element name="hour" type="xsd:int"/>
      <xsd:element name="minute" type="xsd:int"/>
      <xsd:element name="second" type="xsd:int"/>
      <xsd:element name="meridiem" type="xsd:token"/>
      <xsd:element maxOccurs="1" minOccurs="0" name="atomic"
        type="atomic"/>
    </xsd:sequence>
    <xsd:attribute name="timezone" type="xsd:token"/>
  </xsd:complexType>
  <xsd:complexType name="atomic">
    <xsd:sequence/>
    <xsd:attribute name="signal" type="xsd:boolean"/>
  </xsd:complexType>
</xsd:schema>
```

Notice the difference between the content models for the atomic element in these two examples. In Example 5-13, the content for atomic is a minOccurs of 0 and a maxOccurs of 1. This is because atomic does not appear in *time1. xml*, so Relaxer interprets it as being optional rather than required.

xmlspy

As with a DTD, you can also generate an XML Schema document from an XML document with xmlspy (*http://www.xmlspy.com*). These instructions show you how to do this with xmlspy 2004 Enterprise Edition (Release 3).

1. Start xmlspy, and with File → Open, open *time.xml* from the working directory where you extracted the book's file archive.

2. Choose DTD/Schema → Generate DTD/Schema. The Generate DTD/Schema dialog box appears. Select the W3C Schema radio button and click OK (Figure 5-7).

3. You are then asked if you want to assign the generated DTD to the document. Click Yes. This adds an XML Schema instance namespace declaration and a `noNamespaceSchemaLocation` attribute to the XML document.

4. Then you are asked to save the schema. Save it as *spytime.xsd* and click the Save button. It is okay to overwrite *spytime.xsd* if it already exists in the working directory.

5. With File → Save As, save *time.xml*—now with a reference to the schema—as *spytimexsd.xml*.

6. Choose XML → Validate or press F8 to validate *spytimexsd.xml* against *spytime.xsd* (Figure 5-8).

You now have in hand a variety of tools to generate schemas for instances or DTDs. At least one of them should work for you!

Create a RELAX NG Schema from an Instance

HACK
#75

Trang and Relaxer can create RELAX NG schemas on the fly, in either XML or compact syntax.

Trang (*http://www.thaiopensource.com/relaxng/trang.html*) can translate XML documents into RELAX NG schemas, in either XML or compact syntax. Likewise, Relaxer (*http://www.relaxer.org*) can produce RELAX NG schemas in XML syntax. This means that you can develop an XML document and then instantly produce a RELAX NG schema for it. The schemas that Trang or Relaxer produce may not be exactly what you want, but they will give you a good start—a schema that you can edit for your own purposes. By the way, Trang can also produce XML Schema documents and DTDs. This hack will walk you through the steps to automatically produce RELAX NG schemas, in either XML or compact formats, from an XML document.

We'll translate the document *newhire.xml*. This document is based on specifications from the HR-XML Consortium (*http://www.hr-xml.org/channels/home.htm*), which develops XML vocabularies for human resource applica-

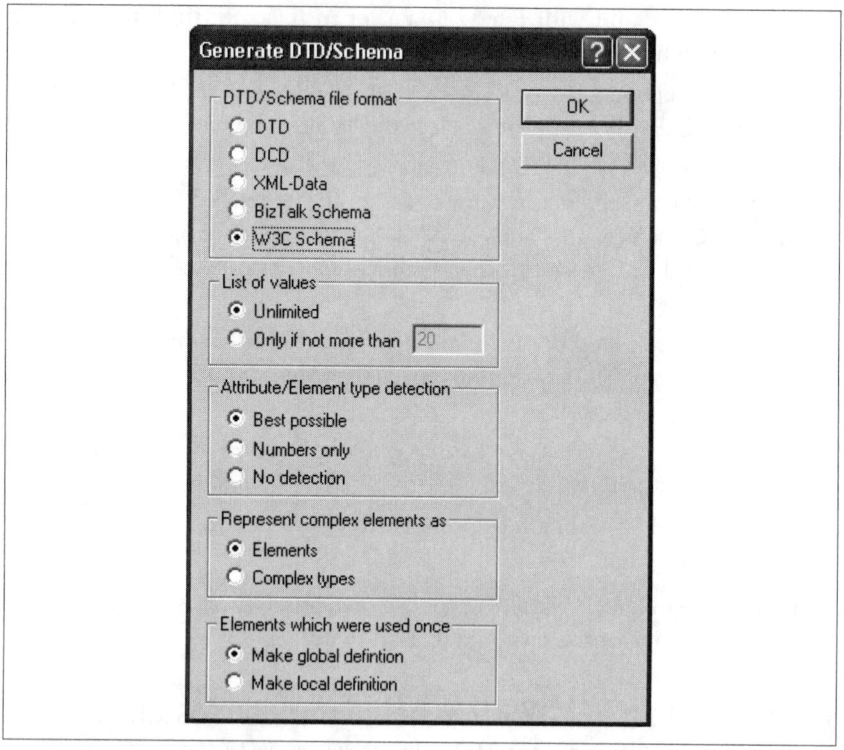

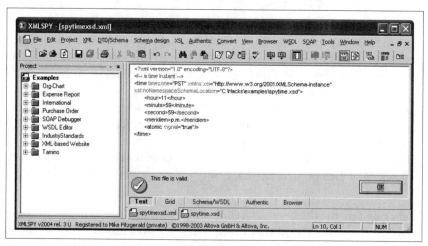

Figure 5-7. *xmlspy's Generate DTD/Schema dialog box with W3C Schema selected*

Figure 5-8. *Validating spytimexsd.xml in xmlspy (text view)*

tions. The file *newhire.xml* contains some personal information about an employee, Floyd Filigree, who lives in New York:

```
<?xml version="1.0" encoding="UTF-8"?>
```

```
<Employee xmlns="http://ns.hr-xml.org">
 <PersonName>
  <GivenName>Floyd</GivenName>
  <FamilyName>Filigree</FamilyName>
  <Affix type="formOfAddress">Mr</Affix>
 </PersonName>
 <PostalAddress>
  <CountryCode>US</CountryCode>
  <PostalCode>10001</PostalCode>
  <Region>NY</Region>
  <Municipality>New York</Municipality>
  <DeliveryAddress>
   <PostOfficeBox>0000</PostOfficeBox>
  </DeliveryAddress>
 </PostalAddress>
</Employee>
```

Trang (XML Syntax)

To translate *newhire.xml* into RELAX NG in XML syntax with Trang, type this command:

```
java -jar trang.jar newhire.xml newhire.rng
```

You can use the Trang JAR that is in the file archive that came with the book, or you can download the latest version of Trang from *http://www. thaiopensource.com/download*, if there is a version later than 20030619.

When you use two arguments, Trang expects that the file type will match a file's suffix (e.g., *.xml* for XML, *.rng* for RELAX NG). You could also type in your command like this, for the same results:

```
java -jar trang.jar -I xml -O rng newhire.xml newhire.rng
```

Either of these commands will produce *newhire.rng*, shown here:

```
1  <?xml version="1.0" encoding="UTF-8"?>
2  <grammar ns="http://ns.hr-xml.org" xmlns="http://relaxng.org/ns/structure/1.0"
3   datatypeLibrary="http://www.w3.org/2001/XMLSchema-datatypes">
4    <start>
5     <element name="Employee">
6      <element name="PersonName">
7       <element name="GivenName">
8        <data type="NCName"/>
9       </element>
10      <element name="FamilyName">
11       <data type="NCName"/>
12      </element>
13      <element name="Affix">
14       <attribute name="type">
15        <data type="NCName"/>
16       </attribute>
```

```
17                    <data type="NCName"/>
18                  </element>
19                </element>
20                <element name="PostalAddress">
21                  <element name="CountryCode">
22                    <data type="NCName"/>
23                  </element>
24                  <element name="PostalCode">
25                    <data type="integer"/>
26                  </element>
27                  <element name="Region">
28                    <data type="NCName"/>
29                  </element>
30                  <element name="Municipality">
31                    <text/>
32                  </element>
33                  <element name="DeliveryAddress">
34                    <element name="PostOfficeBox">
35                      <data type="integer"/>
36                    </element>
37                  </element>
38                </element>
39              </element>
40          </start>
41        </grammar>
```

Trang makes decisions on how to lay out the schema based on the document information, and then you can edit its results by hand. For example, you may not want the NCName datatype (lines 8, 11, 15, 22, and 28), so you could edit *newhire.rng* and replace all occurrences of NCName with string.

Relaxer (XML Syntax)

Another option for translating an XML document into RELAX NG schema in XML syntax is Relaxer. Assuming that you have downloaded and installed Relaxer **[Hack #37]**, translate *newhire.xml* into a RELAX NG schema in XML syntax with the command:

```
relaxer -dir:out -rng newhire.xml
```

which will produce *newhire.rng* in the *out* subdirectory:

```
1   <?xml version="1.0" encoding="UTF-8" ?>
2   <grammar xmlns="http://relaxng.org/ns/structure/1.0"
3            xmlns:a="http://relaxng.org/ns/compatibility/annotations/1.0"
4            xmlns:java="http://www.relaxer.org/xmlns/relaxer/java"
5            xmlns:relaxer="http://www.relaxer.org/xmlns/relaxer"
6            xmlns:sql="http://www.relaxer.org/xmlns/relaxer/sql"
7            datatypeLibrary="http://www.w3.org/2001/XMLSchema-datatypes"
8            ns="http://ns.hr-xml.org"
9            >
10    <start>
11      <ref name="Employee"/>
```

```
12    </start>
13    <define name="Employee">
14      <element name="Employee">
15        <ref name="PersonName"/>
16        <ref name="PostalAddress"/>
17      </element>
18    </define>
19    <define name="PersonName">
20      <element name="PersonName">
21        <element name="GivenName">
22          <data type="token"/>
23        </element>
24        <element name="FamilyName">
25          <data type="token"/>
26        </element>
27        <ref name="Affix"/>
28      </element>
29    </define>
30    <define name="Affix">
31      <element name="Affix">
32        <attribute name="type">
33          <data type="token"/>
34        </attribute>
35        <data type="token"/>
36      </element>
37    </define>
38    <define name="PostalAddress">
39      <element name="PostalAddress">
40        <element name="CountryCode">
41          <data type="token"/>
42        </element>
43        <element name="PostalCode">
44          <data type="int"/>
45        </element>
46        <element name="Region">
47          <data type="token"/>
48        </element>
49        <element name="Municipality">
50          <data type="token"/>
51        </element>
52        <ref name="DeliveryAddress"/>
53      </element>
54    </define>
55    <define name="DeliveryAddress">
56      <element name="DeliveryAddress">
57        <element name="PostOfficeBox">
58          <data type="int"/>
59        </element>
60      </element>
61    </define>
62    </grammar>
```

The namespace declaration on line 3 is for the RELAX NG DTD Compatibility spec (*http://www.oasis-open.org/committees/relax-ng/compatibility-20011203.html*).

This spec integrates default attribute values, IDs, and documentation into RELAX NG processing, but it is a separate spec with different conformance requirements than straight RELAX NG 1.0. Though Relaxer declares this namespace, it does not use it. Relaxer adds several other namespace declarations for its own purposes (lines 4, 5, and 6), which the document does not use.

Relaxer organizes nodes into named templates (lines 13, 19, 38, and 55), unlike Trang's output. In addition, Relaxer uses the token datatype, which is one of two built-in RELAX NG datatypes (lines 22, 25, 33, 35, 41, 47, and 50). The other is string (XML Schema has a string datatype, too). Relaxer uses the int XML Schema datatype (*http://www.w3.org/TR/xmlschema-2/#int*) on lines 44 and 58 for PostalCode and PostOfficeBox, where Trang uses the larger integer instead (*http://www.w3.org/TR/xmlschema-2/#integer*).

Trang (Compact Syntax)

To translate *newhire.xml* into RELAX NG's compact syntax, type this command:

```
java -jar trang.jar newhire.xml newhire.rnc
```

You could also type the command using the switches -I and -O to produce the same results:

```
java -jar trang.jar -I xml -O rnc newhire.xml newhire.rnc
```

Either of these commands will produce *newhire.rnc*:

```
1   default namespace = "http://ns.hr-xml.org"
2
3   start =
4     element Employee {
5       element PersonName {
6         element GivenName { xsd:NCName },
7         element FamilyName { xsd:NCName },
8         element Affix {
9           attribute type { xsd:NCName },
10          xsd:NCName
11        }
12      },
13      element PostalAddress {
14        element CountryCode { xsd:NCName },
15        element PostalCode { xsd:integer },
16        element Region { xsd:NCName },
17        element Municipality { text },
18        element DeliveryAddress {
19          element PostOfficeBox { xsd:integer }
20        }
21      }
22    }
```

Convert a RELAX NG Schema to XML Schema

If you like working with RELAX NG but you need XML Schema too, Trang is the answer. Trang converts RELAX NG schemas (in both XML and compact syntax) to XML Schema.

If you are like me, you prefer to work with RELAX NG when developing schemas for XML, but out of necessity you may need to provide schemas in XML Schema format. Trang can help you out because it allows you to translate RELAX NG schemas in XML or compact syntax into XML Schema. This hack shows you how.

Here is the command to convert the RELAX NG schema *time.rng* (in XML syntax) to *newtime.xsd*:

```
java -jar trang.jar time.rng newtime.xsd
```

Example 5-14 shows the XML Schema that is the result of the translation (*newtime.xsd*):

Example 5-14. newtime.xsd

```
1  <?xml version="1.0" encoding="UTF-8"?>
2  <xs:schema xmlns:xs="http://www.w3.org/2001/XMLSchema"
3      elementFormDefault="qualified">
4    <xs:element name="time">
5      <xs:complexType>
6        <xs:sequence>
7          <xs:element ref="hour"/>
8          <xs:element ref="minute"/>
9          <xs:element ref="second"/>
10         <xs:element ref="meridiem"/>
11         <xs:element ref="atomic"/>
12       </xs:sequence>
13       <xs:attribute name="timezone" use="required"/>
14     </xs:complexType>
15   </xs:element>
16   <xs:element name="hour" type="xs:string"/>
17   <xs:element name="minute" type="xs:string"/>
18   <xs:element name="second" type="xs:string"/>
19   <xs:element name="meridiem" type="xs:string"/>
20   <xs:element name="atomic">
21     <xs:complexType>
22       <xs:attribute name="signal" use="required"/>
23     </xs:complexType>
24   </xs:element>
25 </xs:schema>
```

The schema element is the document element and http://www.w3.org/2001/ XMLSchema is the namespace URI (line 2). The attribute elementFormDefault with a value of qualified means that an instance is expected to have a default namespace declaration on its document element and that all of its child elements will be in that default namespace or in no namespace, if one is not declared in the instance.

The element time declared on line 4 is followed by a sequence of other child elements and the declaration of an attribute timezone (line 13). This sequence is held in a complexType element wrapper that wraps complex content (i.e., content that can have attributes, etc.). These definitions refer to the elements that appear later in the schema (lines 16–20). The atomic element adds an attribute signal, and so is embedded in a complexType element. Trang does not give the attributes timezone and signal types.

Trang can also take as input a compact syntax schema, such as *time.rnc*. Here is how to translate a compact syntax schema to XML Schema:

```
java -jar trang.jar time.rnc timec.xsd
```

And here is the outcome of the translation, which is the same as the outcome that came from the XML syntax version:

```
1   <?xml version="1.0" encoding="UTF-8"?>
2   <xs:schema xmlns:xs="http://www.w3.org/2001/XMLSchema"
3       elementFormDefault="qualified">
4     <xs:element name="time">
5       <xs:complexType>
6         <xs:sequence>
7           <xs:element ref="hour"/>
8           <xs:element ref="minute"/>
9           <xs:element ref="second"/>
10          <xs:element ref="meridiem"/>
11          <xs:element ref="atomic"/>
12        </xs:sequence>
13        <xs:attribute name="timezone" use="required"/>
14      </xs:complexType>
15    </xs:element>
16    <xs:element name="hour" type="xs:string"/>
17    <xs:element name="minute" type="xs:string"/>
18    <xs:element name="second" type="xs:string"/>
19    <xs:element name="meridiem" type="xs:string"/>
20    <xs:element name="atomic">
21      <xs:complexType>
22        <xs:attribute name="signal" use="required"/>
23      </xs:complexType>
24    </xs:element>
25  </xs:schema>
```

HACK #77   Use RELAX NG and Schematron Together to Validate Business Rules

There are few issues regarding XML validation that cause as many headaches as validation of business rules (constraints on relations between element and attribute content in an XML document). This hack helps relieve that headache.

Even after the release of the new, grammar-based schema languages XML Schema and RELAX NG, it remains difficult to express restrictions on relations between the contents of various elements and attributes. This hack introduces a method that makes it possible to validate these kinds of rules by combining two XML Schema languages, RELAX NG (*http://www.relaxng.org/*) and Schematron (*http://www.ascc.net/xml/resource/ schematron/*).

W3C XML Schema (*http://www.w3.org/XML/Schema*) lacks much support for co-occurrence constraints, and RELAX NG supports them only to the extent that the presence or absence of a particular element or attribute value changes the validation rules. On the other hand, Schematron provides good support for these types of constraints. Schematron is a rule-based language that uses path expressions instead of grammars to define what is allowed in an XML document. This means that instead of creating a grammar for an XML document, a Schematron schema makes assertions applied to a specific context within the document. If the assertion fails, a diagnostic message that is supplied by the author of the schema is displayed.

One drawback of Schematron is that, although the definition of detailed rules is easy, it can often be a bit cumbersome to define structure. A better language for defining structure is RELAX NG, so the combination of the two is perfect to create a very powerful validation mechanism.

As an example, here is a simple mathematical calculation modeled in XML (*add.xml*):

```
<addition result="3">
 <number>1</number>
 <number>2</number>
</addition>
```

This example shows a simple addition between two numbers, each modeled with a number element, and the result of the addition specified in the result attribute of the surrounding addition element.

A RELAX NG schema (in XML syntax) to validate this little document is very easy to write and can, for example, look like *add.rng* in Example 5-15.

Example 5-15. add.rng

```
<grammar xmlns="http://relaxng.org/ns/structure/1.0"
datatypeLibrary="http://www.w3.org/2001/XMLSchema-datatypes">

<start>
 <element name="addition">
  <ref name="number"/>
  <ref name="number"/>
```

Example 5-15. add.rng (continued)

```
    <attribute name="result">
     <data type="decimal"/>
    </attribute>
   </element>
  </start>

  <define name="number">
   <element name="number">
    <data type="decimal"/>
   </element>
  </define>

 </grammar>
```

The schema defines the structure for the document as well as specifying the correct datatype for the number element and the result attribute. The problem is that the previous schema will also validate the following instance, which is structurally correct but mathematically incorrect (*badadd.xml*):

```
    <addition result="5">
        <number>1</number>
        <number>2</number>
    </addition>
```

In RELAX NG, there is no way to specify that the value of the result attribute should equal the sum of the values in the two number elements except by faking it using value elements. By "faking it" I mean that during RELAX NG validation the actual addition does not take place, just the checking of values against a schema. Schematron, on the other hand, is very good at specifying these kinds of relationships. Before explaining how to embed Schematron rules in the RELAX NG schema, let's backtrack and briefly look at how Schematron works.

As mentioned earlier, Schematron uses path expressions to make assertions applied to a specific context within the instance document. Each assertion specifies a test condition that evaluates to either true or false. If the condition evaluates to false then a specific message, specified by the schema author, is given as a validation message. In order to implement the Schematron path expressions, XPath is used with various extensions provided by XSLT. This is very good in terms of validation purposes because it means that the only thing needed for validation with Schematron is an XSLT processor.

In order to define the context and the assertions, a basic Schematron schema consists of three layers: *patterns*, *rules*, and *assertions*. In its simple form, the pattern works as a grouping mechanism for the rules and provides a pattern name that is displayed together with the assertion message if the assertion fails. The rule specifies the context for the assertions, and the assertion itself specifies the test condition that should be evaluated. In XML terms, the pattern is defined using a pattern element, rules are defined using rule elements as children of the pattern element, and assertions are defined using assert elements as children of the rule element.

A Schematron rule for validation of the addition constraint above could look something like this (*add.sch*):

```
<sch:schema xmlns:sch="http://www.ascc.net/xml/schematron">
 <sch:pattern name="Validate calculation result">
  <sch:rule context="addition">
   <sch:assert test="@result = number[1] + number[2]"
    >The addition result is not correct.</sch:assert>
  </sch:rule>
 </sch:pattern>
</sch:schema>
```

The rule has a context attribute that specifies the addition element to be the context for the assertion. The assertion has a test attribute that specifies the condition that should be evaluated. In this case, the condition is to validate that the value of the result attribute has the same value as the sum of the values in the two number elements. If this Schematron rule were applied to the erroneous XML instance *badadd.xml*, a validation message similar to this would be displayed:

```
From pattern "Validate calculation result":
    Assertion fails: "The addition result is not correct." at
        /addition[1]
        <addition result="2">...</>
```

So, now we have one RELAX NG schema to validate the structure and one Schematron rule to validate the calculation constraint, and the only thing left is to combine them by embedding the Schematron rule in the RELAX NG schema (dropping the sch:schema document element). This is made possible because a RELAX NG processor will ignore all elements that are not declared in the RELAX NG namespace. The combined schema will then look like this (*addsch.rng*):

```
<?xml version="1.0" encoding="UTF-8"?>
<grammar xmlns="http://relaxng.org/ns/structure/1.0"
datatypeLibrary="http://www.w3.org/2001/XMLSchema-datatypes"
xmlns:sch="http://www.ascc.net/xml/schematron">

<start>
 <element name="addition">
  <sch:pattern name="Validate calculation result">
   <sch:rule context="addition">
    <sch:assert test="@result = number[1] + number[2]"
```

```
     >The addition result is not correct.</sch:assert>
    </sch:rule>
   </sch:pattern>
   <ref name="number"/>
   <ref name="number"/>
   <attribute name="result">
    <data type="decimal"/>
   </attribute>
  </element>
 </start>

 <define name="number">
  <element name="number">
   <data type="decimal"/>
  </element>
 </define>

</grammar>
```

The exact location of the embedded Schematron rule does not matter—it can be placed anywhere in the RELAX NG schema. A good location for the embedded rule is within the definition of the element that is the context for the Schematron rule (shown emphasized in the combined schema). The finished RELAX NG schema with embedded Schematron rules is ready for validation, and the only thing left is an explanation of the validation process.

You can use the Topologi Schematron Validator (*http://www.topologi.com/ products/validator/download.php*) to validate *add.xml* against *addsch.rng* (Figure 5-9). This validator not only validates against Schematron schemas, but also XML Schema, DTDs, and RELAX NG with embedded Schematron schemas. After downloading and installing the application, open it and then select the working directory for both the XML document and schema. Select the XML document *add.xml* and the schema *addsch.rng*, and then click Run. Results are displayed in a dialog box. Try it with *badadd.xml* to see the difference in results.

Without a validator like Topologi to validate the embedded Schematron rules, you can extract them from the RELAX NG schema and validate them separately using normal Schematron validation.

Pulling Schematron Out of RELAX NG

Luckily, this is very easy to do with an XSLT stylesheet called *RNG2Schtrn. xsl* (*http://www.topologi.com/public/Schtrn_XSD/RNG2Schtrn.zip*), which will merge all embedded Schematron rules and create a separate Schematron schema. This stylesheet is already in the working directory where you unzipped the file archive.

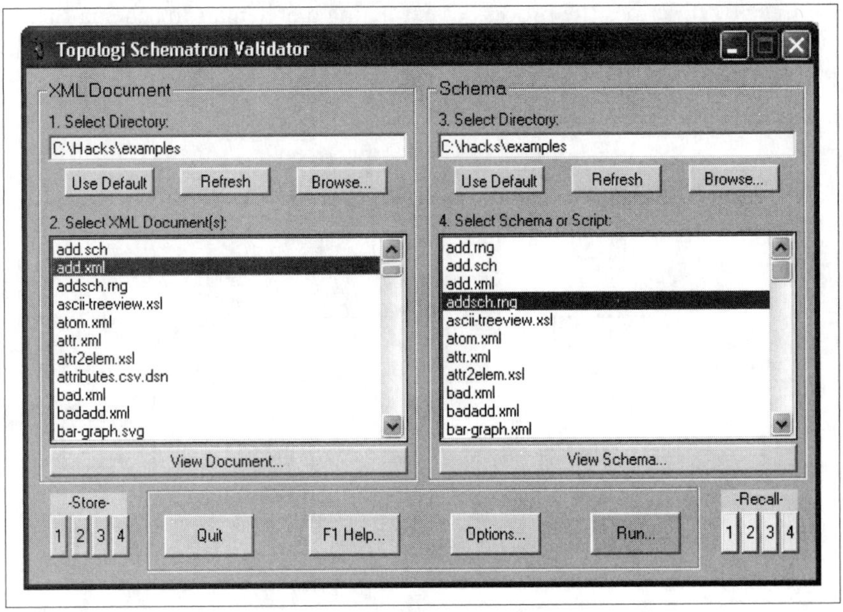

Figure 5-9. Topologi Schematron Validator

Apply this stylesheet to the RELAX NG schema with the embedded stylesheet with Xalan C++ **[Hack #32]**:

```
xalan -o newadd.sch addsch.rng RNG2Schtrn.xsl
```

When successful, this transformation will produce this result (*newadd.sch*):

```
<?xml version="1.0" encoding="UTF-8" standalone="yes"?>
<sch:schema xmlns:sch="http://www.ascc.net/xml/schematron"
xmlns:rng="http://relaxng.org/ns/structure/1.0">
<sch:pattern name="Validate calculation result"
xmlns="http://relaxng.org/ns/structure/1.0">
 <sch:rule context="addition">
  <sch:assert test="@result = number[1] + number[2]">The addition
     result is not correct.</sch:assert>
 </sch:rule>
</sch:pattern>
<sch:diagnostics/>
</sch:schema>
```

Then you can use Topologi to validate *add.xml* against *newadd.sch*, or you can use Jing to do it (Version 20030619 of the JAR—not *jing.exe*—offers provisional support of Schematron):

```
java -jar jing.jar newadd.sch add.xml
```

Figure 5-10 describes the process of extracting a Schematron schema that is embedded in a RELAX NG schema (XML syntax), and then processing the RELAX NG and Schematron schemas separately.

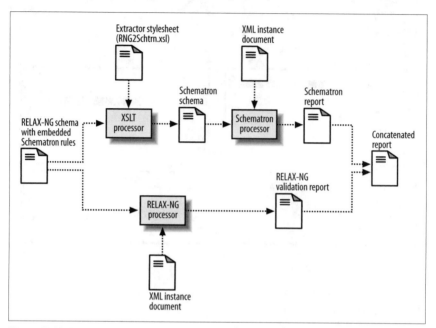

Figure 5-10. Processing a RELAX NG schema with embedded Schematron rules

See Also

- "An Introduction to Schematron," by Eddie Robertsson, on XML.com: *http://www.xml.com/pub/a/2003/11/12/schematron.html*
- "Combining RELAX NG and Schematron," by Eddie Robertsson, on XML.com: *http://www.xml.com/pub/a/2004/02/11/relaxtron.html*

—Eddie Robertsson

Use RELAX NG to Generate DTD Customizations

RELAX NG enables you to create a customized subset or extension of a DTD much more easily than doing it the old-fashioned way.

You may find at some point in your XML work—especially if you're working with a large, complex XML vocabulary such as DocBook (*http://www.docbook.org*)—that you don't use or want the full set of elements that the

XML vocabulary provides, and would much rather work with a smaller, custom subset that excludes the elements you don't need.

If you're working with a RELAX NG schema, you'll be happy to find out that making a subset of it is a relatively trivial task, especially if you're using a RELAX NG compact syntax (RNC) schema instead of a RELAX NG XML-syntax (RNG) schema. You basically just need to create a file in which you include (by reference) the schema you want to subset, and then list out all the elements you want to exclude, giving the notAllowed pattern for the content of the element.

On the other hand, if you're working with a DTD, you'll find that trying to create a subset of it the old-fashioned way (by making a DTD customization layer or by editing the DTD directly) can be a much more complicated and time-consuming task.

The good news is that you don't need to do it the old-fashioned way because you can use some existing free software to quickly and easily generate a custom DTD: Norm Walsh's Perl script *flatten.pl* (*http://cvs.sourceforge.net/ viewcvs.py/*checkout*/docbook/cvstools/flatten*), James Clark's Trang and Jing (*http://www.thaiopensource.com/relaxng/*), and David Tolpin's XSLT stylesheet *incelim.xsl* (*http://ftp.davidashen.net/incelim/*).

The problem with trying to subset a DTD the old-fashioned way is that it requires you to:

- Search through the documentation for the DTD (or through the DTD itself) to identify all the parameter entities and/or parent-element content models that contain the elements you want to exclude.

- Redefine all content models and parameter entities that contain any of the elements you want to exclude.

That can be much more of a hassle than it sounds, and those are just the steps that you need to take to make a subset. If you want to add any elements, it can end up being a lot more complicated.

The solution to all that customization hassle is to instead use a RELAX NG compact-syntax schema along with a couple of very clever tools. This enables you to generate a subset of a DTD using a process that:

- Does not require you to know or care what parent elements contain the elements you want to exclude.

- Does not require you to redefine the content of any of the parent elements that contain the elements you want to exclude.

The first part of the process, getting some tools installed and doing a couple of preliminary steps, is the only part that takes any real amount of time, and even then it doesn't really take long. The remaining steps, creating the customization file to describe your subset and generating your custom DTD, take very little time at all.

Generating an RNC Schema

To make creating your DTD subset as easy as possible, you need to have a flattened RELAX NG compact-syntax (RNC) version of the DTD you want to subset. This section describes a simple process you can use to do that. (If you already have an RNC version of your DTD, you can just skip this section and go to the next.) The process requires a few tools that you'll need to download, but they're all relatively easy to install and use.

Flattening your DTD. To ensure that everything works as expected, you need to generate a flattened version of your DTD source; i.e., a standalone version of the DTD in which all entity references to external files have been replaced with the contents of the referenced files. (If you're not working with a modular DTD—if your DTD does not use entity references to include other files—you can skip this section and go on to the next.)

To flatten your DTD source:

1. Locate Norm Walsh's Perl script *flatten.pl* in the working directory of examples, or check for a later version (download it and place it in the working directory).

2. Run the following command:

   ```
   perl flatten.pl docbook.dtd > docbook-flat.dtd
   ```

   flatten.pl generates the file *docbook-flat.dtd* in the same directory as your *docbook.dtd* file.

Generating an RNC schema from your flattened DTD. To create an RNC schema from a flattened DTD:

1. Make sure Trang and Jing are available (*http://www.thaiopensource.com/download/*).

2. With Trang in the classpath, run the following command:

   ```
   java -jar trang.jar docbook-flat.dtd docbook.rng
   ```

   Trang generates *docbook.rng* in the same directory as your *docbook.dtd* file.

3. Run the following:

   ```
   java -jar trang.jar docbook.rng docbook.rnc
   ```

Trang generates *docbook.rnc* in the same directory as your *docbook.rng* file.

The reason for the two-step process of first creating an RNG version and then an RNC version is that you'll need to have both versions around to get things to work smoothly. You need the RNG version in order to be able to convert back to DTD syntax, and you could actually do everything you need to do using only the RNG version. But having a version in the RNC syntax—which is designed for ease of authoring and readability—makes the customization process easier.

Creating an RNC Schema Customization File

The elegance and simplicity of the design of RELAX NG and its compact syntax makes the process of creating your actual RNC customization file the quickest and easiest part of this whole solution.

To make your RNC schema customization file, simply create a *custom.rnc* file similar to Example 5-16, replacing *docbook.rnc* with your own RNC file and replacing the element names on the left of the equals signs with the names of the elements you want to exclude.

Example 5-16. RNC customization file custom.rnc

```
include "docbook.rnc" {
  confdates = notAllowed
  confgroup = notAllowed
  confnum = notAllowed
  confsponsor = notAllowed
  conftitle = notAllowed
  contractnum = notAllowed
  contractsponsor = notAllowed
  msg = notAllowed
  msgaud = notAllowed
  msgentry = notAllowed
  msgexplan = notAllowed
  msginfo = notAllowed
  msglevel = notAllowed
  msgmain = notAllowed
  msgorig = notAllowed
  msgrel = notAllowed
  msgset = notAllowed
  msgsub = notAllowed
  msgtext = notAllowed
  simplemsgentry = notAllowed
}
```

That's it. Really.

Compiling Your Customization File

James Clark's Trang is an extremely powerful tool for converting among various schema types: from RNG, RNC, DTD, or XML to RNG, RNC, DTD, or XSD. One of Trang's current limitations is that it can't convert RELAX NG schemas to DTDs if those schemas include other schemas by reference and also override element definitions from those referenced schemas. What that means is that Trang, on its own, can't convert your RNC customization file to a DTD.

This is where the next tool in the chain comes in: David Tolpin's *incelim.xsl* stylesheet. The name of the stylesheet describes what it does: it resolves any includes in RELAX NG schemas by literally inserting the contents of them into its output, and then it eliminates from its output all definitions of elements that are overridden in a customization file.

It is basically doing something very similar to what Norm Walsh's *flatten.pl* tool does for DTDs, but Tolpin prefers to describe the process as creating a "compiled" version of the schema. In his own words:

> *incelim* is a RELAX NG splicer. It takes a RELAX NG grammar in XML syntax, expands all includes and externalRefs, and optionally replaces references to text, empty, or notAllowed with the patterns. The result is a "compiled" schema convenient for distribution, as well as for consumption by tools which do not yet support include and externalRef.

Note the part that says it "takes a RELAX NG grammar in XML syntax." That means you'll first need to transform your RNC customization file into RNG syntax before using *incelim.xsl*.

Converting Your RNC Customization File to RNG XML Syntax

Like all XSLT stylesheets, *incelim.xsl* needs well-formed XML as input. So, because RELAX NG compact syntax (RNC) is non-XML syntax, you'll need to convert your RNC customization file into RELAX NG XML syntax (RNG) before using *incelim.xsl*. This is another task for Trang.

To transform your *custom.rnc* RNC customization file to RNG, just run the following command:

```
java -jar trang.jar custom.rnc custom.rng
```

Trang generates *custom.rng* in the same directory as your *custom.rnc* file. It'll look something like Example 5-17 .

Example 5-17. RNG customization file custom.rng

```
<grammar xmlns="http://relaxng.org/ns/structure/1.0">

<include href="docbook.rng">
```

Example 5-17. RNG customization file custom.rng (continued)

```
<define name="beginpage">
 <notAllowed/>
</define>
<define name="confdates">
 <notAllowed/>
</define>
<define name="confgroup">
 <notAllowed/>
</define>
<define name="confnum">
 <notAllowed/>
</define>
<define name="confsponsor">
 <notAllowed/>
</define>
<define name="conftitle">
 <notAllowed/>
</define>
</include>
</grammar>
```

Compare Example 5-17 to Example 5-16 and you'll see why most people prefer to create and edit RELAX NG using the RNC syntax, and just convert that to RNG syntax when they need to.

Using incelim.xsl to Compile Your RNG Customization File

To compile your RNG customization file with *incelim.xsl*, you'll need to use an XSLT engine—either Michael Kay's Saxon or Daniel Veillard's *xsltproc*. You can download Saxon from *http://saxon.sourceforge.net*; if you are running Cygwin or a Linux distribution that includes *libxml2*, you already have *xsltproc*.

> Make sure to use the latest version of *xsltproc*, because *xsltproc* compiled against *libxml* v20604, *libxslt* v10102, and *libexslt* v802 and earlier versions cannot be used with *incelim.xsl*. This is due to a bug in the implementation of exsl:node-set( ) in those earlier versions.

To use *incelim.xsl*:

1. *incelim.xsl* and other stylesheets are in a subdirectory (*incelim*) of the file archive and should already be in your working directory. If you want the latest version, download *incelim.xsl* again and place it in the *incelim* subdirectory. It's actually a set of stylesheets with the *incelim.xsl* stylesheet

just acting as a core file, so make sure to keep all the files in the same directory.

2. Run the following command, using whichever XSLT engine (Saxon or *xsltproc*) you prefer, and replacing the pathname with an appropriate path. In Saxon:

```
java -jar saxon7.jar custom.rng incelim/incelim.xsl >
    custom-compiled.rng
```

or in *xsltproc*:

```
xsltproc incelim/incelim.xsl custom.rng > custom-compiled.rng
```

Either command generates a *custom-compiled.rng* file in the same directory as your *custom.rng* file. If you look at the contents of that file, you'll see that it represents the complete contents of your original DTD/schema, minus all the elements you excluded in your customization file.

Generating Your DTD Subset

The final step—getting your customization file back into DTD syntax—is another easy one. Just run the following command:

```
java -jar trang.jar custom-compiled.rng custom.dtd
```

Trang generates a *custom.dtd* in the same directory as your *custom-compiled.rng* file.

It's possible that Trang may fail to convert your customization, but instead just emit one or more error messages similar to the following:

```
custom-compiled.rng:1329:error: sorry, cannot handle this kind of
"oneOrMore"
```

If you get an error message like that, don't panic: it probably just indicates that your customization has left behind an element that no longer has any real content because you've removed all of its possible child elements. That is, it's probably an element you wanted to remove but just overlooked.

The fix is to:

1. Go to the part of your *custom-compiled.rng* file where Trang says it's having a problem (the number in the error message is a line number in the file).

2. Identify the name of the problem element.

3. Go back to the earlier section "Creating an RNC Schema Customization File" and add the problem element to the list of excluded elements in your customization file.

4. Repeat the previous steps to regenerate the *custom.rng*, *custom-compiled.rng*, and *custom.dtd* files.

Once you begin using *custom.dtd*, you'll see that it omits all elements you excluded in your RNC customization file.

—Michael Smith

Generate Instances Based on Schemas

Use xmlspy or Sun's Instance Generator to create instances of DTDs or other schemas.

Perhaps you need to generate XML instances of a given schema to create a test suite or you want a collection of instance files for some other reason. xmlspy (*http://www.xmlspy.com*) can create a single instance of a DTD or XML Schema document, but the Sun Instance Generator, a Java program, can create many XML instances based on a DTD, RELAX NG, Relax, or XML Schema. If you want a quick look at a single instance, xmlspy may be adequate for you. However, if you need a set of files, including some with intentional errors in them, Sun's tool is probably the way to go. This hack shows you how to use both tools.

Generating an Instance with xmlspy

These instructions assume that you have already downloaded and installed xmlspy 2004 Professional or Enterprise Edition (this won't work with the Home Edition). Follow these steps to create an instance of the DTD *time. dtd*:

1. Open xmlspy.

2. Choose File → Open and the Open dialog box appears. Navigate to the working directory of files from the book file archive and select the file *time.dtd*. Then click the Open button.

3. Choose DTD/Schema → Generate sample XML file. The Generate sample XML file dialog box appears. All the radio buttons should be selected by default, and the repeatable elements text box should contain the number 1. This means that xmlspy will generate a document that includes all non-mandatory elements and attributes, the first choice of a choice (|) will be used, only one instance of repeatable elements will be used, and the elements and attributes will be filled with sample data. Now click OK.

4. The sample XML document is generated. Choose File → Save As and save the file as *timegen.xml* in the working directory.

5. Click the Text tab. xmlspy should appear similar to Figure 5-11.

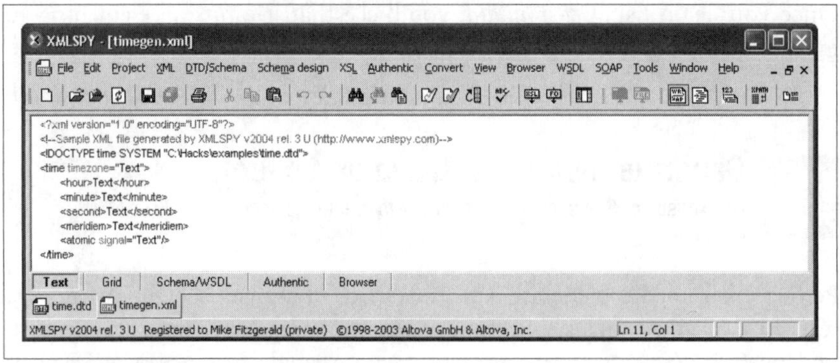

Figure 5-11. Generated XML document in xmlspy

Generating an Instance with the Sun Instance Generator

Kawaguchi Kohsuke developed the Sun Instance Generator, which is written in Java. Download the latest version of the ZIP archive from the address given earlier and extract the contents into the working directory. You will need to register on the Sun site (if you have not done so already) to download the generator. The following have been tested with Version 20040601, available from *https://msv.dev.java.net/servlets/ProjectDocumentList?folderID=101* (but it might be outdated by the time you read this).

While at a command prompt, enter this command:

```
java -jar xmlgen.jar
```

The generator will give you a usage summary. Table 5-1 summarizes the possible options.

Table 5-1. Sun Instance Generator options

Command-line option	Description
-dtd *file.dtd*	Use a DTD file as the model schema.
-ascii	Use US-ASCII for element and attribute content or values. Without -ascii, the generator uses a broader range of Unicode characters.
-seed *n*	Set a random seed *n*.
-depth *n*	Determine cut-back depth of document, based on occurrence restraints. Once limit *n* is reached, the generator limits depth.
-width *n*	Tell generator the maximum number of times that the occurrence constraints zero or more (*) and one or more (+) are repeated.
-n *n*	Generate *n* number of instances.
-warning	Show warnings.

Table 5-1. Sun Instance Generator options (continued)

Command-line option	Description
-quiet	Don't show progress messages.
-root {namespaceURI}elementname	Fix the root element to the given element.
-encoding	Java-style character encoding, such as UTF8.
-example *file.xml*	Provide an example file to guide the generator. You can use this option more than once.
-error *m/n*	Set the error ratio; that is, generate *n* number of errors per *m* elements (average).
-nocomment	Suppress the insertion of comments that indicate generated errors.

Let's get right to work. To generate an instance from the RELAX NG schema *time.rng* using US-ASCII content for elements and attributes, enter this command:

```
java -jar xmlgen.jar -ascii time.rng
```

The result will look like Example 5-18.

Example 5-18. Output of Sun Instance Generator

```
parsing a grammar: time.rng
generating document #1
<?xml version="1.0" encoding="UTF-8"?>
<time timezone="s{8Ty[^QpD;Wg*" xmlns:ns1="">
    <hour>z#BJIr4&lt;</hour>
    <minute>U&apos;</minute>
    <second>Ln&quot;X])&quot;&apos;#06</second>
    <meridiem>jCj&quot;R}Mt8z`</meridiem>
    <atomic signal="ka: ^p-1LazDC&gt;"/>
</time>
```

Try this to generate an instance from the XML Schema document, *time.xsd*:

```
java -jar xmlgen.jar -ascii time.xsd
```

And this to generate an instance from the DTD *time.dtd* (note -dtd switch):

```
java -jar xmlgen.jar -ascii -dtd time.dtd
```

Use the -example option to include the whole document in DTD output. The example file *time.xml* shows the tool the structure you are seeking to describe.

```
java -jar xmlgen.jar -ascii -example time.xml -dtd time.dtd
```

You can generate a number of instances by using the -n option (this example produces 10 instances):

```
java -jar xmlgen.jar -ascii -n 10 time.rng
```

Introduce errors in your instances by including an error ratio; e.g., -error 1/ 5 means output one error for every five elements (a relatively high occurrence of errors):

```
java -jar xmlgen.jar -ascii -error 1/5 time.rng
```

Comments in the output note the errors, unless you use the -nocomment option. Finally, to generate a series of 100 files with a low occurrence of errors and save them to disk, use the $ character in the output filename:

```
java -jar xmlgen.jar -n 100 -error 1/100 time.rng time-$.xml
```

This will create 100 files (*time-00.xml*, *time-01.xml*, *time-02.xml*, etc.) with occasional errors. You now have a test suite!

See Also

- For more information on how to use the Sun Instance Generator, see the document *HowToUse.html* that comes with the software download

## CHAPTER SIX

RSS and Atom
Hacks 80–90

Syndication lets sites share information across the Web, making it easy to do things like display headlines from a site or collection of sites. Most of the syndicated feeds are written in RSS, a simple XML vocabulary (in several varieties) for summarizing information about a site. Several popular flavors of RSS are leading the pack, with upstart Atom growing in acceptance. This chapter contains hacks that can help you get a handle on the web site syndication trend.

We start with a hack that explains how to get started subscribing to RSS feeds [Hack #80], followed by a series of hacks that show you how to create RSS 0.91 [Hack #81], RSS 1.0 [Hack #82], RSS 2.0 [Hack #83], and Atom [Hack #84] documents. Read in succession, these four hacks may seem a little repetitive; however, they are necessary to spell out clearly the formats of each of these vocabularies. You'll also validate feeds online [Hack #85].

You'll learn how to generate RSS feeds with Perl [Hack #86] and with popular blogging software from Movable Type [Hack #87]. You'll also learn how to post RSS headlines on your own site [Hack #88] and create feeds from Google [Hack #89] and from Amazon [Hack #90].

Most of the files mentioned in this chapter are in the book's file archive, available for download from *http://www.oreilly.com/catalog/xmlhks/*.

Subscribe to RSS Feeds

#80 You've heard the RSS buzz and you figure you ought to do something about it. This hack introduces you to RSS and shows you how to start subscribing to RSS feeds today.

RSS is an XML vocabulary, now taking several forms. It first emerged from Netscape's My Netscape Network in the late 1990s and has grown into a ubiquitous format for syndicating web content. Sites generate RSS documents that essentially are summaries of web sites and include, among other things, headlines, content descriptions, and links to web pages, blogs, and graphics.

At the moment, the most popular versions of RSS are the following (see *http://www.syndic8.com/stats.php?Section=rss#RSSVersion*):

- RSS 0.91 **[Hack #81]** *http://backend.userland.com/rss091* and *http://www.scripting.com/netscapeDocs/RSS%200_91%20Spec,%20revision%203.html*, also called *Rich Site Summary*

- RSS 1.0 **[Hack #82]** *http://web.resource.org/rss/1.0/spec*, also called *RDF Site Summary*

- RSS 2.0 **[Hack #83]** *http://blogs.law.harvard.edu/tech/rss*), also called *Really Simple Syndication*

- Atom **[Hack #84]** *http://atomenabled.org/*, which is gaining popularity

The political history of these specs takes a few twists and turns that I won't get into here, except to say that there was a camp (Dave Winer, et al) that preferred simple markup over a more complex approach.

These RSS documents are treated as newsfeeds that can be aggregated or gathered by sites like *http://www.bloglines.com*, *http://www.syndic8.com*, and O'Reilly's own *http://www.oreillynet.com/meerkat/*. You can also subscribe to these feeds with an RSS reader such as these well-known examples:

- Radio UserLand, probably the most popular RSS news reader for Windows and the Mac: *http://www.userland.com/*

- Amphetadesk, another popular RSS news reader that is open source and works on multiple platforms: *http://www.disobey.com/amphetadesk/*

- NetNewsWire, a three-paned RSS reader for Mac OS X: *http://ranchero.com/netnewswire/*

- FeedReader, a free, open source RSS news reader for Windows 95 or later: *http://www.feedreader.com/*

- NewsGator, an RSS news reader for Microsoft Outlook: *http://www.newsgator.com*

In this hack, I'll show you how to get several of the news readers and subscribe to newsfeeds with them.

Radio UserLand

Radio is more than just a news reader: it's also a launchpad for publishing blogs. You can get it for 30 days free, and then after that pay $39.95 USD. Download it from *http://radio.userland.com/download*.

Once you have downloaded Radio and installed it, open the application and you'll go to your main blogs page in your default browser. Click the link for news aggregator (where you can read your RSS newsfeeds) and then click the link for subscriptions.

There you can subscribe to a newsfeed by entering a URL manually in an address box at the top of the window and clicking the Add button (see Figure 6-1). You can unsubscribe to newsfeeds by clicking a checkbox on the left side of the window and then clicking the Unsubscribe button at the bottom of the page.

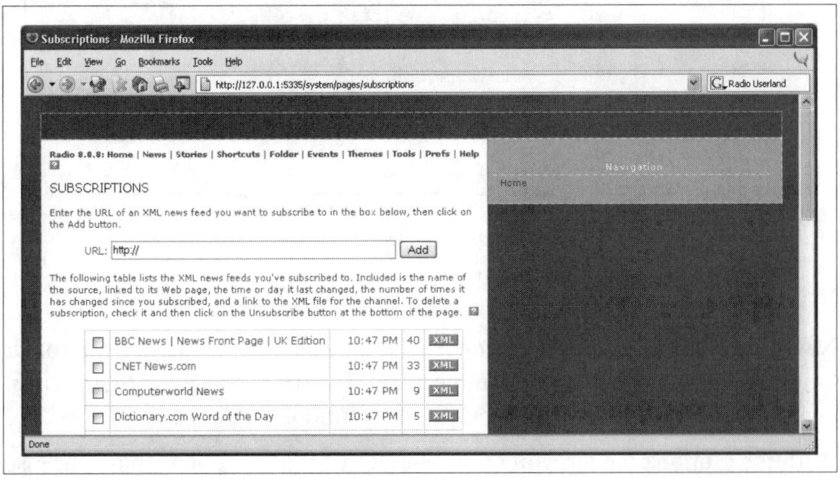

Figure 6-1. Radio UserLand subscription page

AmphetaDesk

When you bring up AmphetaDesk, a small console browser window is opened and the application is displayed in your default browser. Your current newsfeeds are displayed there. Click the Add a Channel link near the top of the browser window and you will go to a view like the one in Figure 6-2. You can either enter a link for a newsfeed in the box provided and then click the Add This Channel button, or you can click the checkbox to the left of the channel you want to subscribe to (hundreds to choose from, arranged in alphabetical order) and then click Subscribe to the Channels I've Checked Below.

If you go to the My Channels page, you can click on the checkboxes to the left of listed subscriptions and then click Remove the Checked Channels to delete that subscription.

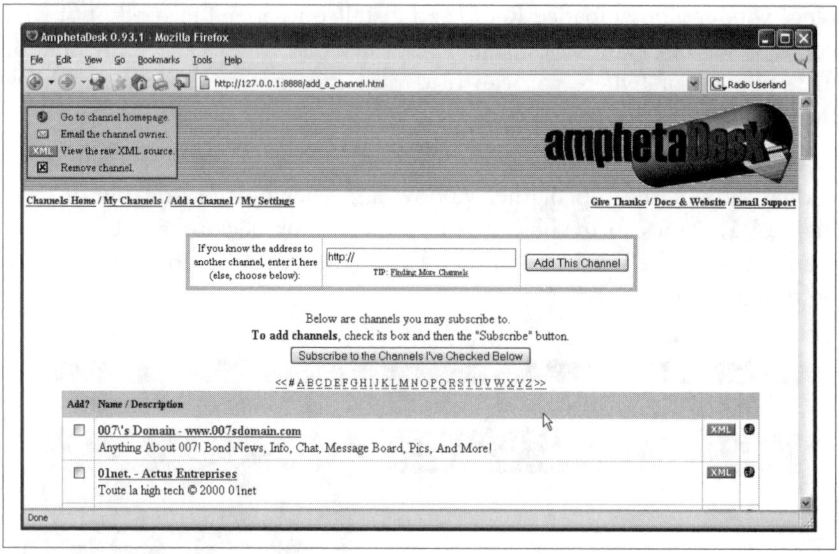

Figure 6-2. AmphetaDesk's Add a Channel page

NewsGator

NewsGator (*http://www.newsgator.com*) is an RSS news reader for Microsoft Outlook. It also offers an online news reader service (*http://services. newsgator.com/*), but we'll look only at the Outlook reader here.

With the Outlook reader, you get a 14-day free trial or you can buy a license for $29 USD. Download it from *http://www.newsgator.com/downloads.aspx*. After downloading the NewsGator executable file, double-click it, and the installation program takes over. Click through the installation steps.

The next time you open Outlook, you will see a dialog box regarding your NewsGator trial. Just click the Continue button for now. Then the News-Gator wizard appears. This will give you an introduction to the news reader, allow you to select the folder where newsfeeds will be organized and stored, and step through a tutorial as well.

When you are all done with the wizard, you will see NewsGator's folder in with your other personal folders, and a NewsGator menu on the toolbar. From that menu, select Subscriptions. You can then click the Add button on the Subscriptions dialog box. Select Add feed, and the dialog box will be displayed (Figure 6-3). You can then add the URLs for your desired feeds and click OK.

After entering a URL (try *http://www.reutershealth.com/eline.rss*) and clicking OK, you will be returned to the Subscriptions dialog box. Click Close

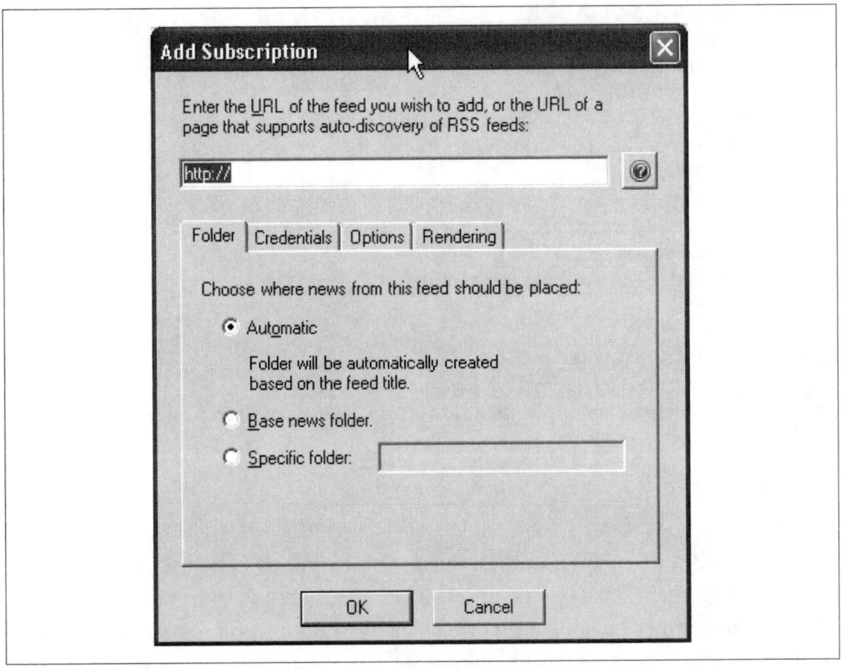

Figure 6-3. NewsGator Add Subscription dialog box

and then return to Outlook. A new subfolder will be added for your new newsfeed. If you use Outlook every day, NewsGator keeps your newsfeeds where you can easily reach them.

See Also

- "Why RSS Is Everywhere," by Xeni Jardin (*Wired*, April 2004): *http://www.wired.com/wired/archive/12.04/start.html?pg=7*

- Read about *Variety*'s approach to RSS, plus click through its links on the RSS phenomena: *http://www.variety.com/index.asp?layout=rss*

—Michael Fitzgerald

HACK #81 Create an RSS 0.91 Document

Create an RSS 0.91 document using a template, and gain a little essential background in RSS history.

RSS 0.91 is probably the most popular RSS format because it is the oldest and is so simple, which, as with so many other technologies, encourages adoption by the teeming masses. Here is a minimal 0.91 document, containing all the required elements and a few optional ones (it is named *news.xml* in the file archive):

```
<rss version="0.91">
 <channel>
  <title>Wy'east Communications</title>
  <link>http://www.wyeast.net</link>
  <description> Wy'east Communications is an XML
     consultancy.</description>
  <language>en-us</language>
  <image>
   <url>http://www.wyeast.net/images/mthood.jpg</url>
   <title>Wy'east</title>
   <link>http://www.wyeast.net</link>
  </image>
  <item>
   <title>Legend of Wy'east</title>
   <link>http://www.wyeast.net/wyeast.html</link>
   <description>The Native American story behind the name
      Wy'east.</description>
  </item>
 </channel>
</rss>
```

RSS 0.91 doesn't declare a namespace for its elements. The rss element is the document element. It has a required attribute, version, whose value is 0.91. This element must have exactly one channel child and one or more item children. Following the channel element are these elements:

title

A descriptive title for this channel. This should usually be the same as the content of the HTML element title on your main site page (such as *index.html*). The maximum number of characters allowed here is 100.

link

A URI for the channel. This should be a link to the web site that originates the feed—in this case, *http://www.wyeast.net*. Maximum length of this element is 500 characters.

description

A description of the channel, usually answering the question "What's this site all about?" Limited to 500 characters.

For a comparison of the required and optional child elements of channel for both RSS 0.91 and 2.0, see Table 6-2 in "Create an RSS 2.0 Document" **[Hack #83]**.

The image is an optional element that has three required child elements: url, which contains a URL for a JPG, GIF, or PNG image representing the channel (500 character limit); title, which contains the alt attribute value from the img element in HTML used for the graphic whose link is in url (100 character limit); and link, a link to the web site represented by the link in url. The elements title and link should have the same content as the elements with the same names that are children of channel (500 character limit).

RSS 0.91 requires the first non-whitespace characters of the content in link and url elements to begin with ftp:// or http://. Others are not permitted. This restriction is lifted by RSS 2.0 [Hack #83].

The optional children of image are description, width, and height. description should contain the same advisory text as might be found in the title attribute on the a element that creates the link associated with the graphic; width and height are the width and height of the graphic. By default, the value of width is 88 with a max of 144; the default value of height is 31 with a max of 400.

This document has only one item element, though it is common to have several (you can only have up to 15 in RSS 0.91 according to *http://blogs.law. harvard.edu/ tech/rss#comments*). A channel element may have one or more item children, which can contain: title, the title of the article or story (100 character limit); link, the URL to the story (500 character limit); and description, which holds a summary of the article or story (500 character limit).

You can find a DTD for RSS 0.91 at *http://my.netscape.com/ publish/formats/rss-0.91.dtd*.

Other optional children of channel are shown in Table 6-1. For more information on these and other RSS 0.91 elements, see *http://backend.userland. com/rss091*.

Table 6-1. Optional children of channel in RSS 0.91

Element	Description
copyright	Copyright notice for the channel
docs	Documentation for the RSS format used by the channel
lastBuildDate	Last time channel content changed, in RFC 822 format, Sat, 01 Jan 05 00:00:27 PST (see *http://www.ietf.org/rfc/rfc822.txt*)
managingEditor	Email address of managing editor for the channel
pubDate	Publication date of channel, in RFC 822 format, Sat, 01 Jan 05 00:00:27 PST (see *http://www.ietf.org/rfc/rfc822.txt*)

Table 6-1. Optional children of channel in RSS 0.91 (continued)

Element	Description
rating	Platform for Internet Content Selection (PICS) rating (*http://www.w3.org/ PICS/*)
skipDays	Days to skip reading channel
skipHours	Hours to skip reading channel
textInput	A text input box for the channel, such as a search box (required children include title, description, name, and link)
webMaster	Email address of webmaster for the channel

Create an RSS 1.0 Document

#82   Create an RSS 1.0 document using a template or with Java.

RSS 1.0 is a branch from RSS 0.91 that incorporates elements from the W3C's Resource Description Framework or RDF (*http://www.w3.org/RDF/*). Some folks didn't particularly like this branch to RDF because they saw it as too complex. Nevertheless, RSS 1.0 is now a popular format for RSS documents, running a close second to RSS 0.91, according to *http://www.syndic8. com/stats.php?Section=rss#RSSVersion*.

Following is a minimal example of an RSS 1.0 document, available in the file archive as *wyeast.rss* and at *http://www.wyeast.net/wyeast.rss*:

```
<?xml version="1.0" encoding="UTF-8"?>
<rdf:RDF xmlns="http://purl.org/rss/1.0" xmlns:rdf="http://www.w3.org/1999/
02/22
-rdf-syntax-ns#">
 <channel rdf:about="http://www.wyeast.net/wyeast.rss">
  <title>Wy'east Communications</title>
  <link>http://www.wyeast.net</link>
  <description>Wy'east Communications is an XML
    consultancy.</description>
  <items>
   <rdf:Seq>
    <rdf:li rdf:resource="http://www.wyeast.net/wyeast.html"/>
   </rdf:Seq>
  </items>
 </channel>
 <item rdf:about="http://www.wyeast.net/wyeast.html">
  <title>Legend of Wy'east</title>
  <link>http://www.wyeast.net/wyeast.html</link>
  <description>The Native American story behind the name
    Wy'east.</description>
 </item>
</rdf:RDF>
```

The rdf:RDF element from the RDF namespace (*http://www.w3.org/1999/02/22-rdf-syntax-ns#*) is the document element. This element must have exactly one channel child and one or more item children (these elements are in the default namespace, http://purl.org/rss/1.0). The rdf:about attribute on channel, from the RDF namespace, identifies the feed with a URI. Following channel are these elements:

title
> A descriptive title for this channel.

link
> A URI for the channel.

description
> A description of the channel.

items
> Contains the RDF elements Seq and li. The resource attribute on rdf:li contains a URI that identifies an item used later in the document.

Like channel, the sole item element holds title, link, and description elements that describe the news item. There can be virtually unlimited item element children after channel here. The rdf:about attribute on item must be unique and should match the content of link.

Two other possible children of channel are image and textinput, which link by means of rdf:resource attributes to other image and textinput elements, optionally used in the document as children of rdf:RDF (i.e., you can have one without the other). The image element links a graphic to the channel and must contain the trio title, link, and url; the textinput element contains a script or form that relates to the site and contains title, link, name, and description elements.

The document *wyeast.rss* was generated by a Java program, *Rss1.java*, available in the file archive. This program was written using the XML Object Model or XOM (*http://cafeconleche.org/XOM/*), an easy-to-use XML API written by Elliotte Rusty Harold.

In order to work, *Rss1.java* needs Xerces and XOM JARs in the classpath at compile time, and the XOM JAR in the classpath at runtime. You can get *xercesImpl.jar* from *http://www.apache.org/dist/xml/xerces-j/* and the XOM JAR from the XOM web site. This program can be adapted to work with any of the RSS or Atom vocabularies.

See Also

- To use a Perl program to generate an RSS 1.0 document; *http://search.cpan.org/~kellan/XML-RSS-1.02/lib/RSS.pm*

Create an RSS 2.0 Document
Create an RSS 2.0 document from a template.

RSS 2.0 is an update of RSS 0.91, and so does not follow the RDF approach taken by RSS 0.91 and RSS 1.0, it is the third most popular RSS format. You can find the spec for RSS 2.0 at *http://blogs.law.harvard. edu/tech/rss*. It is similar to RSS 0.91, but offers some clarifications and additional elements.

The following, *news.xml*, is a minimal example of RSS 2.0:

```
<rss version="2.0">
 <channel>
  <title>Wy'east Communications</title>
  <link>http://www.wyeast.net</link>
  <description> Wy'east Communications is an XML consultancy.</description>
  <item>
   <title>Legend of Wy'east</title>
   <link>http://www.wyeast.net/wyeast.html</link>
   <description>The Native American story behind the name Wy'east.</
description>
  </item>
 </channel>
</rss>
```

Like RSS 0.91, RSS 2.0 doesn't declare a namespace for its own elements. Also like 0.91, rss is the document element. It must have a version attribute with a value of 2.0.

The channel element is required, as are its children title, link, and description. The language element is required as a child of channel by 0.91, but under 2.0 it is optional. The image element is also required by 0.91; it's optional under 2.0. Table 6-2 compares the required and optional elements of channel in 2.0 and 0.91. The purpose of each is briefly described.

Table 6-2. Child elements of channel in RSS 2.0 and RSS 0.91

Element	Purpose	RSS 2.0	RSS 0.91
title	Title of channel	Required	Required
link	Link to channel	Required	Required
description	Description of channel	Required	Required
language	Language code for channel	Optional	Required
image	Image that represents the channel (required children url, title, and link; optional children description, width, and height)	Optional	Required
copyright	Copyright notice for the channel	Optional	Optional
managingEditor	Email address of managing editor	Optional	Optional

Table 6-2. Child elements of channel in RSS 2.0 and RSS 0.91 (continued)

Element	Purpose	RSS 2.0	RSS 0.91
webMaster	Email address of webmaster	Optional	Optional
pubDate	Publication date of channel in RFC 822 format, Sat, 01 Jan 05 00:00:27 PST; though not specified in RFC 822, a four-digit year is allowed (see *http://www.ietf.org/rfc/rfc822.txt*)	Optional	Optional
lastBuildDate	Last time channel content changed in RFC 822 format, Sat, 01 Jan 05 00:00:27 PST; though not specified in RFC 822, a four-digit year is allowed (see *http://www.ietf.org/rfc/rfc822.txt*)	Optional	Optional
rating	Platform for Internet Content Selection (PICS) rating (*http://www.w3.org/PICS/*)	Optional	Optional
docs	Documentation for the RSS format used by channel	Optional	Optional
textInput	A text input box for the channel, such as a search box (required children include title, description, name, and link)	Optional	Optional
skipDays	Days to skip reading channel	Optional	Optional
skipHours	Hours to skip reading channel	Optional	Optional
category	One or more channel categories	Optional	N/A
generator	Name of generator program	Optional	N/A
cloud	Specifies a protocol for publishing and subscribing to feeds	Optional	N/A
ttl	Time to live in minutes	Optional	N/A

Under the item element in RSS 2.0, a description element can contain entity-encoded HTML. In other words, it can hold an article or story in itself, written in HTML (with & for & and < for <). Table 6-3 compares the 0.91 and 2.0 children of item.

Table 6-3. Child elements of item in RSS 2.0 and RSS 0.91

Element	Purpose	RSS 2.0	RSS 0.91
title	Title of item	Optional /Required	Required
link	Link to item	Optional /Required	Required
description	Description of item	Optional /Required	Optional
author	Email address of author of item	Optional	N/A
category	One or more item categories (optional attribute domain)	Optional	N/A
comments	URL for comment page for item	Optional	N/A
enclosure	Describes an object attached to item (required attributes url, length, and type)	Optional	N/A

Table 6-3. *Child elements of item in RSS 2.0 and RSS 0.91 (continued)*

Element	Purpose	RSS 2.0	RSS 0.91
guid	Globally unique identifier	Optional	N/A
pubDate	Publication date in RFC 822 format	Optional	N/A
source	RSS channel the item came from (required attribute url)	Optional	N/A

An item element may represent a story such as an article from a newspaper or a magazine. In such a case, the item's description child should contain a synopsis of the story, with a URI in the link element pointing to the full story. On the other hand, an item may also contain a complete story. In this case, the description child of item will contain the text of the whole story (which may be entity-encoded HTML), so the link and title children of item don't have to be included. Though all elements of item are optional in 2.0, at least one title or description must be present.

> RSS 2.0 restricts the first non-whitespace characters in the content of link and url elements. This content must begin with a URI scheme registered at IANA (*http://www.iana.org/ assignments/uri-schemes*), such as ftp://, http://, https://, mailto:, or news://. RSS 0.91 allows only http:// and ftp://.

See Also

- With Radio UserLand, you can generate an RSS 2.0 document for your Radio weblog by going to Prefs and then clicking RSS Configuration under Weblogs. A link to this RSS document will appear on your weblog home page.

HACK #84 Create an Atom Document

Atom is gaining ground as a feed format, and we should be paying attention to it. This hack guides you through the creation of an Atom document from a template.

Atom is an emerging syndication format for newsfeeds, an attempt to evolve from and improve on the current RSS scene. You can find a draft of the specification at *http://www.mnot.net/drafts/draft-nottingham-atom-format-02. html*. The Atom forum folks are also creating an Atom API to support Atom newsfeeds (*http://bitworking.org/projects/atom/draft-gregorio-09.html*).

The goals of the forum are that Atom will be 100 percent vendor-neutral, freely extensible by anybody, cleanly and thoroughly specified, and implemented by everybody (*http://www.intertwingly.net/wiki/pie/RoadMap*). The

Atom spec certainly is more concise than its competitors, and I like that. More and more aggregators are supporting Atom, so I'll say with some confidence that Atom is headed in the right direction, if not to the head of the pack—all in due time, of course.

The following template may be used to create your own Atom feed. *atom. xml* is a brief example of an Atom document:

```
<feed version="0.3" xmlns="http://purl.org/atom/ns#" xml:lang="en">
  <title>Wy'east Communications</title>
  <link rel="alternate" type="text/html"
   href="http://www.wyeast.net/"/>
  <author>
    <name>Mike Fitzgerald</name>
  </author>
  <tagline>Wy'east Communication is an XML consultancy.</tagline>
  <modified>2004-08-14T02:43:00-07:00</modified>
  <entry>
    <title>Legend of Wy'east</title>
    <link rel="alternate" type="text/html"
     href="http://www.wyeast.net/wyeast.html"/>
    <id>http://www.wyeast.net/wyeast.html</id>
    <issued>2004-08-14T02:43:00-07:00</issued>
    <modified>2004-08-14T02:43:00-07:00</modified>
  </entry>
</feed>
```

The document element of an Atom document is feed. This element and its children must be in the namespace http://purl.org/atom/ns# (either a default namespace or prefixed). RSS 0.91 and RSS 2.0 avoid namespaces, but Atom cannot do so. feed must have a version attribute; currently, the appropriate value is 0.3, but I expect that to change by the time you are reading this. An xml:lang attribute (*http://www.w3.org/TR/2004/REC-xml-20040204/#sec-lang-tag*) is recommended but not mandatory. Values of xml:lang must conform to RFC 3066, "Tags for the Identification of Languages" (*http://www.ietf.org/rfc/rfc3066.txt*).

 The order of the child elements of feed doesn't matter in Atom.

A feed element must contain exactly one title element, which is a title for the resource. It should match the content of the title element in an HTML document, if that is the kind of resource the Atom document is talking about. This corresponds to the title element used in RSS 0.91, RSS 1.0, and RSS 2.0.

A feed element must also contain exactly one link element that has a rel attribute with a value of alternate. (Unlike Atom's predecessors, link elements must be empty, that is, they must not have any content.) feed can have more than one link element child, but its rel attribute value must be something other than alternate; for example, start, next, or prev (rel attribute values are specified at *http://bitworking.org/projects/atom/draft-gregorio-09.html#rfc.section.5.4*). The type attribute is mandatory and provides a media type (such as text/html) for the linked resource according to the guidelines in RFC 2045, "Multipurpose Internet Mail Extensions (MIME) Part One: Format of Internet Message Bodies" (*http://www.ietf.org/rfc/rfc2045.txt*). In addition, a link element must have an href attribute that contains a URI for the resource in question. Finally, link may have a title attribute giving the title of the link.

A feed element must have exactly one author element, or, as an alternative, all the entry element children of feed must have an author element. An author element must have exactly one name child element, and may also have one url and/or one email child. url contains a URI associated with the named author, and email is an RFC 822 (*http://www.ietf.org/rfc/rfc822.txt*) email address for the same author. The order of the child elements of author is not significant. An author element is said to be a Person construct.

The document contains one tagline element, an optional element that holds a description of the feed and is a child of feed. tagline is a Content construct. A Content construct may have a type attribute and a mode attribute. type has a media type as a value, following the guidelines in RFC 2045 (*http://www.ietf.org/rfc/rfc2045.txt*). A mode attribute can have one of three values: xml (the default if mode is not present), escaped, or base64. If the value is xml, it means that the element's content is XML, such as XHTML (namespace qualified); if escaped, the content is an escaped string that must be unescaped by the feed processor; if base64, the content is base64-encoded (see also RFC 2045).

In addition, feed must contain exactly one modified element that contains a Date construct. A Date construct is formed according to the Date and Time Formats note published by the W3C (*http://www.w3.org/TR/NOTE-datetime*).

Consequently, a feed element may contain these additional optional elements:

- One or more contributor elements that, like author, is a Person construct

- One id element that contains a globally unique identifier that must be a URI and not change; for example, a tag URI (*http://www.taguri.org/*)

- One generator element that states what software generated the feed
- One copyright element containing a copyright statement (a Content construct)
- One info element explaining the feed format (a Content construct)

Feed Entries

An Atom document may contain zero or more entry elements as children of feed. An entry element roughly corresponds to an item element in the earlier RSS specs. entry may contain any namespace-qualified child elements. As with feed, entry must contain a title element, a link element, and an author element, which have the same specs as those in feed.

Each entry element must have modified and issued child elements, which are both Date constructs. The difference is that issued states when the entry was issued, and modified states the last time the entry was modified. An entry may also have a created child (also a Date construct) which gives the entry's creation date.

Finally, an entry element may have one or more contributor child elements, defined just as in feed. It also may have a summary element that contains a summary, excerpt, or abstract of the entry, plus it may have one or more content children (Content constructs), which can contain the actual payload of the entry—in XML, escaped, or base64 format— rather than being just a link to it.

See Also

- General information about Atom: *http://www.atomenabled.org*
- Wiki site for developers: *http://www.intertwingly.net/wiki/pie/FrontPage*

HACK #85   Validate RSS and Atom Documents

Use an online validator to check your RSS and Atom documents.

You can check RSS 0.91, RSS 1.0, RSS 2.0, and Atom documents online using Mark Pilgrim and Sam Ruby's Feed Validator (*http://feedvalidator.org*). The project is hosted on SourceForge (*http://sourceforge.net/projects/feedvalidator/*). This hack will use Feed Validator to check an RSS or Atom document.

Go to *http://feeds.archive.org/validator/* and in the text box, enter the URL http://www.wyeast.net/news.rss (0.91) as shown in Figure 6-4, or an Atom document, http://www.wyeast.net/atom.xml. (The scheme name http:// is

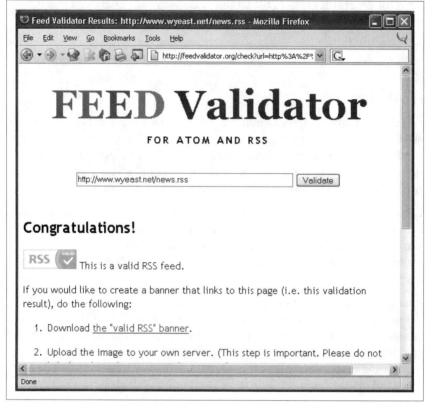

Figure 6-4. Feed Validator in Firefox

already provided in the text box.) Click the Validate button. The file is processed and the results are posted to the browser (Figure 6-5).

If the validator generates errors, you can read more about these errors at *http://feedvalidator.org/docs/*. For example, if your RSS document is not well-formed, it will generate an XML parsing error, which you can read about at *http://feedvalidator.org/docs/error/SAXError.html*.

If you want to parse an RSS 1.0 feed, you can validate it with the W3C RDF validator because it is written as RDF. Go to *http://www.w3.org/RDF/Validator/* and enter the URL http://www.wyeast.net/wyeast.rss, as shown in Figure 6-6. (You can also paste RDF markup into the text box directly to validate it.) Click Parse URI. If the parse is successful, you will see results like those shown in Figure 6-7.

```
W3C RDF Validation Service - Mozilla Firefox                    [_][□][X]

File  Edit  View  Go  Bookmarks  Tools  Help                      ↳

(←) ▾ (→) ▾ 🔄 🔲 🏠 📄 🔲  http://www.w3.org/RDF/Validator/    ▾  [G.]

W3C® RDF Validation Service RDF
                                       Powered

Note: this online service has been updated and now supports the Last Call Working
Draft specifications issued by the RDF Core Working Group, including datatypes.
Deprecated elements and attributes of the standard RDF Model and Syntax
Specification are no longer supported.

Online Service

Enter a URI or paste an RDF/XML document into the following text field and a 3-tuple
(triple) representation of the corresponding data model as well as an optional graphical
visualization of the data model will be displayed.

┌─────────────────────────────────────────────────────────────────┐
│                                                                   │
│                                                                   │
│                                                                   │
└─────────────────────────────────────────────────────────────────┘

[ Parse RDF ] [ Restore the original example ] [ Clear the textarea ]
or
[ Parse URI: ] [http://www.wyeast.net/wyeast.rss            ]  [ Clear the URI ]

Done
```

Figure 6-5. Results of validating an RSS document with Feed Validator

See Also

- Another face of Feed Validator is shown as RSS Validator: *http://rss. scripting.com/*
- Yet another face of Feed Validator is Walidator: *http://www.walidator. com/*
- Leigh Dodd's downloadable Schematron RSS validator: *http://www. ldodds.com/rss_validator/*

—Michael Fitzgerald

Create RSS with XML::RSS

#86 By using the popular syndication format known as RSS, you can use your newly scraped data in dozens of different aggregators, toolkits, and more.

Due to the incredible popularity of RSS, folks are starting to syndicate just about anything one might be interested in following—recipes, job listings, sports scores, and TV schedules to name but a few.

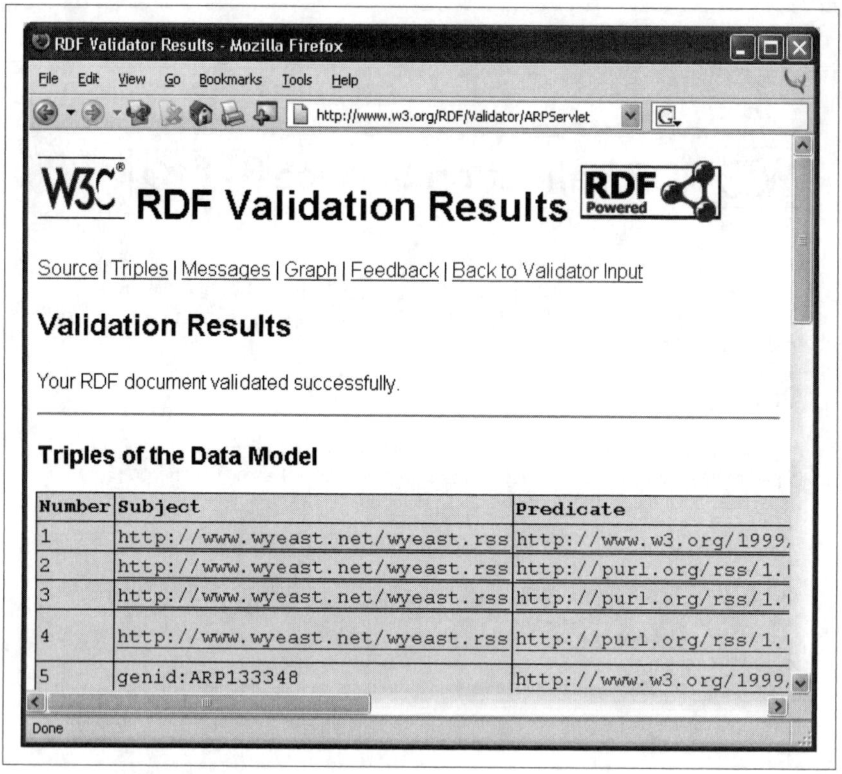

Figure 6-6. W3C RDF validator

Here's a simple RSS 0.91 file:

```
<?xml version="1.0"?>
<rss version="0.91">

  <channel>
    <title>ResearchBuzz</title>
    <link>http://www.researchbuzz.com</link>
    <description>News and information on search engines... </description>
    <language>en-us</language>

    <item>
     <title>Survey Maps of Scotland Towns</title>
     <link>http://researchbuzz.com/news/2003/jul31aug603.shtml</link>
    </item>

    <item>
     <title>Directory of Webrings</title>
     <link>http://researchbuzz.com/news/2003/jul31aug603.shtml</link>
    </item>

  </channel>
</rss>
```

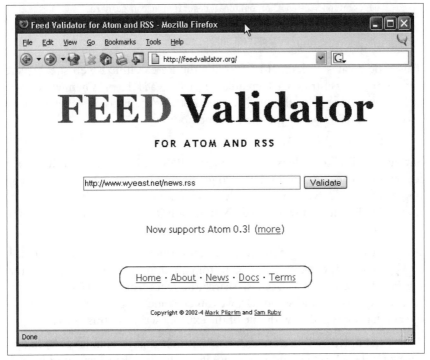

Figure 6-7. Results of parse in W3C RDF validator

Thankfully, we don't have to worry about creating these files by hand. We can create RSS files with a simple Perl module called XML::RSS (*http://search.cpan.org/author/KELLAN/XML-RSS/*). Here's how (*rss.pl*):

```perl
#!/usr/bin/perl -w
use strict;
use XML::RSS;

my $rss = new XML::RSS(version => '0.91');
$rss->channel(
    title       => 'Research Buzz',
    link        => 'http://www.researchbuzz.com',
    description => 'News and information on search en...',
);

$rss->add_item(
    title       => 'Survey Maps of Scotland Towns',
    link        => 'http://researchbuzz.com/news/2003/etc/etc/etc#etc',
    description => 'An optional description can go here.'
);

$rss->add_item(
    title       => 'Directory of Webrings',
    link        => 'http://researchbuzz.com/news/2003/yadda/yadda#etc',
```

```
        description => 'Another optional description can go here.'
);
```

```
print $rss->as_string;
```

This code creates a channel to describe the ResearchBuzz web site, replete with some story entries, each created by a call to add_item. When we're done adding items, we print the final RSS to STDOUT. Alternatively, if we want to save our RSS to a file, we use the save method:

```
$rss->save("file.rss");
```

Saving your RSS to a file is *very* important. RSS is likely to be downloaded a lot by users checking for updates, so generating it on the fly each time will bog down your server unnecessarily. It's common for a mildly popular site to have its RSS feed downloaded six times a minute. You can automate the creation of your RSS files with a cron job [Hack #90].

Because the call to add_item always creates a new RSS entry with a title, link, and description, we can feed it from anything available, such as iterating over the results of a database search, matches from an HTML parser or regular expression, and so on. Or, we can do something much more interesting and hack it together with one of the existing scripts in this book.

In this example, we'll use an aggregated search engine from [Hack #85] in *Spidering Hacks* (O'Reilly) and repurpose its results into RSS instead of its normal format.

You'll need the XML::RSS module installed, as well as the code from "Aggregating Multiple Search Engine Results" [Hack #85], in *Spidering Hacks*, available from *http://www.oreilly.com/catalog/spiderhks/*. Note that most fields within an RSS feed are optional, so this code (*agg2rss.pl*) outputs only a title and link, not a description:

```
#!/usr/bin/perl -w

# agg2rss - aggregated search to RSS converter
# This file distributed under the same licence as Perl itself
# by rik - ora@rikrose.net

use strict;
use XML::RSS;

# Build command line, and run the aggregated search engine.
my (@currentPlugin, @plugins, $url, $desc, $plugin, %results);
my $commandLine = "aggsearch " . join " ", @ARGV;
open INPUT, "$commandLine |" or die $!;
while (<INPUT>){ chomp;
    @currentPlugin = split / /, $_;
    push @plugins, $currentPlugin[0];
```

```perl
    while (<INPUT>){
        chomp;
        last if length == 0;
        s/</&lt;/; s/>/&gt;/;
        ($url, $desc) = split /: /, $_, 2;
        $url =~ s/^ //; $desc =~ s/^ //;
        $results{$currentPlugin[0]}{$url} = $desc;
    }
}
close INPUT;

# Results are now in the @plugins,
# %results pair. Put the results into RSS:
my $rss = XML::RSS->new(version => '0.91');

# Create the channel object.
$rss->channel(
        title       => 'Aggregated Search Results',
        link        => 'http://www.example.com/cgi/make-new-search',
        description => 'Using plugins: ' . join ", ", @plugins
);

# Add data.
for $plugin (@plugins){
    for $url (keys %{$results{$plugin}}){
        $rss->add_item(
                title       => $results{$plugin}{$url},
                link        => $url,
        );
    }
}

# Save it for later, in our RSS feed for our web site.
$rss->save("/rss/index.rdf");
```

Okay, we've created the RSS and placed it on our web site so that others can
consume it. What now? XML::RSS not only generates RSS files, but it can
also parse them. In this example, we'll download the RSS feed for the front
page of the BBC and print a nice, readable summary to STDOUT (most likely
your screen):

```perl
#!/usr/bin/perl -w

# get-headlines - get the BBC headlines in RSS format, and print them
# This file distributed under the same licence as Perl itself
# by rik - ora@rikrose.net

use strict;
use LWP::UserAgent;
use XML::RSS;

my $url = "http://www.bbc.co.uk/syndication/feeds/".
```

```
        "news/ukfs_news/front_page/rss091.xml";

    # get data
    my $ua = LWP::UserAgent->new( );
    my $response = $ua->get($url);
    die $response->status_line . "\n"
      unless $response->is_success;

    # parse it
    my $rss = XML::RSS->new;
    $rss->parse($response->content);

    # print each item
    foreach my $item (@{$rss->{'items'}}){
        print "title: $item->{'title'}\n";
        print "link: $item->{'link'}\n\n";
    }
```

This code is saved as *bbc.pl*. Its results look similar to this:

```
% perl bbc.pl

title: UK troops attacked in Basra
link: http://news.bbc.co.uk/go/click/rss/0.91/public/-
      /1/hi/world/middle_east/3137779.stm

title: 'More IVF' on the NHS
link: http://news.bbc.co.uk/go/click/rss/0.91/public/-
      /1/hi/health/3137191.stm

...etc...
```

See Also

- *Google Hacks* (O'Reilly) for much more information on search engines.
- *Spidering Hacks* (O'Reilly) for much more on scraping data from web sites.

—*Richard Rose*

HACK #87   Syndicate Content with Movable Type

Movable Type (MT) is a very flexible personal publishing system that is
extremely popular in the weblogging world. One of its most powerful features
is its ability to output content into any markup form you may need for easy
syndication of content.

While the possible uses for Movable Type's (*http://www.movabletype.org/*)
template engine are vast, for this hack we'll focus on the syndication formats that MT supports by default and some of the many things you can do
with them. MT ships with templates for RSS 1.0 and 2.0 in addition to the
current version of the emerging Atom format, Version 0.3. The RSS tem-

---

plates produce a syndication feed containing the last 15 posts for the weblog including the post title, link, primary category, author, issue date, and an excerpt. (MT has an excerpt field for each post. If that field was not populated it will automatically generate one from the body text. The length depends on the parameter set in the weblog configuration.) The Atom format provides the same information, but it also includes the full content of the post amongst other refined pieces of metadata. Let's walk through some common extensions and specialized syndication feeds.

Syndicating the Whole Post

Let's begin by adding the full text of the post to the RSS templates. In order to include both an excerpt and the full text, we need to use the content module so we can use its encoded tag. To do so, we would add this namespace declaration:

```
xmlns:content="http://purl.org/rss/1.0/modules/content/"
```

In the RSS 1.0 template you'll end up with:

```
<rdf:RDF
  xmlns:rdf="http://www.w3.org/1999/02/22-rdf-syntax-ns#"
  xmlns:dc="http://purl.org/dc/elements/1.1/"
  xmlns:sy="http://purl.org/rss/1.0/modules/syndication/"
  xmlns:admin="http://webns.net/mvcb/"
  xmlns:cc="http://web.resource.org/cc/"
  xmlns:content="http://purl.org/rss/1.0/modules/content/"
  xmlns="http://purl.org/rss/1.0/">
```

In the RSS 2.0 template you'll end up with:

```
<rss version="2.0"
  xmlns:dc="http://purl.org/dc/elements/1.1/"
  xmlns:sy="http://purl.org/rss/1.0/modules/syndication/"
  xmlns:admin="http://webns.net/mvcb/"
  xmlns:rdf="http://www.w3.org/1999/02/22-rdf-syntax-ns#"
  xmlns:content="http://purl.org/rss/1.0/modules/content/"
  >
```

With the content module namespace declaration in place, we can now insert some MT template tags to insert the full text into the RSS feeds. Go down toward the end of the templates and add this line between the item tags:

```
<content:encoded><$MTEntryBody encode_xml="1"$></content:encoded>
```

Save the template and then rebuild it. Your RSS feeds now will include the full text of your entries.

MT provides two body fields that some people like to use. If you are one of those people you would add this line instead:

```
<content:encoded><$MTEntryBody encode_xml="1"$><$MTEntryMore encode_
xml="1"$></content:encoded>
```

This inserts the content of both fields into the feed.

Including Trackback Links

Trackback pings are a means of remote hyperlinking. They were first introduced in MT and have been adopted by many other weblog tools since. Here is how we could include the Trackback ping URLs for each item and the Trackback pings that were made from them.

We begin by declaring the Trackback syndication module namespace in our root element.

```
xmlns:trackback="http://madskills.com/public/xml/rss/module/trackback/"
```

Next we go down into the item tag and insert this markup:

```
<MTEntryIfAllowPings>
  <trackback:ping rdf:resource="<MTEntryTrackbackLink encode_xml="1">"/>
  <MTPings>
    <trackback:about rdf:resource="<$MTPingURL encode_xml="1"$>" />
  </MTPings>
</MTEntryIfAllowPings>
```

By wrapping this block in the MTEntryIfAllowPings tags, only items that allow Trackback pings will have these tags inserted.

Creating Specialized Feeds

We can continue adding MT content to our feed by using the many syndication modules in existence. For an example of a very meta rich feed, see Ben Hammersley's "Making Feature-Rich, Movable Type RSS Files" (*http://www.oreillynet.com/pub/a/javascript/2003/02/28/rss.html*).

Let's go a different direction and focus on creating different specialized feeds. Rather then include both an excerpt and the full text in the same feed, you may opt to offer separate feeds. Start with one of the default templates, copy the template text, and create a new template. Paste the template text into the new record and follow the previous steps, but replace the item description element with content:encoded. (Be sure to use a different filename for the output.)

Even with the description available, it is a good practice to use content: encoded because some versions of RSS define description as a plain-text excerpt with a limit of 500 characters. Any capable aggregator will be able to handle this tag and have a chance to handle the full text differently.

If you are providing a full text feed, you may want to consider cutting down on the number of entries you include in the feed to conserve bandwidth. To do so is just a matter of adjusting the lastn attribute of the MTEntries element. For example, to reduce the number of items to the last three, change the MTEntries element to:

```
<MTEntries lastn="3">
```

Now your full text RSS feeds would include only 3 items, substantially reducing its size and saving bandwidth each time an aggregator retrieves the file.

Category Feeds

Assuming you assign categories to your posts, MT can be used to create separate syndication feeds for the latest entries in each.

To begin, copy one of the default syndication templates to your clipboard. Setting up per-category feeds doesn't require making any changes to the template, but you may make changes anyway depending on preference and effect. Go to the Templates listing by clicking the Templates button in the left-hand navigation bar. Scroll down and click the "Create new archive template" link. Give your template a title and paste the template code from your clipboard into the Template Body field. Click Save.

Archive templates need to be associated with an archive type. To make this assignment, click Weblog Config in the left-hand toolbar and then click Archiving from the links at the top of the page.

Make sure Category archives are checked so they are activated. If they are not, check them at this time and press Save.

Click the "Add new" button, and a pop-up will appear with two drop-down boxes. Select the Category archive type the name of the Category syndication template you created, and then click the Add button.

That's it. The pop-up will close and the archive configuration page will refresh to list the new template as a Category archive template. At this time you can define the filenaming scheme if you like. See the MT documentation for more information.

Syndicating Comments

If you have an active comments board on your Movable Type weblog, you can provide readers with a syndication feed of the most recent comments, which they can track with their aggregator.

Begin by creating a new index template and pasting the default RSS template into the template body. Give it a unique and descriptive name and press Save.

You will probably want to add the content namespace declaration and modify the channel information to reflect the nature of this syndication feed. These modifications are trivial, so we'll skip over them and get to the heart of the matter in the item tags.

We replace the MTEntries element and its contents with the following template code:

```
<MTComments lastn="20">
<item>
        <title><$MTCommentAuthor$>: <MTCommentEntry><$MTEntryTitle$>
            </MTCommentEntry> (<$MTCommentDate
            format="%Y-%m-%dT%H:%M:%S"$><$MTBlogTimezone$>)</title>
        <content:encoded><$MTCommentBody
            encode_xml="1"$></content:encoded>
        <link><$MTCommentEntryLink$>#<$MTCommentID
            zero_pad="5"$></link>
        <dc:contributor><$MTCommentAuthor$></dc:contributor>
        <dc:date><$MTCommentDate
            format="%Y-%m-%dT%H:%M:%S"$><$MTBlogTimezone$></dc:date>
</item>
</MTComments>
```

This will insert the last 20 comments made in the weblog. Since comments don't have titles, we create our own with various bits that make it easily scannable and unique.

If you have decided to use RSS 1.0, you will have to modify the items element block also.

```
<items>
    <rdf:Seq><MTComments lastn="20">
      <rdf:li rdf:resource="<$MTCommentEntryLink$>#<$MTCommentID
          zero_pad="5"$>" />
    </MTComments></rdf:Seq>
</items>
```

Click the Save button and then Rebuild. Presto! Your readers can now track the comments with their aggregators.

As you can see, MT has a very flexible and powerful means of creating markup, so there are a lot of other options we could have explored. You'll have to explore its potential on your own.

If you are looking to insert syndication content into your weblog layout, look to the mt-feed plug-in (formerly mt-rss-feed).

—*Timothy Appnel*

Post RSS Headlines on Your Site

Place other sites' syndicated headlines on your own pages, periodically.

Including syndicated newsfeeds is a nice way of adding some compelling content to your site. The problem is that sometimes the news feed gets over-run during heavy news days, goes offline, and/or suffers a host of other con-nectivity issues. These problems make *your* site load slowly, because the software holds your user hostage while the feed retrieval portion of the application waits to time out.

A simple way around this problem is to use a program that periodically retrieves the feed and slices and dices it into an easy-to-include file on your host. Doing this achieves five goals:

- User page loads are not penalized when feeds go down.
- Failures to connect do not harm the existing include file.
- Multiple attempts to read the feed do not penalize the user.
- Feeds can be mirrored for local/private use.
- Content can be formatted to taste.

The Code

This is a little program (*getap.pl*) I wrote to repurpose news from an AP Wire feed:

```
#!/usr/bin/perl -w
# ------------------------------------------------------------------------
# copyright Dean Peters © 2003 - all rights reserved
# http://www.HealYourChurchWebSite.org
# ------------------------------------------------------------------------
#
# getap.pl is free software. You can redistribute and modify it
# freely without any consent of the developer, Dean Peters, if and
# only if the following conditions are met:
#
# (a) The copyright info and links in the headers remains intact.
# (b) The purpose of distribution or modification is non-commercial.
#
```

```
# Commercial distribution of this product without a written
# permission from Dean Peters is strictly prohibited.
# This script is provided on an as-is basis, without any warranty.
# The author does not take any responsibility for any damage or
# loss of data that may occur from use of this script.
#
# You may refer to our general terms & conditions for clarification:
# http://www.healyourchurchwebsite.com/archives/000002.shtml
#
# For more info. about this code, please refer to the following article:
# http://www.healyourchurchwebsite.com/archives/000760.shtml
#
# combine this code with crontab for best results, e.g.:
# 59 * * * * /path/to/scriptname.pl > /dev/null
#
# --------------------------------------------------------------------------

use XML::RSS;
use LWP::Simple;

# get content from feed -- using 10 attempts.
# replace the URL with whatever feed you want to get.
my $content = getFeed("http://www.goupstate.com/apps/pbcs.dll/".
                        "section?Category=RSS04&mime=xml", 10);

# save off feed to a file -- make sure you
# have write access to file or directory.
saveFeed($content, "newsfeed.xml");

# create customized output.
my $output = createOutput($content, 8);

# save it to your include file.
saveFeed($output, "newsfeed.inc.php");

# download the feed in question.
# accepts two inputs, the URL, and
# the number of times you wish to loop.
sub getFeed {
    my ($url, $attempts) = @_;
    my $lc = 0; # loop count
    my $content;
    while($lc < $attempts) {
        $content = get($url);
        return $content if $content;
        $lc += 1; sleep 5;
    }

    die "Could not retreive data from $url in $attempts attempts";
}

# saves the converted data ($content)
# to final destination ($outfile).
```

```
sub saveFeed {
    my ($content, $outfile) = @_;
    open(OUT,">$outfile") || die("Cannot Open File $outfile");
    print OUT $content; close(OUT);
}

# parses the XML file and returns
# a string of custom content. You
# can pass the number of items you'd
# like as the second argument.
sub createOutput {
    my ($content, $feedcount) = @_;

    # new instance of XML::RSS
    my $rss = XML::RSS->new;

    # parse the RSS content into an output
    # string to be saved at end of parsing.
    $rss->parse($content);
    my $title = $rss->{channel}->{title};
    my $output  = '<div class="title">GoUpstate/AP NewsWire</div>';
        $output .= '<div class="newsfeed">\n';

    my $i = 0; # begin our item loop.
    foreach my $item (@{$rss->{items}}) {
        next unless defined($item->{title}) && defined($item->{link});
        $i += 1; next if $i > $feedcount; # skip if we're done.
        $output .= "<a href=\"$item->{link}\">$item->{title}</a><br />\n";
    }

    # if a copyright and link exists, then post it.
    my $copyright = $rss->{channel}->{copyright};
    my $link = $rss->{channel}->{link};
    my $description = $rss->{channel}->{description};
    $output .= "<a href=\"$link\" title=\"$description\" >".
                "$copyright</a>\n" if($copyright && $link);
    $output .= "</div>";
    return $output;
}
```

Running the Hack

Running this code creates two new files in the current directory: *newsfeed.xml* is the raw data we've downloaded, and *newsfeed.inc.php* is our repurposed data for use on our own site. Using the following crontab syntax, the program is executed every hour:

```
59 * * * * /path/to/scriptname.pl > /dev/null
```

The nice thing about this approach is that this particular feed does get busy from time to time and, at one point on a Friday, it went offline. My users did not notice because, in most cases, I was able to get by the "busy signal" on the second or third attempt out of 10. In the case where the entire remote site went offline, my users merely viewed an older include file without interruption or delay.

—Dean Peters and Tara Calishan

HACK   Create RSS 0.91 Feeds from Google
#89
A .NET program can help you create an RSS feed based on a query to Google. You have to be a registered developer at Google to use this program, but the possibilities are rich.

Peter Drayton (*http://www.razorsoft.net/*) has created a .NET program called *google2rss* that uses a Google API (*http://www.google.com/apis/*) query to create an RSS 0.91 feed [Hack #81] with the top 10 hits it finds on Google. You first have to go to the Google API web page to register so that you can get a license key. You cannot perform this hack without getting the license key. You will also need to install Microsoft .NET on your system. You can download .NET from Microsoft's MSDN site, *http://msdn.microsoft.com/netframework/technologyinfo/howtoget/*, or you can get it from *http://www.gotdotnet.com*. You'll need to download both the .NET Framework Version 1.1 Redistributable Package (about 24 MB) and the .NET Framework SDK Version 1.1 (about 108 MB).

Download the *google2rss* software from *http://www.razorsoft.net/downloads/google2rss.zip*. You can also read background information at *http://www.razorsoft.net/weblog/stories/2002/04/13/google2rss.html*.

Fortunately, the *google2rss* download includes source code, because after I extracted the archive, I discovered that I had to recompile the program to get it to work with .NET v1.1. That's because the binary in the archive was compiled with .NET v1.0. A copy of the recompiled program is in the file archive that is offered with the book. The compilation process has several steps, which include the .NET *xsd.exe* and *wsdl.exe* programs. These programs compile XML Schema and WSDL files into executable programs [Hack #99] that can be used by the main program. See the *make* file in the *google2rss* archive for details.

With *google2rss* and .NET installed, and while you are in the working directory, type the command:

```
google2api
```

You will see a long list of possible options, five of them required, ten optional, and seven default. The five required options are as follows:

-key *your Google API key*
> Your Google account key, which you get by registering with Google as a developer.

-query *query string*
> The subject you are querying about.

-title *title of the feed*
> The title of the RSS 0.91 document.

-link *feed's home URL*
> The link to where the RSS document will live.

-description *feed description*
> A description of the feed.

Here is a sample *google2rss* command that queries on the term *RSS*:

```
google2rss -key "your-google-key-goes-here" -query "RSS" -safesearch true
-filter true -title "RSS on Google" -link http://www.example.com/rss
-description "Tracking RSS on Google" -outfile google.rss
```

You already read about the required options. The -safesearch option with a value of true screens for adult or indecent content. The -filter with true option hides similar results from the search. The -outfile sets the output filename.

The program goes out and does its query and then saves the RSS 0.91 output as *google.rss*, which is about 60 lines long (line length should vary from day to day and from query to query). Example 6-1 shows the RSS 0.91 document.

Example 6-1. google.rss

```
<?xml version="1.0" encoding="utf-8"?>
<rss xmlns:xsd="http://www.w3.org/2001/XMLSchema" xmlns:xsi="http://www.w3.org/
2001/XMLSchema-instance" version="0.91">
  <channel>
    <title>RSS on Google</title>
    <link>http://www.wyeast.net/rss</link>
    <description>Tracking RSS on Google</description>
    <language>en-us</language>
    <lastBuildDate>Thu, 08 Apr 2004 00:38:27 GMT</lastBuildDate>
    <item>
      <title>&lt;b&gt;RSS&lt;/b&gt; 2.0 Specification</title>
      <description>Technology at Harvard Law. Internet technology
hosted by Berkman Center. &lt;b&gt;RSS&lt;/b&gt; 2.0&lt;br&gt;
Specification. Contents. &lt;b&gt;...&lt;/b&gt; is &lt;b&gt;RSS&lt;
/b&gt;? &lt;b&gt;RSS&lt;/b&gt; Directory. About this website.
Specifications. &lt;b&gt;...&lt;/b&gt;  </description>
      <link>http://blogs.law.harvard.edu/tech/rss</link>
    </item>
    <item>
```

Example 6-1. google.rss (continued)

```
    <title>XML.com: What is &lt;b&gt;RSS&lt;/b&gt;? [Dec. 18, 2002]
    </title>
    <description>In Mark Pilgrim&amp;#39;s inaugural Dive Into XML
column, he reviews the history&lt;br&gt; and technical details of the
varieties of &lt;b&gt;RSS&lt;/b&gt; on the Web. &lt;b&gt;...&lt;/b&gt;
 What is &lt;b&gt;RSS&lt;/b&gt;? &lt;b&gt;...&lt;/b&gt; </description>
    <link>http://www.xml.com/pub/a/2002/12/18/dive-into-xml.html
    </link>
  </item>
  <item>
    <title>RDF Site Summary (&lt;b&gt;RSS&lt;/b&gt;) 1.0</title>
    <description>RDF Site Summary (&lt;b&gt;RSS&lt;/b&gt;) 1.0.
Official Specification. The &lt;b&gt;RSS&lt;/b&gt; 1.0 specification
&lt;br&gt; was released on 2000-12-06. It was published &lt;b&gt;...
&lt;/b&gt;  </description>
    <link>http://www.purl.org/rss/1.0/</link>
  </item>
  <item>
    <title>RDF Site Summary (&lt;b&gt;RSS&lt;/b&gt;) 1.0</title>
    <description>RDF Site Summary (&lt;b&gt;RSS&lt;/b&gt;) 1.0.
Abstract. RDF Site Summary (&lt;b&gt;RSS&lt;/b&gt;) is a lightweight
&lt;br&gt; multipurpose extensible metadata description and
syndication format. &lt;b&gt;...&lt;/b&gt;  </description>
    <link>http://www.purl.org/rss/1.0/spec</link>
  </item>
  <item>
    <title>Introduction to &lt;b&gt;RSS&lt;/b&gt; -
       WebReference.com</title>
    <description>Introduction to &lt;b&gt;RSS&lt;/b&gt;. &lt;b&gt;
...&lt;/b&gt; Then you need an &lt;b&gt;RSS&lt;/b&gt; news feed. To
start all you need&lt;br&gt; is content you want broadcast, and one
&lt;b&gt;RSS&lt;/b&gt; text file. What is &lt;b&gt;RSS&lt;/b&gt;? &lt;b&gt;...
&lt;/b&gt;  </description>
    <link>http://www.webreference.com/authoring/languages/xml/rss/
       intro/</link>
  </item>
  <item>
    <title>Feed Validator for Atom and &lt;b&gt;RSS&lt;/b&gt;
    </title>
    <description>FEED Validator. for Atom and
&lt;b&gt;RSS&lt;/b&gt;. Jump to&lt;br&gt; navigation. Now supports
Atom 0.3! (more). &lt;b&gt;...&lt;/b&gt;  </description>
    <link>http://feedvalidator.org/</link>
  </item>
  <item>
    <title>Feedster :: &lt;b&gt;RSS&lt;/b&gt; Search Engine</title>
    <description>Feedster, the fast search engine for &lt;b&gt;RSS
&lt;/b&gt; content including weblogs,&lt;br&gt; now with myFeedster,
your custom web-based newsreader. Feedster. &lt;b&gt;...&lt;/b&gt;
    </description>
```

Example 6-1. google.rss (continued)

```
    <link>http://www.feedster.com/</link>
  </item>
  <item>
    <title>Latest &lt;b&gt;RSS&lt;/b&gt; News (&lt;b&gt;RSS&lt;/b&gt; Info)
</title>
    <description>The &lt;b&gt;RSS&lt;/b&gt; format allows quick and
easy syndication of news, headlines, and more. &lt;b&gt;...&lt;/b&gt;
&lt;b&gt;RSS&lt;/b&gt;&lt;br&gt; Info. News and information on the
&lt;b&gt;RSS&lt;/b&gt; format. News. Readers. Tools. Resources. &lt;b&gt;...&lt;/
b&gt;  </description>
    <link>http://blogspace.com/rss/</link>
  </item>
  <item>
    <title>&lt;b&gt;RSS&lt;/b&gt; 0.92</title>
    <description> &lt;b&gt;...&lt;/b&gt; &lt;b&gt;RSS&lt;/b&gt;
0.92. Mon, Dec 25, 2000; by Dave Winer. New version available,
October&lt;br&gt; 2002 &lt;b&gt;RSS&lt;/b&gt; 2.0 is the current
version. It is upward compatible &lt;b&gt;...&lt;/b&gt;
    </description>
    <link>http://backend.userland.com/rss092</link>
  </item>
  <item>
    <title>&lt;b&gt;RSS&lt;/b&gt; Tutorial for Content Publishers
and Webmasters</title>
    <description>&lt;b&gt;RSS&lt;/b&gt; Tutorial. for Content
Publishers and Webmasters. This tutorial explains&lt;br&gt; the
features and &lt;b&gt;...&lt;/b&gt; Introducing &lt;b&gt;RSS&lt;/b&gt;.
Think about all of the information &lt;b&gt;...&lt;/b&gt;
    </description>
    <link>http://www.mnot.net/rss/tutorial/</link>
  </item>
  </channel>
</rss>
```

Now play around with the options the program offers, saving your result in a different file each time.

HACK #90 Syndicate a List of Books from Amazon with RSS and ASP

Someday all data will be available as RSS. Get a head start by syndicating Amazon search results.

With the wide audience for RSS data, just about everything is being turned into an RSS feed. This hack turns any Amazon Web Services (AWS) query result into an RSS feed.

What You Need

This hack uses ASP, which runs on Windows servers running IIS. The logic is straightforward, though, and could be translated to any scripting language. You also need an Amazon developer token and an Amazon associates tag, both available from *http://www.amazon.com/associates*.

The Code

The file *amazon_rss.asp* is in the file archive for the book. Be sure to change the Const declarations to match your setup.

```
<%
''  AMAZON-RSS.ASP
''  Sean P. Nolan
''  http://www.yaywastaken.com/
''
''  This code is free for you to use as you see fit. Copy it, rewrite it,
''  run it yourself, whatever. But no warranties or guarantees either. Who
''  knows what the hell it does. Not me, that's for sure!
''
''  Generates an RSS 0.91 feed from an Amazon book query
''
''''''''''''''''''''''''''''''''''''''''''''''''''''''''''''''''''''''''''
        Const MAX_PAGES_DEFAULT = 10
        Const DEV_TOKEN = "insert developer token"
        Const AFFILIATE_CODE = "insert associate tag"
        Const XSL_FILE = "amazon_lite.xsl" 'change to heavy for more info.

        Dim szTitle, szMaxPages, nMaxPages

        Response.ContentType = "text/xml"
        Server.ScriptTimeout = 60 * 4 ' 4-minute maximum
        Response.Expires = 0

        szMaxPages = Request.QueryString("maxpages")
        If (szMaxPages = "") Then
            nMaxPages = MAX_PAGES_DEFAULT
        Else
            nMaxPages = CLng(szMaxPages)
        End If

        szTitle = "Amazon Books: " & XMLify(Request.QueryString("keywords"))

        %><?xml version="1.0" encoding="ISO-8859-1" ?>
    <rss version="0.91">
        <channel>
            <link>http://www.yaywastaken.com/amazon/</link>
            <title><%= szTitle %></title>
            <description>Create your own custom Amazon RSS feed!</description>
            <language>en-us</language>
        <%
```

```
RenderItems Request.QueryString("keywords"), _
            Request.QueryString("browse") , _
            Request.QueryString("author") , _
            Request.QueryString("shortdesc"), _
            nMaxPages
%>

    </channel>
</rss>
    <%

    ..........................................................................

    ' RenderItems

    Sub RenderItems(szKeywords, szBrowseNode, szAuthor, szShortDesc, ↵
nMaxPages)
        Dim szURLFmt, szURL, xmlDoc, ipage, http, xmlErr
        Dim fParsed, xslDoc, szXSLPath, szOutput

        'On Error Resume Next

        If (szShortDesc <> "") Then
            szXSLPath = "amazon-lite.xsl"
        Else
            szXSLPath = "amazon-heavy.xsl"
        End If

        Set xslDoc = Server.CreateObject("Msxml2.DOMDocument")
        xslDoc.async = False
        xslDoc.load(Server.MapPath(szXSLPath))

        If (szBrowseNode <> "") Then
            szURLFmt = "http://xml.amazon.com/onca/xml?v=1.0&" & _
                        "t=" & AFFILIATE_CODE & _
                        "&dev-t=" & DEV_TOKEN & "&BrowseNodeSearch=" & _
                        Server.URLEncode(szBrowseNode) & _
                        "&mode=books&type=heavy&page=%%%PAGE%%%&f=xml"
        ElseIf (szAuthor <> "") Then
            szURLFmt = "http://xml.amazon.com/onca/xml?v=1.0&" & _
                        "t=" & AFFILIATE_CODE & _
                        "&dev-t=" & DEV_TOKEN & "&AuthorSearch=" & _
                        Server.URLEncode(szAuthor) & _
                        "&mode=books&type=heavy&page=%%%PAGE%%%&f=xml"
        Else
            szURLFmt = "http://xml.amazon.com/onca/xml?v=1.0&" & _
                        "t=" & AFFILIATE_CODE & _
                        "&dev-t=" & DEV_TOKEN & "&KeywordSearch=" & _
                        Server.URLEncode(szKeywords) & _
                        "&mode=books&type=heavy&page=%%%PAGE%%%&f=xml"
        End If

        ipage = 1
        Do
```

```
                szURL = Replace(szURLFmt, "%%%PAGE%%%", ipage)

                Set http = Server.CreateObject("Msxml2.ServerXMLHTTP")
                http.open "GET", szURL, False
                http.send ""

                If (http.status <> 200) Then
                    Exit Do
                End If

                Set xmlDoc = Server.CreateObject("Msxml2.DOMDocument")
                xmlDoc.async = False
                xmlDoc.validateOnParse = False
                xmlDoc.resolveExternals = False
                fParsed = xmlDoc.loadXML(http.responseText)

                If (Not fParsed) Then
                    Exit Do
                End If

                Set xmlErr = Nothing
                Set xmlErr = xmlDoc.selectSingleNode("ProductInfo/ErrorMsg")
                If (Not xmlErr Is Nothing) Then
                    Exit Do
                End If

            Set xslDoc = Nothing
                Set xslDoc = Server.CreateObject("Msxml2.DOMDocument")
                xslDoc.async = False
                xslDoc.validateOnParse = False
                xslDoc.resolveExternals = False
            xslDoc.load(Server.MapPath(XSL_FILE))

                szOutput = xmlDoc.transformNode(xslDoc)
                Response.Write szOutput

                ipage = ipage + 1
                If (ipage > nMaxPages) Then
                    Exit Do
                End If
        Loop
    End Sub

    ' ............................................................
    ' Helpers

    Function XMLify(sz)
        XMLify = Replace(sz, "&", "&amp;")
        XMLify = Replace(XMLify, "<", "&lt;")
        XMLify = Replace(XMLify, ">", "&gt;")
        XMLify = Replace(XMLify, """""""", """""")
        XMLify = Replace(XMLify, "'", "&apos;")
    End Function
%>
```

This file makes an Amazon Web Services XML/HTTP request based on querystring variables passed in the URL, and transforms the XML locally with an XSL stylesheet. Depending on how much detail you want in the RSS feed, there are two different stylesheets. The first, for light data, is called *amazon_lite.xsl*.

```
<?xml version='1.0'?>
<xsl:stylesheet version="1.0"
    xmlns:xsl="http://www.w3.org/1999/XSL/Transform">
<xsl:output omit-xml-declaration="yes" />
<xsl:template match="ProductInfo/Details">
    <item><link>
    <xsl:value-of select="@url" />
    </link><title>
    <xsl:value-of select="ProductName" />
    </title><description>
        <xsl:text>Author: </xsl:text>
        <xsl:value-of select="Authors/Author[1]" />
        <xsl:text>; </xsl:text>
        <xsl:value-of select="OurPrice" />
        <xsl:if test="Availability">
            <xsl:text> (</xsl:text>
            <xsl:value-of select="Availability" />
            <xsl:if test="Availability = 'Pre Order'">
                <xsl:text>: release date </xsl:text>
                <xsl:value-of select="ReleaseDate" />
            </xsl:if>
            <xsl:text>)</xsl:text>
        </xsl:if>
    </description></item>
</xsl:template>

<xsl:template match="/">
    <xsl:apply-templates select="ProductInfo/Details" />
</xsl:template>

</xsl:stylesheet>
```

Another stylesheet, appropriately titled *amazon_heavy.xsl*, provides more detailed information in the feed.

```
<?xml version='1.0'?>
<xsl:stylesheet version="1.0"
    xmlns:xsl="http://www.w3.org/1999/XSL/Transform">
<xsl:output omit-xml-declaration="yes" />
<xsl:template match="ProductInfo/Details">
    <item><link>
    <xsl:value-of select="@url" />
    </link><title>
    <xsl:value-of select="ProductName" />
    </title><description>
        <br />
```

```
        <xsl:element name="a">
            <xsl:attribute name="href">
                <xsl:value-of select="@url" />
            </xsl:attribute>
            <xsl:element name="img">
                <xsl:attribute name="src">
                    <xsl:value-of select="ImageUrlMedium" />
                </xsl:attribute>
                <xsl:attribute name="border">0</xsl:attribute>
                <xsl:attribute name="hspace">4</xsl:attribute>
                <xsl:attribute name="vspace">4</xsl:attribute>
                <xsl:attribute name="align">left</xsl:attribute>
            </xsl:element>
        </xsl:element>

        <font size="+1">
        <xsl:element name="a">
            <xsl:attribute name="href">
                <xsl:value-of select="@url" />
            </xsl:attribute>
            <xsl:value-of select="ProductName" />
        </xsl:element>
        </font>
        <br />
        <xsl:text>Author: </xsl:text>
        <xsl:value-of select="Authors/Author[1]" />
        <xsl:text>; </xsl:text>
        <xsl:value-of select="OurPrice" />
        <xsl:if test="Availability">
            <xsl:text> (</xsl:text>
            <xsl:value-of select="Availability" />
            <xsl:if test="Availability = 'Pre Order'">
                <xsl:text>, release date </xsl:text>
                <xsl:value-of select="ReleaseDate" />
            </xsl:if>
            <xsl:text>)</xsl:text>
        </xsl:if>
        <br clear="all" />

        <xsl:for-each select="Reviews/CustomerReview">
            <xsl:choose>
                <xsl:when test="Rating = 1">
                    <img src="http://g-images.amazon.com/images/G/01/⏎
detail/stars-1-0.gif" border="0" hspace="2" vspace="2" />
                </xsl:when>
                <xsl:when test="Rating = 2">
                    <img src="http://g-images.amazon.com/images/G/01/⏎
detail/stars-2-0.gif" border="0" hspace="2" vspace="2" />
                </xsl:when>
                <xsl:when test="Rating = 3">
                    <img src="http://g-images.amazon.com/images/G/01/⏎
detail/stars-3-0.gif" border="0" hspace="2" vspace="2" />
                </xsl:when>
```

```
        <xsl:when test="Rating = 4">
            <img src="http://g-images.amazon.com/images/G/01/↵
detail/stars-4-0.gif" border="0" hspace="2" vspace="2" />
        </xsl:when>
        <xsl:when test="Rating = 5">
            <img src="http://g-images.amazon.com/images/G/01/↵
detail/stars-5-0.gif" border="0" hspace="2" vspace="2" />
        </xsl:when>
    </xsl:choose>
    <b><xsl:value-of select="Summary" /></b>
    <br />
    <xsl:value-of select="Comment" />
    <br /><br />
  </xsl:for-each>
</description></item>
</xsl:template>

<xsl:template match="/">
    <xsl:apply-templates select="ProductInfo/Details" />
</xsl:template>

</xsl:stylesheet>
```

Running the Hack

The main file *amazon_rss.asp* accepts a few querystring variables. One of these is required each time you run the script.

keywords
> The subject of the books in the RSS feed.

browse
> Use this if you know the browse node code you'd like to syndicate.

author
> Set to the author's name to syndicate a list of that author's books.

Make all three files available on a web server, and then browse to *amazon_rss.asp* with a variable included. For example:

```
http://example.com/amazon_rss.asp?keywords=hacks
```

Now anyone can add this URL to their RSS news reader!

—Sean Nolan

CHAPTER SEVEN

Advanced XML Hacks
Hacks 91–100

In this chapter, we present a handful of somewhat more advanced hacks, some of which require Java and C# programming experience. We start out learning how to use the Java build tool Ant as an XML pipeline [Hack #91]. Next, we get some help avoiding the amp explosion problem [Hack #92], then take a test flight with Cocoon [Hack #93], and then we move text from Wiki to SGML to XML [Hack #94].

The remaining hacks deal with programming. First, we create well-formed XML with JavaScript [Hack #95]; second, we use DOM with Java [Hack #96] and SAX in Java [Hack #97]; third, we process XML with C# [Hack #98]; we use several tools to generate Java and C# code based on an XML instance and a schema [Hack #99]. and generate XML with Genx [Hack #100].

All the example files mentioned in this chapter are available from the file archive, which is downloadable from *http://www.oreilly.com/catalog/xmlhks/*.

#91 Pipeline XML with Ant

Ant is an extensible, open source build tool written in Java and sponsored by Apache. It can also be used as a framework for performing a large variety of operations—including XML-related tasks—in a single step.

Ant (*http://ant.apache.org*) uses build files that are written in XML, and takes advantage of XML in a variety of ways. It's a suitable (if not ideal) framework for XML pipelining—it's open, mature, stable, readily available, widely known and used, easily extensible, and already amenable to XML processing. What else could you ask for?

In this hack, I'll show you the XML structures in an Ant build file, named *build.xml* by default; talk about some common XML-related tasks that Ant can perform; and end with an example of XML pipelining.

To get the examples in this hack to work, you'll need to download and install Ant Version 1.6.1 (or later) binaries from *http://ant.apache.org/ bindownload.cgi*. Because you'll be using an external task that validates with RELAX NG (*http://www.relaxng.org*) schemas, you'll also need James Clark's Jing (*http://www.thaiopensource.com/relaxng/jing.html*).

Validating an XML Document

Ant has a task for validating XML documents called xmlvalidate. By default, Ant validates with Xerces. The XML document *valid.xml* is shown in Example 7-1.

Example 7-1. valid.xml

```
<?xml version="1.0" encoding="UTF-8"?>
<!DOCTYPE time SYSTEM "time.dtd">

<!-- a time instant -->
<time timezone="PST">
 <hour>11</hour>
 <minute>59</minute>
 <second>59</second>
 <meridiem>p.m.</meridiem>
 <atomic signal="true"/>
</time>
```

It points to the DTD *time.dtd* (Example 7-2).

Example 7-2. time.dtd

```
<!ELEMENT time (hour,minute,second,meridiem,atomic)>
<!ATTLIST time timezone CDATA #REQUIRED>
<!ELEMENT hour (#PCDATA)>
<!ELEMENT minute (#PCDATA)>
<!ELEMENT second (#PCDATA)>
<!ELEMENT meridiem (#PCDATA)>
<!ELEMENT atomic EMPTY>
<!ATTLIST atomic signal CDATA #REQUIRED>
```

You can validate *valid.xml* with the build file *build.xml*, which uses the xmlvalidate task (Example 7-3).

Example 7-3. build.xml

```
<?xml version="1.0"?>

<project default="valid">
 <target name="valid">
  <xmlvalidate file="valid.xml"/>
 </target>
</project>
```

The target element is a child of project and must have a name attribute. The value of this attribute matches the value of the default attribute of project, i.e., valid. When there is more than one target in a build file, the value of default only matches the value of one name attribute in one target. The target element also has several other attributes not shown here. On the xmlvalidate element, the file attribute specifies the document to validate (in this case, *valid.xml*).

In the working directory, and with Ant installed and in the path, issue the command:

```
ant
```

Ant knows to look for the *build.xml* file, and to take its orders from there. The ant command produces the following output, if successful:

```
Buildfile: build.xml

valid:
[xmlvalidate] 1 file(s) have been successfully validated.

BUILD SUCCESSFUL
Total time: 1 second
```

In Ant, *types* are elements that can help perform tasks, especially on groups of files. For example, using the fileset type as a child of xmlvalidate, you can validate a series of XML documents, as shown in *build-fileset.xml* (Example 7-4).

Example 7-4. build-fileset.xml

```
<?xml version="1.0"?>

<project default="valid">
 <target name="valid">
  <xmlvalidate>
   <fileset file="*ternal.xml"/>
  </xmlvalidate>
 </target>
</project>
```

The file attribute of fileset allows you to specify a series of files with wildcards. If you run this build file, you will see that Ant validates both the *internal.xml* and *external.xml* documents in one step.

The xmlvalidate task has several features I haven't mentioned, but are worth looking at, such as checking a document only for well-formedness by using lenient="yes" (see *http://ant.apache.org/manual/OptionalTasks/xmlvalidate.html*).

The Jing Task

One way that you can extend Ant is by writing your own task (instructions on how to do this are found at *http://ant.apache.org/manual/develop. html#writingowntask*). James Clark has written a task for Jing that allows you to use Ant to validate XML documents against RELAX NG schemas, using either XML or compact syntax. This task is documented at *http:// www.thaiopensource.com/relaxng/jing-ant.html*.

Jing's source code (*JingTask.java*) is available for download from *http:// www.thaiopensource.com/download/jing-20030619.zip*, but for convenience I have included a copy of *JingTask.java* in the example file archive for easy inspection (along with a copy of Jing's license, *jing-copying.txt*).

The document *time.xml* is valid with regard to the RELAX NG schema *time.rng*, shown in Example 7-5.

Example 7-5. time.rng

```
<element name="time" xmlns="http://relaxng.org/ns/structure/1.0">
 <attribute name="timezone"/>
 <element name="hour"><text/></element>
 <element name="minute"><text/></element>
 <element name="second"><text/></element>
 <element name="meridiem"><text/></element>
 <element name="atomic">
  <attribute name="signal"/>
 </element>
</element>
```

To validate *time.xml* against *time.rng* with Ant, use the build file *build-jing.xml* (Example 7-6).

Example 7-6. build-jing.xml

```
<?xml version="1.0"?>

<project default="rng">

 <taskdef name="jing" classname="com.thaiopensource.relaxng.util.JingTask"/>

 <target name="rng">
  <echo message="Validating with RELAX NG schema using Jing..."/>
  <jing rngfile="time.rng" file="time.xml"/>
 </target>

</project>
```

The taskdef element defines the jing task in the name attribute, and the classname attribute identifies the class that executes the task. The compiled class is stored in *jing.jar*. If you place *jing.jar* in Ant's *lib* directory, Ant will be able to find the task. (For example, on my Windows machine, I've placed *jing.jar* in *C:\Java\Ant\apache-ant-1.6.1\lib*.)

The echo task echoes the text in the message attribute. Jing is silent upon success, so you can throw in an echo task to send a message of some sort, as shown in Example 7-6. The jing task's rngfile attribute identifies a RELAX NG schema, and the file attribute names the instance of the schema. You can also use a fileset type as a child of jing, allowing you to validate more than one document at a time.

Run this build file with this command:

```
ant -f build-jing.xml
```

and you will get a result like this:

```
Buildfile: build-jing.xml

rng:
     [echo] Validating with RELAX NG schema using Jing...

BUILD SUCCESSFUL
Total time: 1 second
```

Jing can also validate against schemas in the compact syntax, RELAX NG's terse, non-XML format. The compact schema *time.rnc* is shown in Example 7-7.

Example 7-7. time.rnc

```
element time {
  attribute timezone { text },
  element hour { text },
  element minute { text },
  element second { text },
  element meridiem { text },
  element atomic {
    attribute signal { text }
  }
}
```

The build file *build-rnc.xml* (Example 7-8) validates *time.xml* against *time.rnc*. Note the addition of the compactsyntax attribute to the jing task element.

Example 7-8. build-rnc.xml

```
<?xml version="1.0"?>

<project default="rng">

  <taskdef name="jing" classname="com.thaiopensource.relaxng.util.JingTask"/>
```

Example 7-8. build-rnc.xml (continued)

```
<target name="rng">
  <echo message="Validating with RELAX NG compact syntax schema using
    Jing..."/>
  <jing compactsyntax="true" rngfile="time.rnc" file="time.xml"/>
</target>

</project>
```

Give the command:

```
ant -f build-rnc.xml
```

and you will get this report:

```
Buildfile: build-rnc.xml

rng:
     [echo] Validating with RELAX NG compact syntax schema using
Jing...

BUILD SUCCESSFUL
Total time: 1 second
```

An XML Pipeline Example

This example places previously discussed tasks together into a single build file and adds a few other targets as well. The resulting file, *build-all.xml*, is an example of a simple XML pipeline. The basic scenario is that a property is set (holding the current directory) using a local XML document (*properties.xml*), and a remote ZIP file (*time.zip*) is downloaded via the get task. The ZIP archive contains four files: two RELAX NG schemas (*time1. rng* and *time1.rnc*), the DTD *time1.dtd*, and an XML instance *time2.xml*. This archive is unzipped and *time2.xml* is validated against *time1.rng*, *time1. rnc*, and *time1.dtd*. Then, *time2.xml* is transformed into a text document with XSLT (*clock.txt*). Granted, more complex operations are possible, but this gives you an idea of how you can put a pipeline together.

The build file is shown in Example 7-9.

Example 7-9. build-all.xml

```
<?xml version="1.0"?>

<project default="xform">

<taskdef name="jing" classname="com.thaiopensource.relaxng.util.JingTask"/>

<target name="init">
  <echo message="Load XML properties..."/>
```

Example 7-9. build-all.xml (continued)

```xml
  <xmlproperty file="properties.xml"/>
  <property name= "MailLogger.from" value="schlomo@example.com"/>
  <property name= "MailLogger.success.to" value="harvey@example.com"/>
  <property name= "MailLogger.failure.to" value="joe@example.com"/>
  <property name= "MailLogger.mailhost" value="mail.example.com"/>
</target>

<target name="get" depends="init">
 <get src="http://www.wyeast.net/time.zip" dest="time.zip"/>
</target>

<target name="unzip" depends="get">
 <unzip src="time.zip" dest="${build.dir}"/>
</target>

<target name="rng" depends="unzip">
 <echo message="Jing validating (XML)..."/>
 <jing rngfile="time1.rng" file="time2.xml"/>
</target>

<target name="rnc" depends="rng">
 <echo message="Jing validating (compact)..."/>
 <jing compactsyntax="yes" rngfile="time1.rnc" file="time2.xml"/>
</target>

<target name="val" depends="rnc">
 <xmlvalidate file="time2.xml" failonerror="no">
  <dtd publicId="-//Wy'east Communications//Time DTD//EN"
       location="file:///C:/Hacks/examples/time1.dtd"/>
 </xmlvalidate>
</target>

<target name="xform" depends="val">
 <echo message="Transforming time2.xml by clock1.xsl..."/>
 <xslt in="time2.xml" out="clock.txt"
       style="clock1.xsl">
  <outputproperty name="method" value="text"/>
  <outputproperty name="encoding" value="US-ASCII"/>
 </xslt>
</target>

</project>
```

To run the pipeline, simply type:

```
ant -f build-all.xml
```

The output will look like this, provided you have a live Internet connection:

```
Buildfile: build-all.xml

init:
```

```
          [echo] Load XML properties...

get:
          [get] Getting: http://www.wyeast.net/time.zip

unzip:
        [unzip] Expanding: C:\Hacks\examples\time.zip into C:\Hacks\examples

rng:
         [echo] Jing validating (XML)...

rnc:
         [echo] Jing validating (compact)...

val:
[xmlvalidate] 1 file(s) have been successfully validated.

xform:
         [echo] Transforming valid.xml by clock.xsl...

BUILD SUCCESSFUL
Total time: 3 seconds
```

Each of the targets, except the one named init, has a depends attribute. The value of this attribute establishes a hierarchy of dependencies between the targets. The default or starting target is xform (identified in the project element); in order for this target to execute, the val target must first execute successfully, and in order for val to execute, rnc must execute, and so forth. So this dependency is not established structurally, as through a parent-child relationship, but rather through attribute values. You can put the targets in any order in the build file. They will still execute according to the order of the values in the depends and name attributes. These dependencies make up the segments of the pipeline.

The build file has an xslt target that transforms *time2.xml* into *clock.txt* according to the XSLT stylesheet *clock1.xsl*. The outputproperty children contribute attributes and values that would normally be supplied by the output element of XSLT.

The xmlvalidate target uses a dtd child to specify a formal public identifier for the DTD and the location of a local copy of that DTD.

The get target gets a URL source, downloading it to a specified location. The xmlproperty target reads the file *properties.xml*:

```
<?xml version="1.0"?>

<build>
 <dir>.</dir>
</build>
```

The arbitrary tags in the properties file determine the name or names for the variable that you can use elsewhere in the build file to reference values, such as ${build.dir}. The first part of the variable name comes from the build tag and the second part from dir. The content of dir becomes the value of the variable.

The property elements in the init target list some properties for the Ant MailLogger (*http://ant.apache.org/manual/listeners.html*), which will send an email containing the Ant build information from schlomo to harvey (on success) or joe (on failure) at example.com, using the mailhost mail.example.com. These are, of course, dummied values. Use email addresses and a mail server that will work for you when running this example.

To get the MailLogger to work, use the -logger switch:

```
ant -logger org.apache.tools.ant.listener.MailLogger -f build-all.xml
```

See Also

- Ant's online manual: *http://ant.apache.org/manual/index.html*
- Ant Wiki: *http://wiki.apache.org/ant/FrontPage*
- "XML Pipelining with Ant," by Michael Fitzgerald. *XML.com*, January 28, 2003: *http://www.xml.com/pub/a/2003/01/29/ant.html*
- "Running Multiple XSLT Engines with Ant," by Anthony Coates. *XML.com*, December 11, 2002: *http://www.xml.com/pub/a/2002/12/11/ant-xml.html*
- *Ant: The Definitive Guide*, by Jesse E. Tilly and Eric M. Burke (O'Reilly)
- *Java Development with Ant*, by Eric Hatcher and Steve Loughran (Manning)

HACK #92   Use Elements Instead of Entities to Avoid the "amp Explosion Problem"

Use replaceable elements as a solution to the "amp explosion problem."

Search for the string & using your favorite search engine. Then search for the string &amp; and then &amp;amp; and so on. You will get lots of hits and see lots of interesting text. Here are some examples I found:

- Why Choose Auto &amp;amp;amp;amp; Home Insurance
- po&amp;amp;eacute;sie, nouvelles, th&amp;amp;eacute;&amp;amp;acirc;tre

These strange incantations can be traced back to the entity structure of XML (and SGML before it). Simply put, XML provides a number of ways in which textual units, known as *entities* [Hack #25], can be spliced into other textual units by an XML parser. The mechanism involves referring to these entities by name. The name is preceded by an ampersand character and followed by a semicolon.

Some of these entities are built into XML itself and thus are built into every XML parser. The five built-in entities (see Table 7-1) provide ways of encoding characters that would otherwise have special meaning to an XML parser because of their roles in markup .

Table 7-1. XML predefined entities

Entity reference	Description
&lt;	Less-than sign (<)
&gt;	Greater-than sign (>)
&apos;	Apostrophe (')
&quot;	Quotation mark (")
&amp;	Ampersand (&)

The troublesome entity here is the ampersand. Note that the escaped version of it features an ampersand character—the very character we are trying to escape. This self-referencing ampersand is the source of the trouble illustrated in the two examples shown earlier. Unless you are very careful in XML processing (especially multistage XML processing), it is very easy to get your ampersand escaping into a muddle.

The simplest muddle is illustrated here again:

```
Why Choose Auto &amp;amp;amp;amp; Home Insurance
```

The base text most probably started out as:

```
Why Choose Auto & Home Insurance
```

A program probably performed a global search and replace operation to escape the ampersand, yielding:

```
Why Choose Auto &amp; Home Insurance
```

So far so good. Later however, another application (or a second invocation of the first application) performed the same operation again, yielding:

```
Why Choose Auto &amp;amp; Home Insurance
```

This happened three more times to yield the final text:

```
Why Choose Auto &amp;amp;amp;amp; Home Insurance
```

Note that the text is well-formed XML syntax every step of the way, which makes detecting this problem more difficult.

This explosion of escaped ampersands acts like the rings in the cross-section of a tree, providing a good guide to the age of the document in terms of document processing steps performed.

The second example is a more complex muddle caused by exactly the same ampersand explosion. Here it is again:

```
po&amp;amp;amp;eacute;sie, nouvelles,
th&amp;amp;amp;eacute;&amp;amp;amp;acirc;tre
```

The original text here was most probably:

```
poésie, nouvelles, théâtre
```

In the first stage of processing, the accented characters were replaced with corresponding entity names commonly used in HTML/XML applications, namely the so-called ISO standard entity sets (*http://www.ascc.net/xml/resource/entities/*). In the ISO entity sets, an accented *é* is represented by the entity reference é and a circumflexed *â* is represented by the entity reference â. Performing these entity replacements yields:

```
po&eacute;sie, nouvelles, th&eacute;&acirc;tre
```

Later, in order to insulate any literal ampersands in the text, a program probably performed a global search and replace operation to escape the ampersands, yielding:

```
po&amp;eacute;sie, nouvelles, th&amp;eacute;&amp;acirc;tre
```

This was repeated twice more to yield the final text:

```
po&amp;amp;amp;eacute;sie, nouvelles,
th&amp;amp;amp;eacute;&amp;amp;amp;acirc;tre
```

The problems of the latter example are compounded by the fact that the é and â entities are not built into XML parsers. Consequently, to get a document to pass a well-formedness parse, it is necessary to define these entities. This can be done in a document itself using a document type declaration subset such as this (*ents.xml*):

```
<!DOCTYPE doc [
<!ENTITY eacute "&amp;eacute;">
<!ENTITY acirc "&amp;acirc;">
]>
<doc>
<p>
This document has an ampersand (&amp;) an apostrophe (&apos;) and a
quotation mark (&quot;). These three entities are built into XML.
</p>
<p>
This document also as an e acute (&eacute;) and an a circumflex (&acirc;).
</p>
</doc>
```

However, defining these entities is more commonly done by adding the entity declarations to the external DTD.

Note that the replacement text for both é and â entities in the previous example is designed to recreate the original entity markup. This is the safest thing to do when you wish to process XML without harming the entity markup. Unfortunately, it involves adding yet more troublesome ampersands to the XML document!

One way to avoid this kind of trouble is to replace all entity references in your documents with elements. As soon as the content is parseable XML, use XML processing exclusively. Do not mix text processing (global search and replace) with XML processing.

Replacing the entity references in your documents with elements is straight-forward. Simply create elements to act as placeholders for the real entity references while document processing is underway. Here is a good sequence to follow when starting out with plain text:

1. Replace all literal ampersand characters with an empty XML element such as <amp/>, and replace all literal less-than signs with an empty XML element such as <lt/>. This is a global search and replace operation.

2. Replace all non–built-in entity references with empty elements named after the entity, such as <eacute/> for the é entity and so on. This is a global search and replace operation.

3. Top and tail your document text with the start and end tags of a single XML element, say, <doc>. You now have well-formed XML.

4. Perform all subsequent text processing using XML tools; i.e., always start with an XML parse, and process the data emitted by the parser. Do not use any further global search and replace operations that involve either of XML's special characters (ampersand or less-than sign). If an ampersand needs to be added to the document during processing, insert an <amp/> element. Likewise, if a less-than sign needs to be added, insert an <lt/> element.

5. At the very last stage of processing, convert the placeholder elements created for entities back into entity syntax.

For example, here is a file, *ents.txt*, that we will mark up in XML, avoiding the use of entities:

```
This document has an ampersand (&) an apostrophe (') and a quotation mark
("). These three entities are built into XML.
This document also as an e acute (é) and an a circumflex (â).
```

Performing steps 1 through 3 of the procedure produces the following XML document (*fixedents.xml*):

```
<doc>
This document has an ampersand (<amp/>) an apostrophe (<apos/>) and a
quotation mark (<quot/>). These three entities are built into XML.
This document also as an e acute (<eacute/>) and an a circumflex (<acirc/>).
</doc>
```

The document is now well-formed XML, and will pass through an XML parser unharmed. Perform all further processing of this document using XML tools and you are unlikely to ever suffer from ampersand explosion.

The only place that literal ampersands can occur with the method I just presented is in attribute values. In my processing pipelines, I tend to model everything in terms of element structure, modeling attributes as sub-elements, and converting them to attribute syntax only at the very end of a processing pipeline.

Note that this approach makes XML parsing easier, as well-formedness checking parsers do not require you to declare element types but do require you to declare any non–built-in entities. Using this technique negates the need to carry around entity declarations, either in internal document type declaration subsets or in external DTDs.

Newer schema languages, such as RELAX NG (*http://www.relaxng.org*) and W3C XML Schema (*http://www.w3.org/XML/Schema*), do not provide facilities for manipulating the entity structure and so this all-element approach plays well with them and with tools based on them.

Finally, when creating a DTD, RELAX NG, or W3C XML Schema model, I make a point of creating amp, quot, 1t, and apos elements so that I can use the aforementioned techniques, even when performing schema-valid XML processing.

See Also

- "Ampersand Attrition in XML and HTML": *http://www.propylon.com/ news/ctoarticles/Ampersand_Attrition_in_XML_and_HTML_ 20020704.html*

—*Sean McGrath*

Use Cocoon to Create a Well-Formed View of a Web Page, Then Scrape It for Data

Cocoon is a popular web development framework from Apache.

To an XML hacker, the Web is a frustrating place. Little islands of well-formed XML content are awash in vast seas of "tag soup" in the form of malformed HTML documents [Hack #49]. Using a technique known as screen-scraping, it's possible to extract information from these pages, relying on knowledge of specific markup practices or document structures to pick out the data items from amongst the presentation elements.

Generally, screen-scraping involves using text processing tools like Perl that ignore the markup completely. However, there are ways to apply screen-scraping techniques using XML tools such as XSLT, the benefit being that one can go a little further with the tools immediately at hand without having to context switch to another environment—good news when you're after fast results.

This hack will demonstrate how to use elements of Cocoon (*http://cocoon. apache.org/*), an open source XML processing framework that can create a well-formed view of any web page and then apply XSLT to the results to extract some useful metadata.

Cocoon in 60 Seconds

For the uninitiated, Cocoon is an open source XML processing framework written in Java. It has a loyal community that is continually enhancing its functionality, but at the core is a very simple but powerful design pattern: the pipeline.

A Cocoon pipeline consists of three basic components: a Generator, responsible for providing the data to be processed; a Transformer that performs some useful processing on that data; and, ultimately, a Serializer that assembles the results. The interface used to glue these components together is the SAX API: a Generator produces SAX events, which are fed into Transformers, which in turn deliver events further down the pipeline until they're finally delivered to a Serializer that constructs the resulting document.

Cocoon is bundled with many different implementations of each of these components, with the most common being: the XML Generator, which is an XML parser; the XSLT Transformer, which applies an XSLT transform to the data passing through the pipeline; and the XML Serializer, which turns the SAX events back into an XML document.

However, among the other varied generators available in Cocoon is the HTML Generator, which is capable of turning any HTML page into well-formed XML that can then be processed by other components in a pipeline. The HTML Generator achieves this using JTidy (*http://jtidy.sourceforge.net/*), a Java port of the command-line tool HTML Tidy [Hack #22].

Cocoon runs as a web application, making it a quick and simple way to publish XML data using XSLT. An individual instance of Cocoon uses a configuration file called a *sitemap.xmap* that describes the required processing pipelines, binding them to a particular request URL that will trigger their processing.

Running the Hack

To run this hack you'll need to download and install Cocoon from *http://cocoon.apache.org*. Cocoon is available only as a source distribution, but the install and setup is very straightforward.

First, ensure that you have Java installed and a JAVA_HOME environment variable pointing to the location of the installation. Then, after unpacking the source distribution, change into the newly created directory and execute the following:

```
./build.sh
./cocoon.sh servlet
```

This will build the Cocoon application and then start it up as a standalone service that will be available at *http://localhost:8888/*. Consult the Cocoon documentation for more information on tweaking the build as well as how to install Cocoon into an existing servlet container. For the rest of this hack we'll refer to the location of the cocoon installation as $COCOON_HOME.

The first step toward implementing this hack is to configure Cocoon using a sitemap. Copy the file in Example 7-10, *sitemap.xmap*, into the directory *$COCOON_HOME/build/webapp*. You'll find *sitemap.xmap* in the working directory where you unzipped the file archive that came with the book.

 Be sure to back up the existing file named *sitemap.xmap* in *$COCOON_HOME/build/webapp* if you want to try out Cocoon demos later.

Example 7-10. sitemap.xmap

```
<map:sitemap xmlns:map="http://apache.org/cocoon/sitemap/1.0">
  <map:components>

  <map:generators default="html">
    <map:generator name="html"
```

Example 7-10. sitemap.xmap (continued)

```
          src="org.apache.cocoon.generation.HTMLGenerator">
    </map:generator>
  </map:generators>

  <map:transformers default="xslt">
   <map:transformer name="xslt"
        src="org.apache.cocoon.transformation.TraxTransformer">
        <use-request-parameters>false</use-request-parameters>
   </map:transformer>
  </map:transformers>

  <map:serializers default="xml">
   <map:serializer mime-type="text/xml"
                   name="xml"
                   src="org.apache.cocoon.serialization.XMLSerializer"/>
  </map:serializers>

  <map:matchers default="param">
   <map:matcher name="param"
        src="org.apache.cocoon.matching.WildcardRequestParameterMatcher">
        <parameter-name>url</parameter-name>
   </map:matcher>
  </map:matchers>

  <map:selectors />

  <map:actions/>

  <map:pipes default="caching">
   <map:pipe name="caching"
        src="org.apache.cocoon.components.
pipeline.impl.CachingProcessingPipeline"/>
  </map:pipes>

 </map:components>

 <map:views/>

 <map:resources/>

 <map:action-sets/>

 <map:pipelines>
  <map:pipeline>
   <map:match pattern="**">
    <map:generate type="html" src="{1}"/>
    <map:transform src="extractMetadata.xsl">
     <map:parameter name="url" value="{1}"/>
    </map:transform>
    <map:serialize type="xml"/>
```

Example 7-10. sitemap.xmap (continued)

```
    </map:match>
   </map:pipeline>
  </map:pipelines>

</map:sitemap>
```

A sitemap consists of two main sections. The first portion of the sitemap is a series of component definitions that declare the different kinds of Generator, Transformer, and Serializer components that will be available for use by pipelines described later in the sitemap. Each component is named so that it can be referred to later; it's possible to declare an implementation as the default for a particular component type.

In this instance there are three component definitions:

- The HTML Generator, which will be responsible for fetching and parsing the required HTML document, applying JTidy to ensure that it's well-formed.

- The XSLT Transform responsible for invoking a stylesheet to process the content.

- The XML Serializer, which will produce the resulting document that will be delivered in response to the request.

The other component worth mentioning is the Matcher. This is used to bind an HTTP request to a particular pipeline that will be used to generate the response. A Matcher uses a wildcard or regular expression to select a given pipeline based on some aspect of the request. In this case, we're using a Matcher that tests for a request parameter named url.

The second half of a sitemap consists of the pipeline definition, which combines the declared components to perform some useful processing. In this simple example there is only a single pipeline definition:

```
<map:pipeline>
  <map:match pattern="**">
  <map:generate src="{1}"/>
  <map:transform src="extractMetadata.xsl">
   <map:parameter name="url" value="{1}"/>
  </map:transform>
  <map:serialize/>
  </map:match>
 </map:pipeline>
```

The pipeline will match any incoming request with a url parameter and will then take the following steps:

1. Generate data for the pipeline by accessing the web page referenced in the url parameter. The HTML Generator will internally run the content of the page through JTidy to generate well-formed HTML.

2. Transform the results using a stylesheet called *extractMetadata.xsl*, passing the original URL as a stylesheet parameter.

3. Serialize the results of the transform as an XML document, which will be returned as the response.

The XSLT stylesheet in Example 7-11, *extractMetadata.xsl*, should be copied from the working directory and stored in *$COCOON_HOME/build/webapp*.

Example 7-11. extractMetadata.xsl

```
<xsl:stylesheet version="1.0"
                xmlns:xsl="http://www.w3.org/1999/XSL/Transform"
                xmlns:rdf="http://www.w3.org/1999/02/22-rdf-syntax-ns#"
                xmlns:dc="http://purl.org/dc/elements/1.1/"
                xmlns:xhtml="http://www.w3.org/1999/xhtml">

<xsl:output method="xml" indent="yes"/>

<xsl:param name="url"/>

<xsl:variable name="lcletters">abcdefghijklmnopqrstuvwxyz</xsl:variable>
<xsl:variable name="ucletters">ABCDEFGHIJKLMNOPQRSTUVWXYZ</xsl:variable>

<xsl:template match="xhtml:body"/>

<xsl:template match="xhtml:html">
   <xsl:apply-templates select="xhtml:head"/>
</xsl:template>

<xsl:template match="xhtml:head">
   <rdf:Description rdf:about="{$url}">
      <xsl:apply-templates select="xhtml:title"/>
      <xsl:apply-templates select="xhtml:meta"/>
   </rdf:Description>
</xsl:template>

<xsl:template match="xhtml:title">
   <dc:title><xsl:value-of select="."/></dc:title>
</xsl:template>

<xsl:template match="xhtml:meta">
   <xsl:variable name="name">
      <xsl:choose>
         <xsl:when test="@http-equiv">
            <xsl:value-of select="translate(@http-equiv, $ucletters,
                               $lcletters)"/>
```

Example 7-11. extractMetadata.xsl (continued)

```
            </xsl:when>
            <xsl:when test="@name">
                <xsl:value-of select="translate(@name, $ucletters, $lcletters)"/>
            </xsl:when>
        </xsl:choose>
    </xsl:variable>
    <xsl:choose>
        <xsl:when test="$name = 'content-type' or $name='dc.format'">
            <dc:format><xsl:value-of select="@content"/></dc:format>
        </xsl:when>
        <xsl:when test="$name = 'content-language' or $name='dc.language'">
            <dc:language><xsl:value-of select="@content"/></dc:language>
        </xsl:when>
        <xsl:when test="$name = 'description' or $name = 'dc.description'">
            <dc:description><xsl:value-of select="@content"/></dc:description>
        </xsl:when>
        <xsl:when test="$name = 'keywords' or $name = 'dc.subject'">
            <dc:subject><xsl:value-of select="@content"/></dc:subject>
        </xsl:when>
        <xsl:when test="$name = 'copyright' or $name = 'dc.rights'">
            <dc:rights><xsl:value-of select="@content"/></dc:rights>
        </xsl:when>
        <xsl:when test="$name = 'dc.title'">
            <dc:title><xsl:value-of select="@content"/></dc:title>
        </xsl:when>
        <xsl:when test="$name = 'dc.publisher'">
            <dc:publisher><xsl:value-of select="@content"/></dc:publisher>
        </xsl:when>
        <xsl:when test="$name = 'dc.date'">
            <dc:date><xsl:value-of select="@content"/></dc:date>
        </xsl:when>
        <xsl:when test="$name = 'dc.creator'">
            <dc:creator><xsl:value-of select="@content"/></dc:creator>
        </xsl:when>
        <xsl:when test="$name = 'dc.type'">
            <dc:type><xsl:value-of select="@content"/></dc:type>
        </xsl:when>
        <xsl:when test="$name = 'dc.contributor'">
            <dc:contributor><xsl:value-of select="@content"/></dc:contributor>
        </xsl:when>
        <xsl:when test="$name = 'dc.coverage'">
            <dc:coverage><xsl:value-of select="@content"/></dc:coverage>
        </xsl:when>
        <xsl:otherwise/>
    </xsl:choose>
</xsl:template>

</xsl:stylesheet>
```

The stylesheet is capable of processing any well-formed HTML page to extract some useful metadata. The stylesheet generates an RDF document as its output. (RDF is the standard way for capturing metadata about web resources.) The Dublin Core project (in the namespace http://purl.org/dc/elements/1.1/) defines a number of standard properties that can be used to describe a web resource using RDF. These properties cover simple items such as title, author, and so forth.

The Dublin Core project also defines a standard way to embed those properties in an HTML document using the meta element. All this stylesheet essentially does is extract that metadata from this standard location (as well as a few other, common, nonstandard ones) to build an appropriate RDF document.

The stylesheet itself is straightforward, consisting primarily of a large conditional block that tests for the presence of different items of metadata, emitting the appropriate RDF property if found.

With both the sitemap and stylesheet in place, it's now possible to try out the hack. Make sure that Cocoon is running and try a URL such as:

```
http://localhost:8888/tidy?url=http://hacks.oreilly.com
```

This will trigger the pipeline and should deliver an RDF document like the one shown in Example 7-12.

Example 7-12. Output from Cocoon hack

```
<?xml version="1.0" encoding="ISO-8859-1"?>
<rdf:Description xmlns:rdf="http://www.w3.org/1999/02/22-rdf-syntax-ns#"
                 xmlns:xhtml="http://www.w3.org/1999/xhtml"
                 xmlns:dc="http://purl.org/dc/elements/1.1/"
                 rdf:about="http://hacks.oreilly.com">
  <dc:title>hacks.oreilly.com -- O'Reilly Hacks Series</dc:title>

  <dc:description>Hacks are tools, tips, and tricks that help users
  solve problems. They are aimed at intermediate-level power users
  and scripters. Each book is a collection of 100 article-length
  hacks, and each one provides detailed examples that show how to
  solve practical problems. Got a hack? Share it with us.
  </dc:description>

</rdf:Description>
```

Substitute any web address for the value of the url parameter to process a different page. Substitute another stylesheet in the pipeline definition to perform a more complex transformation.

Extending the Hack

There are several ways that this hack could be extended. One example is to exploit more of Cocoon's functionality to build a full-fledged application or web service that harvests some or even all of its data by scraping web pages and other data sources.

The example stylesheet is also fairly generic. It attempts to provide some useful basic metadata about any web page. However, in some cases the required data may be part of the actual page body, requiring a more complex transform. This extension can be used to extract data from services that don't currently offer an XML interface.

Extracting data using only XSLT can be quite tricky. By adopting Cocoon as the basic framework it's possible to take advantage of additional features as you require them—for example, writing a custom Transformer component to process the data using the SAX API rather than relying on just XSLT. The mark of any good framework is that there's room for growth.

—Leigh Dodds

From Wiki to XML, Through SGML
#94   Wikis are nice for typing. XML is nice for processing. SGML is a standard language for specifying conversions from one to the other.

Wikis exploded onto the scene in the late 1990s but have been quieter recently. A Wiki is a site written using a very simplified syntax without tags (e.g., a blank line means start a new paragraph). The nice thing about Wiki formats is that they reduce the number of keystrokes needed to mark up a document (to the level of very simple HTML) to the same number as a nice, swanky, custom application needs. Today I am writing this in Mozilla Composer: in order to put in a link I need to type ^L to open the link editor, type the text, then Tab, then the URL, then Enter: three characters overhead. In a Wiki, I type [and then the text, a > character followed by the URL, and then]. Pretty much identical to Mozilla Composer, but with the advantage that one doesn't need to learn any special keystrokes or customize an editor to cope with them.

WikiWikiWeb (*http://c2.com/cgi/wiki?WikiWikiWeb*) provides a simple rich text format based on visual cues rather than HTML tags. This is convenient for hand editing and has the virtue that the raw text gives a rough indication of the formatted text. Wiki-like syntaxes are useful, for example, for creating documents in mail programs or PDAs, where terseness is important and there is no well-formedness checking or validation available.

SGML: A Language for Describing Wikis

Now that Wiki and XML are both fairly established, it gives us nice end-points for suggesting where SGML fits in: SGML is a language for defining the syntaxes of Wiki-like languages and parsing them into HTML-like documents with missing tags, then filling in the gaps to reveal XML-like structured documents.

The idea is as old as the hills, so old that I expect it will be patented soon. SGML provided many facilities to support this kind of terse markup. XML removed support in the name of ease of implementation, but the strict mantra of "all structure should be explicitly tagged with elements" is not always the best answer.

This hack shows how to describe Wiki content using SGML. This technique converts a Wiki page into XML using the open source SP software from James Clark (*http://www.jclark.com/sp/*). Using this technique, you can provide your users with low-keystroke ways to send structured data with less opportunity for syntax errors and no reliance on the editing system at their end. The data does not need to be rich text—it could even be simple records of data.

An SGML Document Type for Wiki

The first step is to describe Wiki as an SGML document type, using HTML names where possible:

```
<!ENTITY % blocks      " p | head | bull1 | bull2 | bull3  | li1 | li2 |
    li3 |  bq  " >
<!ENTITY % inlines     " b | i | bi | tt " >
<!ELEMENT page         o o ( keyword |%blocks; | pre | dl | hr )* >
<!ELEMENT ( dt | dd | pre | %blocks;  )
           o o ( #PCDATA | %inlines; | link  )* >
<!ELEMENT ( text | ref | %inlines;   )
           o o ( #PCDATA )* >

<!ELEMENT dl           o o ( dt, dd? )+>
<!ELEMENT hr           o o EMPTY >
<!ELEMENT link         o o (text, ref? ) >
<!ELEMENT keyword      o o (#PCDATA) >
```

If you are used to XML DTDs, you can see this is a little terser. For example, the same element declaration can declare multiple element types, and you can use a parameter entity reference. The various - and o symbols, also unavailable in XML, describe whether the start and end tags can be implied by the parser (o means "omissible").

There are some differences in this document type from HTML. The top-level element is page. List items are not nested, but indented according to their number: bull*n* means a bullet list at indent level *n*. li*n* means a list with no indent at that level. There is an element link instead of the a or img elements from HTML.

Which Wiki?

There are many Wiki dialects. In this hack, we use a fairly generic one that falls between the readily parseable WikiWorks dialect and the original Wiki, and is tweaked to be suitable for blogs. The fact that there are already many mutually incompatible dialects of Wiki should be no surprise: the optimal shortcuts for you depend on the kinds of text you have to deal with.

Let's first describe the various rules for the Wiki in rough English, and then we can figure out the declarations for them to get them into our SGML vocabulary:

- Start-of-line followed by ---- means a hr
- A blank line starts a new paragraph except in a pre
- A start of line followed by a space means a pre
- In a pre, a blank line or a line starting with a space continues the pre
- Start-of-line followed by * means a bull1; start-of-line followed by ** means a bull2; and start-of-line followed *** means a bull3
- Start-of-line followed by # means an li1 indented list with no bullet or number; start-of-line followed by ## means an li2 indented list with no bullet or number; start-of-line followed ### means an li3 indented list with no bullet or number
- Start-of-line followed by a tab means a dl followed by a dt
- In a dt element, a : starts a dd
- Start-of-line followed by a tab, space, :, and another tab starts a bq
- Start-of-line followed by # means a numbered list li1
- '' starts and ends an i element (or end-of-line)
- ''' starts and ends a b element (or end-of-line)
- '''' become a single quote
- ''''' starts and ends bold italic text (or end-of-line)
- ** starts and ends a tt section (when not in a pre)
- [and] delimit a link
- In a link, a > means the text to its left is a title and to the right is the reference; otherwise; the text is the reference

- [[to escape [in normal text
- Start-of-line followed by ! is a heading
- Start-of-line followed by = is a keyword (metadata)

Some Wiki dialects also allow tables and automatic link recognition. The first is left as an exercise to the reader; the second is more than SGML can handle. Once you have described your Wiki dialect in terms of SGML, you can easily add more shortcuts as needed.

Wiki as SGML

Now that we have a description of our Wiki dialect, and of the abstract grammar of a Wiki page, we need a way of parsing one in terms of the other.

SGML's short references provide just that. We can tell the parser to substitute a particular tag for a particular delimiter string. SGML provides four features to make this feasible:

- You can recognize different delimiter strings in different contexts (using different delimiter maps).
- An SGML parser is pretty smart about filling in the gaps for missing tags (tag implication).
- SGML (like any decent text processing system) allows us to distinguish between end-of-line and start-of-line positions (let's call them RE and RS for Record Start and Record End).
- The parser adopts a longest-match-first approach to delimiter matching.

First, we define entity references for all the start tags and some end tags. We will use these later. We use a special form of the entity reference that doesn't need to be reparsed, shown in Example 7-13. Examples 7-13 through 7-15 (including the fragments shown) are all in the file *wiki.sgm*.

Example 7-13. STARTTAG entity references

```
<!ENTITY bull1-s STARTTAG "bull1" >
<!ENTITY bull2-s STARTTAG "bull2" >
<!ENTITY bull3-s STARTTAG "bull3" >
<!ENTITY li1-s STARTTAG "li1" >
<!ENTITY li2-s STARTTAG "li2" >
<!ENTITY li3-s STARTTAG "li3" >

<!ENTITY p-s STARTTAG "p" >
<!ENTITY pre-s STARTTAG "pre" >
<!ENTITY bq-s STARTTAG "bq">
<!ENTITY hr-s STARTTAG "hr" >
<!ENTITY head-s STARTTAG "head" >
<!ENTITY key-s STARTTAG "keyword">
<!ENTITY key-e ENDTAG "keyword" >
```

Example 7-13. STARTTAG entity references (continued)

```
<!ENTITY b-s STARTTAG "b">
<!ENTITY bi-s STARTTAG "bi">
<!ENTITY i-s STARTTAG "i">
<!ENTITY b-e ENDTAG "b">
<!ENTITY bi-e ENDTAG "bi">
<!ENTITY i-e ENDTAG "i">
<!ENTITY tt-s STARTTAG "tt">
<!ENTITY tt-e ENDTAG "tt">

<!ENTITY ref-s STARTTAG "ref">
<!ENTITY link-s STARTTAG "link">
<!ENTITY link-e ENDTAG "link">

<!ENTITY dt-s "</><dt>" >
<!ENTITY dd-s STARTTAG "dd" >
```

We also add a few funnies:

```
<!ENTITY fourQuot CDATA "'" >
<!ENTITY lsb CDATA "[">
```

Next we define maps (sets) of these in Example 7-14.

Example 7-14. Maps to entity references

```
<!SHORTREF imap
    "'" i-e
    "&#RE" i-e >
<!SHORTREF bmap
    "''" b-e
    "&#RE" b-e >
<!SHORTREF bimap
    "'''" bi-e
    "&#RE" bi-e >
<!SHORTREF linkmap
    "]" link-e
    ">" ref-s >
<!SHORTREF dtmap
    ":" dd-s >
<!SHORTREF ttmap
    "**" tt-e
    "&#RE;" tt-e >
<!SHORTREF keymap
    "&#RE;" key-e >

<!SHORTREF pagemap
    "&#RS;----" hr-s

    "&#RS;*" bull1-s
    "&#RS;**" bull2-s
    "&#RS;***" bull3-s
```

Example 7-14. Maps to entity references (continued)

```
    "&#RS;#" li1-s
    "&#RS;##" li2-s
    "&#RS;###" li3-s

    "&#RS;&#RE;&#RS;*" bull1-s
    "&#RS;&#RE;&#RS;**" bull2-s
    "&#RS;&#RE;&#RS;***" bull3-s
    "&#RS;&#RE;&#RS;#" li1-s
    "&#RS;&#RE;&#RS;##" li2-s
    "&#RS;&#RE;&#RS;###" li3-s

    "&#RS;&#RE;&#RS;" p-s
    "&#RS;!" head-s
    "&#RS;=" key-s
    "&#RS;&#TAB;" dt-s
    "&#RS;&#TAB;&#SPACE;:" bq-s
    "&#RS;&#SPACE;" pre-s

    "&#RS;&#RE;&#RS;&#RE;&#RS;" p-s
    "&#RS;&#RE;&#RS;!" head-s
    "&#RS;&#RE;&#RS;&#TAB;" dt-s
    "&#RS;&#RE;&#RS;&#TAB;&#SPACE;:" bq-s
    "&#RS;&#RE;&#RS;&#SPACE;" pre-s

    "''" i-s
    "'''" b-s
    "''''" fourQuot
    "'''''" bi-s
    "**" tt-s

    "[" link-s
    "[[" lsb
>

<!-- the difference with pmap is that a blank does not start a para -->

<!SHORTREF premap
    "&#RS;----" hr-s

    "&#RS;*" bull1-s
    "&#RS;**" bull2-s
    "&#RS;***" bull3-s
    "&#RS;#" li1-s
    "&#RS;##" li2-s
    "&#RS;###" li3-s

    "&#RS;&#RE;&#RS;*" bull1-s
    "&#RS;&#RE;&#RS;**" bull2-s
    "&#RS;&#RE;&#RS;***" bull3-s
    "&#RS;&#RE;&#RS;#" li1-s
    "&#RS;&#RE;&#RS;##" li2-s
```

Example 7-14. Maps to entity references (continued)

```
"&#RS;&#RE;&#RS;###" li3-s

"&#RS;!" head-s
"&#RS;&#TAB;" dt-s
"&#RS;&#TAB;&#SPACE;:" bq-s
"&#RS;&#SPACE;" pre-s

"&#RS;&#RE;&#RS;!" head-s
"&#RS;&#RE;&#RS;&#TAB;" dt-s
"&#RS;&#RE;&#RS;&#TAB;&#SPACE;:" bq-s
"&#RS;&#RE;&#RS;&#SPACE;" pre-s

"'" i-s
"''" b-s
"''''" fourQuot
"''''''" bi-s

"[" link-s
"[[" lsb
>
```

There are some extra declarations to handle the common case of someone typing two blank lines. This will reduce the number of spurious elements with no content.

And finally, we define when each map is active (which delimiters get recognized in which elements) in Example 7-15.

Example 7-15. Define maps as active

```
<!USEMAP imap i>
<!USEMAP bmap b>
<!USEMAP bimap bi>
<!USEMAP ttmap tt>
<!USEMAP linkmap ( link | ref | text ) >
<!USEMAP dtmap dt >
<!USEMAP keymap keyword >

<!USEMAP pagemap ( page | %blocks; | dd ) >
<!USEMAP premap pre >
```

How does it work? Example 7-16 is a Wiki document:

Example 7-16. A Wiki document (page.txti)

```
!An Example Document
=Wiki
=SGML
=XML

This is an
```

Example 7-16. A Wiki document (page.txti) (continued)

```
example document.

*It has some
kind of list
**with some kinds of nested list
* and also
#some
##type of
###indentation

But that is '''not''' ''all''!
You can link by URL alone
[http://www.topologi.com], by name plus **URL**,
[Schematron>http://www.ascc.net/xml/schematron]
or by an existing name only
[Schematron] (in the last case, the [[system] must fill
in the gap from a linkbase, so it mightn''''t work
the first time a document is link-indexed.)
----
 And here we have some preformatted text
which should be '''OK'''

And still ''should'' be preformatted.
----
!Now Another Head

    A term: a definition

    Another term: another definition
with wrapped text
    : This is supposed to be a block quote now
but...

I am not sure how useful it is.

And here is another paragraph.
```

Example 7-17 shows the document in XML (*page.xml*), after the text has been parsed as SGML and re-emitted as XML.

Example 7-17. page.xml

```
<?xml version="1.0"?>
<page><head>An Example Document
</head><keyword>Wiki</keyword><keyword>SGML</keyword><keyword>XML</keyword><p>
This is an
example document.
</p><bull1>It has some
kind of list
</bull1><bull2>with some kinds of nested list
</bull2><bull1> and also
```

Example 7-17. page.xml (continued)

```
</bull1><li1>some
</li1><li2>type of
</li2><li3>indentation
</li3><p>But that is <b>not</b> <i>all</i>!
You can link by URL alone
<link><text>http://www.topologi.com</text></link>, by name plus
<tt>URL</tt>,
<link><text>Schematron</text><ref>http://www.ascc.net/xml/schematron
</ref></link> or by an existing name only
<link><text>Schematron</text></link> (in the last case, the [system]
must fill in the gap from a linkbase, so it mightn't work
the first time a document is link-indexed.)
</p><hr/><pre>And here we have some preformatted text
which should be <b>OK</b>
And still <i>should</i> be preformatted.
</pre><hr/><head>Now Another Head
</head><dl><dt>A term</dt><dd> a definition
</dd><dt>Another term</dt><dd> another definition
with wrapped text
</dd></dl><bq> This is supposed to be a block quote now
but...
</bq><p>I am not sure how useful it is.
</p><p>And here is another paragraph.</p></page>
```

The following command line was used:

```
sx -wno-all -xno-nl-in-tag -xlower -xempty wiki.sgm page.txt > page.xml
```

When we parse the Wiki page, we will need to prepend the SGML declaration as well as the appropriate DOCTYPE declaration, which should say we are starting with a page element. Actually, we are going a little beyond strict SGML and relying on SP's particular error recovery to handle definition lists; however, the point is not that SGML could describe all Wikis but that it gets pretty close.

We're using SX, an SGML-to-XML converter. Part of the SP package, it is available as open source C++ code at the OpenJade Project or directly from James Clark's site (*http://jclark.com/SP/*), which includes premade binaries for Windows. Linux users may find their system already comes with SP: try the command man sx or man osx to check.

What this does not implement is that Wikis should allow & and < anywhere. In this Wiki dialect, use & and < to get them, or use a numeric character reference. (SGML does allow these delimiters to be remapped, but this confuses SX; in any case, having character references available is a net win.)

Is SGML worth it? It all depends on your skills and preferences. If you were doing this in Java, you would need to alter the JavaCC grammar (if you used that), adjust the mapping functions to create the XML, and then adjust the

XML's DTD when validating, which isn't necessarily less work at all. The SGML approach also has the benefit that DTDs can be written and maintained by technical people who are not programmers.

SGML's weak spot here is definitely the need to predeclare the short reference delimiters in the SGML declarations. Without that we could have an all-DTD solution, which would be easier and more fun.

—Rick Jelliffe

HACK #95 Create Well-Formed XML with JavaScript

Use Javascript to ensure that you write correct, well-formed XML in web pages.

Sometimes you need to create some XML from within a browser. It is easy to write bad XML without realizing it. Writing correct XML with all its bells and whistles is not easy, but in this type of scenario you usually only need to write basic XML.

There is a kind of hierarchy of XML:

1. Basic: Elements only; no attributes, entities, character references, escaped characters, or encoding issues
2. Plain: Basic plus attributes
3. Plain/escaped: Plain with special XML characters escaped
4. Plain/advanced: Plain/escaped with CDATA sections and processing instructions

The list continues with increasing levels of sophistication (and difficulty).

This hack covers the basic and plain styles (with some enhancements), and you can adapt the techniques to move several more steps up the ladder if you like.

The main issues with writing basic XML is to get the elements closed properly and keep the code simple. Here is how.

The Element Function

Here is a Javascript function for writing elements:

```
// Bare bones XML writer - no attributes
function element(name,content){
    var xml
    if (!content){
        xml='<' + name + '/>'
    }
    else {
```

```
        xml='<'+ name + '>' + content + '</' + name + '>'
    }
    return xml
}
```

This basic hack even writes the empty-element form when there is no element content. What is especially nice about this hack is that you can use it recursively, like this:

```
var xml = element('p', 'This is ' +
    element('strong','Bold Text') + 'inline')
```

Both inner and outer elements are guaranteed to be closed properly. You can display the result for testing like this:

```
alert(xml)
```

You can build up your entire XML document by combining bits like these, and all the elements will be properly nested and closed.

The element( ) function does not do any pretty-printing, because it has no way to know where line breaks should go. If that is important to you, just create a variant function:

```
function elementNL(name, content) {
    return element(name,content) + '\n'
}
```

More sophisticated variations are possible but rarely needed.

Adding Attributes

At the next level up, the most pressing problems are to format the attribute string properly, to escape single and double quotes embedded in the attribute values, and to do the least amount of quote escaping so that the result will be as readable as possible.

We modify the element( ) function to optionally accept an associative array containing the attribute names and values. In other languages, an associative array may be called a dictionary or a hash.

```
// XML writer with attributes and smart attribute quote escaping
function element(name,content,attributes){
    var att_str = ''
    if (attributes) { // tests false if this arg is missing!
        att_str = formatAttributes(attributes)
    }
    var xml
    if (!content){
        xml='<' + name + att_str + '/>'
    }
    else {
        xml='<' + name + att_str + '>' + content + '</'+name+'>'
```

```
        }
        return xml
}
```

The function `formatAtributes()` handles formatting and escaping the attributes.

To fix up the quotes, we use the following algorithm if there are embedded quotes (single or double):

1. Whichever type of quote occurs first in the string, use the other kind to enclose the attribute value.

2. Only escape occurrences of the kind of quote used to enclose the attribute value. We don't need to escape the other kind.

Here is the code:

```
var APOS = "'"; QUOTE = '"'
var ESCAPED_QUOTE = { }
ESCAPED_QUOTE[QUOTE] = '&quot;'
ESCAPED_QUOTE[APOS] = '&apos;'

/*
    Format a dictionary of attributes into a string suitable
    for inserting into the start tag of an element.  Be smart
    about escaping embedded quotes in the attribute values.
*/
function formatAttributes(attributes) {
    var att_value
    var apos_pos, quot_pos
    var use_quote, escape, quote_to_escape
    var att_str
    var re
    var result = ''

    for (var att in attributes) {
        att_value = attributes[att]

        // Find first quote marks if any
        apos_pos = att_value.indexOf(APOS)
        quot_pos = att_value.indexOf(QUOTE)

        // Determine which quote type to use around
        // the attribute value
        if (apos_pos == -1 && quot_pos == -1) {
            att_str = ' ' + att + "='" + att_value +  "'"
            result += att_str
            continue
        }

        // Prefer the single quote unless forced to use double
        if (quot_pos != -1 && quot_pos < apos_pos) {
```

```
                    use_quote = APOS
            }
            else {
                    use_quote = QUOTE
            }

            // Figure out which kind of quote to escape
            // Use nice dictionary instead of yucky if-else nests
            escape = ESCAPED_QUOTE[use_quote]

            // Escape only the right kind of quote
            re = new RegExp(use_quote,'g')
            att_str = ' ' + att + '=' + use_quote +
                att_value.replace(re, escape) + use_quote
            result += att_str
        }
        return result
    }
```

Here is code to test everything we've seen so far:

```
function test( ) {
    var atts = {att1:"a1",
        att2:"This is in \"double quotes\" and this is " +
        "in 'single quotes'",
        att3:"This is in 'single quotes' and this is in " +
        "\"double quotes\""}

    // Basic XML example
    alert(element('elem','This is a test'))

    // Nested elements
    var xml = element('p', 'This is ' +
    element('strong','Bold Text') + 'inline')
    alert(xml)

    // Attributes with all kinds of embedded quotes
    alert(element('elem','This is a test', atts))

    // Empty element version
    alert(element('elem','', atts))
}
```

Open the file *jswriter.html* (Example 7-18) in a browser that supports Java-Script (the script is also stored in *jswriter.js* so you can easily include it in any HTML or XHTML document).

Example 7-18. jswriter.html

```
<html xmlns="http://www.w3.org/1999/xhtml">
<head><Title>Testing the Well-formed XML Hack</head>
<script type='text/javascript'>
// XML writer with attributes and smart attribute quote escaping
function element(name,content,attributes){
```

Example 7-18. jswriter.html (continued)

```
    var att_str = ''
    if (attributes) { // tests false if this arg is missing!
        att_str = formatAttributes(attributes)
    }
    var xml
    if (!content){
        xml='<' + name + att_str + '/>'
    }
    else {
        xml='<' + name + att_str + '>' + content + '</'+name+'>'
    }
    return xml
}
var APOS = "'"; QUOTE = '"'
var ESCAPED_QUOTE = {}
ESCAPED_QUOTE[QUOTE] = '&quot;'
ESCAPED_QUOTE[APOS] = '&apos;'

/*
    Format a dictionary of attributes into a string suitable
    for inserting into the start tag of an element.  Be smart
    about escaping embedded quotes in the attribute values.
*/
function formatAttributes(attributes) {
    var att_value
    var apos_pos, quot_pos
    var use_quote, escape, quote_to_escape
    var att_str
    var re
    var result = ''

    for (var att in attributes) {
        att_value = attributes[att]

        // Find first quote marks if any
        apos_pos = att_value.indexOf(APOS)
        quot_pos = att_value.indexOf(QUOTE)

        // Determine which quote type to use around
        // the attribute value
        if (apos_pos == -1 && quot_pos == -1) {
            att_str = ' ' + att + "='" + att_value +  "'"
            result += att_str
            continue
        }

        // Prefer the single quote unless forced to use double
        if (quot_pos != -1 && quot_pos < apos_pos) {
            use_quote = APOS
        }
        else {
            use_quote = QUOTE
```

Example 7-18. jswriter.html (continued)

```
            }

            // Figure out which kind of quote to escape
            // Use nice dictionary instead of yucky if-else nests
            escape = ESCAPED_QUOTE[use_quote]

            // Escape only the right kind of quote
            re = new RegExp(use_quote,'g')
            att_str = ' ' + att + '=' + use_quote +
                att_value.replace(re, escape) + use_quote
            result += att_str
        }
        return result
    }
    function test() {
        var atts = {att1:"a1",
            att2:"This is in \"double quotes\" and this is " +
            "in 'single quotes'",
            att3:"This is in 'single quotes' and this is in " +
            "\"double quotes\""}

        // Basic XML example
        alert(element('elem','This is a test'))

        // Nested elements
        var xml = element('p', 'This is ' +
        element('strong','Bold Text') + 'inline')
        alert(xml)

        // Attributes with all kinds of embedded quotes
        alert(element('elem','This is a test', atts))

        // Empty element version
        alert(element('elem','', atts))
    }
    </script>
    </head>

    <body onload='test()'>
    </body>
    </html>
```

When the page loads, you will see the following in four successive alert boxes, as shown in Figure 7-1. The lines have been wrapped for readability.

First alert:

```
<elem>This is a test</elem>
```

Second alert:

```
<p>This is <strong>Bold Text</strong>inline</p>
```

Third alert:
```
<elem att1='a1'
att2='This is in "double quotes" and this is
in &apos;single quotes&apos;'
att3="This is in 'single quotes' and this is in
&quot;double quotes&quot;">This is a test</elem>
```
Fourth alert:
```
<elem att1='a1'
att2='This is in "double quotes" and this is in
&apos;single quotes&apos;'
att3="This is in 'single quotes' and this is in
&quot;double quotes&quot;"/>
```

Figure 7-1. jswriter.html in Firefox

Extending the Hack

You may want to escape the other special XML characters. You can do this
by adding calls such as:

```
content = content.replace(/</g, '&lt;')
```

Take care not to replace the quotes in attribute values, since
`formatAttributes()` handles this so nicely. Because the parameters to
`elements()` and `formatAttributes()` are strings, they are easy to manipulate
as you like.

Creating Large Chunks of XML

If you create long strings of XML, say with more than a few hundred string
fragments, you may find the performance to be slow. That's normal, and
happens because JavaScript, like most other languages, has to allocate memory for each new string every time you concatenate more fragments.

The standard way around this is to accumulate the fragments in a list, then join the list back to a string at the end. This process is generally very fast, even for very large results.

Here is how you can do it:

```
var results = [ ]
results.push(element("p","This is some content"))
results.push(element('p', 'This is ' +
    element('strong','Bold Text') + 'inline'))
// ... Append more bits

var end_result = results.join(' ')
```

See Also

- *JavaScript: The Definitive Guide,* by David Flanagan (O'Reilly)

—Tom Passin

HACK #96   Inspect and Edit XML Documents with the Document Object Model

The W3C Document Object Model was an early effort to gain fine-grained control over a document in memory. This hack introduces you to how DOM works.

The Document Object Model or DOM (*http://www.w3.org/DOM/*) is a W3C-specified recommendation set that provides facilities to "allow programs and scripts to dynamically access and update the content, structure and style of documents. The document can be further processed and the results of that processing can be incorporated back into the presented page" (*http://www.w3.org/DOM/#what*). In other words, DOM is a tree-based API that allows you to pick an XML document (or HTML document) apart into its constituent parts, examine those parts, change them, and stuff them back into a document.

The first release of DOM came out in 1998 as a single document, with a second edition appearing in 2000 (*http://www.w3.org/TR/2000/WD-DOM-Level-1-20000929/*). Level 2 of DOM appeared later in 2000 and consists of not less than six modules: Core, Views, Events, Style, Traversal, Range, and HTML. You can get the whole package in a single ZIP archive at *http://www.w3.org/2001/05/level-2-src.zip*. Level 3 just reached recommendation status. It adds a Validation module (*http://www.w3.org/TR/ DOM-Level-3-Val/*) and a Load and Save module (*http://www.w3.org/TR/DOM-Level-3-LS/*). It also updates the Core module (*http://www.w3.org/TR/DOM-Level-3-Core/*).

DOM represents documents as a hierarchy or tree of nodes. These nodes include Document, Element, Comment, and Text. These nodes are specified as interfaces that can be implemented by an application of DOM. Usually, the methods specified by these interfaces can manipulate the nodes in some way. Here is a sampling of a few of the methods specified in the Element interface:

getAttribute *and* setAttribute, getAttributeNS *and* setAttributeNS
> getAttribute lets you retrieve an attribute by name, and setAttribute adds a new attribute with a value. The NS variants let you retrieve an attribute by local name and namespace URI, plus add an attribute with qualified name, namespace URI, and a value.

getElementsByTagName *and* getElementsByTagNameNS
> These return a list of all descendent elements with the give tag name. The NS version uses a local name and a namespace URI.

hasAttribute *and* hasAttributeNS
> hasAttribute returns true when it finds an attribute with the given name; likewise, hasAttributeNS returns true when it finds an attribute with the given local name and namespace URI.

In general, DOM stores whole documents in memory, which works fine when you are dealing with small or even medium size files; however, with large files you are likely to experience performance hits. Other APIs—such as SAX **[Hack #97]**, which is event-based—are a better choice for processing large documents.

DOM is implemented in a number of languages, such as Java and Python (*http://www.python.org*). This hack demonstrates a few small applications that use DOM: DOM Inspector, and Python and Java programs that are run at the command line.

DOM Inspector

The Mozilla and Firefox browsers offer a feature called DOM Inspector (*http://www.mozilla.org/projects/inspector/*). DOM Inspector provides a handy, straightforward DOM view of a document. With DOM Inspector, you can examine and even edit attributes in any web document using DOM techniques, and you can navigate through the hierarchy of the document with a two-paned window that allows a variety of document and node views.

In Firefox, you can access this feature by choosing Tools → DOM Inspector. If you were already viewing *time.xml* in Firefox, it would appear in the DOM Inspector when you invoke the tool. If not, you could enter the URL for the file in the address bar and then click Inspect. *time.xml* is shown in DOM Inspector in Figure 7-2. (I have turned off anonymous content, and the detection of whitespace nodes under the View menu, plus the display of id and class attributes by clicking the small window button on the upper-right of the left pane.)

> If you close the browser, run DOM Inspector separately, and bring up a new document, that document will appear in a small browser window at the bottom of DOM Inspector.

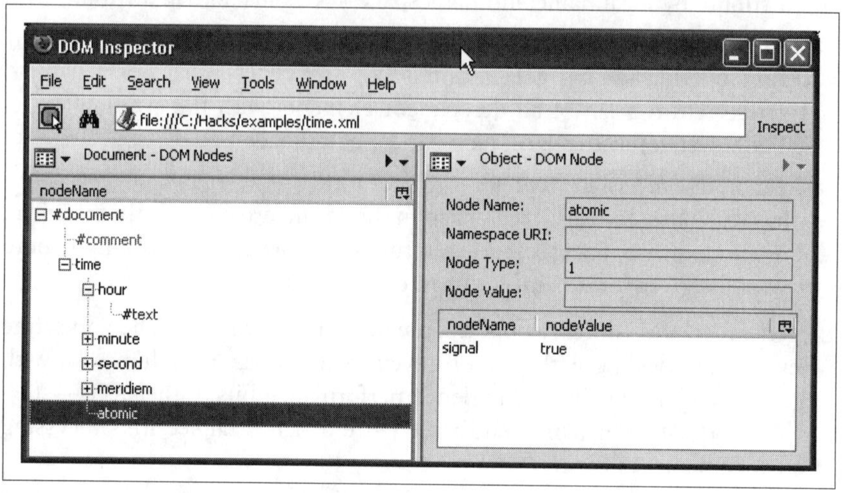

Figure 7-2. time.xml in the Firefox DOM Inspector

The nodes in *time.xml* are represented in tree form in the left pane, and the atomic node (an element) is highlighted. Information about the atomic node is displayed in the right pane. There, for example, you can see that atomic has a signal attribute node with a value of true. The representation of node names as #document, #comment, or #text, with the preceding #, comes from the DOM specification.

You can edit attribute values with DOM Inspector. Select a node with attributes in the left pane, and then select an attribute from that node in the right pane. Right-click and select Edit from the menu. You can then change the value of the attribute, but only temporarily—that is, only for the document in memory (you can't write your changes to disk). Try a document such as *time.html* that uses style attributes with CSS values. When you edit such values, you can see the change immediately in the browser window.

With the browser window in the background, click on a node name such as hour or minute in the DOM Inspector, or right-click on the name and select Blink Element from the menu. When you click on the name, watch in the browser window: you will see a red, blinking box surrounding the node whose name you clicked. So DOM Inspector is a navigation aid. This will be helpful when you are looking at larger, more complex documents.

Click through some of the other menus to see what other features DOM Inspector has. Then, open a more complex document to see a more intricate representation of the file in DOM. For example, go to *http://www.w3.org/* and bring up DOM Inspector. Navigate through the nodes in the left pane and select h2. Then, in the right pane, click on the menu button next to the words Object-DOM Node in the pane's title bar. Choose CSS Style Rules and you will see a listing of style information that applies to the subject node.

Python's minidom

The Python programming language is growing in popularity. It is easy to learn—if you have any programming background—and is easy to use. Python handles XML well, and has a number of modules to do so; for example, xml. dom.minidom, which is one of Python's implementations of DOM (*http://www. python.org/doc/current/lib/module-xml.dom.minidom.html*). Our first example will show how to use minidom with Python's command-line interface.

Assuming that you have downloaded (*http://www.python.org/download/*) and installed Version 2.3.3 (or later) of Python, type the command python while in the working directory to see the following prompt:

```
Python 2.3.3 (#51, Dec 18 2003, 20:22:39) [MSC v.1200 32 bit (Intel)]
on win32
Type "help", "copyright", "credits" or "license" for more information.
>>>
```

Now, for each line prefixed by >>> in Example 7-19, enter the given command, and the command will be followed by the given output; for example, after you enter lines 1, 2, and 3, you should get the output on lines 4, 5, and 6.

Example 7-19. Python minidom line-by-line example

```
1  >>> from xml.dom import minidom
2  >>> doc = minidom.parse("time.xml")
3  >>> doc.toxml()
4  u'<?xml version="1.0" ?>\n<!-- a time instant --><time timezone="PST">\n <hour>1
5  1</hour>\n <minute>59</minute>\n <second>59</second>\n <meridiem>p.m.</meridiem>
6  \n <atomic signal="true"/>\n</time>'
7  >>> print doc.toxml()
```

Example 7-19. Python minidom line-by-line example (continued)

```
 8  <?xml version="1.0" ?>
 9  <!-- a time instant --><time timezone="PST">
10    <hour>11</hour>
11    <minute>59</minute>
12    <second>59</second>
13    <meridiem>p.m.</meridiem>
14    <atomic signal="true"/>
15  </time>
16  >>> hr = doc.getElementsByTagName("hour")[0]
17  >>> print hr.toxml( )
18  <hour>11</hour>
19  >>> ^Z
```

Line 1 imports the minidom package. On line 2, minidom's parse( ) method places the document *time.xml* in a DOM structure named doc. On line 3, minidom's toxml( ) method outputs the document, as stored, to standard output (lines 4–6). Without the print command, the contents of doc are printed out in raw form; however, with print, you get the nicely formatted output seen on lines 8 through 15. Line 16 uses the getElementsByTagName( ) method to grab the hour node ([0] specifies the first item in the structure holding the element), and line 17 prints it out. The Ctrl-Z on line 19, followed by Enter, ends the Python command-line session.

Here's another example. In the file archive you will find the document *time.py* (Example 7-20), a program that uses the minidom module to convert *time.xml* into an HTML document.

Example 7-20. time.py

```
 1  import xml.dom.minidom
 2
 3  dom = xml.dom.minidom.parse("time.xml")
 4  hour = dom.getElementsByTagName("hour")[0]
 5  minute = dom.getElementsByTagName("minute")[0]
 6  second = dom.getElementsByTagName("second")[0]
 7  meridiem = dom.getElementsByTagName("meridiem")[0]
 8
 9  def getText(nodelist):
10      rc = ""
11      for node in nodelist:
12          if node.nodeType == node.TEXT_NODE:
13              rc = rc + node.data
14      return rc
15
16  def doTime(time):
17      print "<html>"
18      print "<title>Time Instant</title>"
19      print "<body>"
20      print "<h2>Time Instant</h2>"
21      print " <ul>"
```

Example 7-20. time.py (continued)

```
22      doHour(hour)
23      doMinute(minute)
24      doSecond(second)
25      doMeridiem(meridiem)
26      print " </ul>"
27      print "</body>"
28      print "</html>"
29
30  def doHour(hour):
31      print "  <li>Hour: %s</li>" % getText(hour.childNodes)
32
33  def doMinute(minute):
34      print "  <li>Minute: %s</li>" % getText(minute.childNodes)
35
36  def doSecond(second):
37      print "  <li>Second: %s</li>" % getText(second.childNodes)
38
39  def doMeridiem(meridiem):
40      print "  <li>Meridiem: %s</li>" % getText(meridiem.childNodes)
41
42  doTime(dom)
```

This program parses *time.xml*, and then uses the getElementsByTagName( ) method to grab four nodes of interest out of dom: hour, minute, second, and meridiem. Each of these is used in the method definitions on lines 30 through 40. In these definitions, the getText( ) method (line 9) is called with the childNodes attribute, which retrieves a list of all the child nodes (only text nodes in these cases). In each print call, %s is replaced by the string value returned by getText( ). getText( ) creates an empty string rc and then uses a for loop to collect all the child nodes, if they are text nodes (node.TEXT_NODE tests for that).

The doTime( ) method on line 16 pulls everything together: the manually printed HTML tags and the method calls doHour( ), doMinute( ), doSecond( ), and doMeridiem( ), which together form the HTML list item (li) elements.

DOM in Java

Finally, here is a little bit of DOM as implemented by Java (*http://java.sun. com*) as part of Sun's Java API for XML Processing, or JAXP (*http://java.sun. com/xml/jaxp/ index.jsp*). Java 1.4 and later come standard with JAXP and DOM built in. The file *BitODom.java*, found in the file archive, has code similar to the command-line Python script shown in Example 7-19.

```
1   import javax.xml.parsers.DocumentBuilder;
2   import javax.xml.parsers.DocumentBuilderFactory;
3   import javax.xml.parsers.ParserConfigurationException;
4   import org.w3c.dom.Document;
```

```
5    import org.w3c.dom.NodeList;
6    import org.w3c.dom.Node;
7    import java.io.File;
8    import java.io.IOException;
9    import org.xml.sax.SAXException;
10
11   public class BitODom {
12
13       static Document document;
14
15       public static void main(String[ ] args)
16           throws IOException, SAXException, ParserConfigurationException {
17
18           DocumentBuilderFactory factory = DocumentBuilderFactory.newInstance(
     );
19           DocumentBuilder builder = factory.newDocumentBuilder( );
20           NodeList list;
21           Node node;
22
23           document = builder.parse(new File(args[0]));
24           list = document.getElementsByTagName("hour");
25           node = list.item(0);
26           System.out.println(node);
27
28       }
29
30   }
```

The classes imported on lines 1, 2, and 3 were added by Sun.
DocumentBuilder allows you to obtain DOM Document instances from an
XML document, and DocumentBuilderFactory lets applications get a parser
that produces DOM object trees. ParserConfigurationException throws an
exception if there is a configuration problem. The interfaces imported on
lines 4, 5, and 6 are APIs specified by the W3C. A Document represents an
entire XML (or HTML) document. NodeList provides an abstract order-list
of nodes, and Node represents an individual node in the DOM. The File
class (line 7) helps the parser accept a file for parsing. IOException and
SAXException (lines 8 and 9) help the program figure out what to do if there
is a problem in main( ) (line 16).

Line 13 instantiates a Document, and lines 18 and 19 build an object from
which we can call the parser( ) method (line 23). The NodeList and Node
(lines 20 and 21) are necessary for actually doing something with the nodes
in document—first placing the hour node in list (line 24), then using the
item( ) method to extract the node from list and put it in node (line 25),
then finally printing the node (line 26).

Both the source and compiled class files are already in the file archive (*BitODom.java* and *BitODom.class*). To recompile the source file, run javac from a command prompt while in the working directory:

```
javac BitODom.java
```

Then run the program with *time.xml*:

```
java BitODom time.xml
```

Your program output should be:

```
<hour>11</hour>
```

Try BitODom on other documents that contain the hour element (find the files with grep "<hour>" *.xml). This little Java program just gives you a starting point with DOM. Now that you have a basic understanding of how DOM works in Java, you can consult the DOM APIs and start adding other method calls or using attributes on your own to manipulate and change your XML documents (*http://java.sun.com/j2se/1.4.2/docs/api/org/w3c/dom/package-summary.html*).

> It should be noted once again that Java objects can use considerable memory, and that object creation and deletion takes time, which can make a system quite sluggish. You will find that loading large XML documents in DOM in Java can try your patience. If you are dealing with a good number of large documents, consider an alternative such as SAX **[Hack #97]**.

See Also

- "Dive into Python," by Mark Pilgrim: *http://diveintopython.org/toc/index.html*
- *Python in a Nutshell*, by Alex Martelli (O'Reilly), pages 494–511
- Java 1.4 DOM APIs: Java Version 1.4 DOM tutorial: *http://java.sun.com/j2ee/1.4/docs/tutorial/doc/JAXPDOM.html*
- Microsoft's *DOM Developer's Guide*, with help for programming in C/C++, Visual Basic, and JScript: *http://msdn.microsoft.com/library/default.asp?url=/library/en-us/xmlsdk/htm/dom_devguide_overview_2g1j.asp*

HACK
#97 Processing XML with SAX

SAX is the de facto standard XML parser interface for Java. You learn how to
use it here with a simple SAX application written in Java.

The Simple API for XML (SAX) is a streaming, event-based API for XML
(*http://www.saxproject.org*). It was (and continues to be) developed by members of the xml-dev mailing list (*http://www.xml.org/xml/xmldev.shtml*). Discussion of a uniform API for XML parsers began on xml-dev in December
1997   (*http://lists.xml.org/archives/xml-dev/199712/msg00170.html*)   and
resulted in the release of the first version of SAX in May 1998 (*http://lists.
xml.org/archives/xml-dev/199805/msg00226.html*), with David Megginson as
the chief maintainer (*http://www.megginson.com/*). SAX 2.0.1, which has
namespace support, was released in January 2002, with David Brownell as
the lead maintainer (*http://lists.xml.org/archives/xml-dev/200201/msg01943.
html*).

SAX provides an interface to SAX parsers. As an event-based API, it
munches on documents and reports, parsing events along the way, usually
in one fell swoop. These reports come directly to the application through
callbacks. This is called *push parsing*. To push these events, an application
must implement event handlers (methods) from the SAX interfaces, such as
startDocument( ) or startElement( ). Without implementing or registering
these handlers, a SAX application won't "see" the results that are pushed up
from its underlying parser.

> *Pull parsing*, on the other hand, allows you to pull events on
> demand. Examples of pull parsers include the C# Xml-
> Reader **[Hack #98]**, Paul Prescod's Python pull parser (*http://
> www.prescod.net/python/pulldom.html*), Aleksander Slomin-
> ski's XML pull parser (*http://www.extreme.indiana.edu/xgws/
> xsoap/xpp/*), and the Streaming API for XML (StAX), which
> is a pull parser API just now emerging from the Sun Java
> Specification Request, JSR 173 (*http://www.jcp.org/en/jsr/
> detail?id=173*).

SAX was originally written in Java and continues to be maintained in Java,
but it is also available in other languages, such as C++, Pascal, and Perl
(*http://www.saxproject.org/?selected=langs*). This hack demonstrates a simple Java program that uses SAX.

A Little Help from SAX

First, have a look at the document *blob.xml*:

```
<time timezone="PST"><hour>11</hour><minute>59</minute><second>59
</second><meridiem>p.m.</meridiem></time>
```

Not much to look at, is it? It's just a blob of elements with only one attribute, no pretty whitespace between elements, no XML declaration, and no comments. Having elements crammed together is not a big problem from a processing standpoint, except that it gives me a headache when I'm looking at it.

When I was first learning Java a few years ago, I searched high and low for simple SAX programs, ones that were reduced down to something I could grasp. I didn't have much luck finding such programs, so I decided to write a few of my own. Example 7-21 is a short SAX program, *Poco.java*. This program does some readily discernible things, just right for someone getting up to speed with SAX. It will also help us do something interesting with *blob.xml*.

Example 7-21. Poco.java

```
1   import org.xml.sax.XMLReader;
2   import org.xml.sax.Attributes;
3   import org.xml.sax.helpers.DefaultHandler;
4   import org.xml.sax.helpers.XMLReaderFactory;
5
6   public class Poco extends DefaultHandler {
7
8       private int depth = -1;
9       private static String parser = "org.apache.crimson.parser.XMLReaderImpl";
10
11      public static void main (String[ ] args) throws Exception {
12
13          XMLReader reader = XMLReaderFactory.createXMLReader(parser);
14          reader.setContentHandler(new Poco( ));
15          reader.parse(args[0]);
16
17      }
18
19      public void startDocument( ) {
20          System.out.println("<?xml version=\"1.0\" encoding=\"ISO-8859-1\"?>\n");
21          System.out.println("<!-- processed with Poco -->");
22      }
23
24      public void startElement (String uri, String name,
25      String qName, Attributes atts) {
26      depth++;
27      if (depth > 0)
28      System.out.print(" ");
29      System.out.print("<" + qName + ">");
30      if (depth == 0)
31      System.out.println( );
32      }
33
34      public void endElement (String uri, String name, String qName) {
```

Example 7-21. Poco.java (continued)

```
35      System.out.print("</" + qName + ">");
36      if (depth == 1)
37      System.out.println( );
38      depth--;
39      }
40
41      public void characters (char ch[ ], int start, int length)
42      {
43      for (int i = start; i < start + length; i++) {
44      System.out.print(ch[i]);
45      }
46      }
47
48  }
```

Compiling this program as shown here requires Java version 1.4 or later:

```
java Poco.java
```

Because 1.4 has JAXP built in, you don't have to place a SAX JAR file (such as *sax2r2.jar*, available from *http://sourceforge.net/projects/sax/*) in the class-path. When the program is compiled, you can run it like this:

```
java Poco blob.xml
```

or like this in Windows:

```
java Poco file:///C:/Hacks/examples/blob.xml
```

The results of processing *blob.xml* with *Poco.class* are shown in Example 7-22.

Example 7-22. Results of processing blob.xml with Poco.class

```
<?xml version="1.0" encoding="ISO-8859-1"?>

<!-- processed with Poco -->
<time>
 <hour>11</hour>
 <minute>59</minute>
 <second>59</second>
 <meridiem>p.m.</meridiem>
</time>
```

An XML declaration and comment are added to the top of the resulting doc-ument. All the elements from the source file are copied, properly indented, and sent to standard output, including their character data content. The attribute on the time element, however, is not processed and so is excluded from the output. Now let's talk about how all this happened.

On line 1 of Example 7-21, the program imports the XMLReader interface from the package org.xml.sax, then on line 4 imports the class XMLReaderFactory from org.xml.sax.helpers. Line 13 creates an XML reader for SAX using the factory. Creating the reader is number one on your list of things to do when writing a SAX program.

The createXMLReader( ) method takes as an argument a string that represents a Java class name. This class name is the entry point for the underlying XML parser. JAXP's default XML parser is Crimson, identified with the class name org.apache.crimson.parse.XMLReaderImpl. If createXMLReader( ) has no argument, you can pass in a class name for the parser using the -D command-line option and the system property org.xml.sax.driver. For example, you could use the -D option on the command line, like this:

```
java -Dorg.xml.sax.driver=org.apache.crimson.parse.XMLReaderImpl
Poco blob.xml
```

and get the same results as placing the class name in the program itself. You might choose the Xerces parser instead of Crimson. In this case, use this command line:

```
java -cp .;xercesImpl.jar -Dorg.xml.sax.driver=org.apache.xerces.parsers.
SAXParser
Poco blob.xml
```

This command assumes that *xercesImpl.jar* is in the current directory (download it from *http://xml.apache.org/xerces2-j/download.cgi*).

The DefaultHandler class (line 3) is also from the helpers package. It implements several other SAX interfaces, and is the default base class for SAX2 event handlers. For example, the DefaultHandler class implements methods from the ContentHandler interface. More precisely, ContentHandler contains only signatures for such methods or event handlers as startDocument( ) and startElement( ), and DefaultHandler provides no-op implementations of these and other methods. The Poco class extends the DefaultHandler class (line 6), and the call to setContentHandler( ) on line 14 registers a content event handler. Without this content handler, all reported events are quietly ignored.

The rubber hits the road when the parse( ) method is called on line 15. The argument (args[0]) is a string that represents the filename from the command line. The argument for parse( ) is of type InputSource (*http://www.saxproject.org/apidoc/org/xml/sax/InputSource.html*), which can be a system identifier (or URI), a bytes stream, or a character stream.

Poco.java provides working implementations for four methods: startDocument( ) (line 24), startElement( ) (line 24), endElement( ) (line 34), and characters( ) (line 41). SAX uses callbacks, which are registered to handle certain events when encounterd, hence we call these methods *event handlers*. If we don't implement them in our program, they actually get called at runtime, but nothing apparent happens! Only by implementing the event handlers do we get into action.

startDocument( ) writes an XML declaration (line 20) and a comment (line 21) to standard output. startElement( ) writes a start tag, and endElement( ) writes an end tag. The only reason why the Attributes interface is imported (line 2) is to satisfy the required method signature for startElement( ), whose fourth argument is of type Attributes.

Both startElement( ) and endElement( ) use the depth variable (line 8) to determine element depth and to add whitespace appropriately, but this is not a general solution because it only works for a depth of 0 or 1! For a solid technique on handling element depth and whitespace, see David Megginson's *DataWriter.java*, available at *http://megginson.com/Software/xml-writer-0.2.zip*. characters( ) (line 44) simply prints any characters it encounters.

> The program is admittedly weak in its exception handling. It only does the minimum by throwing Exception from main( ). SAXException and SAXParseException are both imported by DefaultHandler, which Poco extends. A more responsible program—and therefore a more complex one—would use try/catch blocks to handle the exceptions intelligently. I have chosen to keep this program simple so it is easier to understand.

Poco.java is only the beginning of you can do, but it should give you a fairly good understanding of the basics of SAX programming in Java.

See Also

- Karl Waclawek's SAX for .NET: *http://sf.net/projects/saxdotnet*
- SAX API reference: *http://www.saxproject.org/apidoc/overview-summary.html*
- *SAX2*, by David Brownell (O'Reilly)
- *The Book of SAX*, by W. Scott Means and Michael A. Bodie (No Starch Press)

Process XML with C#

Even if you aren't a C# programmer, you can get up to speed on processing XML with C# in short order with this hack.

C# is an object-oriented programming language that comes as part of Microsoft's .NET framework (*http://www.microsoft.com/net/*), which was introduced in 2000. C# has taken a lot of lessons from C, C++, and Java, but I won't get into a comparison of these languages here. (For a good discussion of this, see Dare Obasanjo's "A Comparison of Microsoft's C# Programming Language to Sun Microsystems' Java Programming Language" at *http://www.25hoursaday.com/CsharpVsJava.html*.) Like any programming language, C# has it proponents and opponents. While I still use Java the most, when XML is concerned, I fall into the camp of C# proponents.

My objective here is to introduce some of C#'s programming facilities for XML, which are legion. C# offers oodles of APIs for you to scratch just about any XML itch you can find. This hack will exercise several programs that use a few of these APIs, enough to get you started writing your own C# programs for processing XML.

Getting C#

C# is compiled into an intermediate code, so you need to have .NET or Mono on your system to even get a compiled C# program to work. You can get C# in several ways. If you are working on Windows, you can download .NET from Microsoft's MSDN site (*http://msdn.microsoft.com/netframework/technologyinfo/howtoget/*) or through *http://www.gotdotnet.com*; or, if you are on Windows or Linux (Red Hat, Debian, and SUSE), you can download the Ximian C# compiler that is part of the open source Mono project (*http://www.go-mono.com/*). Borland also offers Borland C# Builder for the Microsoft .NET Framework (*http://www.borland.com/csharpbuilder/*).

If you opt for .NET, you have to download both the .NET Framework Version 1.1 Redistributable Package (about 24 MB) and the .NET Framework SDK Version 1.1 (about 108 MB). The programs used in this hack have been developed with .NET on Windows, and have not been tested with the Ximian compiler.

As far as documentation resources, .NET comes with a large parcel of good HTML documentation. You can also find a reference manual for C# on the MSDN site (*http://msdn.microsoft.com/library/en-us/csref/html/vcoriCProgrammersReference.asp*). Mono also provides online documentation at *http://www.go-mono.com:8080/*.

Writing an XML Document with XmlTextWriter

The System.Xml namespace in C# has a class called XmlTextWriter that provides properties and methods for writing XML documents. The C# program *inst.cs* takes input from the command line and writes an XML document either to standard output or to a file. It is shown in Example 7-24.

Both source (*inst.cs*) and binary (*inst.exe*) versions of this program are available in the file archive for the book. With the .NET C# compiler installed and in the path, you can recompile this program with this command:

```
csc inst.cs
```

To run the program, type:

```
inst
```

You will get this usage information:

```
Inst: generates a time instant in XML
Usage: inst hr min sec am|pm [file]
```

To generate XML with *inst.exe*, enter a line such as:

```
inst 10 43 56 am
```

which generates the output shown in Example 7-23.

Example 7-23. Output of inst.exe

```
<?xml version="1.0" encoding="IBM437"?>
<!-- a time instant -->
<time timezone="PST">
 <hour>10</hour>
 <minute>43</minute>
 <second>56</second>
 <meridiem>am</meridiem>
 <atomic signal="false" />
</time>
```

To write the output of the program to a file, use this syntax:

```
inst 10 43 56 am timeout.xml
Writing XML to file timeout.xml
```

The XML is written to the file *timeout.xml*, as reported by the program.

Example 7-24 shows *inst.cs*, the source code for *inst.exe*.

Example 7-24. inst.cs

```
1  using System;
2  using System.Text;
3  using System.Xml;
4
5  class Inst {
```

Example 7-24. inst.cs (continued)

```
 6
 7        // Output file flag
 8        static bool file = false;
 9
10        // Usage strings
11        static string name = "Inst: generates a time instant in XML";
12        static string usage = "\nUsage: inst hr min sec am|pm [file]";
13
14        static void Main(String[ ] args) {
15
16            // Test arguments
17            if (args.Length == 0) {
18                Console.WriteLine(name + usage);
19                Environment.Exit(1);
20            } else if (args.Length == 5) {
21                // Fifth argument = output to file
22                file = true;
23            } else if ((args[1] == "0") || (args[2] == "0")) {
24                Console.WriteLine("Use 00 for hr or min; exit.");
25                Environment.Exit(1);
26            } else if (args.Length > 5) {
27                Console.WriteLine("Too many arguments; exit.");
28                Environment.Exit(1);
29            }
30
31            // Test argument values
32            byte hr = System.Convert.ToByte(args[0]);
33            byte min = System.Convert.ToByte(args[1]);
34            byte sec = System.Convert.ToByte(args[2]);
35            if (!((hr >= 1) && (hr <= 24))) {
36                Console.WriteLine("Arg 1 must be 1-24; exit.");
37                Environment.Exit(1);
38            } else if (!((min >= 0) && (min <=59))) {
39                Console.WriteLine("Arg 2 must be 00-59; exit.");
40                Environment.Exit(1);
41            } else if (!((sec >= 0) && (sec <=59))) {
42                Console.WriteLine("Arg 3 must be 00-59; exit.");
43                Environment.Exit(1);
44            }
45
46            switch(args[3]) {
47                case "am":
48                    break;
49                case "a.m.":
50                    break;
51                case "pm":
52                    break;
53                case "p.m.":
54                    break;
55                default:
56                    Console.WriteLine("Arg 4 must be am|a.m.|pm|p.m.; exit.");
```

Example 7-24. inst.cs (continued)

```
57                    Environment.Exit(1);
58                    break;
59            }
60
61            // Create the XmlTextWriter
62            XmlTextWriter w;
63            if (file) {
64                // Output to file with US-ASCII encoding
65                w = new XmlTextWriter(args[4], Encoding.ASCII);
66                Console.WriteLine("Writing XML to file " + args[4]);
67            } else {
68                // Output to console with IBM437 encoding
69                w = new XmlTextWriter(Console.Out);
70            }
71
72             w.Formatting = Formatting.Indented;
73             w.Indentation = 1;
74             w.WriteStartDocument();
75             w.WriteComment(" a time instant ");
76             w.WriteStartElement("time");
77             w.WriteAttributeString("timezone", "PST");
78              w.WriteElementString("hour", args[0]);
79              w.WriteElementString("minute", args[1]);
80              w.WriteElementString("second", args[2]);
81              w.WriteElementString("meridiem", args[3]);
82              w.WriteStartElement("atomic");
83                w.WriteAttributeString("signal", "false");
84              w.WriteEndElement();
85             w.WriteEndElement();
86            w.WriteEndDocument();
87            w.Flush();
88            w.Close();
89
90        }
91
92  }
```

On the first three lines, the using declaration declares the namespaces System, System.Text, and System.Xml, making it possible to use methods and properties from these namespaces without prefixing them. On lines 7 through 29, the program handles arguments to the program. If, for example, there are no arguments (line 17), the program prints the name and usage strings (lines 11 and 12), and if there are five arguments, the fifth argument is taken to be a filename (line 20). Lines 31 through 59 perform various tests on the input strings, to make sure they are suitable for the application. For example, the hr argument must be in the range 1 through 24 (line 35).

Starting on line 62, the actual XML comes into play when the XmlTextWriter class is declared; the class is instantiated in different ways, depending on whether a filename is provided as an argument to the program (line 65). If a filename is not given, the XML is just written to the console (line 69).

The Formatting and Indentation properties on lines 72 and 73 set the indentation to 1 (the default is 2). The method WriteStartDocument( ) on line 74 begins the document and writes an XML declaration, and WriteComment( ) writes a comment (line 75). WriteStartElement( ), seen on lines 76 and 82, creates start tags for elements without character data content; calls to this method should be coupled with calls to WriteEndElement( ), which writes end tags (lines 84 and 85). WriteAttributeString( ) produces attributes with values (lines 77 and 83). WriteElementString( ) calls write elements with text content from command-line arguments (lines 78–81).

The WriteEndDocument( ) method on line 86 is not required, but it closes any open elements or attributes, so it is generally good practice to use it. Flush( ) flushes the buffer, and Close( ) closes the stream (lines 87 and 88).

Reading XML

System.Xml provides several classes for reading documents, such as the XmlDocument class, which represents an XML document in DOM [Hack #96]. You use XmlDocument's Load method to read the actual document. Other options include XmlReader, XmlTextReader, and XmlValidatingReader. This example will demonstrate XmlTextReader, which is used on line 22 of *read.cs* (shown in Example 7-26). This program reads an XML document and then creates a generalized RELAX NG schema based on the input document.

As with *inst.cs*, both source (*read.cs*) and binary (*read.exe*) code for this program are in the file archive for this book, but you can compile this program yourself with:

```
csc read.cs
```

Run the program by typing:

```
read
```

You will then get this usage information:

```
Read: read an XML document, create a RELAX NG schema
Usage: read file
```

Reading the document *time.xml* like this:

```
read time.xml
```

will yield the rudimentary RELAX NG schema shown in Example 7-25.

By the way, XmlTextReader expects well-formed XML as input. If you submit a malformed file like *bad.xml*, the program will throw an unhandled exception.

Example 7-25. Output of read.exe when it processes time.xml

```
<grammar xmlns="http://relaxng.org/ns/structure/1.0">

<start>
 <ref name="body"/>
</start>

<define name="body">
<element name="time">
<attribute name="timezone"/>
<element name="hour">
<text/>
</element>
<element name="minute">
<text/>
</element>
<element name="second">
<text/>
</element>
<element name="meridiem">
<text/>
</element>
<element name="atomic">
<attribute name="signal"/>
</element>
</element>
</define>

</grammar>
```

To write the output of the program to a file, redirect the output:

```
read time.xml > timeout.rng
```

With the redirect, the schema is written to the file *timeout.rng*. Then you could validate *time.xml* against *timeout.rng* with Jing **[Hack #72]**:

```
java -jar jing.jar timeout.rng time.xml
```

Now that you know how to use it (the easy part), let's talk about the program itself, shown here in Example 7-26.

Example 7-26. read.cs

```
1  using System;
2  using System.Xml;
3
4  public class Read {
5
```

Example 7-26. read.cs (continued)

```
6     // Usage strings
7     static string name = "Read: read an XML document, create a RELAX NG schema";
8     static string usage = "\nUsage: read file";
9
10    public static void Main(String[ ] args) {
11
12        // Test arguments
13        if (args.Length == 0) {
14            Console.WriteLine(name + usage);
15            Environment.Exit(1);
16        } else if (args.Length > 1) {
17            Console.WriteLine("Too many arguments; exit.");
18            Environment.Exit(1);
19        }
20
21    XmlTextReader r = new XmlTextReader(args[0]);
22
23    Console.WriteLine("<grammar xmlns=\"http://relaxng.org/ns/structure/1.0\">
       \n");
24    Console.WriteLine("<start>");
25    Console.WriteLine(" <ref name=\"body\"/>");
26    Console.WriteLine("</start>\n");
27    Console.WriteLine("<define name=\"body\">");
28
29        while (r.Read()) {
30            if (r.MoveToContent() == XmlNodeType.Element) {
31                Console.WriteLine("<element name=\"" + r.Name + "\">");
32                if (r.IsEmptyElement && r.HasAttributes) {
33                    for (int i = 0; i < r.AttributeCount; i++) {
34                        r.MoveToAttribute(i);
35                        Console.WriteLine("<attribute name=\"" + r.Name + "\"/>");
36                    }
37                    r.MoveToElement();
38                    Console.WriteLine("</element>");
39                } else if (r.HasAttributes) {
40                    for (int i = 0; i < r.AttributeCount; i++) {
41                        r.MoveToAttribute(i);
42                        Console.WriteLine("<attribute name=\"" + r.Name + "\"/>");
43                    }
44                    r.MoveToElement();
45                }
46            }
47            if (r.MoveToContent() == XmlNodeType.EndElement)
48                Console.WriteLine("</element>");
49            if (r.MoveToContent() == XmlNodeType.Text)
50                Console.WriteLine("<text/>");
51        }
52    Console.WriteLine("</define>");
53    Console.WriteLine("\n</grammar>");
54    }
55 }
```

Earlier I said that the program *read.cs* creates a *generalized* RELAX NG schema. What I mean by *generalized* is that, without paying a lot of attention to details, it analyzes an XML document and places the resulting schema in a single named definition, body. It has not been optimized, there is no exception handling, it has not been tested extensively, it can't handle complex content models (for example, no support for content and values other than text), and it doesn't use built-in XML writing facilities, opting to just write to the console with the methods Write( ) and WriteLine( ). However, the program does achieve the important goal of demonstrating, in simple terms, what can be done when reading XML with the pull parser XmlTextReader (line 21).

Like *inst.cs*, *read.cs* uses the first part of the program to declare namespaces System and System.Xml (lines 1 and 2) and handle arguments from the command line (lines 6 through 19). Lines 23 through 27 write the tags for the beginning of a RELAX NG grammar, including a namespace declaration.

The real action begins with the while loop on line 29. The Read( ) method reads the next node from the stream, as long as there are nodes to read, using recursive descent. The MoveToContent( ) method (line 30) checks the current node. This is a pull. It checks whether the current node is text (non-whitespace), an element, end of an element, an entity reference, the end of an entity, or a CDATA section. If the node is not one of these, the reader skips ahead to the next node of interest or to the end of the file. It skips over processing instructions, document type declarations, comments, and whitespace.

Line 30 also checks if a node is an element (XmlNodeType.Element); if it is, it creates a start tag for element (a RELAX NG element), then further tests if the element is empty with the IsEmptyElement property, and whether it has attributes with the HasAttributes property (line 32). If the element does have attributes, it moves through the attributes in succession with MoveToAttribute( ) (lines 33 and 34), writes the RELAX NG attribute element (line 35), and then moves to the next element and writes an element end tag (lines 37 and 38). The process is basically repeated for non-empty elements on lines 39 through 44.

Line 47 tests for the end of an element (XmlNodeType.EndElement) and if found, line 48 writes an element end tag. Lines 49 and 50 test if a node is a text node (XmlNodeType.Text) and if so write an empty RELAX NG text element. Finally, lines 52 and 53 close up the RELAX NG schema by writing the end tags for define and grammar.

That's it. As you can see, C# makes quick work of writing and reading XML documents. It's been worth my investment to get up to speed with C# and put it to use. (But I still like my Java and C, too.)

See Also

- *.NET and XML*, by Niel M. Bornstein (O'Reilly)
- Chapter 17 in *C# Cookbook*, by Stephen Teilhet and Jay Hilyard (O'Reilly)

Generate Code from XML

Tools are readily available that can convert XML into Java code, which in turn can allow you to easily manipulate markup from code rather than by hand in an editor or with something like XSLT. This hack walks you through an XML-to-code conversion scenario, and shows you how you can use the code after producing it.

This hack will demonstrate one tool that can generate code from either XML documents or a schema. Relaxer (*http://www.relaxer.org*) is a free Java tool that, among many other things, can generate Java code from XML documents, RELAX NG schemas (*http://www.relaxng.org*), or Relax Core schemas (*http://www.xml.gr.jp/relax/*).

Using Relaxer to Generate Java

With Relaxer, you can generate Java source code from an XML document or from a RELAX NG schema. In this example, we'll generate code based on the instance *time.xml*. Assuming that Relaxer is installed and ready to roll [Hack #37], type this command while in the working directory where the book files were extracted:

```
relaxer -verbose -java -useJAXP time.xml
```

From this command, Relaxer produces the following five Java files—11,358 lines of code in a matter of seconds:

- *Time.java*
- *Atomic.java*
- *RStack.java*
- *UJAXP.java*
- *URelaxer.java*

Time.java and *Atomic.java* are based on *time.xml*. These Java classes provide a set of constructors for creating objects based on this data model. For example, both *Time.java* and *Atomic.java* provide a default constructor (no arguments), another constructor that accepts a DOM document as an argument of type org.w3c.dom.Document, and another that accepts a URL argument of type *java.net.URL*.

Time.java and *Atomic.java* also provide methods that allow you to access the content of the elements in a document that match this form. For example, you can use the getHour( ) and setHour( ) methods to retrieve or change the content of elements. These methods accept arguments of type int. Relaxer chose this type based on its evaluation of the content of the hour element. Another method is makeTextDocument( ) which outputs a representation of the object as an XML document. The other three Java files were generated automatically by Relaxer and support underlying functionality. The fields and methods in these files are not user-accessible.

To easily view the Java source that Relaxer produces, apply Javadoc to the source files with this command:

```
javadoc -d relaxerdoc Time.java Atomic.java RStack.java UJAXP.java
URelaxer.java
```

This command puts Javadoc output files in the subdirectory *relaxerdoc*. To view these files, open the file *relaxerdoc/index.html* in a browser. Now you can see the documentation for all these classes, including fields, constructors, and methods that Relaxer created.

To compile these Java files, use *javac*:

```
javac Time.java
```

This compiles *Time.java*, *Atomic.java*, *RStack.java*, *UJAXP.java*, and *URelaxer.java* all at once. In the working directory, you will find another Java file, *ChangeTime.java*, shown in Example 7-27. This application uses the Relaxer-generated code to access and set the value of an attribute and the content of elements in *time.xml*.

Example 7-27. ChangeTime.java

```
1   import java.io.File;
2   import java.io.IOException;
3   import javax.xml.parsers.ParserConfigurationException;
4   import org.xml.sax.SAXException;
5
6   public class ChangeTime {
7
8       public static void main(String[ ] args)
9       throws IOException, SAXException, ParserConfigurationException {
10
11          // Instantiate an Time object
12          Time inst = new Time(new File(args[0]));
13
14          // Get current
15          System.out.println("Current Time");
16          System.out.println("Hour: " + inst.getHour());
17          System.out.println("Minute: " + inst.getMinute());
18          System.out.println("Second: " + inst.getSecond() + "\n");
19
```

Example 7-27. ChangeTime.java (continued)

```
20          // Set content
21          inst.setTimezone("MDT");
22          inst.setHour(12);
23          inst.setMinute(23);
24          inst.setSecond(05);
25          inst.setMeridiem("p.m.");
26
27          // Print the new XML
28          System.out.println("New Time");
29          System.out.println(inst.makeTextDocument());
30
31      }
32
33  }
```

You can compile and run this program with these commands:

```
javac ChangeTime.java
java ChangeTime time.xml
```

The output from this program will look like Example 7-28.

Example 7-28. Output from the ChangeTime program

```
Current Time
Hour: 11
Minute: 59
Second: 59

New Time
<time timezone="MDT">
 <hour>12</hour>
 <minute>23</minute>
 <second>5</second>
 <meridiem>p.m.</meridiem>
 <atomic signal="true"/>
</time>
```

The output you see will be different from this. That's because I went into *Time.java* and *Atomic.java* and tweaked the code so it would do what I wanted. For example, I edited the makeTextElement( ) method in *Time.java* so that the output would have the line breaks and indentation I wanted.

Using xmlspy to Generate C#

xmlspy 2004 Enterprise Edition for Windows has the capability of generating Java, C++, and C# classes from XML Schema. You can customize C++ generation to support MSXML, Xerces, and so forth. You can also create projects for Visual Studio .NET (*http://msdn.microsoft.com/vstudio/*), Borland C# Builder for the Microsoft .NET Framework (*http://www.borland.com/*

csharpbuilder/), and Mono, an open source C# implementation (*http://www. go-mono.com/*). While we can generate Java and C++ with xmlspy, we'll just illustrate xmlspy's capabilities by generating C#.

To generate C# code, open the XML Schema file *moment.xsd* in xmlspy from the *spycode* subdirectory of the working directory (Figure 7-3). This, of course, assumes that you have already downloaded and installed xmlspy 2004 Enterprise Edition and that you have extracted the book's files into your working directory.

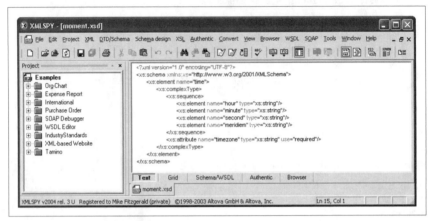

Figure 7-3. moment.xsd in xmlspy

Now choose DTD/Schema → Generate program code, and a dialog box appears that allows you to choose a code template (Figure 7-4). Click the C# Settings tab and click the Mono Makefile radio button. Then click the Choose Template tab, click the C# radio button as shown in the figure, and then click OK.

You are shown the Browse for Folder dialog box. Navigate to the working directory where you will find the *spycode* directory. Select it and click OK. The code is generated there. You are then asked if you want to open the directory where the code was just written. If you click Yes, Windows Explorer opens the *spycode* directory.

Let's have a look at the files that xmlspy produced. Under *spycode*, you will find the directories *Altova*, *moment*, *momentTest*, and the *makefile* that xmlspy created. (*makefile* is for compiling all the files under Mono and we won't be using that, though if you have Mono on your system, you're welcome to use it.) The XML Schema file after which the code was modeled (*moment. xsd*) is there, plus *makeit.bat*, *moment1.xml*, and *momentTest.exe*, all of which we will discuss in due course.

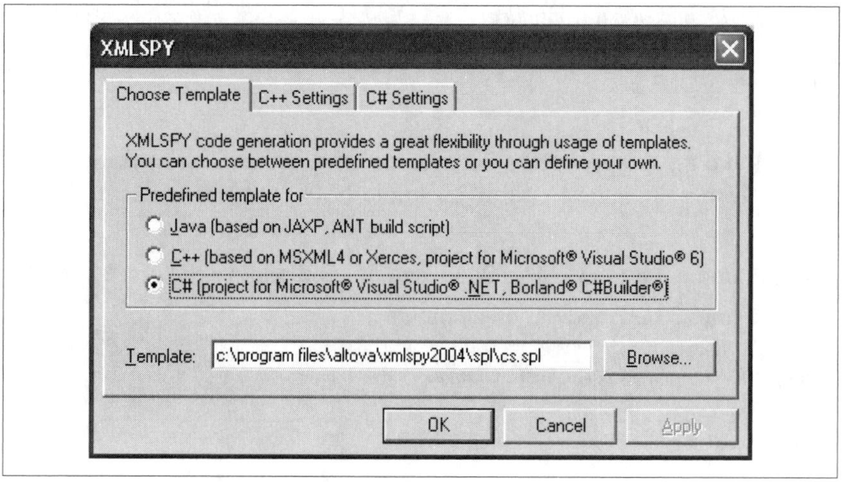

Figure 7-4. xmlspy code template dialog box

In the *Altova* directory are the following files: *Altova.dll*, *AssemblyInfo.cs*, *Node.cs*, *Document.cs*, and *SchemaTypes.cs*. In the *moment* directory are *AssemblyInfo.cs*, *moment.dll*, *momentDoc.cs*, and *timeType.cs*. And in the *momentTest* directory are *AssemblyInfo.cs*, *momentTest.cs*, and *momentTest.exe*. I am not going to go into a lot of detail about the code, but I will point out that the code under *Altova* is undergirding for the other code in *moment*. The main code that applies to *moment.xsd* is found in *moment*, where the *timeType.cs* code offers many methods for accessing nodes in instances of *moment.xsd*. The file *momentTest.cs* in *momentTest* uses some of these methods, as you will see in Example 7-30.

I won't assume that you have Visual Studio, Mono, or Borland installed, just that you have the Microsoft .NET framework installed [Hack #98]. You will notice another file in *spycode* called *makeit.bat* (Example 7-29). This batch file will compile all the C# files that xmlspy created with the *csc* compiler.

Example 7-29. makeit.bat

```
@echo off
rem cheater make file for Altova C# files
pushd Altova
csc /t:library /out:Altova.dll *.cs
popd
pushd moment
csc /t:library /r:../Altova/Altova.dll /out:moment.dll *.cs
popd
pushd momentTest
csc /r:../Altova/Altova.dll /r:../moment/moment.dll *.cs
```

Example 7-29. makeit.bat (continued)

```
copy momentTest.exe ..
popd
echo Done
```

Before building an application, let's go into the *momentTest* directory, open *momentTest.cs* in a text editor (Example 7-30), and make the following changes:

- Uncomment lines 31, 32, 39, 40, and 46 (i.e., remove the preceding //).
- Add lines 33–37 and 41–45 as shown.

Example 7-30. momentTest.cs with changes

```
1  //
2  // momentTest.cs
3  //
4  // This file was generated by XMLSPY 2004 Enterprise Edition.
5  //
6  // YOU SHOULD NOT MODIFY THIS FILE, BECAUSE IT WILL BE
7  // OVERWRITTEN WHEN YOU RE-RUN CODE GENERATION.
8  //
9  // Refer to the XMLSPY Documentation for further details.
10 // http://www.altova.com/xmlspy
11 //
12
13
14 using System;
15 using Altova.Types;
16
17 namespace moment
18 {
19     /// <summary>
20     /// Summary description for momentTest.
21     /// </summary>
22     class momentTest
23     {
24         protected static void Example( )
25         {
26             //
27             // TODO:
28             //    Insert your code here...
29             //
30             // Example code to create and save a structure:
31                 momentDoc doc = new momentDoc( );
32                 timeType root = new timeType( );
33                 SchemaString hour = new SchemaString("10");
34                 SchemaString min = new SchemaString("14");
35                 SchemaString sec = new SchemaString("29");
36                 SchemaString am = new SchemaString("a.m.");
37                 SchemaString mdt = new SchemaString("MDT");
38             //    ...
```

Example 7-30. momentTest.cs with changes (continued)

```
39              doc.SetRootElementName("", "time");
40              doc.SetSchemaLocation("moment.xsd"); // optional
41              root.Addtimezone(mdt);
42              root.Addhour(hour);
43              root.Addminute(min);
44              root.Addsecond(sec);
45              root.Addmeridiem(am);
46              doc.Save("moment1.xml", root);
47          //
48          // Example code to load and save a structure:
49          //   momentDoc doc = new momentDoc( );
50          //   timeType root = new timeType(doc.Load("moment1.xml"));
51          //   ...
52          //   doc.Save("moment1.xml", root);
53          //
54      }
55
56      /// <summary>
57      /// The main entry point for the application.
58      /// </summary>
59      [STAThread]
60      public static int Main(string[ ] args)
61      {
62          try
63          {
64                  Console.WriteLine("moment Test Application");
65                  Example( );
66                  Console.WriteLine("OK");
67                  return 0;
68          }
69          catch (Exception e)
70          {
71                  Console.WriteLine(e);
72                  return 1;
73          }
74      }
75   }
76 }
```

Now move back up to the parent directory (*spycode*), and type *makeit* at a command prompt. If you have entered the changes to *momentTest.cs* correctly, the build should be successful. *makeit* also copies the complied file *momentTest.exe* into the *spycode* directory. Now type *momentTest* at the command prompt, and you should get this feedback:

```
moment Test Application
OK
```

momentTest generated a new copy of *moment1.xml* (Example 7-31), which is valid with regard to *moment.xsd*. If you want, you can test it with either *xmllint* or *xsv* [Hack #69].

Example 7-31. moment1.xml

```xml
<?xml version="1.0" encoding="UTF-8"?>
<time xmlns:xsi="http://www.w3.org/2001/XMLSchema-instance" xsi:
noNamespaceSchemaLocation="moment.xsd" timezone="MDT">
  <hour>10</hour>
  <minute>14</minute>
  <second>29</second>
  <meridiem>a.m.</meridiem>
</time>
```

xmlspy generated over 1,900 lines of C# code in less than a second or two. This code can quickly be put to good use in manipulating markup program-matically, as you have seen. Have a look at the methods and so forth in *timeType.cs* under *moment*, then try experimenting with some of these meth-ods in *momentTest.cs*, or try generating different kinds of code (Java or C++) with xmlspy based on *moment.xsd* or some other schema.

See Also

- .NET Version 1.1 offers several programs, such as *wsdl.exe* and *xsd.exe*, that generate C# code based on XML and schema files. Search for *wsdl. exe* or *xsd.exe* in the .NET documentation.

HACK 100   Create Well-Formed XML with Genx

If you prefer the C language, Genx provides a fast, efficient C library for generating well-formed and canonical XML. On top of that, it's well documented and a real pleasure to use.

Genx (*http://www.tbray.org/ongoing/When/200x/2004/02/20/GenxStatus*) is an easy-to-use C library for generating well-formed XML output. In addi-tion to its output being well-formed, Genx writes all output in canonical form. It was created by Tim Bray with help from members of the xml-dev mailing list (*http://xml.org/xml/xmldev.shtml*) over the first few months of 2004. Some of the benefits of Genx include size, efficiency, speed, and the integrity of its output. Genx is well documented (*http://www.tbray.org/ ongoing/genx/docs/Guide.html*) and it's fairly easy to figure out what's going on just by looking at the well-commented source code.

This hack shows you how to download, install, and compile Genx, then walks you through two example programs. The hack assumes that you are familiar the C programming language, and that you have a C compiler and the make build utility available on your system. The example programs in this hack have been tested under Version beta5 of Genx.

Setting Up Genx

The first thing you have to is download Genx. It comes in a tarball only. After you download it to the working directory for the book, you need to extract the files. While at a shell or command prompt in the working directory, if you are on a machine that runs a Unix operating system, decompress the Genx tarball with:

```
gzip -d genx.tgz
```

Then extract the tar file *genx.tar* with:

```
tar xvf genx.tar
```

This creates a *genx* subdirectory where all the files from the archive will be extracted. (If you are on Windows without Cygwin, you can use a utility like WinZip to extract the GZIP archive.)

Compiling Genx

Genx comes with a *Makefile* for building the project. While in the *genx* subdirectory, just type make, and the process begins. The build will compile the needed files *genx.c* and *charProps.c. genx.c* includes the *genx.h* header file; *charProps.c* is where character properties are stored, and it is used to test for legal characters in XML.

The ar (archive) command is invoked to create an archive from object files *genx.o* and *charProps.o* The archive is called *libgenx.a*. The *ranlib* utility is also invoked to create an index for the archive. You will need to use *libgenx.a* when you compile your own Genx files. One other program, *tgx.c*, is also compiled and run. This program runs a number of tests on Genx and reports on what it finds so you know everything is working.

A First Example

Several test programs are provided in the Genx package and are stored under the *docs* subdirectory. I have written two sample programs that I'll highlight here. You can find these programs in the *genx-examples* subdirectory wherever the example file archive for this book was extracted. Change directories to *genx-examples* and type make again (the Genx examples have their own *makefile*). After you invoke make in *genx-examples*, the example programs will be built and ready to go.

Example 7-32 is a simple C program called *tick.c* that uses functions from the Genx library.

Example 7-32. tick.c

```c
1  #include <stdio.h>
2  #include "../genx/genx.h"
3
4  int main()
5  {
6    genxWriter w = genxNew(NULL, NULL, NULL);
7
8    genxStartDocFile(w, stdout);
9     genxStartElementLiteral(w, NULL, "time");
10     genxAddAttributeLiteral(w, NULL, "timezone", "GMT");
11     genxStartElementLiteral(w, NULL, "hour");
12      genxAddText(w, "23");
13     genxEndElement(w);
14     genxStartElementLiteral(w, NULL, "minute");
15      genxAddText(w, "14");
16     genxEndElement(w);
17     genxStartElementLiteral(w, NULL, "second");
18      genxAddText(w, "52");
19     genxEndElement(w);
20    genxEndElement(w);
21   genxEndDocument(w);
22  }
```

Line 2 of the program is an #include directive for the copy of the *genx.h* header file that is located in the *genx* directory above *genx-examples*, provided that Genx and was installed as directed.

> You can also place a copy of *genx.h* in the location for system include files (on my Cygwin system, for example, the location is *c:/cygwin/usr/include*). If a copy of *genx.h* is in the system include location, you can change the #include directive on line 2 to #include <genx.h>.

The first statement inside main( ) creates a writer for the output of the program. The variable w is of type genxWriter, and it is initialized by the genxNew function (see line 6). Looks like a Java constructor, doesn't it? genWriter is a pointer to the struct genxWriter_rec, which stores all kinds of information about the document being built. The three arguments to the genxNew function are for memory allocation and deallocation. When all three arguments are set to NULL, we are instructing Genx to use its default memory handling (that is, with malloc( ) and free( )).

Following this initialization of a writer is a series of function calls, each with a small job. Notice that the first or only argument to each of these functions is w, the writer structure. The call to genxStartDocFile( ) on line 8 starts the writing process. The second argument, stdout, indicates that the document will be written to standard output. (The document could otherwise be written to a file, as you will see in the next example.) At the end of the program (line 21) is a call to genxEndDocument( ), which signals the end of the document and flushes it.

The program also contain four calls to genxStartElementLiteral( ) (lines 9, 11, 14, and 17), each of which is terminated by a call to genxEndElement( ) (lines 13, 16, 19, and 20). genxStartElementLiteral( ) has three arguments. The first is the writer structure (w) explained previously, next is a namespace name or URI (NULL if none), and the third is the element name, such as time or hour.

If you give an element a namespace URI in the second argument, Genx writes the namespace URI on the element with an xmlns attribute and automatically creates a prefix, which is used on any child elements that have the same namespace declared.

The text content for a given element, if any, is created with genxAddText( ) (lines 12, 15, and 18), with the second argument containing the actual text, such as 23 or 14.

You can probably guess that genxAddAttributeLiteral( ) (line 10) writes an attribute on the element that is created immediately before it. It has four arguments. The first is the writer structure, and the second is a namespace URI, which is NULL if no namespace is used. The third argument is the attribute name and the fourth is the attribute value.

To run the program, just type tick at the prompt (it was compiled with *make* previously). The output of the program should look like this:

```
<time timezone="GMT"><hour>23</hour><minute>14</minute><second>52</second></
time>
```

This output is an example of canonical XML. Some obvious marks are no XML declaration and double quotes rather than single quotes around attribute values. Now let's look at a Genx example that is a little more complex.

Declare Markup for Better Performance

In the next example we will explore a different approach for writing an XML document with Genx. The program *tock.c* declares elements, an attribute, and a namespace *before* it uses them, then writes elements and an attribute with different functions that are more efficient than their *literal* counterparts. It also write its non-canonical output to a file. Example 7-33 shows the code for *tock.c*.

Example 7-33. tock.c

```
1   #include <stdio.h>
2   #include "../genx/genx.h"
3
4   int main( )
5   {
6     genxWriter w = genxNew(NULL, NULL, NULL);
7     FILE *f = fopen("tock.xml", "w");
8     genxElement time, hr, min, sec;
9     genxAttribute tz;
10    genxNamespace tm;
11    genxStatus status;
12    tm = genxDeclareNamespace(w, "http://www.wyeast.net/time", "tm", &status);
13    time = genxDeclareElement(w, tm, "time", &status);
14    tz = genxDeclareAttribute(w, NULL, "timezone", &status);
15    hr = genxDeclareElement(w, tm, "hour", &status);
16    min = genxDeclareElement(w, tm, "minute", &status);
17    sec = genxDeclareElement(w, tm, "second", &status);
18
19    genxAddText(w, "<?xml version=\"1.0\" encoding=\"UTF-8\"?>\n");
20    genxStartDocFile(w, f);
21    genxPI(w, "xml-stylesheet", " href=\"tock.xsl\" type=\"text/xsl\" ");
22    genxComment(w, " the current date ");
23    genxAddText(w, "\n");
24    genxStartElement(time);
25     genxAddAttribute(tz, "GMT");
26     genxAddText(w, "\n ");
27     genxStartElement(hr);
28      genxAddText(w, "23");
29     genxEndElement(w);
30     genxAddText(w, "\n ");
31     genxStartElement(min);
32      genxAddText(w, "14");
33     genxEndElement(w);
34     genxAddText(w, "\n ");
35     genxStartElement(sec);
36      genxAddText(w, "52");
37     genxEndElement(w);
38     genxAddText(w, "\n");
39    genxEndElement(w);
40   genxEndDocument(w);
41
42  }
```

Line 7 creates a FILE object by calling the fopen( ) function with a filename
(*tock.xml*) where the output is to be written and the stream or writer object
(w) from which the data will be supplied. Following that, four elements
(time, hr, min, and sec) are declared to be of type genxElement (line 8). The
attribute tz is declared to be of type genxAttribute (line 9), and the

namespace tm is declared with genxNamespace (line 10). status is of type genxStatus (line 11), an enum that helps keep track of the status of things, such as GENX_SUCCESS and GENX_BAD_NAME, and so forth. status is used as the last argument of the functions that are on lines 12 through 17, with the address-of operator &.

After the initial declarations, all these variables are initialized with an appropriate function: genxDeclareNamespace( ) (line 12), genxDeclareElement( ) (lines 13, 15, 16, and 17), and genxDeclareAttribute( ) (line 14). The namespace variable tm is given a namespace name (*http://www.wyeast.net/ time*) and a prefix (tm) with the genxDeclareNamespace( ) function.

The genxAddText( ) function inserts strings—an XML declaration and newline characters and spaces—into the file output stream (lines 19, 23, 26, 30, 34, and 38). The addition of the XML declaration is what makes the output non-canonical.

The functions genxPI( ) (line 21) and genxComment( ) (line 22) write an XML stylesheet processing instruction and a comment, respectively. Then the functions genxStartElement( ) (lines 24, 27, 31, and 35) and genxAddAttribute( ) (line 25) begin writing the markup. The functions use an object rather than text to write the markup literally, with better performance than their counterparts genxStartElementLiteral( ) and genxAddAttributeLiteral( ). Other elements, such as genxAddText( ) (lines 28, 32, and 36) and genxEndElement( ) (lines 29, 33, 37, and 39), may be used with both variations of the element and attribute creation elements, or just for inserting interelemental whitespace, and so on.

To run the program, type tock at a command or shell prompt. Genx will then create the file *tock.xml*, shown in Example 7-34.

Example 7-34. tock.xml

```
<?xml version="1.0" encoding="UTF-8"?>
<?xml-stylesheet  href="tock.xsl" type="text/xsl" ?>
<! the current date -->

<tm:time xmlns:tm="http://www.wyeast.net/time" timezone="GMT">
 <tm:hour>23</tm:hour>
 <tm:minute>14</tm:minute>
 <tm:second>52</tm:second>
<tm:time>
```

Just for fun, this non-canonical output can be transformed with the XSLT stylesheet *tock.xsl* and validated with the RELAX NG schema *tock.rng*. Both files are in the *genx-examples* subdirectory.

There are a number of other Genx functions that I have not touched on—such as the memory management functions genxGetAlloc( ), genxSetAlloc( ) and such like. My take is that Tim Bray is on the right track, and that if you use C and you need to generate XML output, you will no doubt find that Genx is an efficient tool.

Index

We'd like to hear your suggestions for improving our indexes. Send email to *index@oreilly.com*.

F

Feed Validator, 353–354
FeedReader, 340
filetype plugin (ftplugin) for vim, 47
FIPS (Federal Information Processing
    Standards) codes, 216
    translation, lookup tables with
      XSLT, 216–221
      putting lookup tables in
        stylesheets, 218
fips_internal_codes.xsl, 219
fips_lu_data.xml, 216
fips_no_keys.xsl, 217
fips_out.xml, 221
fips.xml, 217
Firefox browser DOM Inspector, 415
flatten.pl, 329, 330
FLOWR, 85
FOAF (Friend of a Friend)
    project, 250–258
    foaf:depiction property, 256
    foaf:knows property, 253
      achieving grain with
        subproperties, 254
    foaf.sxw, 259
    Person class, 251
    rdfs:seeAlso property, 253
    Wiki, 251
for-each-group function, 226
formatAtributes( ) function
    (JavaScript), 408
Friend of a Friend project (see FOAF)

G

generated.xsd, 313
generate-id( ) function, 223
Genx, 442
    compiling, 442
    download and installation, 442
    well-formed XML, creation
      using, 442–447
      declaration of markup,
        advantages, 445
      example programs, 443–447
gen.xml, 142
gen.xsl, 143
getAttribute and getAttributeNS, 414
getElementsByTagName( )
    method, 414, 419

getElementsByTagNameNS( )
    method, 414
getText( ) method, 419
global element declarations, 286
Google, running feed from, 368–371
    software and licensing
      requirements, 368
google2rss, 368
google.rss, 369–371
gradient, 267
grad.svg, 266
graphical editors, 17–21
    <oXygen/>, 18, 39–41
    xmlspy 2004, 17, 67–70
    xRay2, 18
grep, 200–203
    -C switch, 203
group2.xml, 226
group2.xsl, 226
group.html, 224
grouping nodes in stylesheets, 221–227
    Muenchian method, 222
    XSLT 1.0, 222–225
    XSLT 2.0, 226, 226–227
group.xml, 222
group.xsl, 223

H

Harold, Elliotte Rusty, 347
hasAttribute and hasAttributeNS, 415
href attribute, 9
HTML, 82–84
    conversion to XML, 76
    iTunes library file, conversion
      to, 171–176
    processing from XML using
      TagSoup, 190
HTML Tidy, 82–84
    -asxhtml switch, 83

I

Ian Davis,, 255
IBM XML Diff and Merge Tool, 111
identity.xsl, 145
Image.rdf, 256
incelim.xsl, 332, 333
Infoset (XML Information
    Set), 114–116

Colophon

Our look is the result of reader comments, our own experimentation, and feedback from distribution channels. Distinctive covers complement our distinctive approach to technical topics, breathing personality and life into potentially dry subjects.

The tool on the cover of *XML Hacks* is a socket wrench. A socket wrench (known as a key or spanner in the U.K.) consists of a shank or rod capable of being fitted with sockets of various sizes, usually with six or twelve points, for handling hex fasteners. A socket wrench is used for turning a nut or bolt head, but is distinguishable from a box wrench in that the socket is circular and can reach a fastener within a narrow or deep recess.

Reg Aubry was the production editor for *XML Hacks*. Derek Di Matteo was the copyeditor. Emily Quill and Genevieve d'Entremont were the proofreaders and, along with Matt Hutchinson and Claire Cloutier, provided quality control. Mary Agner and James Quill provided production assistance. John Bickelhaupt wrote the index.

Hanna Dyer designed the cover of this book, based on a series design by Edie Freedman. The cover image is a stock photograph taken from the Photos.com collection. Emma Colby produced the cover layout with QuarkXPress 4.1 using Adobe's Helvetica Neue and ITC Garamond fonts.

David Futato designed the interior layout. This book was converted by Joe Wizda and Julie Hawks to FrameMaker 5.5.6 with a format conversion tool created by Erik Ray, Jason McIntosh, Neil Walls, and Mike Sierra that uses Perl and XML technologies. The text font is Linotype Birka; the heading font is Adobe Helvetica Neue Condensed; and the code font is LucasFont's TheSans Mono Condensed. The illustrations that appear in the book were produced by Robert Romano and Jessamyn Read using Macromedia FreeHand 9 and Adobe Photoshop 6. This colophon was written by Reg Aubry.